D1215579

AFRICAN HISTORICAL DICTIONARIES
Edited by Jon Woronoff

Historical Dictionary
of
TANZANIA

by

LAURA S. KURTZ

African Historical Dictionaries, No. 15

The Scarecrow Press, Inc.
Metuchen, N.J. & London
1978

042557

Ref
DT
444
. K87
1978

Library of Congress Cataloging in Publication Data

Kurtz, Laura S
    Historical dictionary of Tanzania.

    (African historical dictionaries ; no. 15)
    Bibliography: p.
    1. Tanzania--History--Dictionaries. I. Title.
II. Series.
DT444.K87   967.8'003   77-25962
ISBN 0-8108-1101-4

To my fellow-teachers, students and friends
who are shaping the current history of Tanzania--
may you find this volume helpful.

CONTENTS

v

EDITOR'S FOREWORD

For various reasons, the United Republic of Tanzania has been one of the most "popular" African countries with both Africans and students of Africa abroad. Its attractiveness may be due to its long-term commitment to a progressive social revolution, one based more on acts than on words, which is a relief from the largely verbal radicalism of so many other countries. It may be due to the gently charismatic nature of its leader, also a relief from the many compulsive charismatics who have, often quite temporarily, presided over their nation's destiny and enjoyed the people's support. Whatever the reason, I am certain the public will be pleased to have this instructive and comprehensive "dictionary" to Tanzania.

The year 1978 is a particularly good one for this volume to appear, coming eleven years after the historic Arusha Declaration, at a time when many institutions, names, and figures of the earlier system have changed, and a key to the new situation is sought. Along with numerous maps, lists of rulers, the chronology and a detailed bibliography, both the new-comer and the long-standing acquaintance will find many things of use. Certainly, for those who know either Tanganyika or Zanzibar better, it is most comforting to find that the author has given each part of the now more united nation a fair share in the entries.

Dr. Laura S. Kurtz first went to Tanganyika in 1958, and stayed for a number of years before returning to New York University to obtain a Ph.D. at the School of Education. She returned in 1971, and since then has been active in the Dar es Salaam College of National Education again as a teacher, a teacher in many forms, including that of teacher to a younger generation of Tanzanian teachers. Her book An African Education: The Social Revolution in Tanzania gives excellent insight into a problem which is also dealt with briefly in this dictionary. Her knowledge of the

vii

country, as well as her attachment to the people, has not failed to give us a very handy and stimulating guide.

Jon Woronoff
Series Editor

ABBREVIATIONS AND ACRONYMS

AIC	African Inland Church
ASP	Afro-Shirazi Party
CCM	Chama Cha Mapinduzi (Revolutionary Party)
CCT	Christian Council of Tanzania
CMS	Church Missionary Society
COSATA	Cooperative Supply Association of Tanzania
EALB	East African Literature Bureau
ELCT	Evangelical Lutheran Church of Tanzania
HMSO	Her Majesty's Stationery Office
KAR	King's African Rifles
KNCU	Kilimanjaro Native Cooperative Union
LEGCO	Legislative Council
MP	Member of Parliament
NUTA	National Union of Tanzania Workers
OAU	Organization of African Unity
OUP	Oxford University Press
RR	Railway
S/S	Secondary School
STD	Standard
TAA	Tanganyika African Association
TAGSA	Tanganyika African Government Servants Association
TANU	Tanganyika African National Union
TAPA	Tanganyika African Parents' Association
TEC	Tanzania Episcopal Conference
TNR	Tanzania Notes and Records
TPDF	Tanzania People's Defence Forces
TYL	Tanganyika African National Union Youth League
UMCA	Universities Mission to Central Africa
UN	United Nations
UTP	United Tanganyika Party
UWT	Umoja Wa Wanawake Wa Tanzania (United Women of Tanzania)
VA	Voluntary Agency (Agencies)
ZNP	Zanzibar Nationalist Party
ZPPP	Zanzibar and Pemba People's Party

ix

RULERS OF TANGANYIKA, ZANZIBAR AND TANZANIA

SULTANS OF KILWA

957-996	Ali bin al-Hasan
996-999	Ali bin Bashat
999-1003	Daudi bin Ali
1003-1005	Khalid bin Baker (usurper of Kilwa)
1005-1042	Hasan bin Sulemani I
1042-1100	Ali bin Daudi I
1100-1106	Ali bin Daudi II
1106-1129	Hasan bin Daudi
1129-1131	Sulaiman bin ?
1131-1170	Daudi bin Sulaiman I
1170-1188	Sulaiman al Hasan bin Daudi
1188-1190	Daudi bin Sulaiman II
1190-1191	Talut bin Sulaiman
1191-1215	Hasan bin Sulaiman II
1215-1225	Khalid bin Sulaiman
1225-1263	? bin Sulaiman (Bony Sulaiman)
1263-1277	Ali bin Daudi III
1277-1294	Hasan bin Talut
1294-1308	Sulaiman bin Hasan
1308-1310	Daudi bin Sulaiman III
1310-1333	Hasan bin Sulaiman
1333-1356	Daudi bin Sulaiman
1356-	Sulaiman bin Daudi (20 days)
1356-1362	Hasan bin Sulaiman
1362-1364	Talut bin Husain
1364-1366	Sulaiman bin Husain
1366-1389	Sulaiman bin Sulaiman
1389-1412	Husain bin Sulaiman II
1414-1421	Muhammed bin Sulaiman
1421-1442	Sulaiman bin Muhammed
1442-1454	Ismail bin Husain
1454-1455	Amir Muhammed bin Sulaiman (usurper)

1455-1456 Ahmed bin Sulaiman
1456-1466 Hassan bin Ismail
1466-1476 Said bin Hasan
1476-1477 Amir Sulaiman bin Muhammed (usurper)
1477-1478 Abdullah bin Hasan
1478-1479 Ali bin Khalib al-Hasan
1479-1484 Hasan bin Sulaiman IV
1485-1486 Sabhat bin Muhamed
1486-1490 Ali bin Khalib al-Hasan
1490-1495 Ibrahim bin Muhammed
1495-1499 Fudail bin Sulaiman
1499-1506 Amir Ibrahim bin Sulaiman
1506   Muhammed bin Rukn al-Din
1506-1507 Hajji Hasan bin Muhammed
1507   Muhammed Mikatu bin al-Amir Muhammed
c1513-1520 Muhammed bin Husain

There were fourteen sultans between 1442 and 1498.
Some of the undated ones are:

Amir Said bin Sulaiman
Hasan bin Ibrahim
Hasan bin Sulamani
Hasan bin Muhammed Ruka
Ibrahim bin Muhammed
Ibrahim bin Muhammed
Ismail bin Husein
Isufu bin Hasan
Isufu bin Ibrahim
Mohamed bin Ali
Mohamed bin Isufu
Muhammed bin Msuatu

SULTANS OF ZANZIBAR
(on partial family tree)

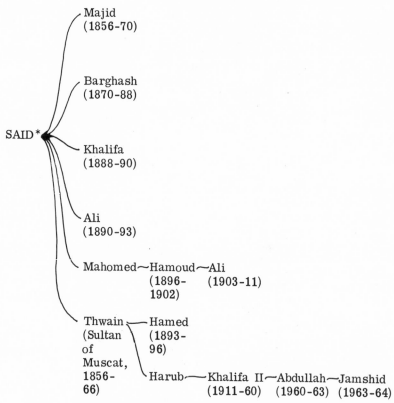

Majid
(1856-70)

Barghash
(1870-88)

SAID*

Khalifa
(1888-90)

Ali
(1890-93)

Mahomed—Hamoud—Ali
(1896-   (1903-11)
1902)

Thwain.——Hamed
(Sultan   (1893-
of   96)
Muscat,
1856-   Harub.——Khalifa II—Abdullah—Jamshid
66)   (1911-60) (1960-63) (1963-64)

*Sultan of Oman and Zanzibar, 1804-56.

GOVERNORS OF TANGANYIKA

1.	Julius von Soden	1891-1893
2.	? Schele	1893-1895
3.	Hermann Wissman	1895-1896
4.	Col. Eduard von Liebert	1896-1901
5.	Count Graf von Gotzen	1901-1906
6.	Baron Freiherr von Rechenberg	1906-1912

7. Heinrich Schnee   1912-1916
8. Sir Horace Byatt (admin. 1916-19)   1919-1924
9. John Scott, acting Gov.   1924
10. Sir Donald Cameron   1925-1931
11. Sir Steward Symes   1931-1934
12. Sir Harold MacMichael   1934-1938
13. Sir Mark Aitchison Young   1938-1942
14. Sir Wilfred Jackson   1942-1945
15. Sir William Batterskill   1945-1949
16. Sir Edward Twining   1949-1958
17. Sir Richard Turnbull   1958-1961

CONSULS-GENERAL IN ZANZIBAR

1. Captain Hamerton   1841
2. Sir Lloyd Mathews-1st Minister   1891
3. Sir Gerald Portal   1891-1892
4. Sir Rennel Rodd   1892-1894
5. Sir Arthur Hardinge   1894-1896
    (in Kenya)   (1895-1900)
6. Sir Charles Eliot   1900-1904
    (also Kenya)
7. Sir Basel Cove   1904-1908
8. Edward Clark   1909-1913

RESIDENTS IN ZANZIBAR

1. Major F. B. Pearce   1914-1922
2. J. H. Sinclair   1922-1924
3. Sir Claud Hollis   1924-1930
4. Sir Richard Rankine   1930-1937
5. Sir John Hull   1937-1941
6. Sir Guy Pilling   1941-1946
7. Sir Vincent Glenday   1946-1952
8. Sir John Rankine   1952-1954
9. H. S. Potter   1954-1959
10. Sir George Mooring   1959-1963

CHRONOLOGY

1000 BC   Original peoples known as Bushmen were disturbed by the Southern Cushites coming down from the North.

Pre-AD   Early traders along the coast were from Egypt, India, Assyria, Phoenicia, Arabia, Persia and Greece.

2d C. AD   The Romans also visited the East Coast. Greek wrote about Rhapta under the King of SW Arabia.

0-1000 AD   Arrival of Bantu; Arab and Persian merchants made their homes in the coastal and island settlements.

ca. 1270   Sultan Hassan bin Sulaiman I ruled Kilwa and probably built the Great Mosque. Began minting coins.

by 1290   Muslims dominated Indian Ocean, spread of Islam at the Coast. Migration of Shiraz.

1000-1300   Bantu migration in Central and Northern Tanganyika and Kilimanjaro. In Central Tanganyika a mixture of Cushites, Highland Nilotes and Bantu.

1300-1500   Afro-Arab coast culture flourished.

ca. 1320   Sultan Hassan bin Sulaiman II ruled Kilwa, conquered the Mafia Islands.

1380-90   Pate invaded southwards and for a short while controlled much of the coast; first mention of Unguja.

xiv

1450   Reemergence of Kilwa. Rebuilding of the Great
            Mosque.

1490   Kilwa had lost her former power.

1500-1600   Arrival of Hinda group from the North to estab-
            lish pastoral dynasties in Karagwe and Bukoba
            (Bahima).

1500   Petro Alvares Cabral reached Kilwa.

1502   Second journey of Vasco da Gama with 10 ships,
            Kilwa forced to pay tribute to Portugal.

1503   Ruy Lawrence Ravasco forced Mafia, Zanzibar and
            other towns to pay tribute.

1504   Kilwa refused to pay tribute to Lopez Suarez.

1505   Francisco d'Almeida attacked Kilwa on way to
            India.

1509   Portuguese occupied Zanzibar, Pemba and Mafia.

1512   Portuguese withdrew their garrisons from Kilwa.

1588   Second visit of Ali Bey, defeated with the help of
            the Zimba.

1600   British East India Company founded to trade with
            the East.

1612   First account of route into interior--Kilwa to
            Zambezi.

1652   Omani attack on Zanzibar and Pate.

1669   Omani attack along the coast almost as far as
            Mozambique.

1678   Viceroy brought a fleet to punish the East Afri-
            can Coast towns.

1700-1800   Cattle raids and wars were normal among the
            small kingdoms SW of Lake Victoria. Kara-
            gwe War with the Bunyoro during the reign of
            Ntare VI.

1700-50   Masai expansion into Tanganyika.

1750-1850 Pastoral Masai dominated a large area of the
           Rift Valley, highlands and plains where they
           held cattle raids with their neighbors.

1753   A Mazrui attempt to conquer Zanzibar was de-
           feated; Zanzibar remained loyal to Oman.

1780   Imam seized Kilwa and put a loyal governor in
           charge to tax the slave traders.

1784   Attempt by Saif bin Ahmad al Busaidi to make a
           separate Sultanate of Kilwa and Zanzibar failed.
           Imam reestablished control of coast.

1804-56   Sultan Said ruled. Slave trade flourished.

1811   Zanzibar slave market established.

1820's   Arab and Swahili merchants penetrated the inter-
           ior.

1822   Moresby Treaty made it illegal to sell slaves out-
           side Said's dominions.

1833   A treaty signed with the Sultan of Zanzibar gave
           American merchants trading rights.

1837   American Consulate established in Zanzibar.

1839   Sultan Said signed a treaty with Chief Fundikira
           for free right of passage of traders through
           Nyamwezi land. Trade treaty with the British.

1840   Sultan Said moved his capital to Zanzibar from
           Muscat.

ca. 1840   Ngoni invasions from the south in two groups.

1844   Sultan signed a trade treaty with France.

1845   Hamerton Treaty made it illegal to ship slaves
           out of East Africa. Rebmann was the first
           white man to see Mt. Kilimanjaro.

1848   Krapf and Rebmann visited Kilwa.

1856-9	R. Burton and Speke travelled to the Lakes Region.
1859	Treaty of commerce between Sultan and Hanseatic Republics.
1860-3	Speke and J. Grant visited area to West and North of Lake Victoria.
1863	Holy Ghost Fathers started a freed slave settlement in Zanzibar.
1864	Universities Mission to Central Africa entered Zanzibar.
1866-73	Dr. Livingstone's last journey.
1868	Holy Ghost Fathers at Bagamoyo.
1870	Sultan Barghash became ruler of Zanzibar.
1871-4	Nyamwezi successfully resisted the Zanzibaris and gained control of the caravan routes.
1872	Inauguration of Wm. Mackinnon's British-India Co. mail service from Zanzibar to Aden.
1872-6	Stanley's explorations in East Africa.
1873	Zanzibar slave market was closed; treaty between the Sultan and Britain abolished slave trade within the Sultan's dominions.
1875-80	UMCA expanded its work among the Yao.
1877	Zanzibar-Aden telegraph cable laid. London Missionary Society in Lake Tanganyika area.
1878	White Fathers at Tabora and Lake Tanganyika.
1882	Burning of Masasi.
1883	H. H. Johnston arrives. Britain did not endorse his treaties.
1884-5	Karl Peters made treaties with chiefs on mainland opposite Zanzibar and had them ratified in Germany.

1886	Anglo-German Agreement of 1886 (Delimitation Treaty). Kirk left Zanzibar.
1887	Mackinnon's Imperial British East Africa Association founded. Proclamation that all children born in Sultan's dominion were free.
1888-9	Abushiri's rebellion at Pangani.
1890	The German government took control of the German East Africa Company.
1891	The Medical Department was established.
1891-3	Resistance by the Zaramo, Chagga and Nyamwezi.
1894	The IBEA Co. was bought out by the British Government.
1895	Land Ordinance; Native Reserves marked out.
1894-8	Risings among the Gogo, Hehe, Yao and Haya.
1896	Khalid bin Barghash's revolt at Zanzibar.
1897	Ocean Road Hospital opened. Status of slavery abolished in Zanzibar and Pemba.
1901	British loan to help Zanzibar economy.
1902	Amani Institute opened. Tanga-Korogwe RR line completed.
1903	Establishment of plantation farming--sisal, coffee, rubber.
1905	Cotton growing school at Mpanganya.
1905-7	Maji-Maji Revolt.
1905-14	Construction of the Central RR Line, Dar es Salaam-Tabora-Kigoma.
1906	Gov. Rechenberg opposed settlers. Consul General assumed almost complete power in Zanzibar.
1907	Administration reforms initiated. British rejected

Arab supremacy. Colonial Department of the
German Gt. formed.

1908   Courts came under British control in Zanzibar.

1909   Slave decree ended slavery in Zanzibar.

1910   Encouragment of coffee growing among Chagga and
        Haya.

1911   Sultan Ali abdicated.

1912   Tanga RR Line extended to Moshi.

1913   Settlers represented on Advisory Council. Sultan
        Khalid regained some influence in Zanzibar.

1918   Sir Horace Byatt made adminstrator of post-WW I
        conquered lands.

1919   Influenza epidemic. Britain took over administra-
        tion of Tanganyika under a mandate of the League
        of Nations.

1920   "Tanganyika" first used. Shillings and cents be-
        came currency.

1921   Native Authority Ordinance.

1922   Slavery ended in Tanganyika. Gold discovered.

1923   Native Authority Ordinance--Masai Reserves
        made. Land Ordinance--Reallocation of Set-
        tlers' Land. Trade Tariffs.

1925   Expansion of education begun. Zanzibar adminis-
        tration separated from Kenya. Indirect rule
        began when D. Cameron became Governor.

1926   Native Authority Ordinance. Legislative Council
        formed.

1927   Clove Growers Association (CGA) formed in Zan-
        zibar.

1928   Tabora-Mwanza RR branch line opened.

1929   Native Courts Ordinance. Moshi-Arusha RR branch
            line opened TAA formed.

1931   Economic collapse.

1932   Beginnings of tea and sugar growing.

1933   Recovery from Depression. CGA attacked Arab
            businessmen. Sukumaland Federal Council of
            Chiefs formed.

1934   Governmental reforms on the local level in Zan-
            zibar.

1937   Indian boycott of Zanzibar trade.

1938   Labour Advisory Board formed.

1939   All German citizens detained. Farms under a
            Custodian.

1942   Wheat growing began.

1945   First two African members on the Legislative
            Council.

1946   East African Airways formed. Became Tanganyi-
            ka Territory under the UN. Three African mem-
            bers on Legco.

1946-50   Groundnut Scheme which ended in failure.

1946-51   Gradual extension of African representation on
            Legco and Executive Council.

1948   East African High Commission formed.

1949   East African Posts and Telegraphs and East Afri-
            can Railways and Harbours formed.

1951   Committee on Constitutional Development recom-
            mended equal racial representation on the unof-
            ficial side of the Legco.

1953   Local Government Ordinance provided for elected
            local councils. A Speaker replaced the Govern-
            or as president of the Legco. Nyerere elected
            President of TAA.

1954   Three African unofficials on the Executive Council.
              7 July, TANU founded. UN Mission recom-
              mended a fixed timetable for Tanganyika's in-
              dependence.

1955   First elections to the Legco. Racial parity among
              the unofficial members. Nyerere presented
              TANU's demand for independence to UN Trustee-
              ship Committee. New Legco with multi-racial
              unofficial representatives in Zanzibar, 3 unof-
              ficial members on Executive Council. Council
              boycotted by Arabs. Council appointed. Legco
              enlarged.

1956   UTP formed, pledged to multi-racial government.
              EAA began regular flights to Britain and India.
              ZNP and ASP formed in Zanzibar.

1957   Elections in Zanzibar won by ASP. Political ri-
              valry led to Arab-African racial clashes.
              Nyerere appointed to Legco, but soon resigned.
              Nyerere's public meetings banned by the govern-
              ment.

1958   Sweeping TANU victories in Legco elections. UTP
              disbanded. Gov. R. Turnbull's arrival. Ramage
              Committee appointed to decide on further con-
              stitutional changes.

1959   Executive Council became Council of Ministers
              which included five TANU representatives. Tan-
              ganyika Elected Members Organization formed,
              the nucleus of a new government.

1960   Election to 70 Legco seats, TANU won 70. EAA
              began jet services to India and Asia. Blood
              Constitutional Committee brought recommenda-
              tions in Zanzibar.

1961   1 May--Full internal self-government in Tanganyi-
              ka with Nyerere as Prime Minister. Legco be-
              came National Assembly. 9 Dec. --Tanganyika
              became fully independent. (Zanz.) Elections in
              Jan. produced an indecisive result. Fresh out-
              break of political and racial violence during the
              June elections. ZNP and ZPPP formed a co-
              alition government under Sheikh Mohammed
              Shamte. EACSO formed from the East African

High Commission. University College of Dar
es Salaam opened with Faculty of Law.

1962   Regional Commissioners appointed. Preventive
            Detention Act. 9 Dec. --Tanganyika became a
            Republic. Zanzibar Constitutional Conference
            in London.

1963   Tanga RR Line linked to main Kenya line. Uni-
            versity of East Africa came into being. (Zanz.)
            24 June--Internal Self-Government gained. Ca-
            binet and National Assembly formed. 10 Dec. --
            Independence.

1964   12 Jan. --Revolution in Zanzibar. 16-20 Jan. --Mu-
            tiny by Tanganyika Rifles 1st Battalion.
            6 Apr. --United Republic of Tanzania formed.

1965   One-Party State policy announced. Tanzania Bank
            of Commerce formed. Interim Constitution
            of Tanzania effective 1 July. Elections for
            President, Local government and National As-
            semby members in Tanzania mainland.

1966   Bank of Tanzania established. Tanzania currency
            in use.

1966-8   Diplomatic relations broken with Britain over
            Rhodesia issue.

1967   5 Feb. --Arusha Declaration, Uljamaa policy stated.
            Nationalization of major industries. East Afri-
            can Community formed. Africanization of Heads
            of Secondary Schools and Teachers Colleges.

1968   All MP's required to sign a financial statement
            confirming that they have only one source of in-
            come. Swahili language became medium of pri-
            mary education to Std. VII.

1970   Adult Education Year. Nationalization of all
            schools. University of Dar es Salaam founded
            and University of East Africa disintegrated.
            Presidential elections held.

1971   Feb. --Four persons sentenced to life imprisonment;
            Treason trial. New Primary school syllabuses

to revolutionize education. Mwongozo--TANU
Guidelines released. Tenth Anniversary of independence celebrated.

1972   President of Zanzibar-Vice President of Union
        Karume assassinated. Decentralization of power
        to regions. Tanzania/Uganda border clashes.

1973   STC disbanded and replaced by regional trade
        companies and a national import corporation.
        Tabora Declaration reasserted both the primacy
        of Ujamaa villages in rural development and of
        rural development in national development.

1974   20 Years of TANU celebrated. Nov. --Musoma
        Resolution called for Universal Primary Educa-
        tion for 1977. Agricultural Campaign--Kufa
        na Kupona.

1975   Presidential elections and National Assembly seats.
        The Great Uhuru Railway completed.

1976   Cooperative marketing policies revised. TANU-
        ASP merger constitution written.

1977   Birth of CCM--the new revolutionary party.
        Tenth Anniversary of Arusha Declaration cele-
        brated.

INTRODUCTION

The United Republic of Tanzania, the thirteenth largest African country, is located mostly between latitude 2° and 12° S. and longitude 30° to 40° E. It contains the highest mountain and the lowest spot in Africa; Mt. Kilimanjaro rises to 19,520 ft. (5,950 m.) and the floor of Lake Tanganyika is believed to be 1,175 ft. (358 m.) below sea level. Tanzania has a land area of 342,171 sq. miles (874,423 sq. km.) and 20,650 sq. miles of inland water. It stretches north to south, east to west with over 700 miles at its greatest length and width. Tanzania's borders touch eight countries: its neighbors on the north are Uganda and Kenya; on the west are Zaïre, Rwanda, Burundi; and on the south are Zambia, Malawi and Mozambique. Tanzania has a coastline of over 500 miles on the east with the Indian Ocean.

Within Tanzania there are a wide variety of land forms, climates and people. The formation of the country has been likened to a giant bowl; a plateau in the center ranging from 3,000 to 5,000 feet in altitude is bounded by the Eastern and Western Rifts of the famous Rift Valley. Most of the plateau is open grassland with a thin cover of trees. Two-thirds of it is uninhabited. The northern belt of the highland areas include the Usambara, Pare, Kilimanjaro and Meru Mountains, the Central and Southern include the Southern Highlands, Livingstone, Uguru and Uluguru Mountains. The highest peaks are volcanic. Ol Donyo L'Engai last erupted in 1966 and Mt. Kilimanjaro has been heard to rumble into the 1970's. Block faulting is responsible for the uplift of the plateau areas as well as for the depressed areas of the Rift Valley, Lakes Tanganyika, Nyasa, Rukwa, Manyara and Eyasi.

The rest of the country has gently sloping plains and plateaus broken by low hill ranges and scattered, isolated hills. At the coast there are areas of sweeping sandy beaches with developed coral reefs. There are extensive areas of mangroves, especially at the mouths of rivers.

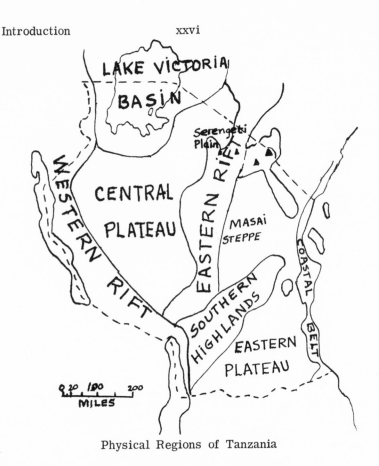

Physical Regions of Tanzania

The coastal 10-40 mile wide lowland is hot and humid. Temperatures in most of Tanzania are temperate due to the high altitude which counteracts its tropical location. Although Tanzania is hotter than Kenya, its climate and vegetation are not "tropical" in the usual sense except along the lush coastal belt. Woodland and bush country occupy most of Tanzania. Desert, semi-desert and arid lands account for the remainder of the land area.

Rainfall is variable from place to place and time to time and is generally lower than expected for the latitude. The central third of the country is rather dry and evaporation exceeds rainfall for nine months of the year.

Due to shortage of water, soil erosion and unreliable rainfall, the population is concentrated in the peripheral areas

of the country.   This makes economic development more difficult and communication and transportation more costly.   The
decision to move the capital from Dar es Salaam to Dodoma
was aimed at developing the interior and reducing distances
and cost.

One of the greatest attractions for visitors is the abun-
dant wildlife and geological formations in Tanzania.   Mt. Kili-
majaro attracts the mountain climber and the National Parks
draw the nature lover.

Tanzania has few natural resources, but it has people
and they are the main aim in its development.   The original
peoples are considered to have been a type of the Bushman
in South Africa.   A few remnants exist.   The "ancient Azanians" described by the explorers and traders, arrived around
1000 B. C.   They were Caucasoid and sometimes called
"Southern Cushites. "   The Bantu who now form the largest
group, came around A. D. 1000.   The Nile-Hamites, more
recently known as Cushitic, were followed by the Nilotes.

Two different historical areas developed, the people of
the Coast and of the Interior.   Very little is recorded about
the interior until it was penetrated by trading caravans to and
from the coast in the 1830's.

The coastal area has a much longer history of trading
contacts with Egypt, India, China, Assyria, Phoenicia, Arabia, Greece and Rome all before A. D. 1000.   Persians then
settled on the coast and the islands later forming the Zanzibar Republic.   Kilwa developed into an important trading center.   The Portuguese pushed northwards and ruled the area
for awhile in the early 16th century only to lose it again to
the Omani Arabs.   Sultan Said moved his capital to Zanzibar
in 1840 after he had already established a flourishing slave
trade there and signed treaties with European countries.   This
attracted the European explorers and missionaries to the
coast and inland, following the major slave trading caravan
routes.   Then came the scramble for Africa and Karl Peters
made treaties with inland chiefs for Germany.   Britain offered
assistance to the Sultan of Zanzibar and the coastal strip of
land.   The Anglo-German Agreements of 1886 and 1890 de-
limited the boundaries of German East Africa and the British
Protectorate.

There were a number of uprisings and resistance to
the German rule on the mainland and they went through a

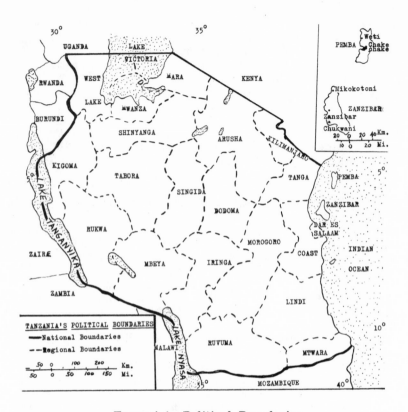

Tanzania's Political Boundaries

period of suppression and then a developmental period which
was cut short by the First World War.

After the War, Britain administered what is now
Tanzania as two separate entities: a mandate under the
League of Nations (the mainland) and a Protectorate hooked
more closely with Kenya (the islands). Indirect rule was the
policy. The mainland became a Trusteeship Territory under
the United Nations after World War II and a more realistic
development of the territory was initiated.

Settlers had never reached even one-half of one percent of the population. Asians did not exceed one percent.
The government policy that developed before independence was
a "separate but equal" one; the three education systems developed side by side and no greater amount of grants went to
the Africans although they constituted 99 percent of the population.

There was and is no tribe among the 120 who could claim to be a majority group; the largest one had one million members, only 10 percent of the total population. Swahili, the lingua franca, is a Bantu language and, as such, united the various groups into a cohesive, nationalist entity much more smoothly than their neighbors. The first political party, TAA, was revamped and TANU went ahead swiftly and surely to independence which was granted on 9 December 1961. Exactly one year later Tanganyika became a Republic.

Zanzibar moved more slowly and less smoothly to independence. They became a sovereign nation on 10 December, 1963. Social and economic relationships came to a head in the Revolution of 12 January, 1964. The governmental power transferred from the minority, Arab community to the Africans. Several days later the Tanganyika Rifles' First Battalion mutineed as a show of their grievances.

On 26 April, 1964, the two sovereign states formed the United Republic of Tanganyika and Zanzibar and by October the name Tanzania was adopted. Each state advocated a single party and a socialist ideology. TANU and ASP operated side by side as the Union consolidated selected matters. Others were dealt with independently. By 1976 the parties decided to amalgate and form one new, revolutionary party, CCM (Chama cha Mapinduzi).

Ninety-five percent of the people live in rural areas and agriculture accounts for 80 percent of the exports. Manufacturing contributed 10 percent to the GDP in 1976, mining and quarrying 1 percent and commerce about 12 percent. Ujamaa villagization mushroomed in the 1970's; the villagers increased from 1.5 million people in 4,500 villages in 1971 to 10.2 million people in over 6,100 villages in 1976.

Islamic influence is strong along the coast and along the early caravan trade routes. Another 3 or 4 million people are Christians, either Roman Catholics or Protestants. Others subscribe to traditional religious beliefs. Ujamaa in Tanzania does not eliminate religion but rather encourages its existence, realizing that religion does not interfere with itself.

Tanzania's cities are not large in comparison with cities of more developed countries. The largest, Dar es Salaam, reached the half-million mark in 1975 and the second largest, Tanga, had not yet hit 100,000 by 1977.

Railways and Towns

A work-study education is deemed best for implement-
ing Education for Self-Reliance and the Arusha Declaration.
Much effort has gone into functional adult education as a
means of accelerating the developmental processes.   An informed, literate population is expected to be more receptive
to change, a requirement for a revolutionary, mobilized society.   Tanzania has been very pragmatic in its policies and
Universal Primary Education was stepped up from 1969 to
1970, and then 1977 when Ujamaa villagers were ready for
greater social services.

Tanzania was linked to Uganda and Kenya in an East
African federation for Common Social Services after World
War II and continued in the partnership after they became

soverign nations.   However, their relationship had its ups and downs, successes and failures.   The East African Community faced a crisis several times in 1976 and gave way to a disintegration process, one service at a time.

Closer ties developed with Zambia through the Great Uhuru Railway transporting much of Zambia's imports via Dar es Salaam harbor.   Tanzania, as one of the Front Line States on the issue of Southern Africa, has great sympathy for the African majorities still under a minority government.   Tanzania has also given a home to refugees and freedom fighters from a number of nations.

It belongs to the Commonwealth and is a member of the OAU and the UN.   It advocates a non-alignment policy in world power politics and supports Pan-Africanism.

President Nyerere has been the mastermind of Tanzania's political philosophy and pragmatism.   He is charismatic, humble and merciful and has an outstanding gift for explaining government policies to the people.   He is casual, lively and straightforward.

Tanzania's ability to experiment with new ideas even in the middle of a Five-Year Plan, has been watched quite closely by a number of African and Third World countries. Its stability has been a challenge to most nations.   May it continue.   Nyerere, in his Introduction to his book, Freedom and Socialism, said it like this:

> By thinking out our own problems on the basis of those principles which have universal validity, Tanzania will make its own contribution to the development of mankind.   That is our opportunity and our responsibility.

THE DICTIONARY

ABDALLAH BIN HEMEDI EL AJJEMY (1840-1912). A distinguished Swahili historian, who was born in Zanzibar to an Arab father and Machinga mother. Abdallah served Kimweri za Nyumbai and later passed from Kilindi to German service. After serving as akida of Sega and Muheza, he was promoted to liwali of Tanga in 1905 when he was sixty-nine years old. This elevation gave him one of the half-dozen highest posts open to a non-European. Abdallah served as liwali of Tanga until 1910. He died at Tanga in 1912.

ABDULLAH BIN KHALIFA, SULTAN (1910-1963). Son of Sultan Khalifa who ruled Zanzibar from 1911 to 1960, was born in 1910 and was fifty years old when he succeeded his father as Sultan. He was a sick man and died three years later on 1 July, 1963.

ABDULLAH BIN NASIBU (?-1882). The Arab leader most disliked by Mirambo. He was one of the foremost Arab warriors of the interior, earning the nickname "Kissessa" (Valiant) from his many victories. He acquired a large and devoted following at Unyanyembe (near Tabora) from his generosity in dividing out the spoils. Disagreement arose among the Arab community at Unyanyembe and the sultan's liwali, Said bin Salim was driven from office by a combination of forces led by Abdullah and Shaykh bin Nasibu, with the support of Chief Isike of Unyanyembe. The liwali fled to Urambo under Mirambo and for years there was distrust between the former and latter liwali, the British and Sultan Barghash as Abdullah bin Nasibu acted as the liwali. In 1881 Abdullah was recalled to Zanzibar and, rather surprisingly, he heeded the order. The supposed reason for his recall was his mistreatment of Emile Sergere, a European trader at Unyanyembe. He is said to have had very heavy debts with the Indian merchants of Zanzibar, so much so that he did not dare to show his face at the

Zanzibar court. His name has also been listed among
members of a faction which had designed to overthrow
Sultan Barghash in Zanzibar. Abdullah bin Nasibu died
in 1882. Some claim that he was poisoned through the
orders of Barghash as he was attempting to return to
Unyanyembe.

ABEDI, SHEIKH AMRI (1924-1964). Born in Ujiji, and educated at Tabora Secondary School from 1937 to 1941, he
took up postal work training (1942-43) and Islamic missionary training (1944-53). He studied in Rabwah College in Pakistan (1954-56). In 1959 he was elected a
member of Parliament, was Mayor of Dar es Salaam
from 1960-62 and Regional Commissioner for Western
Region in 1962. He held ministerial posts in the Justice
Department (1963) and was appointed Minister of Community Development and National Culture in 1964.

ABUSHIRI BIN SALIM AL-HARTHI   see   BUSHIRI

ADULT EDUCATION. By the late 1940's the Social Welfare
Department started to conduct adult education courses in
towns and by 1952 these services were extended to the
rural areas. In the rural areas the emphasis was on the
eradication of illiteracy while town dwellers attended
evening courses. Most of the services were carried out
by voluntary agencies. The Three Year Development
Plan for 1961 to 1964 set aside £230,000 for community
development schemes. These were to be used to eradicate illiteracy by a mass campaign. Extra-mural
classes were offered at the Institute of Adult Education
which was under Makerere College until it opened in
1963. Evening classes were carried on in the larger
towns such as Dar es Salaam, Tanga, Morogoro, Iringa
and Moshi. Also Saturday seminars were conducted.
Those who benefitted most from these beginnings had had
a secondary education or greater. The Institute of
Adult Education opened in 1963 and carried on the extra-
mural classes, but added a second emphasis after 1964:
study and research in adult education and the professional training of adult education teachers and administrators.
Informal education for adults in literacy classes continued
under the auspices of the Community Development Division and the voluntary agencies. There were 300,000
enrolled in literacy classes in 1962 and 600,000 in 1965.
The number exceeded 600,000 adult learners in 1969.
    In the Education Act of 1969, adult education was

placed under the Ministry of National Education. That
same year the Commission of Enquiry into the University of Dar es Salaam advocated that adult education be
extended to the rural areas. So correspondence courses,
radio programs and adult literacy classes have received
greater emphasis. "Functional literacy" was stressed
with many activities of learning provided for adults with
literacy as one of the activities.
     President Nyerere declared 1970 as Adult Educa-
tion Year. The Directorate of Adult Education became
a division of the education department of the Ministry
in 1973. By the end of 1974 literacy had risen to 50
percent. The September 1974 enrollment in classes of
arithmetic, Swahili, history, political education, farming methods, health and domestic science was between
250,000 and 500,000 in each and a total of 3.4 million.
However, some may have been double-counted. In 1975
there were over 5 million registered in classes. An
examination was given to adults in 1975 to see which
standard each pupil had reached. By June 1976, 61 percent of the adults were believed to be able to read or
write.

ADVISORY COMMITTEE ON AFRICAN EDUCATION. The
     Committee was established in 1926 in accordance with
     the Colonial Office Memorandum of 1925. It consisted
     of three government officials, two Africans, two repre-
     sentatives of trade and commerce and no less than eight
     missionaries. The one African was a missionary ap-
     pointee and the other a government servant. There was
     no Muslim representative. The Committee had regular
     and profitable meetings until 1934. It did not meet after
     1934 and was later replaced by a Central Advisory Com-
     mittee which had twice the official and half the mission-
     ary membership of the original Committee. The Edu-
     cation Ordinance of 1961 repealed the separate Advisory
     Committees and instead formed a multiracial Advisory
     Council of Education.

ADVISORY COUNCIL OF EDUCATION. Replaced the sepa-
     rate Advisory Committees on education by the Education
     Ordinance of 1961. It was multiracial and considered
     very important to the Minister of Education. The Chief
     Education Officer was the Chairman of the Council which
     consisted of 12 or more members with perhaps only the
     Chairman and Secretary being Government officials. It
     met at least once a year. Its powers could not be over-

ridden by the Minister of Education without special permission from the President, Cabinet and National Assembly.

AFRICAN ASSOCIATION. Formed in 1930 to safeguard the
interests of the African civil servants. It moved into
the political sphere in Bukoba as early as 1937 and in
Pare in 1942.

AFRICAN ASSOCIATION (in Zanzibar). Formed in 1934 and
asked for official recognition as an affiliation of TAA.
It was formed by mainlanders to protect laborers and
squatters. It did not become politically active until after
World War II.

AFRICAN INLAND MISSION/CHURCH (AIM/AIC). Entered
Tanzania from Kenya in 1909 with a group led by Rev.
E. Sywulka. They settled in Nassa north of Mwanza and
divided the area with the CMS, but the greater expansion
took place in Sukumaland. Pastors were chosen and ordained and in 1966 Pastor Jeremiah Kisaula was ordained
to the office of Bishop. Although the AIM had handed
over authority to the AIC in 1957, the name was not officially changed until 1965. By 1976 there were 70 pastors, 500 evangelists and around 70,000 Christians. The
Church operates two Bible schools, a print shop and
bookstores, a hospital at Kolandoto and ten dispensaries.
The general church office is located in Mwanza.

AFRICAN NATIONAL CONGRESS. Formed as Tanganyika
African Congress in 1958 and registered under the name
ANC. The founder was Zuberi Mtemvu, a former provincial secretary of TANU. The main difference between
ANC and TANU was their emphasis on Africa for the
Africans. ANC put up three candidates in the 1960 election for Legislative Council. Mtemvu opposed Nyerere
as Presidential Candidate. The ANC folded up soon afterwards as they were greatly defeated and Tanganyika opted
to become a one-party state.

AFRICAN TEACHERS EXAMINATION BOARD. Created in
1950. It was concerned with sitting and correcting professional written examinations and with the conditions
governing practical teaching. Its name was changed in
1958 to Teacher Training Advisory Board.

AFRICANIZATION. The process of "localizing" the leadership

positions; in most cases it was an African taking over
from a non-African. In 1951 there was only one African
top-level civil servant. By 1959 only five were Africans
in the 4000 top- and middle-level jobs. By July 1960,
the Africans totalled 380. There were 13 African doctors,
no African judges or magistrates, no African assistant
principal secretaries or permanent secretaries. In 1961
Africans held 14 percent of the jobs in Government services and 15 percent of the top-level. District Commissioners were replaced by Africans very rapidly--from
only one African in the 58 districts in 1959 to five in
1961 and fifty-three by Independence date. By January
1963, 40 percent of the civil servants were locals. Even
this was too slow for many people and was a source of
the mutiny of January 1964 among the troops. Only 17
out of 685 secondary school teachers in 1964 were Africans. In 1967 all heads of boys' secondary schools and
teacher training colleges were replaced by Africans. By
that time 78 percent of the business licenses were held
by African businessmen. Also at least 70 percent of the
civil servants were African and over 1000 were studying
for degree courses in the East African University in the
hope of filling many more of the remaining posts. The
name changed to "localization" when citizens of any ethnic
group were given responsibilities. In 1974, 67 percent
of the top posts were filled by Tanzanians and the estim-
ate for 1980 was 90-95 percent.

AFRO-SHIRAZI PARTY (ASP). The result of a merger between the African Association and the Shirazi Association
(Zanzibar branch) on 5 February, 1957, and was first
called Afro-Shirazi Union (ASU). Even though they had
joined, they continued in separate identities. ASP took
part in the 1957 elections. The goal of the ASP was the
achievement of independence and subsequent government
of an African Zanzibar by an all-African government. It
was anti-Arab. In December 1959, the Zanzibar and
Pemba People's Party under Sheikh Shamte split off from
ASP. The ASP lost the 1961 elections because of poor
organization and lack of cohesion as a disciplined political movement. It had no formal constitution and thus internal conflicts were not solved. These weaknesses were
overcome by 1963. During the 1963 elections ASP won
the majority of the votes but lost the election and a co-
alition of ZNP/ZPPP formed the government. Arabization
was fostered and a large number of lower-level African
policemen were dismissed. This developed into a crucial

force responsible for its own fall. Many dismissed policemen took part in the Revolution of 12 January, 1964,
which resulted in a new government under the ASP. The
People's Republic of Zanzibar was led by Sheikh Karume.
The goals of the ASP and TANU were practically the
same, so a union between Zanzibar and Tanganyika was
enacted on 26 April, 1964. The parties did not merge,
however, due to the apprehension of the Zanzibari's that
they would be swallowed up by the mainland. So ASP
carried on in Zanzibar as the only party there until 1976
when agreement was reached with TANU to merge and
form a new party. A 20-man TANU-ASP Commission
met in October and laid the foundation for the CCM which
was born officially on 5 February, 1977.

AGE-SETS. Groupings of similar age within a tribe or clan
whose members share certain duties and responsibilities.
The Nilo-Hamitic-speaking tribes support this system in
which the men of a tribe belong to one of several graded
age-sets. These age-sets exist entirely separate from
the neighborhoods or kin groups. Male members become
members of a specific named set after passing through
an initiation ceremony, usually involving circumcision,
during their youth. They are bound together for the duration of their mature lifetime. They are equals or peers.
If one is designated spokesman, he is first among equals.
The opening of a new set every 3 to 4 years signals the
shift of the sets with older members to a higher grade.
There are 5 grades of age-sets: junior warrior, senior
warrior, junior elder, senior elder, and retired elder.
Each grade has its own responsibilities. As junior warriors, the men usually marry and settle down to raise a
family. All warriors are active in herd management and
herd protection, but each level has its own particular
duties. Junior elders participate in neighborhood affairs
and fulfill certain political and jural duties. Elevation
from warriorhood to elderhood is very significant and
elaborate ceremonies mark the event. At the same time
senior elders must be willing to retire and other grades
must have sufficient members. Senior warriors enjoy
high esteem and are reluctant at times to move on to
another grade.

AGRICULTURE. About 10 percent of the land is under cultivation, another 10 percent fallow land or pastureland.
Approximately 27 percent of grassland and woodland is
potentially suited for cultivation if developed. About

one-third of Tanzania has a water supply adequate for
cultivation.   About 95 percent of the population live in
rural areas and are subsistence farmers.   For the first
time in 1966, the value of all cash crops sold in the market was estimated to exceed the total value of crops consumed on the farm.   Since then, agriculture has represented around 40-45 percent of the GNP and accounts for
80 percent of the exports, with cotton, coffee and sisal
leading.
        Bananas, yams and coconuts were brought to Afri-
ca from Southeast Asia not later than A. D. 500.   Maize,
cassava, groundnuts and sweet potatoes were introduced
in Africa during the 15th century from the Americas by
the Portuguese and European traders.   Sisal was introduced by the Germans in 1892.   In 1902 the German government began communal farming in the Dar es Salaam
area.   Villagers were forced to work in rotation on a
common field using cotton seeds and tools provided by the
government.   Coffee was developed in Bukoba and the
Chagga areas.   Groundnuts were taken by the Germans to
Nyamwezi and Sukumaland.   Rubber was produced.   Other
cash crops are cashew nuts, tea, pyrethrum, tobacco and
cloves.   Agricultural diversification has received a good
deal of attention due to the fluctuating world market
prices.
        Village settlement schemes were designed around
1960 to enable the farmer to change from subsistence
farming to contributing to the national economy.   This
transformation approach was abandoned for the improvement approach aimed at gradual and progressive improve-
ments in the methods of small farmers where results have
been much better.   Ujamaa (q. v.) villages have provided
an easier contact with the people for developing improvement methods and concentrating effort.   State farms are
also a part of the agricultural program.   See also VIL-
LAGE SETTLEMENT SCHEME; STATE FARMS; UJAMAA
VILLAGES; and the various crops under their own entries.

AKIDAS.   Under the German administration, akidas were the
    Arabs, Swahilis or recognized chiefs in a large area who
    were given authority over 20,000 to 30,000 people.   They,
    with jumbes under them, collected taxes, administered
    local justice and prepared the people for economic develop-
    ment.   The use of the akida aided the growth of Swahili
    in the hinterland.   The methods they used and their treat-
    ment of the people sometimes aroused bitter feelings.
    Akidas often erected a barrier between ruler and ruled

causing a lack of understanding of each other.   They became one of the Africans' grievances because of their
alien background, Islamic culture, power to tax and quasi-
military status.

ALI BIN HAMOUD, SULTAN.   Sultan of Zanzibar from 1902
until he abdicated in 1911.   He became Sultan at seventeen years of age when his father, Sultan Hamoud bin
Mohammed died.   Ali was still fresh from school in London.   Since he was still a minor, the First Minister took
the opportunity to consolidate British control and exercised all the powers of the Sultan.   The Zanzibar army
was disbanded in 1907 and two companies of the KAR
were given control.   In 1908 import duties were increased
from 5 to 7.5 percent.   Compensation to slaves was to
be paid from 1909-1911.   So he began to spend more
time travelling abroad.   While he was in Europe during
1911, he abdicated.   He died in Paris in 1918.

ALI BIN AL-HASSAN BIN ALI.   The first great ruler or Sultan at Kilwa.   The Arab historians date his reign from
957-996, while most others claim it was two centuries
later according to our Western calendar.   He most likely
arrived at Kilwa around 1200 and established a new 'Shirazi' dynasty at this trading post.   He built a strong fortress and raided other towns.   He gained the nickname
Nguo Nyingi (Many Clothes).   Sultan Ali put his son Muhammed in charge of Mafia.

ALI BIN SAID, SULTAN (1855-1893).   The last of Sultan
Said's sons, ruled from 1890-1893 and died at thirty-
eight years of age on 5 March, 1893, after frequent
periods of prostration.   He requested the protection of
Great Britain.   On 1 August, 1890, he was persuaded to
sign the Anti-Slavery Decree.   The Protectorate was established on 4 November, 1890.   He agreed that relations
with foreign powers shall be conducted through the British Government channels.   It was binding forever on himself, his heirs and his successors.   He died on 5 March,
1893.

ALL-MUSLIM NATIONAL UNION OF TANGANYIKA (AMNUT).
Formed in 1957 but never put itself forward as a political party.   It did act, however, as a Muslim pressure
group.   It was critical of TANU for not supporting Islamic education, and, as a whole, was conservative to
social changes, such as the emancipation of women

and secular education.   TANU threatened to ban the AM-
NUT on several occasions.   In September 1959 its leaders urged that Tanganyika should not become independent
until all Muslims had greater educational opportunities,
but the organization was denounced by Muslim leaders.

AMANI INSTITUTE.   This biological-agricultural institute in
Usambara was established in 1902 to tackle problems of
tropical agriculture.   They experimented with soils, crops
and fertilizers and hunted ways to combat disease.   The
government spent £10,000 a year.   Cotton was fostered.
Quinine was made here as well as at Mpwapwa.   During
World War I they prepared many varieties of foodstuffs,
spices, medicines, soap, oils and liquors.   The agricultural research on an East African basis began in 1927 at
Amani.   The Institute was moved to Nairobi, Kenya in
1948.

ANGLICAN CHURCH IN TANZANIA.   The Anglican Church began in Tanzania under two different groups--The Church
Missionary Society and the Universities Mission to Central Africa.   Discussions concerning unity were seriously
given thought in a meeting between the Bishops of both
groups of Tanzania and of neighboring Kenya in 1958.   So
in 1960 the Anglican Church of East Africa was formed
directly under the Archbishop of Canterbury.   There were
four dioceses in Tanzania and one in Kenya.   Ten years
later, in 1970, there were two branches made--Tanzania
and Kenya.   In Tanzania there were eight dioceses formed.
One year later the Southwestern Diocese was established
and it was joined to the Tanzania Anglican Church.   John
Sepeku is the Archbishop of the church.

ANGLO-GERMAN AGREEMENT OF 1886.   Affected Britain,
Germany and Zanzibar.   It defined the islands and northern East African coastal towns for the Sultan.   The country between Tana and Ruvuma Rivers was divided by a
line from the Umba River to Lake Victoria in the Northwest: the northern half (modern Kenya) went to Britain,
the southern half went to Germany.   They also agreed to
settle rival claims in Kilimanjaro peacefully.   The Sultan's Territory was limited to a ten-mile coastal strip.
Germany also gained control of Witu outside Africa.

ANGLO-GERMAN AGREEMENT OF 1890 (The Heligoland Treaty).
Germany recognized Britain as authority in Uganda (an-
nulled Peter's treaty with Kabaka Mwanga), abandoned

her territory of Witu and accepted the British Protectorate over Zanzibar and Pemba. The Northern boundary
of the German area was drawn across Lake Victoria at
latitude one degree south and the borders with Rhodesia
and Nyasaland were agreed upon. Britain agreed to ar-
range for the cession to Germany of all the Sultan's possessions on the mainland and also Mafia. Germany also
acquired Heligoland in the North Sea from Britain.

ANTI-SLAVERY DECREE. Signed by Sultan Ali on 1 August,
1890, it prohibited all sale, exchange or purchase of
slaves; closed down slave markets with immediate effect;
declared slaves of a childless master free on his death;
forbade the wives of Indians to hold slaves; threatened
punishment of masters for ill-treatment; and permitted
slaves to purchase their freedom.

ARAB ASSOCIATION (Zanzibar). Formed to work for com-
pensatory payments to ex-slaveowners. A split in the
Association occurred over ethnic representation as proposed by the British Resident in March 1954. Almost
all its executive members were arrested by the British.
The ensuing Arab boycott of all government organizations
for $1\frac{1}{2}$ years was successfully carried out.

ARABS. In the 1800's Arabs led caravan traders into the
interior of Tanganyika in search of ivory and slaves.
They developed a large slave trade. Arab-trading posts
were situated at or near African towns. These Arab-
Muslim kingdoms gradually Islamicized the population.
Arabs in Tanzania are a heterogenous group but are all
Islamic. During the 1950's, 78.1 percent of the employed
Arabs were in wholesale and retail trade. The 1965 es-
timate was given as 25,600 Arabs on the mainland and
around 50,000 in Zanzibar. The majority of Arabs in
Zanzibar were peasant farmers, lived in wattle huts and
cultivated small plots of cassava, pineapples and bananas.
The Arabs have been more backward in education than
Indians and Europeans. Some of their main contributions
to East Africa are: Islam, social customs and dress
styles adopted in many places, the development of many
African cultures, their language influenced the development of Swahili. Polygyny is desired and practiced among
the Arabs. Zanzibar Africans felt oppressed when the
Arabs were in political power and vice versa.

ARCHEOLOGICAL FINDINGS see OLDUVAI GORGE; ZIN-
JANTHROPUS

ARMY.   Tanganyikans in the KAR fought in World War I and
    World War II, even gaining a good reputation in serving
    abroad in Somalia and Ethopia, Madagascar and Burma.
    In 1929 the KAR was reorganized and the 1st, 2nd and
    6th Battalions were located in Tanganyika.   The Supply
    and Transportation Brigade was also organized.   By 1960,
    the 2000 soldiers were still equipped with World War I
    rifles.
            On January 20, 1964, the soldiers of the First Bat-
    talion of the Tanganyika Rifles conducted a mutiny.   Al-
    though the Tabora and Tanga units threatened to support
    it, the mutiny was confined to Dar es Salaam and was
    soon put down with the help of the British Royal Marines.
    The Mutiny stemmed from grievances over Africaniza-
    tion of the service and salaries.   These demands were
    met and the Army was kept non-political.
            The National Service Act was passed in 1966.
    Military service is voluntary, but graduates of secondary
    schools and the university are required to do a year ($1\frac{1}{2}$
    years from 1967-75) in nation-building activities and mili-
    tary training at a camp.
            By 1968 there were 4 battalions, 4000-5000 men,
    an air wing with 100 men in the training unit and no or-
    ganized reserves.   A naval unit was then in the planning
    stages.   By the mid-1970's the armed forces totalled
    14,600 with 13,000 in the army, 600 in the navy and 1000
    in the airforce.   National Service trainees are reservists
    if required and the People's Militia also consists of work-
    ers who have been trained after working hours.   At in-
    dependence Israel was training the army.   Since then
    Canada and China have carried the greater responsibility
    for the training program.   The army is also busy with
    national self-reliance programs.

ARUSHA (town).   Located exactly half-way between Capetown
    and Cairo on the Great North Road.   Arusha is a fast-
    growing town, an important business center at the head
    of the railway line from Tanga.   It is an important cen-
    ter for tourism because it is well-located to serve those
    interested in visiting Serengeti and Arusha National Parks,
    the Masai, Ngorongoro Crater and the Olduvai Gorge.
    Its selection in 1967 as the Headquarters of the East Afri-
    can Community also boosted its importance.   It has an
    altitude of 4600 feet and a pleasant climate which is con-
    ducive to business and farming.   This town situated on
    the Great North Road is also a center of a productive
    area.   Slaughtering and refrigeration of cattle and pigs
    and wheat-milling are its main industries and the main

crops are coffee, sisal, wheat, and pyrethrum. Its population was estimated to be 10,000 in 1959, over 32,000
by 1967, and 104,000 in 1977.

ARUSHA (tribe). Sometimes referred to as "agricultural Masai" and are engaged in a mixed farming system. As a
settled and established tribe the Arusha date from about
1930, at which time a few small groups of Masai-speak-
ing peoples came to settle near the upper Burka River
at the Southwestern edge of the rain forest of Mt. Meru.
They began cultivation and have very few or no livestock.
They prospered as farmers and pushed up the mountain
slope, clearing the forest as they went. Their language
and many customs are similar to the Masai. Coffee is
their cash crop while bananas, corn and beans are also
grown on the same land. The parish is an important
unit. Although land is owned by the household heads, the
members of the parish have a strong sense of duty and
cultivate the land in their parish. They mend their
roads, handle internal disputes and deal vis-a-vis with
other parishes. In 1957 there was an average of 2000
people in a parish which averaged 2 square miles in size.
There is less and less land available for each parish.
The Arusha have an autonomous age-set system. If a
person moves from one parish to another, he joins the
age-set in the new parish which is equivalent to the one
he was first initiated in.

ARUSHA DECLARATION. Contained the goals of TANU in a
major policy statement in February 1967 by President
Nyerere. It was not a new policy but a call for the people of Tanzania to unite and work together for their own
economic and social welfare. Its main aims were: self-
reliance using local resources, not depending too much
on external aid and assistance; 'Ujamaa,' national service
and sacrifice, popular participation in the process of nation building; the removal of all distinctions based on
class, wealth, status; and the control by the people of
all major sources and means of production.

ARUSHA NATIONAL PARK. Gazetted in 1970. It has an
area of 137 sq. km. and is famous for its beautiful Ngurdoto Crater, Mt. Meru and the Momela Lakes. The top
of Mt. Kilimanjaro can be easily viewed from here. The
most common animals present are elephants, giraffes,
rhinos, colobus monkeys and buffaloes. It has no lions,
no tsetse flies or mosquitoes.

ASIANS. Most of them were called Indians until India and
    Pakistan split in 1947. They played a key role in open-
    ing and developing the interior: they financed much of
    the slave trade; introduced imported consumer goods; and
    have acted as middlemen and money lenders for African
    agricultural producers and European importers and pro-
    ducers.
        In 1948 they numbered around 58,000 or 0.9 per-
    cent of the population. By 1957 there were over 100,000.
    Half of them were employed in wholesale and retail trade,
    14 percent in manufacturing, 13 percent in public ser-
    vices, and 5 percent in forestry, agriculture and fishing.
    They were mainly an urban group.
        They do not form a single cohesive community due
    to their differences in language, religion and place of
    origin. From late 1961 through 1963 other Tanganyika-
    born Asians were permitted to register as citizens. Ap-
    proximately one-half or more did so. The Aga Khan or-
    dered all Ismailis to take out Tanganyikan citizenship,
    but by 1967 it was not known how many had done so.
    Thousands left Zanzibar after 1964 and quite a substantial
    number left the mainland after nationalization of property
    and industries began in 1970. The Asian Associations
    contribute to the community welfare by erecting schools,
    clinics and providing other services. Over 60 percent
    live in cities and towns and are three times the European
    population. They reside all over Tanzania, but primarily
    in Dar es Salaam and Zanzibar.

AUGUSTANA MISSION. When the Lutheran Church was asked
    to carry on the work of the Leipzig Mission in Iramba
    area because the German missionaries had to vacate dur-
    ing World War I, the Augustana Mission took over. This
    later became known as the Central Synod of the Luther-
    ans. In seven years' time, planning was done by mis-
    sionaries and local church leaders. Pastors were or-
    dained and the church was granted independence from the
    Mission. In 1963 the church spread out to the Barabaig
    tribe and in 1967 on to the Kindiga and Sukuma. The
    President of the Diocese is Zefania Gunda. There are
    around 65,000 Christians, about 300 worship centers,
    30 African pastors and 60 evangelists, 1 Bible School,
    1 hospital and 14 dispensaries.

AVIATION. Tanzania was served by the East African Airways
    and around 20 foreign airlines which hold regular ser-
    vices from Tanzania to all parts of the world. The East

African Airways Corporation came into being on 1 January, 1946, when the Directorate of Civil Aviation was
established for Uganda, Kenya and Tanzania. In 1956
EAA began regular flights to Britain and India. By 1960
EAA began jet services to India and Asia. It had become one of the world's most successful airlines. There
were 30 airfields in use in Tanzania in 1957. EAA had
22 landing airports in Tanzania in the 1970's, some so
small that the dropping of the DC-3 fleet in 1976 required
construction at some of the airports to enable them to
handle the DC-9 planes. In 1975 the EAA made a net
profit of 41.1 million shillings. It was one of the few
airlines to operate with a 9-yr. successive profit. Yet
in December 1976, it reached a crucial breaking-up point.
The Chairman of EAA in 1976 was Ndugu Kilewo. On
22 January, 1977, Kenya formed its own national airlines
and Tanzania established Tanzania Airlines mid-year.

AZANIA. The name given to the Coast of East Africa by the
Greek writers.

AZANIANS. Probably the first inhabitants in the interior.
Huntingford dates this civilization about A. D. 700 or
earlier. They were skilled in using dry stone for building, some of the settlements showing as many as a hundred houses clustered together. One archeological discovery of ruins is a city along the hills of the Kenya-
Tanzania border. Another characteristic of the Azanian
civilization was the elaborate terracing of cultivated land.
They also dug irrigation canals, raised cattle, mined
iron and other minerals and worked them both for their
own needs and for export. Trading appears to have been
on a small scale. Huntingford believes the civilization
came to an end around the 14th or 15th century. There
are indications that they were overwhelmed by the pastoral nomads who were militarily superior to them; they
were slowly destroyed by the more primitive groups.

-B-

BABU, AHMED MOHAMMED ABDULRAHMAN (1922-   ).
Born of mixed Arab-Comorian descent. After an education in Zanzibar, he enrolled in Makerere University
College and later in London University, specializing in
English literature, philosophy, social psychology and
journalism. His active participation in Zanzibar politics
began in 1957 after six years with the Zanzibar Clove

Growers' Association and six years in a savings bank
counter in West London.   He became a leader of the
Zanzibar National Party (ZNP) and won successive victories by linking the Arab, Asian and African groups
through Islam.   His political activities between 1957 and
1964 were interrupted by a prison sentence in 1962-63
for a minor offense of sedition.   After a two-year struggle to turn the conservative, pro-Sultanate ZNP away
from Koranic principles towards strict socialism, Babu
resigned before the July 1963 elections and founded UMMA
(Masses) Party which was Marxist organized.   UMMA
was banned one week before the January 1964 revolution
in Zanzibar.   Babu was in Tanganyika mainland during
the Zanzibar Revolution.   He became the Minister of Defense and External Affairs in the new Zanzibar government and his party UMMA merged with ASP.   After the
Union of Zanzibar and Tanganyika in April 1964, he held
the portfolios of the Minister of State, then Minister for
Commerce and Cooperatives, Minister for Health, Minister for Commerce and Industries and Minister of Economic Affairs and Planning.   In February 1972 he was
dropped from the Cabinet.   On 7 April, 1972, he was detained after the assassination of Zanzibar's President and
the Union's First Vice President Karume.   He has been
imprisoned on the mainland and not returned to Zanzibar
for trial or sentencing.

BAGAMOYO.   The first capital of the mainland, it is situated
75 kilometers north of Dar es Salaam.   (See HOLY
GHOST FATHERS for the first missionary activities there.)
The German governor's residence was built at Bagamoyo,
but the capital was later moved to Dar es Salaam in 1891.
The town site was once the hub of the infamous slave
trade, the terminus of the slave caravan route from Lake
Tanganyika.   The name Bagamoyo ("Here I lay down my
heart") possibly stems from the slaver's activities.   Old
stone pens, shackle rings and other relics of this evil
trade can still be seen.   At present Bagamoyo is a quiet,
almost 100 percent Islamic town depending on fishing and
coconuts.   The last vestiges of its former importance
vanished when Dar es Salaam became the country's capital.

BAHAYA ASSOCIATION.   The first tribal association formed
on a modern basis.   Its forerunner was the Bahaya Union
begun by Klemens Kiiza in 1924 to establish an institution
which would develop the country and seek a system for

the simple way to civilize to the African's advantage.
The Union became the center of opposition to the Chief's
privileges.   Kiiza bought a coffee-hulling machine and organized the Haya into an African Association.   The Growers' Association collapsed when the Chiefs issued orders
controlling methods of growing coffee.   When the Bahaya
Association was organized in 1937, based in Bukoba, it
was initiated to protest the regulations imposed by the
Native Authorities for the Government which required
sanitation on the coffee farms of the Bahaya growers.
Until World War II, the Association was concerned with
a great variety of activities.   A secondary society, the
Bukoba Cooperative Union, was formed in 1950.

BAHIMA.   A more advanced people than the Bantu to the
south of them around Lake Victoria.   They are half-Ham-
itic.   From the 14th century they carried on a peaceful
invasion into Northwestern Tanganyika; they were accepted
as chiefs in Bukoba, Uha, Ujinja, Uvinza and Sukumaland
and Nyamwezi.   The further south they travelled, the
more democratic and less powerful they became.   Around
1750 more groups of Bahima moved east and south into
Ugogo and Usagara.   The Gogo, Hehe and Sambaa are
Bahima descendants.

BANANAS.   Probably introduced into Africa from Southeast
Asia before A. D. 500.   They are grown for eating raw
and cooked, as a major cash crop, for brewing beer; the
stalks provide fodder for cattle and thatching material
for houses.   Bananas grow in the wetter areas--the northwest and the southwestern areas.   They are the staple
food for the Chagga and Haya tribes.

BANK OF TANZANIA.   The central bank which issues and
controls currency.   It was created in June 1966, and had
as its first task the responsibility of introducing a new
Tanzanian currency to replace the East African currency
formerly in use.   One of the aims of the establishment
of this bank was to give monetary authorities greater
flexibility and independence in determing the total supply
of money and credit, thus decreasing one aspect of the
country's dependence on foreign trade.   The third function
of the Bank was to regulate the country's gold and foreign
exchange reserves.

BANTU.   Late arrivals on the scene, having been preceded
by a type of Bushman and the Caucasoid "ancient

Azanians. " They are thought to be Negroes moving south
as the Sahara became a desert. They intermarried with
Hamites. They are a racially diverse people with common origins as proved by the similarity of their language,
which is known as Bantu. A great number of them moved
into East Africa from Southern Congo in the first century
A. D. while others appear to have moved in from the
coast. In Northeastern Tanzania, the Chagga, Shambaa
and Sagara show affinities to those immediately to the
North in Kenya.

  The Eastern Bantus have been profoundly influenced
by the contact with Azanians and Nilo-Hamitic. They accepted certain social institutions, copied their weapons
and hairstyles and intermarried. In the 18th century
chieftainship emerged among the Chagga and the Shambaa.
The Western Bantu are patrilineal and reveal a definite
kinship with the Bantu of Uganda. Their reverence for
their ruling authority was very great. The Southern Tanzania Bantu--the Hehe, Bena, and Gogo--are matrilineal.
Their origin is in Central Africa west of Lake Tanganyika.

BAPTIST CHURCH. The first missionaries were sent by the
  Southern Baptists of USA in 1956. They began work in
  Dar es Salaam and opened a hospital in Mbeya. Rugwe
  Station was opened in 1958 and there they specialized in
  agriculture. Other stations opened in 1961 were Kigoma,
  Tanga and Arusha. Since then they have added Mwanza,
  Moshi, Chunya and Mbozi. The Church operates one
  hospital and three dispensaries, has a seminary to train
  pastors at Arusha, a Social Center in Dar es Salaam and
  four Bible schools. Their members total 12,000. The
  head office is at Tukuyu and the church head is Ishmael
  Sibale.

BARABAIG (tribe) A tribe of around 20,000 members, are
  one of the few surviving 'cattle complex' people. The
  use of and attitudes towards cattle and cattle products
  influence their culture: milk and milk products, hides,
  drawn blood, cow dung, meat and urine are all used.
  They had an unusual custom of murdering strangers.
  The male is tall, muscular and well-developed; women
  are self-possessed, aggressive and independent, old women exert a great influence on clan proceedings. The
  Tanzanian Government has initiated transformations by:
  banning the wearing of the red-ochred toga; a shift from
  herding and nomadism to sedentary horticulturalism;
  severely punishing ritual murder; and forceably reeduca-
  ting young people.

BARAGUYU (tribe). Sometimes called Kwavi. The warriors
   spend much of their time on self-adornment like the
   Masai. They are famous for their necklaces, hair adornment and earpieces.

BARGHASH BIN SAID, SULTAN or SEYYID (1833-1888). An
   energetic and enlightened prince who travelled much. He
   ruled Zanzibar from 1870 to his death in 1888. His reign
   was marked by great opulence in Zanzibar. He ordered
   the construction of a conduit to supply pure drinking-water
   to the town. During his reign the indigenous peoples of
   the islands were brought under effective Arab rule. Muslim judges were sent into the interior. He made Zanzibar a state of world interest by developing steamship and
   cable connections. At first he was pleased with the British for they helped him to power, then he became angry
   with them when they pressed him to stop the slave trade.
   In 1872 he signed a treaty to terminate trade in slaves,
   but it was not effective. He argued all profit came from
   trade and the Koran allowed slavery. Barghash was invited to England in 1875 and met Queen Victoria and the
   Prime Minister. In 1877 he offered to Great Britain a
   70-year lease over all commercial activities in his kingdom. The offer was not accepted. During the same
   year he formed a proper army and chose British officers
   to command and train it. The army was used to spread
   peace in the interior and to stop chiefs from closing the
   trade routes. Barghash experienced humiliating losses
   of his dominion on the mainland. Germany began making
   inroads in 1884 and by 1885 had annexed 60,000 square
   miles of mainland territory. When Barghash protested,
   the Germans lined up warships opposite Zanzibar city.
   He agreed. In 1886 Germany and Britain signed the Delimitation Treaty which only left a 10 by 600 mile strip
   on the coast. Barghash died in 1888 of consumption and
   elephantiasis.

BARONGO, EDWARD (1928-   ). Born in Bukoba District in
   1928 and educated locally through district school level.
   He joined the East Africa Army Medical Corps and served
   four years, then served on the police force from 1951-54,
   as a coffee instructor in Bukoba Native Co-operative
   Union. He entered politics as an ordinary correspondent
   in 1955 and transformed Bukoba TAA branches into a
   TANU branch. He served as District Secretary, Provincial Secretary and Provincial Chairman all of West Lake
   until independence. He entered the national scene as a

member of the National Assembly in 1960, served as
Deputy General Secretary of TANU 1961, Parliamentary
Secretary in the Ministry of Agriculture 1962, Regional
Commissioner in Northern Region and in Ruvuma, served
as Executive Chairman of Tanganyika Tobacco Board and
in 1975 of National Milling Corporation when he was appointed to the office of Junior Ministry in the Ministry
of Agriculture.

BARWANI, SHEIKH ALI MUHSIN.   A journalist and ZNP leader at the time of the 1957 elections in Zanzibar, belongs
to a long-established Arab family in Zanzibar.   He studied
agriculture at Makerere College and was editor of a weekly newspaper Mwongozo.   He lost in the 1957 election to
Karume, but won support of Nkrumah of Ghana; he visited
Ghana and Peking.

BAYI, FILBERT (1953-   ).   Has set world records in long
distance running.   He left secondary school to join the
army at 17 when urged by the Chief of Staff, an old run-
ner, who saw his potential.   Had he completed secondary
school and joined the university, a great possibility, he
may never have been able to develop his running.   He
joined the army in 1970 as a technician with the TPDF
air wing.   On 24 January, 1973, he was promoted to
Sergeant and became a Lieutenant in April 1974 after he
set the world record on 3 February, 1974, for the 1500
meter race during the 10th Commonwealth Games in New
Zealand, completing in 3 min. 32.2 sec.   On 18 May,
1975, in Jamaica, he set a new world record for the
mile: 3 min. 51 sec.   He won the 5000 meter race in
1976.   Bayi has spurned pro offers and runs where the
government organizes his running.

BEESWAX.   Tanzania is the world's largest exporter.   Around
1960 about 400 tons were exported.   The amount increased
and brought in more than £250,000 in foreign currency in
a year.

BENA (tribe)   Their original home is the plateau of Iringa.
They were agriculturalists and herders.   During repeated
feuds with the Hehe, one part of the Bena tribe emigrated
to the Ulanga plains.   They still carry on agricultural
activity, herd cattle and do some fishing.

BENEDICTINE MISSION OF ST. OTTILIEN CONGREGATION.
The first German Roman Catholic missionaries to reach

Tanganyika.   They began their first work in November
1887 about 12 miles west of Dar es Salaam at Pugu.   In
January 1889 the Arab rebels headed by Abushiri raided
their Pugu Station and two brothers and one sister were
murdered.   They courageously carried on the work and
founded a mission house and a sisters' convent at Dar es
Salaam in 1890 and Kurasini Mission in 1894.

Since they had southeastern Tanganyika in mind as
their major area, they pushed into the Southern Highlands
in 1894 and erected the Madibira Station.   The following
year they opened two more stations north of Masasi, one
later destroyed by the Maji-Maji Uprising, and moved to
Ndanda.   By 1903 the Central School had 150 pupils including the son of a Paramount Chief.   In 1905 when Bishop Cassian Spiess was travelling from Kilwa Kivinje to
Peramiho he was attacked and killed by the Maji-Maji
Africans who had grievances against their German rulers
and made no distinction between the Germans in the government and German missionaries.   Two brothers and
two sisters of his party were killed.

In 1906 the name of Benedictine Vicariate was
changed to Vicariate Apostolic of Dar es Salaam.   After
the Maji-Maji Rebellion was suppressed, a period of
peace lasted only about eight years until World War I
made interruptions.   German missionaries had to leave.
In 1920 the western half, the now Diocese of Iringa, was
handed over to the Consolate Fathers from Italy.   The
rest was handed over to the Swiss Capuchin Fathers.   In
turn, the orders amalgamated in the 1950's to form the
now known Tanzania Episcopal Conference (TEC).

BENJAMIN, SETH (1945-1967).   He died while on a marathon
walk in support of socialism after the Arusha Declaration
had been announced in 1967.   The walk, which began in
Arusha, was expected to end in Dar es Salaam.   Benjamin was born in Singida Region in July 1945 and attended
local primary schools.   Although he had been a Head
Prefect, he was not selected to Standard V.   His family
moved to Usa River, Arusha, in 1955.   There he joined
the TYL and became the leader of the Usa River branch.
After working for Doli Sisal Estate, he joined National
Service on 14 October, 1965.   On completion, he was
employed as a messenger at Arusha Regional TANU office.   When Tanzanians began demonstrating their agreement with the Arusha Declaration by walking, he organized
a group at Arusha.   He became so ill on the walk that
he was sent on to Mawenzi Hospital at Moshi.   When

the rest of the group got there by midnight, they learned
that their leader had died.

BERLIN EVANGELICAL MISSIONARY SOCIETY.   A German
Lutheran group, began their work in Dar es Salaam in
1887, opened a station at Kisarawe in 1888 and another
at Maneromango in 1895.   They handed over these stations to the Berlin Mission in 1903.

BERLIN MISSION (Lutheran).   At work by 1870 and entered
Tanzania in September 1891 from the South.   The Nyaku-
sya chiefs welcomed them as traders.   They settled
among the Bena, Kinga and Hehe as well as Nyakyusa and
began what was later called the Synod of Southern Tanzania.   They were hindered by the uprisings between the
Hehe and German rulers from 1891-98 and the Maji-Maji
War in 1905-06.   Also, World War I affected the German
missionaries and many had to leave their stations.   In
spite of the many hindrances, they built churches,
schools, hospitals, dispensaries and a trade school.
There were 2226 converts by 1913.   The first African to
assume leadership of the Synod was Yuda Kiwovele and
the second William Mwakagali.   Due to the great expansion in the Synod of Southern Tanzania, a second Synod
was created for the Ulanga Kilombero area and Rev. Ki-
poroza was given its leadership responsibilities.   There
are around 190,000 members, 1000 worship centers, 4
hospitals, 18 dispensaries, 1 medical school, 1 Bible
school, 56 African pastors and 789 evangelists.
         In 1903 the Berlin Evangelical Missionary Society
handed over to the Berlin Society the Dar es Salaam and
Zaramo areas.   There were problems and by 1913 the
converts totalled only 382.   World Wars I and II also disrupted the mission staff.   However, the work continued
and became the Synod of Eastern Tanzania and Coast Region.   In 1970 the Rev. E. E. Sendoro became its first
African Synod President.   There are approximately 27,000
members with 36 worship centers, 22 African pastors,
52 evangelists and 2 dispensaries.

BERTELSEN, PAUL HENRY.   The first director of the Institute of Adult Education in Dar es Salaam when it opened
in 1963.   Bertelsen was born in 1925 in Denmark and
educated in Copenhagen and Cambridge Universities from
1945-50.   After filling positions of tutor and lecturer at
Birmingham and Copenhagen, he began his first foreign
work in Ghana at the Amudome Residential Adult College

from 1960-63. That provided him with a background for
his directorship at the Institute which was attached to the
University College of Dar es Salaam. He served as Director from 1963 to 1967.

BETHEL MISSION. Founded the Lutheran Church in the Vuga-
Usambara and Tanga areas. The missionaries arrived
in Tanga to begin their work in 1890. Mlolo, Vuga, Lu-
tindi, Bumbuli and Irete are some of their stations. In
1912 they began printing books on their press installed
at Vuga. Bible training was begun at Mlalo in 1946 and
continued until 1954 when it was moved to Makumira near
Arusha. A medical school was opened in 1952 at Bumbuli. The Diocese is now known as the Northeastern and
is in the hand of Bishop Sabestian Kolowa. There are
approximately 45,000 Christians, 39 African pastors, 75
evangelists, 1 Bible school, 3 hospitals and 5 dispensaries.
        Some of the Bethel Missionaries decided to move
on to Ruanda in 1910 where some of their colleagues had
already begun a work. When they got as far as Bukoba,
they found some CMS Christians. The CMS had contacted
these Christians from Uganda, but had not been able to
place any missionaries in Bukoba area. The Bethel missionaries accepted an invitation to remain there and
served at Kigarama, Kashasha, Gubulanga, Kanyangereko
and Ndologe. Later they scattered farther. During
World War I the church work was carried on by the indigenous people of the area until the missionaries were
permitted to return. A few were allowed to remain at
work in schools and in the hospital during World War II.
They were joined by missionaries from America, Sweden
and Denmark. They built churches, schools, hospitals,
dispensaries and an agricultural school. This became
known as the Diocese of Northwestern Tanzania. Bishop
Josiah Kibira is in charge. There are about 100,000
Christians, 270 worship centers, 65 African pastors, and
271 evangelists, 1 Bible school, 2 hospitals, 9 dispensaries and 1 medical school.

BEY, ALI. A Turkish pirate, stirred up many coastal towns
in the 1580's to revolt against the Portuguese. After Ali
Bey's departure, the Viceroy sent solders from Goa to
punish disobedient towns. In 1588 he returned and captured Mombasa in Kenya. The Zimba invaded and recaptured the town with the Portuguese.

BIBLE SOCIETY OF TANZANIA.   First a part of the British
   and Foreign Bible Society.   In 1965 the name was changed
   to The Bible Society in East Africa with headquarters in
   Nairobi.   After Uganda had withdrawn in 1968, the Society was again revised and since November 1970, Tanzania has begun its own Bible Society branch with laws
   and by-laws common to Tanzania.   It was officially installed at Luther House on 31 January, 1971.   The Society is interdenominational.   Its main function is to provide Bibles, Testaments and Bible literature at a reason-
   able price to the population.   Pastor R. K. Ngota is its
   general secretary and N. E. Manongi is Financial Manager.   The head office has been moved to Dodoma.   The
   Bible Society is a member of CCT.

BILHARZIA (Schistosomiasis).   A debilitating, infectious disease endemic in many areas of the mainland and the islands where slow-moving water is contaminated by human
   waste.   It is transmitted by water harboring infected
   snails and infects the intestinal or urinary tract.   Eradication of the disease requires health education, elimination
   of the snails and treatment by drugs.   Irrigation schemes
   for agricultural purposes have not shown any decrease, but
   rather increase, of the contamination.

BINNS COMMISSION, THE. The first comprehensive survey
   on Tanganyika's education since the Phelps-Stoke Commission Report in 1924.   The Binns Study Group of 1951 emphasized practical education and terminal education for
   each level and sought a more liberal education for Africans based on their environment and own way of life.
   They prematurely suggested a Unified Teaching Service.

BLOOD CONSTITUTIONAL COMMITTEE.   In Zanzibar headed
   by Sir Hilary Blood, decided on an elected majority in the
   Legislative Council and that the leader of the majority
   group should join the Executive Council as Chief Minister.
   Sir Blood was appointed Constitutional Commissioner in
   early 1960 and, as a result of his report, Zanzibar received a new constitution and second elections were
   planned for January 1961.

BOMA.   1) A ring fence, as in "cattle boma," and 2) an administrative center, e.g., the offices occupied by an
   Area Commissioner and his District Team.

BOMANI, EMMANUEL (1930-   ).   Born of a Protestant

pastor in Musoma. He was educated locally and at the
Ikizu Teacher Training Centre, then joined Bwiru Secondary School and later St. Mary's Roman Catholic School
at Tabora. He joined the government Cooperative Development Department in 1953 as an inspector. After completing a commercial course in Kenya, he joined the Victoria Federation as acting secretary at its Mwanza Headquarters in 1956. He spent two years as an apprentice
manager of a ginnery, then studied from 1958 to 1960 in
the Northwest Polytechnic in London and earned a Diploma in Business Education. He was posted to the new
ginnery at Buyago on his return. He has been a director
for Smith MacKenzie, Tanganyika, Sisal Marketing Association, Tasnini Textiles, a Councillor of Makerere University College, General Manager of Victoria Federation
of Cooperatives Union and President of COSATA (Cooperative Supplies Association of Tanganyika).

BOMANI, MARK (1932-   ). The first Tanzanian to become
Attorney General. His father was a Protestant minister
and his older brothers, Paul and Emmanuel, have held
high positions in the Victoria Federation of Cooperatives
Union at Mwanza. Mark was born in Musoma, educated
locally and in Bwiru and Tabora Secondary Schools. He
received his B.A. in 1957 from Makerere College in
Uganda. He studied law in Holland, then at London University where he was granted a B.A. and LL.B. degree.
He was called to the Bar at Lincoln's Inn. After several
years in the office of Deputy Solicitor-General, he was
appointed Attorney General in 1965, a post he held until
1976 when he was appointed to the U.N. Institute for
Namibia and located at Lusaka, Zambia.

BOMANI, PAUL (1925-   ). Born on 1 January, 1925, in
Musoma, the son of a Protestant minister. After an
elementary education and a teacher training course at
Ikizu SDA, he refused to teach, although he held a Grade
II Teachers' Certificate. He joined Tabora Government
Secondary School. The Teacher Training Centre cut his
Tabora studies short due to this refusal to teach. Bo-
mani then took up a job from 1945-57 at Williamson Di-
mond Mines as a cashier and learned accounting by a
correspondence course. At twenty-two, in 1947, he be-
came Secretary of the Cooperative Wholesale Society in
Mwanza. He organized a cotton cooperative and regis-
tered it in 1952 as Lake Province Growers Association.
After the passing of the Cooperative Ordinance, the

Society was registered as Victoria Federation of Cooperative Unions. He was the General Manager of this largest marketing cooperative in Africa. By 1965 the Federation had bought up eight cotton ginneries from Asians (only three remained with the Asians).

His political career began early and he was elected the Provincial Chairman of TAA for Mwanza in 1952. After studies in England, Governor Twining appointed Bomani to the Legislative Council and, until September 1957, was TANU's only mouthpiece there. He returned to the Legislative Council in 1959 as an elected TANU member. He has held a number of positions both national and international: Minister for Agriculture and Cooperative Development; Minister for Finance; a Director of the International Monetary Fund; a Governor of the World Bank; Vice Chairman of the African Development Bank; Minister for Economic Affairs; Minister of Commerce and, unfortunately, became the first minister without a constituency when he lost his National Assembly seat during the 1965 elections. Since 1972 he has been Tanzania's Ambassador to the U. S. A.

BROWN, ROLAND GEORGE MacCORMACK (1924-   ). Born in London and educated at Ampleforth College (1938-42) and Cambridge University (1942-43 and 1946-48) and, in 1949 became barrister at law in Gray's Inn, London. He first came to Africa in 1953 in the Uganda-Mutesa disputes. He was the Constitutional Adviser to Chief Minister Nyerere at the March 1961 Conference in Dar es Salaam. From independence until 1965 he filled the office of Attorney General for Tanzania. When a Tanzanian succeeded him, he became Legal Consultant on International and Commercial Affairs to the Tanganyika Government. In 1966 President Nyerere seconded him to President Kaunda in Zambia to head an inquiry into the wave of strikes in the Copper Belt.

BRYCESON, DEREK NOEL MacLEAN (1922-   ). Born in China on 31 December, 1922. He received his education at St. Paul's School in London and Trinity College at Cambridge. At the age of seventeen he joined the RAF and in 1942 was shot down over the Western Desert and his survival was almost a miracle. Complications set in around his pelvis and he became permanently crippled. He emigrated to Kenya to farm in 1947 and moved south to Tanganyika in 1951-52 and settled on a 1200 acre farm near Mt. Kilimanjaro. He was appointed Assistant

Minister for Social Services on 1 July, 1957, and became
the unofficial minister for Mines and Commerce in 1959.
A week before the September 1959 election day, he had
a bad car accident in which he broke his polio-weakened
leg and several ribs.   He was unconscious for many hours
and spent the election in a hospital.   He won the election
on TANU votes against the UTP opponent, John Hunter.
He has held many ministerial positions in the independent
nation: Minister of Health and Labour, of Agriculture
(Forests, and Wildlife added later).   In 1972 he became
the Director of National Parks and has continued in that
capacity.

BUKOBA (town).   Emin Pasha's expedition reached Bukoba by
1890 and Langheld established stations at Bukoba and
Mwanza.   By 1924 a special school for chiefs' sons was
operating on the primary education level.   Bukoba's population was 8000 by 1967, 12,000 in 1975 and 13,000 in
1977.   It grew from a small fishing village on the west
of Lake Victoria and is situated in a valley of seven hills.
It has an instant coffee factory and coffee curing works.

BUKOBA COOPERATIVE UNION.   Formed in 1950, it became
the forerunner of the Bukoba Native Cooperative Union.
In 1960, 48 coffee societies joined to form the BNCU.
They sent staff abroad for training, built a large headquarters building, and operated a coffee-curing plant.   By
1966 it was one of the best organized, best financed and
most prominent cooperative in handling of important shares
of a large export crop--coffee.

BURTON, SIR RICHARD FRANCIS (1821-90).   A famous explorer in East Africa, was born in Hertfordshire on 19
March, 1821.   He joined the East Indian Company's military service in 1842.   This hot-tempered, tall, dark man
had visited Mecca and Ethiopia before his arrival at Zanzibar in 1856.   He spoke Arabic and aimed at exploring
the interior of Africa.   He was selected to be a leader
of an expedition to Central Africa financed by the Royal
Geographic Society.   They proposed to penetrate inland
from the East Coast to the reputed great lake in the interior.   He joined Speke on a journey to Somaliland and
then to Lake Tanganyika.   In June 1857 they set off on
an Arab route from Bagamoyo to Kazeh.   He suffered re-
current bouts of fever and had to be carried on a ham-
mock the last part of the way.   They reached Lake Tanganyika by February 1958.   Speke was blinded by fever

from February to May 1858 at the Lake.   They were dis-
appointed to learn that this was not the source of the
Nile as the water flowed southwards.   Burton was too
sick to go on to Mwanza with Speke.   His descriptions of
his travels and observations show a great interest in the
customs of the people he met.   He then joined the consular services and was stationed in a number of West
African countries.

BUSH SCHOOLS.   A sub-grade of school with or without religious instruction, providing a secular instruction ap-
proximating Std. I and Std. II of the primary course.
They were required by the Education (African) Ordinance
of 1954 to be registered as Part II Schools and that their
teachers be registered.   Around 1960 if a vacancy occurred in a Part I Primary School and a pupil in a bush
school had passed an examination successfully, he could
be admitted to the appropriate standard in the primary
school.   Bush schools received no government grants-in-
aid.

BUSHIRI BIN SALIN AL-HARTHI (sometimes referred to as
ABUSHIRI) (?-1889).   A half-Arab who led the revolt of
the coastal Arabs in August 1888 against German control.
He was a hereditary enemy of the Sultan.   Peoples from
around Pangani and the Zigua tribe around Morogoro re-
volted in fear of losing profits from the slave trade.
Abushiri was successful in capturing all coastal towns
from German East Africa except Bagamoyo and Dar es
Salaam.   He moved first six miles, then forty miles inland and before his death had attacked Mpwapwa.   His
power was broken when Wissman established a fort at
Mpwapwa.   Chief Magaya betrayed him to the Germans
and he was publicly hanged at Pangani on 15 December,
1889.

BWANA HERI BIN JUMA.   A Segu chief, succeeded his father
as ruler of Sadani during Sultan Majid's reign (1856-70).
He had a great influence over the Zigua tribe and was
one of the political leaders of the coast.   He defeated the
Sultan's troops in 1882 and was independent of the Sultan.
He and Bushiri were the leaders of the rebellion against
the German rule at Pangani and Bagamoyo in 1888-89.
He resisted the Germans in his own right; he worked
more or less independently with Bushiri.   He foiled many
of the German offensives against him in January 1889.
Bwana Heri, who was treated as an independent native

chief rather than a rebel, came to terms with the Germans in 1890 after having built forts inland with the support of the Hehe and was unsuccessful.   When he tried
to rise again in power in 1894, the Germans defeated
him and he fled.   He died in Zanzibar years later.

BYATT, SIR HORACE (1875-1933).   Coming from service in
Somaliland, he was the Civil Administrator of the northern sector of German East Africa from 1916 to 1919 during World War I.   On 31 January, 1919, he was made
Administrator of the mandated territory and in 1920 the
Governor.   Being a cautious man, he was convinced that
there should be no sudden innovations to disturb the African population.   Under his administration the 22 districts
of the Germans were retained as well as some of the experienced akidas.   He realized that the future of the country depended chiefly on native production and carried his
"obsession" to the point of refusing either to see representatives of the plantations or to visit their estates.   In
April 1924 he left Tanganyika and was Governor of Trinidad and Tobago from 1924-1929.

-C-

CAMERON, SIR DONALD (1872-1948).   Governor of Tanganyika from 1925 to 1931, had earlier been the Chief Secretary to the Government of Nigeria.   This tall, thin man
with a severe set of countenance, left lasting impressions
on Tanganyika: he established the Legislative Council
which had a high proportion of unofficial members (14
official and up to 10 unofficial members nominated by
the Governor); he introduced Indirect Rule and agreed
with most of the settlers who opposed a federation with
Kenya as he feared his native authority policy would be
ended; he created eleven provinces; a Secretary for Native Affairs was appointed; a Labour Department was set
up in 1926; and he took part in the formation of Tanganyika African Association in 1929.   He left Tanganyika in
1931 and was Governor of Nigeria from 1931-35.

CAPUCHIN FATHERS.   The Swiss Capuchin Fathers received
the eastern part of the Benedictine Fathers' area when
the German missionaries had to leave during World War
I.   In 1953 the Vicariate of Dar es Salaam was raised
to the rank of an Archdiocese and Metropolitan See of
Ecclesiastical Province of Eastern Tanganyika with

Archbishop Edgar Maranta in charge. The Capuchins'
progress was rapid and in March 1956 a local Auxiliary
Bishop, Elias Mchonde was nominated. They amalgamated with other orders to form the present Tanzania
Episcopal Conference (TEC).

CASHEWS. Tanzania is second in world production to Mozambique. The Cashew Association of Tanzania (CATA)
opened up a factory, TANITA, in 1966. They plan to
open up five new factories in Southeastern Tanzania where
most of the cashews grow. These new ones are expected
to have a total processing capacity of 40,000 tons and the
Tanita one is to take up to 25,000 tons of raw nuts by
1980. At end of 1976 the capacity of production was at
20,500 tons. There were 11,000 tons produced in 1951,
28,000 in 1961, 118,000 in 1970 and 115,000 in 1974/75.
The 1974 export value of 213 m. Shs. of raw and processed nuts dropped to 178.5 m. Shs. in 1975 due to
flowers being affected by dry weather in August/Septem-
ber. The average annual production was 150,000 tons.
In terms of quality Tanzania's product is said to be the
best in the world. About 80 percent of the crop is exported to India.

CASSAVA or MANIOC. Introduced in Africa from America
around the 15th century by the Portuguese or other European traders. It was probably brought to the East Coast
of Tanganyika by the Portuguese during their rule which
ended by 1740. Speke found cassava widely grown in
Zanzibar and implies that it was also encountered on the
way to Lake Tanganyika. V. L. Cameron in 1872 reported sweet manioc near Morogoro. It seems likely
that it was absent or non-important in most of East Africa in 1850 except right along the coast and along Lake
Tanganyika where it had been brought from the West.
Europeans and Arabs expanded the growing of cassava
after 1850; they saw it as a valuable safeguard against
the frequent hunger periods and famines.
        Cassava is a major edible rootcrop, not as pop-
ular in the diet as grains, but is the principal reserve
crop. It is easy to plant, cultivate and harvest, is
drought resistant, growth is vigorous, yield is certain.
It can be stored in the ground more than a year. There
are many varieties, including sweet and bitter types.
The root and leaves are both edible. Cassava is relatively free from disease and not eaten by locusts. An over-
dependence on cassava produces deficiency in protein and

in vitamins especially of the B group. By 1956 the crop
had become important in some provinces for cash. The
total annual production in the 1960's was 1 million metric
tons or over. In the 1975/76 year there were 17,635
metric tons purchased by the National Milling Corporation.

CASTOR SEED. Dodoma Region is the greatest producer for
the market. However, the market varies; 1971-73 had
the highest production in the first half of the 1970's with
over 10,000 metric tons in a year and the export value
reaching 19.7 m. Shs. in the best market year.

CATTLE. Animal husbandry, both commercial and for subsistence purposes, occurs in approximately one-third of
the country which is free of the tsetse fly. Some tribes,
such as the Masai, value herding as their economic base.
The Sukuma raise cattle in large numbers. Many tribes
of NW Tanzania have cattle in conjunction with farming.
    Over 90 percent of the cattle are Tanganyika Short-
horn Zebu, a few are Boran and Ankole. Dairy cattle
have been introduced in the Northern regions. The number of cattle have constantly increased from 5.7 million
in 1944 to 6.6 million in 1954, 11 million in 1967, 13
million in 1975, to 15 million in 1976. The government
emphasizes the danger of overgrazing land and advocates
a 10 percent destocking. Under an agreement signed between LIDA and Heifer Project International of USA around
500 heifers had already arrived by end-1976 of the 1000
promised in a 2-year agreement.
    The consumption of meat has risen. In Dar es
Salaam alone the number of cattle slaughtered in 1968
was 46,781 and in 1971 was 81,764. About 400,000 cattle are slaughtered annually at the abbatoirs. The dairy
business produced 40 million gallons of milk in 1961,
50 million in 1966 and in 1974 the Coastal Dairies Industries Ltd. in Dar es Salaam was providing approximately
45,000 liters of milk daily. Three percent of the exports
of Tanzania are tinned meat products. From 1972-75 the
exports of hides and skins averaged 38 m. Shs. yearly.
    On 1 October, 1974, the Cattle Authority was
formed with four main branches: National Ranch Companies; Tanganyika Meat Marketing Corporation; Tanganyika Meat Processing Co.; and the Dairy Companies
(Coast, Mara, Arusha). Mara also exports ghee.

CENTRAL COMMITTEE. Part of TANU, it was under the
National Executive Committee and responsible to it. It

was composed of about twenty senior TANU officers and presidential appointees.   The Central Committee met about once a month and oversaw party administration.

CENTRAL DEVELOPMENT COMMITTEE.   Established in December 1938 to plan a large-scale development program.   It was responsible for examining and reporting "on methods whereby the development of the Territory by non-native and native enterprise may be encouraged" and "to make Tanganyika a country. "   It assessed chances of natural and potential resources.   The main conclusion-- development could not be effected unless communications were much improved.   Its work was interrupted in September 1939 by World War II.

CENTRAL LEGISLATIVE ASSEMBLY.   Emerged along with the East African High Commission after World War II which was responsible for interterritorial transport, communications and taxation.   The Legislative Council was composed of a speaker, seven High Commission civil servants, an appointed Arab and five representatives from each territory of East Africa (one officer appointed by the governor, three unofficial members--one from each race--and one member elected by the territorial legislature).   Africans and Asians held an adverse reaction to the Assembly because it did not live up to its original proposal of equal representation among the races.   But because it concerned itself mainly with economic affairs, it was later generally accepted by most people.

CENTRAL LINE OF TANGANYIKA RAILWAY.   Runs from Dar es Salaam on the coast to Kigoma on the eastern shore of Lake Tanganyika, a distance of 780 miles or 1250 km.   One of its intended roles was to siphon off some of the Katanga mineral traffic, but it has done little of that.   It does carry some imports to eastern Zaïre.   Work on the railway was begun from Dar es Salaam in 1905 and reached Morogoro in 1907, Tabora in 1912 and Kigoma in 1914.   The Central Line runs through large stretches of bushland.   It has few feeder lines, the main one from Tabora stretching to Mwanza along southern Lake Victoria was opened in 1928.   In 1948 a short spur was built from Shinyanga to Mwadui to meet equipment and supply needs of Williamson Diamonds. Another more recent spur stretches to Mpanda to serve the lead mines.   The branch line from Manyoni to Singida closed down since Singida goldfields ceased production.

Morogoro is connected by RR bus and lorry to Tanga line
at Korogwe. Dodoma's RR buses connect to Iringa and
Mbeya in the south and Moshi in the north.

CENTRAL PLATEAU. Situated between the Eastern and
   Western branches of the Rift Valley and varies from 3000
   to 5900 feet above sea level. The Western part covers
   half of the country and bends southeast to Mozambique.
   This huge, uplifted basin is about 4000 feet in the greater
   part and is a hot, dry, hard plain dotted with granitic
   outcrops. Humidity is low and the rainfall reliable from
   20" to 30". Droughts are common. Most of it is so
   dry that it is only fit for open range grazing. There are
   large empty areas. The northern part slopes down to
   3700 feet to form the depression containing the Lake Victoria Basin. There agriculture is rather intense although
   that is not the pattern on most of the Plateau. Soils vary
   from yellowish sandy to dark brown clays with low to
   moderate fertility. Over two-thirds of the plateau is
   covered with miombo woodland which provides a breeding
   place for the tsetse fly. The mean temperature falls
   between 70° and 75°F. The daily and yearly variations
   may be greater than 36°F.

CENTRAL SCHOOL. One in which not less than four standards of English were taught or approved courses of industrial instruction were given. Local primary schools
   fed into these town schools. There were eight Central
   Schools by 1930. No tuition fees were levied, a 4 to 10
   shilling maintenance fee was required.

CHAGGA (tribe). The fifth largest tribe, one of the wealthiest, most highly organized and most modern tribe. They
   live in the best agricultural region, the slopes of Mt.
   Kilimanjaro, where rainfall is good. Around A.D. 1300
   the Chagga alone of the Coastal Bantu had developed a
   centralized monarchic government. They developed a
   great irrigation system with tiny tunnels of water from
   the main stream down Kilimanjaro. They also learned
   to make houses in the ground when tribal wars became
   dangerous. These were called "bolt" or "safety" holes.
   There were around 20 chiefs and considerable inter-
   chiefdom fighting. Power shifted from one chief to an-
   other--Orombo, Rindi (Mandara), Sina, and Marealle II.
        The Chagga Council was established in 1932.
   Three Superior Chiefs each were given a Native Authority
   area. In 1952 Divisional Chiefs and a Paramount Chief

were set up.   In 1960 the Paramount Chief's position gave
way to the President of the Chagga.   The Divisional
Chiefs lost their offices in 1961 when their posts were
abolished.

In 1919 there were around 100,000 Chaggas.   By
1960 there were more than 300,000 and 75 percent of the
young people were literate, a high figure for Tanzania
youth.   In 1964 the Chagga made up six percent of the
population and contributed 12 percent to the leadership
(elite) sample.   By 1976 they numbered around 400,000.

Bananas and coffee are their main crops.   The
Kilimanjaro Native Planters Association was formed in
1925 to organize the marketing of coffee.   Kilimanjaro
Citizen's Union was also established.   By 1932 Kilimanjaro Native Cooperative Union, Ltd. took over the KNPA
and developed to a large, prosperous cooperative which,
in turn, provided services to the Chagga.   See also
Chiefs RINDI, OROMBO, SINA, MAREALLE, and KNCU.

CHAGULA, DR. WILBERT KUMALIJA (1926-   ).   Born near
Shinyanga.   After an elementary education locally and
secondary at Tabora Government Secondary School from
1939-44, he studied at Makerere University College until
1952 when he received his licentiateship in medicine and
surgery.   His internship was done at Sewa Haji Hospital
in Dar es Salaam in 1952.   He studied at King's College,
Cambridge, England from 1953-55 and was awarded a
B.A. in Anatomy with Honors.   After an assistant lectureship in Anatomy at Makerere University College Medical School, he returned to Cambridge University for his
M.A. in 1960, was in Jamaica at the University College
of West Indies in 1961 and the following year at Yale
University School of Medicine in U.S.A. as a fellow of
the Rockefeller Foundation (Jamaica and U.S.A.).   On
return to Tanzania, he became Registrar and Vice Principal of the University College of Dar es Salaam, President of the East African Academy and later Principal of
the University College.

In 1970 he went into active politics and became
Minister of Water Development and Power, and held the
positions of Minister for Economic and Development Planning and for Water, Energy and Minerals.   The last responsibility taken up was East African Minister for Finance and Administration, in February 1977.   He has also served as a member of the U.N. Advisory Council on
the Application of Science and Technology to Development,
a member of TANU National Executive Council, and

Chairman of Tanganyika National Scientific Research
Council and of Tanganyika Society of African Culture.

CHAMA CHA MAPINDUZI (CCM).   The new, revolutionary
party formed when TANU and ASP decided to merge.   It
was officially inaugurated on 5 February, 1977, exactly
ten years to the day that Arusha Declaration was announced, and the twentieth anniversary of the birth of
ASP.

CHESHAM, LADY MARION (1903-73).   American-born.   Her
British husband, Lord Chesham, had been granted in 1936
a 110,000 acre concession for his Southern Highland
Scheme.   He had the land cleared and surveyed, roads
made and a clubhouse built, complete with golf and ten-
nis courts near Mafinga.   It was a well-conceived colonial settlement scheme, designed to fulfill local demands
on a cooperative basis.   In 1939 they were among the
first settlers to go back to England.   Lord Chesham
joined the RAF Fighter Command and Lady Chesham took
up war work   in London.   Lord Chesham died in 1952.
        Lady Chesham returned to Tanganyika in 1956 and
introduced coffee growing at Mafinga.   She stood as an
independent candidate in the election of 1958 and was
backed by TANU.   She took out Tanganyikan citizenship
in 1961.   That same year she founded the Community
Development Trust Fund which was aided by large donations from her American friends.   It actually sponsored
the building of wells, village centers, day care centers
and libraries in small towns.   It also had an emergency
assistance fund.   She held the position of Executive Director of the Fund until 1971.   She died at seventy years
of age in London on 6 September, 1973.

CHIEF JUSTICE.   The head of the judicial branch of government, is appointed to his position by the president and
consults with the President concerning the appointment of
the eight or more associate judges of the High Court.
The Chief Justice is also an appointed member to the
Judicial Service Commission.   He has the power to declare the President unfit to discharge his duties and cer-
tifies the President's resignment if he desires to leave
office before termination of his full time in office.

CHIEFS ORDINANCE OF 1954.   Provided for selected chiefs
to be sent overseas or to the newly established school
of local government at Mzumbe, Morogoro, for additional

training and administrative experience.

CHRISTIAN COUNCIL OF TANZANIA (CCT).   Formed in 1948
    to replace the Tanganyika Missionary Council which had
    organized most of the activities of the Protestant churches.
    The Education Secretary General of the CCT was a liai-
    son officer between the Director of Education and the VA
    schools.   Affiliated churches are: AIC, Anglican, Bap-
    tist, Salvation Army, the Gospel Furthering Fellowship,
    Lutheran, Mennonite, Moravian, Presbyterian and SDA.
    Other organizations with affiliation are: Bible Society;
    Every Home Evangelism; Scripture Union; Target and
    Lengo; YMCA and YWCA.   The departments in CCT are:
    Relief; Finance; Literature; Urban Christian Service;
    Family and Social Welfare; and Development Planning and
    Relief Service.   When all schools were nationalized in
    1970, much of the heavy responsibilities in public educa-
    tion fell to the government.   CCT remained active in
    many other areas and, indirectly, in education.

CHUMA.   One of Livingstone's porters who helped carry his
    body back 1400 miles overland to the coast of East Afri-
    ca.   Chuma had been brought up by the UMCA on his
    release from slavery.   He worked for the UMCA for
    three years after Livingstone's death (1875-78) and died
    when he was only thirty years old.

CHURCH MISSIONARY SOCIETY (CMS).   Dr. and Mrs. Krapf
    were the first CMS missionaries sent to East Africa in
    1844.   Rev. Rebmann also settled first in Rabai, Kenya.
    Then other explorers arrived at Bagamoyo in 1876 and
    made a number of stops through Tanzania on their way
    to Uganda.   By 1878 a mission was opened up at Mpwap-
    wa, one of the stopping-over places.   This mission was
    under the CMS of Equatorial East Africa which consisted
    of the stations in Kenya, Uganda and Tanganyika.   As the
    mission grew, a need arose to make two groups; Uganda
    and western Kenya fit into one and Tanganyika with Coast-
    al Kenya made up the second.
        The Diocese of Central Tanganyika progressed and
    six stations were opened.   There were over 200 evange-
    lists.   A school at Kongwa began training evangelists and
    teachers in 1908 and medical training was offered at
    Mvumi and Kilimantinde.   There were two African pas-
    tors ordained in 1921.   In 1927 the CMS Australia were
    given the Diocese of Central Tanganyika.   The Rt. Rev.
    G. A. Chambers was appointed Bishop of Central Tangan-
    yika in November 1928.

          In the twenty years of Bishop Chambers' service,
stations increased to 15, pastors to 28, the Cathedral
was built at Dodoma and consecrated in 1933. Mvumi
Girls School and the Boys Secondary School at Dodoma
had good reputations.
          Bishop Chambers resigned in 1947 and Bishop
Wynn-Jones took over until his death in 1950. Bishop
Alfred Stanway was the third bishop. The first African
bishop, Yohana Omari, was consecrated in 1955. He
was Assistant Bishop until he died in 1963. One year
later, 1964, Bishop Yohana Madinda was called to be the
Assistant Bishop. Due to the great expansion of the
church, the Diocese of Victoria Nyanza was created in
1963 and Bishop Melvin Wiggins was given the charge.
In 1965 the Diocese of Morogoro was formed under Bishop Gresford Chitemo. The following year the Western
Diocese was made with Bishop Musa Kahurananga in
charge. Bishop Stanley resigned in the Diocese of Central Tanzania in 1971 and Bishop Madinda took his place
as Archbishop. See ANGLICAN CHURCH where the explanation of the merger of CMS and UMCA is given.

CITY-STATES. Grew up along the coast. The most impor-
    tant one was Kilwa Kisiwani. From the 13th to the 15th
    century it had gained an ascendancy over the coastal area.
    In the 15th century it was overtaken by Zanzibar and
    Mombasa. Other city states which developed much like
    Kilwa were Pemba, Zanzibar and Mombasa, Malindi and
    Lamu in Kenya. The towns depended on the monsoons
    and African slaves provided by the African traders. At
    the coast these products were taken by Arabs, Persians
    and Indian traders to be resold in Asia and Europe. The
    intensive trade brought a higher standard of living in
    these areas.

CLOVE GROWERS' ASSOCIATION (C. G. A.) was formed in
    1927 as an attempt by the Zanzibar Government to organ-
    ize growers, large and small, along cooperative lines.
    The idea was to unite owners to reduce laborers' wages,
    to provide marketing and storage facilities, and to give
    harvesting loans to reduce interest rates. Government
    made membership a condition of payment for the bonus
    on young clove trees and 9000 joined C. G. A. When the
    clove duty was reduced and the bonus abolished soon after-
    ward, membership decreased sharply. The C. G. A. felt
    the effect of World Depression more on the price of
    cloves than on the quantities exported. The C. G. A. had

continuously demanded government control to organize
clove-growing along cooperative lines. Prices were not
covering harvesting costs. In 1934 the Government established C.G.A. as a privileged corporation, authorized
it to levy a compulsory contribution on all clove exports
and gave a guarantee to its funds. It became the "licensing authority." The Arab and Swahili population
strongly supported the government while the Indian National Association accused the government of deliberately trying to drive Indians away. A decree in 1937 eliminated
all other dealers in cloves. In August of that year the
Indians of Zanzibar and India organized a successful boycott of the clove trade and, by the end of 1937, the clove
export duty was decreased by £30,000. In February 1938
an agreement was reached and Indians were readmitted to
a share in the clove trade. In 1941 the Zanzibar Government set up the Economic Control Board and granted it
powers which were even greater than the C.G.A. had advocated or even dreamed.

CLOVES. The single most important export since the slave
trade was abolished in Zanzibar. More than 80 percent
of the world's production is grown in Tanzania and approximately 85 percent of the crop is grown on Pemba
Island. Although a governor introduced the crop to the
islands, it was Sultan Said in 1818 who had large areas
of wasteland cleared and dispossessed many small African farmers in order to plant cloves as they were in
great demand. He made plantation owners forsake their
coconut growing in favor of the newest crop. By the end
of his reign, they were producing three-fourths of the
world's supply of cloves. Most of the cloves were destroyed by hurricane in 1872 but were immediately reestablished. The trees are approximately 40 feet high,
normally yield 25-30 pounds of cloves a year and have
an average life of 50-60 years.
        Cloves are exported to India, U.S.A., Britain, Ger-
many and Indonesia. They are used for spices, oil for den-
tists and, in Indonesia, mixed with tobacco for smoking.
About 80,000 acres are under cloves with about 4 million
trees. Cloves and clove oil form more than half of Zanzibar's exports and about 90 percent of its export earnings.

COAL. Large deposits of good quality coal which could be
mined without much difficulty are known to exist near
Songea. Coal and iron ore are found close together.
The Ruhuhu River basin east of Lake Nyasa is believed

to have 285 million tons of good quality non-coking coal
and 116 million tons of lesser grade coal found. The
Kiwira-Songea field near the northwest end of Lake Nyasa
has reserves of 20 million tons. With the Great Uhuru
Railway now completed, the problem of transportation has
been greatly decreased. There were 850 metric tons
mined in 1976.

COCONUTS. Introduced into Africa from Southeast Asia by
A. D. 500. Many new coconut plantations appeared in
Mafia Island in 1890 and they increased greatly along the
coast up to 1900. Coconuts are mainly grown in Mtwara,
Coast and Tanga Regions on the mainland and on Mafia
and Zanzibar Islands. It is estimated that there are more
than 5 million palms. In 1960 10,000 tons of copra were
exported. The amount increased to 14,000 tons in 1967
along with 2400 tons of coir that year. The local consumption has exceeded 50,000 tons per year.

COFFEE. Although European settlers, government workers
and missionaries introduced coffee in many parts of Tanganyika, Speke and Grant had found "robusta" coffee
growing in Bukoba during the mid-1800's. Coffee did not
succeed in Usambara from 1890 to 1900. Roman Catholic missionaries introduced it at Kilimanjaro in 1893 and
it had expanded so much that by 1907 local planters protested against danger of disease and the threat to their
labor supply. Robusta, grown in West Lake, was indigenous and had a ceremonial significance; it had been
grown only by chiefs and was exported first in 1898.
Arabica was introduced in Morogoro by missionaries.
Most of Tanzania's coffee is now Arabica and three-fifths
of Arabica is grown by the Chagga in the Kilimanjaro Region. A European settler introduced it in Sukumaland
and it had become popular by 1911. Most of the seed
brought at that time came from Java. Sir Charles Dundas, the first British administrator in Moshi, encouraged
coffee growing and it had proved to be profitable by 1910.
The 1913 production for export was 1,059 tons, in 1928
was over 10,000 tons. At independence (1961) exports in
coffee reached 20,000 metric tons, 1970 was 55,000 metric tons and in 1975 Tanzania exported 845,104 bags
worth Shs. 383,572,241. Coffee exports in the 1975/76
season brought over one billion shillings. In June 1928
a Coffee Ordinance was passed requiring the registration
of all plantation and coffee dealers and empowering the
Agriculture Department to inspect all plantations.

Subsequent regulations permitted strong action against diseased estates.

COLE, J. S. R. An Attorney General from Ireland who could not be stopped by Twining in the libel case against Nyerere. He was appointed Attorney General in the independent Tanzania and was succeeded by Mark Bomani in 1965.

COLLEGE OF BUSINESS EDUCATION. Built in Dar es Salaam and begun through agreement between Tanganyika and the Federal Republic of Germany. The College opened in 1965 and offers a full-time, residential diploma course and a non-residential course leading to a certificate. Both of these courses run for two years. In December 1975 there were 105 full-time and in June 1976, 609 part-time students. There were 335 graduates and a staff of 5 expatriates and 13 Tanzanians.

COLONIAL DEVELOPMENT AND WELFARE ACT OF 1945. Differed from the 1929 and 1940 acts in that it introduced a new and revolutionary policy, i.e. development for the sake of the colony rather than for the colonizers. It meant, in practice, large expenditures on under-developed areas, a new concept in colonialism. By implication, it also meant a more rapid approach of independence as Britain could not carry a heavy load for a long time.

COMMUNICATIONS. In 1890--Dar es Salaam to Zanzibar cable opened telegraph service; 1904--telegraph lines connected Tanga and Korogwe, Dar es Salaam with Tabora and Mwanza; 1966--a count of 25,000 telephones; 1968-- International cable service handled by a private British company under Government supervision; 1977--all districts received telephone service and an International Telephone Exchange (ITE) was being built at Dar es Salaam to be operational by 1978.

COMMUNITY DEVELOPMENT TRUST FUND. Founded in 1962 by Lady Chesham. It was financed mainly from funds contributed in U.S.A. or other countries. Some of the projects undertaken were: the building of wells; day care centers; village centers; and libraries in small towns.

CONSOLATA FATHERS. From North Italy, they were given the western half of the Benedictine missionary work when the Germans left during World War I. This later became

the Diocese of Iringa.   They amalgamated with others to
form the present Tanzania Episcopal Conference (TEC).

CONSTITUTIONS.   1) Constitution of Tanganyika at Independence, 1961; 2) Constitution for the Republic of Tanganyika, 1962; 3) Constitution for Zanzibar at Independence,
1963; and 4) Interim Constitution adopted in 1965 for the
United Republic of Tanzania.

COOPERATIVE SOCIETIES.   The foundation of the cooperative
movement was laid in 1932 when the first legislation, Cooperative Societies Ordinance, was enacted to provide for
the registration of cooperative societies.   The ordinance
also required annual auditing of accounts and official supervision of the societies.   The first society, registered
on 1 January, 1933, was the Kilimanjaro Native Cooperative Union, Ltd. with eleven primary affiliated societies
for the marketing of coffee.   Other major cooperatives
registered were: 1936--Matengo Cooperative Marketing
Union and three affiliated societies in Songea for the sale
of tobacco: 1936--Bugufi Coffee Cooperative Society of
Ngara for coffee; 1949--The Mwakaleli Coffee Growers
Association in the Southern Highlands with ten affiliated
societies (forerunner of Rungwe African Cooperative
Union); 1950--Bukoba Native Cooperative Union and 48
affiliated primary societies; the Lake Province Growers
Association was the forerunner of the Victoria Federation
of Cooperatives Union Ltd.   By 1957 there were 462 marketing societies and 5 consumer societies.   In 1960 there
were 579 registered societies with 326,000 members.
Just as the number of registered societies had greatly increased from 62 in 1948 to 579 in 1960, the number kept
rising swiftly in the decade of the 1960's.   All cooperative societies were required to register and become affiliated with the Cooperative Union of Tanganyika (CUT)
in 1962.   CUT is an affiliate of TANU.   The number
raised from 1200 in 1963 to 1600 to 1966 and a total
membership of 500,000.   The most prominent societies
were the Victoria Federation of Cooperative Unions, KNCU
and Bukoba Native Cooperative Union.   Coffee and cotton
involved 90 percent of their activities.
        On the national level COSATA (the Cooperative
Supplies Association of Tanganyika) was formed in 1962
for retailing, an area held by Asians earlier.   It was
composed of 41 member societies at its formation.   It
supplied cooperatives and producers and organized retail
trade.   It operated at a loss in all branches during 1966,

according to the Presidential Special Commission of Enquiry.   The training program was intensified.   In 1967
COSATA was amalgamated with several nationalized ex-
port-import firms into the State Trading Corporation.
With the Government's new marketing policies in 1976,
large firms were granted jurisdiction over transportation
of crops for particular regional areas.

COOPERATIVE UNION OF TANGANYIKA (CUT).   An affiliate
of TANU, had its Secretary-General as a representative
on the National Executive Council of TANU as an ex officio member.   See COOPERATIVE SOCIETIES for its
history.

COTTON.   Moved to first place in Tanzania's exports in 1966.
It was in 1902 when the German government ruled that
cotton should be developed in the south of the colony.
Each headman was to have a communal plot and villages
were forced to work in rotation on the common field
using seeds and tools provided by the government.   The
Rufiji valley project failed due to bad organization, poor
land, a mixture of good and bad seeds and crop disease.
It is believed that this system was a cause of the Maji-
Maji Rebellion.
        In 1905 a cotton cultivation school was set up at
Mpanganya.   Restriction on cotton seed was applied.
From 1906-14 a number of cotton estates were established.
Ninety percent of the cotton production comes from Sukumaland.   It was first introduced to this area by a settler
on a share-cropping scheme.   Cotton was popular already
by 1911 and was exported to Europe via the Uganda Railway.
        The annual income from cotton in 1945 was £17
million and in 1949 was £52 million.   By the 1970's over
300 million shillings of foreign exchange are earned yearly
from cotton lint and cotton seed cake.   This is 17 percent of all foreign earnings.   Cotton production rose
steadily from 36,000 bales in 1949 to 167,200 bales in
1961/62 on to 434,400 in 1966/67 which was the peak
year.   Production dropped each year to 250,000 bales in
1975.   Therefore, a campaign was launched in 1975/76
to raise the production again after several years of
drought.   Some of the major enemies of cotton are:
Blackarm, Jassids, Stainers, Red Bollworm, Pink Bollworm, American Bollworm or Budworm, aphis and Helo-
peltis.   The Tanzania Cotton Authority was formed on
1 July, 1973.

COX COMMISSION. Headed by Christopher Cox, a former
education advisor to the British Secretary of State for
the Colonies. The Commission drew up educational plans
in 1947 for the Ten-Year Plan which aimed at expanding
education on all stages to increase the literacy rate, as
well as to enable an increasing number of pupils to benefit from secondary and higher education.

CURRENCY. A coin of Ptolemy VIII (116-80 B.C.) was found
in association with a dagger not far from Dar es Salaam.
Over 176 Chinese coins dating from the 7th to the 13th
century have been found in Zanzibar. Chinese cash had
been exported from China, presumably for metal. About
2000 coins of Kilwa and Zanzibar have also been found.
Kilwa had captured the gold trade from Sofala about 1300
and began minting their own coins.
        The right to issue a paper currency was first con-
ferred on the Deutsch Ostafrikanische Gesellschaft by the
Sultan of Zanzibar in 1888. The Deutsch Ostafrikanische
Bank was created in 1905 with head offices in Berlin.
The first notes issued by the bank were the five rupee
notes. Fifteen rupees were the equivalent of twenty German marks or one English pound. An East African Currency Board was established in 1920 and the currency
changed from rupees to shillings. In 1921 the Metallic
Currency Ordinance was enacted. The East African shilling was adopted as a subsidiary coinage. German silver
coins were redeemed and withdrawn from circulation in
1923. Other coins ceased to be legal tender in 1925.
The Standard Bank was opened in Dar es Salaam in 1916
and National and Grindlays Bank was opened in Tanga and
Dar es Salaam that same year.
        Tanzania currency was created in 1964. In 1966
the Currency Board was dissolved. Up to this time the
East African currency was based on the British sterling
with the shilling on par with the British one. Tanzania's
currency was based on the dollar. On 25 October, 1975,
it was devalued and removed from the dollar to the International Monetary Fund. See also NATIONAL BANK OF
COMMERCE; BANK OF TANZANIA

-D-

DAILY NEWS. Succeeded The Tanganyika Standard in 1972.
It is a government newspaper with a circulation of over
30,000 and covers national and international items of

interest, advertisements, has feature articles and editori-
als. It is generally in an 8-page format. Letters to the
editor are popular. On April 1973 the Daily News
launched a monthly sports magazine Sportscene. Its Sunday edition has more feature articles and photos included
and is called the Sunday News. Its circulation exceeds
35,000. See PERIODICALS.

DAR ES SALAAM. The capital for many years (until the end
1970's) was originally bush, then plantations of cassava,
millet, maize and sesame, a place of ships and canoes
and fishing grounds. Its original name Mzizima means
"healthy town."
        Sultan Said Majid took possession of the coast and
ruled through the Jumbes of Mzizima. He decided to
build a new port--Haven of Peace (Dar es Salaam)--and
work began in the 1860's towards moving his capital there.
Sultan Barghash, his successor, abolished the rule of
the Jumbes and substituted that of Zanzibar. A German
by the name of Loya, bought Dar es Salaam from Jumbe
Tambaza for 15 rupees. When the liwali informed the
Sultan, he was recalled to Zanzibar.
        The Germans took Dar es Salaam on 25 May,
1887, and transferred their seat of Government from Bagamoyo to Dar es Salaam in 1891.
        It is estimated that there were around 900 inhabi-
tants in 1867 and 10,000 by 1894. The population of 1928
was 25,000--800 Europeans, 4500 Asians and 20,000
Arabs. From this point the population rose swiftly to:
35,000 in 1930; 67,000 in 1945; 100,000 in 1952; 129,000
in 1957; 275,000 in 1967; 517,000 in 1975 and 609,000 in
1977.
        The Dar es Salaam Municipal Council was created
1 January, 1949, and a mayor was elected yearly from
their own number. City status was granted on 10 December, 1961. It has a 32 square mile area.
        Dar es Salaam has been the focus of government
and commercial activity, but after a government decision
to move the capital to Dodoma, various departments began moving slowly, the Prime Minister's office paving
the way on 5 October, 1974. Dar es Salaam is a dominant industrial center, the terminus of the Central Line
RR and main port of Tanzania. Its harbor is as near
to being landlocked as any in the world. The three deepwater berths constructed for ocean-liners were opened in
1956. Much of the goods are loaded and unloaded by
lighters. Dhows cater to the coastwise and Persian Gulf
area trade.

The mean daily temperature is around 20° C. or
79° F. with a mean seasonal range of 4° C. or 7° F. and
mean daily range of 8° C. or 14° F. The relative humidity reaches 100 percent on nearly every night of the year
and rarely drops below 55 percent during the day. The
average rainfall is just below 1100 mm., or 43", a year.

DAR ES SALAAM COLLEGE OF NATIONAL EDUCATION.
Often thought of as the "big sister college," opened in
1965. Courses offered at the college are: Diploma in
Education for training of Secondary School teachers; Diploma in Education--Commerce--for Secondary School teachers; Diploma in Education--Domestic Science--for Secondary School teachers; Grade A teacher training for
Primary School teachers; Cooks' Course for Inservice
Cooks in institutions; and Swahili and English in the Foreign Languages Department for Koreans, Chinese, etc.
Education and Up-Grading Grade A to Diploma in Education courses have been transferred to other institutions.

DAR ES SALAAM TECHNICAL COLLEGE. Founded in 1958
as a Technical Institute to provide a secondary commercial and secondary technical course. The latter was
transferred to Ifunda Technical Secondary School in 1964.
In 1965 Dar es Salaam Technical College was founded
with USAID help and provided technician training. It offers Ordinary Technician Diploma for Form IV graduates
and an Engineering Diploma after the Ordinary Technician
Course and several years of experience. An education
option is given in coordination with the Dar es Salaam
College of National Education. Civil, electrical and me-
chanical engineering are all offered.

DE LA WARR COMMISSION see WARR COMMISSION

DECENTRALISATION OF GOVERNMENT ADMINSTRATION
ACT OF 1972. Provided for the movement of much power and autonomy to regional centers from the central
government. The Act was amended in October 1976 in
conformity with the purposes and provisions of the Villages and Ujamaa Villages Act of 1975 and the Urban
Wards (Administrative) Act of 1976, to provide for the
representation of villages, ujamaa villages and urban
wards on the district development councils.

DELIMITATION COMMISSION. Began work in January 1886
with one representative each from Great Britain, Germany

and France. They were charged with the responsibility
to "investigate the Sultan of Zanzibar's claims to certain
territories in East Africa and to determine precise limits
of his territory." They found the Sultan's government
was firmly established everywhere along the ports and a
10-mile strip inland. They did not consult Sultan Barghash for his views. The partition agreement, known as
the Anglo-German Agreement of 1886, was written on 1
November, 1886.

DEVELOPMENT PLAN FOR TANGANYIKA, 1961-64. Largely
    a product of expatriate influence. It restricted expansion
    of primary education in lieu of development of the se-
    condary education, especially Forms I to IV. During its
    implementation, an 8-4-2 cycle was adopted and selected
    primary schools extended Stds. V and VI towards a full-
    primary course. The Plan's targets were not met due
    to various phenomena, including nature. The worst
    drought in years (1961-62) killed crops and cattle and put
    half a million people on famine lists. Although the plan
    was considered unsuccessful, an external factor, self-
    reliance projects, had proved helpful and formed the basis
    for later plans and policies.

DIAMONDS. Found in a 3500-foot by 5000-foot source, one
    of the largest known in the world. Diamonds were re-
    ported near Mabuki in the Kwimba country south of Lake
    Victoria before World War I and were produced on and
    off between the wars. In the Williamson era diamonds
    became big business. Dr. J. T. Williamson discovered
    the Mwadui deposit in 1940. The output expanded rapidly.
    Production has come from super-imposed gravels. The
    annual income (which paid a 15 percent royalty to the
    Treasury) in 1945 was £638,000 and in 1949 reached the
    £1 million mark. In 1960 they brought £4.65 million in
    export value. The diamonds are sent to London for pro-
    cessing and grading, then resold to different companies
    for cutting them. Tanzania Diamond Cutting Co., Ltd.
    (TANCUT) in Iringa, formed in 1966 is one of the buyers.
    TANCUT has sold Shs. 60 million cut diamonds annually;
    it is the world's largest diamond cutting factory under
    one roof. They cut 5200 stones daily. The mines are
    headed towards exhaustion. The output began lowering
    in the 1970's. By mid-1970's the yearly average sale
    was 95,000 gm. at £150 million lowering diamonds from
    90 percent to 88 percent of the total mineral income.

DISTRICT COUNCILS. Directly controlled by the Regional
Commissioner. Most of the members were locally elected
but technical officers and other government officers were
appointed to them. TANU tried to offer recommendations
in the appointments made by the District Councils for the
cells, as well as the Area Commissioner's recommeda-
tions. District Councils were sometimes caught between
the two, but they maintained their independence in most
cases. The District Development Committee and the District Council tended to merge because the same members
were generally involved in both.

DISTRICT SCHOOLS. Developed after World War II and consisted of Std. V and Std. VI and were either attached to a
local primary school of Std. I-IV or were boarding schools
of Stds. V and VI only. These were terminal. Others
were attached as a preparatory course to a secondary
school or teacher-training center. The District Schools
were replaced in the late 1950's by Middle Schools with
Stds. V to VIII in one institution.

DOCKWORKERS' UNION. Organized on the docks in Dar es
Salaam in 1947. Just like the emerging political movements, it was underground and secret. Its initial long-
shoremen's demands on the employers were anonymous
and futile. Pursuing these unheeded demands, they called
for a strike and gained recognition for the organization
from the British Administration. The Dockworkers' Union
was registered and had a brief existence, but it became
dormant in 1950. Its reorganization in 1952 marked the
beginning of the independent trade movement.

DODOMA. The city of 3700 feet altitude, selected to become
Tanzania's capital by the 1980's, has had chief importance
as a route town on the Central RR Line and on the Great
North Road. It did not exist in pre-European days; it
grew up with the construction of the railway and road.
It is located in an area which has frequent droughts, the
height reached in 1941-43. This condition was exacer-
bated by an invasion of hordes of queleas, the resulting
famine led to 115 deaths in the district. Massive relief
services were set up.
    In the 1920's Dodoma was an upcoming communi-
cations center with the Central Line taking post to Dar es
Salaam and airplanes from Cairo to Capetown landing
there. When the Cathedral was dedicated in 1933, it was
raised to town status. The Dodoma Town Council was

established in 1955. The 1948 census reported a population of 9144. In 1952 there were 9375 Africans, 2113
Indians, 360 Europeans, 311 Arabs and 58 Somalis. The
total population was estimated at 13,000 in 1959.

Rice and flour milling and soap manufacturing
were the main industries. With vineyards introduced to
the Ujamaa villages, Dodoma wine has become famous.

The Prime Minister's Office was the first to move
to the new Capital, moving in November 1974. The Party
Headquarters followed shortly afterwards. Population
rose to 37,000 in 1975 and 41,000 by 1977.

DOROBO (tribe). A hunting and gathering tribe living among
the Masai who have a special social and economic relationship with the Masai; they mutually depend upon each
other. They admire and imitate the Masai dress style.
They depend upon the Masai for iron work and cereals
and food (in years of drought). In return the Dorobo provided services for the Masai and provide them with honey
and, sometimes, game meat. They have mixed so well
with the cultures about them that they sometimes lose
their language and adopt from their contacts. Dorobo
show resemblances of the physical features characteristic
of the Bushmen populations. There were less than 2000
in 1957. Their diet is meat and honey. They collect
roots, leaves, berries and tubers of all kinds for food.

DUNDAS, SIR CHARLES (1884-1956). The first British administrative officer in Moshi. He was selected as a
member of the British political staff during the East African Campaign because of the intimate knowledge of German which he had acquired during seventeen years spent
in Hamburg as the son of a British consular official.
During World War I he had been in charge of Wilhelmstal
(Lushoto), then at Pangani before becoming the Moshi District Administrator. While in Moshi he was concerned
with the infant mortality rate. The 34 chiefs in Chaggaland had 9 wives apiece. Each wife averaged 2.5 children and 2 of 3 survived infancy. He introduced coffee
as an economic crop rather than subsistence. In 1924
the Chagga formed the Kilimanjaro Native Planters Association. In 1926 Dundas was appointed the first Secretary for Native Affairs in Tanganyika. As such he represented the African interests in the early Legislative
Councils. He later became Governor of the Bahamas and
Uganda. After World War II he was given an honorary
chieftaincy title before his death which occurred in 1956.

-E-

EAST AFRICA EXAMINATION COUNCIL. Established to gradually take over the responsibility for the East African
version of the Cambridge Overseas Examinations. Beginning in 1968, the certificate awarded was known as the
East African Certificate of Education. After Tanzania had
nationalized its educational institutions on all levels in
1970, it withdrew from the council to provide its own examinations more in line with its National policies of education.

EAST AFRICAN ACADEMY. Founded in 1963 with branches
in Kampala, Nairobi and Dar es Salaam. Its purpose is
to act as a forum for research workers and scholars of
all disciplines. It arranges symposia for discussion of
academic and world problems. The 12th symposium was
held in Arusha, August/September 1976, and studied the
energy sources in East Africa.

EAST AFRICAN AIRWAYS see AVIATION

EAST AFRICAN COMMON SERVICES ORGANISATION (EACSO).
Preceded by the East African High Commission before
independence. The EACSO Authority was comprised of
principal elected members from each of Kenya, Tanganyika and Uganda who also sat as ex officio members in
the Central Legislative Assembly. The Secretary-General and a Legal Secretary ran the permanent secretariat
as officials of the organization. The Assembly had power
to pass measures on civil aviation, custom and excise,
income tax, inter-territorial research, university education, communications and public service commissions.
        In 1965 the Philips Commission was set up to ex-
amine the economic cooperation in East Africa. They
recommended the East African Community which came into being on 1 December 1967, as an outgrowth of EACSO.

EAST AFRICAN COMMUNITY. Preceded by the East African
High Commission and the East African Common Services
Organisation. It was founded by Kenya, Uganda and Tanganyika on 1 December, 1967, as an outgrowth of the
EACSO "to strengthen and regulate the industrial, commercial and other ties among the three with a view to
bringing about accelerated, harmonious and balanced development. " Its main tasks were to establish and maintain a common customs and excise tax, to abolish

generally trade restrictions between Partner States, to coordinate economic planning and transport policies, and to establish a common agricultural policy (in the long run).

The three Heads of States make up the East African Authority, the highest body. The Chairmanship rotates. The EAC Headquarters moved to Arusha, Tanzania, but the head offices of the various departments are located in towns all over East Africa. The East African Legislative Assembly is responsible to the East African Authority, and under the assembly are five councils: Common Market Council; Communications Council; Finance Council; Economic Consultation and Planning Council; and Research and Social Council.

The largest single corporation of the EAC is the East African Railways. Other corporations are: East African Airways; East African Harbours; Cargo Handling Services; East African Posts and Telecommunications; External Communications; Development Bank; Court of Appeal; Fishery-Marine-Freshwater; Malaria and Medical Research-TB-Leprosy-Sleeping Sickness; Pests; Industry; Agriculture and Animal Husbandry; Customs and Excise Department; Meteorology; Literature Bureau; Statistics; Examinations Council (local after 1973); East African Inter-University Commission; and Community Training Centre for their secretariat.

The EAC has had its upheavals resulting in certain organizations splitting up into national bodies. In 1976 an East African Community Treaty Review Commission was appointed to study the feasibility of its continuance or need to reorganize.

EAST AFRICAN HIGH COMMISSION (EAHC). Preceded in 1929 by the East African Meteorological Department, the first East African service. The EAHC was established in 1947, the work of Arthur Creech-Jones, the Colonial Secretary from 1946. The EAHR was formed to coordinate and control communications, taxes, postal services, customs and excise, meteorology, statistics, currency, medical and veterinary research, and higher education in the East African colonies. All races were represented on its Central Legislative Assembly.

Four months after its existence, it amalgamated the East African Railways. In 1949 the East African Posts and Telecommunication (EAP&T) and the East African Railways and Harbours (EAR&H) were formed. At independence, 1961, the EAHC gave birth to the East

African Common Services Organisation (EACSO).

EAST AFRICAN LITERATURE BUREAU. An organization of
the East African Community, was established in 1947 at
the birth of the East African High Commission. The
Bureau aims at promoting African writing, publishes books
for literary and cultural works in East Africa, distributes
them, guides young authors, runs the Central Printing
Section for the EAC, and participates in literacy campaigns organized in each Partner State. The EALB was
the pioneer of the public library movement in East Africa
and from it the Tanganyika Library Services Board inherited 11 members of staff, 50,000 books, Shs. 8259 and
equipment in early 1964.

EAST AFRICAN POSTS AND TELEGRAPHS. Was amalgamated
in Kenya, Uganda and Tanganyika in one common service
with one Postmaster General in 1933. The communications system has grown; subscribers can dial their own
trunk calls and international telephone and cable services
are available 24 hours a day. An International Telephone
Exchange (ITE) built at Dar es Salaam is operational as
of December 1977. The name which it was given later
on was East African Posts and Telecommunications.

EAST AFRICAN VETERINARY RESEARCH. A corporation of
the East African Community, was formed inter-territori-
ally in 1939 as the Central Research Organisation at
Kabete in Uganda.

EDUCATION see PRIMARY EDUCATION; TECHNICAL EDU-
CATION; SECONDARY EDUCATION; TEACHER TRAINING;
PRIMARY SCHOOL LEAVING CERTIFICATE; EDUCATION
SECRETARY GENERAL; HIGHER EDUCATION; EUROPEAN
EDUCATION; and GENERAL ENTRANCE EXAMINATION

EDUCATION ACT OF 1969. Placed all government and public schools under the management and administration of
the Director of National Education, except primary schools
which are the responsibility of the Local Education Authorities. Voluntary agencies were required to hand over
their assisted schools to government and VA teachers became employees of the Government. In the 1969 Act,
the Director was given the responsibility of approving
fees set by the private schools. Adult education and
higher education were brought directly under the Director's
control as well.

EDUCATION ACT SUPPLEMENT NO. 62. OF 1968.   It gave
    the Director of Education power to set up Boards of
    Governors for private schools.   This delegation of power
    enabled him to gain control over these non-aided institu-
    tions.

EDUCATION CONFERENCE OF 1925.   Was attended by gov-
    ernment and missions educators to set up a charter of
    education.   It convened shortly after Governor Cameron's
    arrival in Tanganyika.   A policy between government and
    missions sprang out of the agreements reached at the
    Conference.   A system of grants-in-aid linked the schools
    of all agencies into one official system holding a coherent
    educational policy.   The Educational Ordinance of 1927
    followed the Conference recommendations.

EDUCATION (AFRICAN) ORDINANCE OF 1927.   1) All schools
    had to be registered where secular instruction was given.
    2) Teachers needed to be registered if a school was to
    receive assistance.   3) Freedom of conscience was guar-
    anteed.   4) A Grade I teacher had to be registered at a
    school before English could be offered.   5) Grants-in-aid
    would be forthcoming to mission schools if they met
    Government requirements.

E(A)O OF 1933.   Set up standards of government for the Na-
    tive Authority Schools.

E(A)O AMENDMENTS: 1954.   Part I and Part II schools and
    their teachers were all to be registered.   (Part II schools
    had been known as Bush Schools).

E(A)O IN LATE 1950's.   1) Native Authority Education Com-
    mittees were set up.   2) A maximum of 45 pupils per
    class was set, a minimum of 30 for Std. I and 18 for
    Std. IV to remain in operation.   A maximum of six years
    was granted to a pupil in Primary School.   3) The Dir-
    ector was granted the authority to close schools and pro-
    hibit certain textbooks if found to be inferior.

EDUCATION ORDINANCE OF 1961.   Had provisions for in-
    tegration, uniformity and decentralization.   It repealed
    former laws in order to provide an integrated system of
    education.   It dealt essentially with the power and limita-
    tions of various bodies to control education in the coun-
    try.   The Minister of Education had complete and effec-
    tive control over staffing, admissions, syllabuses,

secular instruction, common standards of discipline and internal organizations and the opening of a school and closure, if necessary, of the VA schools as well as government schools. VAs owned and managed the schools and helped in administration. The Local Education Authority was granted more powers than the former NAECs. The Board of Governors for post primary institutions were created for greater efficiency in management and greater integration in the community. The four separate advisory councils were replaced by one advisory council.

EDUCATION SECRETARIES GENERAL. Originally two in number--one for all the Protestant denominations and one for the various Roman Catholic Orders. The Protestant EDSECGEN represented the Christian Council of Tanzania (CCT) and the Roman Catholic EDSECGEN represented the Tanzania Episcopal Conference (TEC). Their function was to control and to administer the VA systems in accordance with Government policy and to handle the two-way traffic in general correspondence, directives, complaints and suggestions from the government and non-government parts of the education system. Three more EDSECGENs were formed after independence; one for His Royal Highness the Aga Khan's Education Department; one for the East African Muslim Welfare Society; and one for the Tanganyika African Parents' Association. When the schools were nationalized in 1970, the EDSECGENs became coordinators for the educational activities of private schools.

ELANDS. Found in many of the national parks. An experiment was done at Nduimat Farm, Kilimanjaro Region to domesticate eight of them. It was discovered that they convert food into weight faster than cattle, they have a low fat content in their milk (good for heart patients), and a low calorie count in meat (good for dieters).

ELECTIONS: TANZANIA. Of 1958, 1960: All candidates backed by TANU in the National elections won an overwhelming victory. All TANU-backed candidates won their Legislative Council seats. Of 1965: Out of 3,360,000 voters registered, two-thirds of them cast votes. Of the votes cast, 96.5 percent said "Yes" for the President. Two-thirds of the National Assembly members and one Minister were voted out of office; only about 10 percent of the National Assembly was a carry over from the preceding one. Of 1970: 40 percent of the population

registered, but 45 percent of the total population were
less than 15 years of age.   Of those registered, 72 percent voted and 95 percent of those cast said "Yes" or 48
percent of the eligibles.   Of 1975:   81. 9 percent of the
registered voters went to the polls.   "Yes" votes were
74. 8 percent of registered voters and "No" votes were 6. 6
percent.

ELECTIONS: ZANZIBAR. Of 1957: Won by ASP.   Of 1961:
Indecisive result in January: June resulted in a ZNP/
ZPPP Government.   Of 1963: Balance of power remained
as in the 1961 result.

ELINEWINGA (1931-).   Born on 9 May, 1931, in Moshi
District and educated in local primary schools, Old Moshi
Secondary School and Tabora Government Secondary School.
He studied at Makerere College specializing in economics
and received a B. A. and then went on to Oslo in Norway
and U. S. A.   After a number of years of teaching in secondary schools, he was appointed Councillor at the Tanzania Embassy in Moscow and later on to the High Commission in Ottawa, Canada.   On returning to Tanzania,
he served as the Regional Education Officer at Arusha
and Principal of the Kivukoni TANU Ideological College.
Since 1970 he has held a number of ministerial portfolios--
Minister of State for Foreign Affairs, Minister for Water
Development and Power, and Minister for National
Education to February 1977.

ELIUFOO, SOLOMON NKYA (1920-1971).   Born near Mount
Kilimanjaro.   After a local education and teachers training at Marangu, he taught in a secondary school near
Moshi from 1938-39 and at Tanga in 1940.   He studied
at Makerere College from 1941-43 where he earned a
Diploma in Education and remained to teach there 1944
and 1945.   He served the Lutheran Church as its secretary and treasurer from 1946 to 1953 when he left for
studies abroad, first to Bethany College, Kansas, U. S. A.
for two years and then to Bristol University in England.
On return to Tanzania, he taught at Marangu Teachers
Training Centre and served as Education Assistant for
the Lutheran Church of Northern Tanzania.   His political
career began when he was elected to Legislative Council
in 1958.   He was appointed on 1 July, 1959, as the unofficial Minister of Health, a post he held to the end of
1960.   He was the first President of the Chagga Council

in 1960 and 1961, then became the second Minister of
Education in 1962, a position he held until 1968 when his
health prevented him from continuing.

EMIN PASHA (1840-1892).   Born as Eduard Schnitzer in Op-
pelu, Prussia and studied medicine in Breslau and Berlin.
He embraced Islam while practicing in Albania and assumed the name Emin, meaning "faithful one. "   In 1876
he entered the Egyptian service and rose to dignity of
Pasha (governor) of Equatoria (Southern part of the Sudan).
He was rescued by Stanley in 1888 when besieged by the
Mahdists.   He came to Bagamoyo in Tanganyika when he
had an accident.   When he recovered, he joined von Wis-
man in a political rather than medical capacity.   Von
Wissman sent him in 1890 to occupy the Lake Victoria
area.   He spread German rule without fighting.   He was
killed by tribesmen on orders of Arab slave traders while
visiting Rwanda.   His daughter Ferida was escorted to
Germany by a nursing sister.   He was a skillful linguist,
an authority on anthropology, zoology, botany and meteorology.

EMPLOYMENT.   Africans working for Europeans in 1909-10
were 70,000 and the number raised to 172,000 in 1912/13
employed by Europeans, Indians or Arabs.   Of the 172,000
there were 80,000 employed on plantations, 20,000 as
porters, 21,000 for Railway companies, 10,000 by commercial firms, 9000 domestic servants and 6000 police.
By 1945 there were some 340,000 Africans in regular
employment; many in migrant labor.   Between 1957 and
1962 the proportion of African population in salaried jobs
went from 4.5 percent to 4.3 percent yet 885 demands
for work on plantations were unfilled.   In 1961, 97 percent of the half million Africans in paid employment were
getting less than $100 a month.   By 1965 only 3.5 per-
cent were employed with salaries.   Jobs are not enough
and there is a tendency to over-employ at times.

EUROPEAN EDUCATION.   Before World War II, European
children were sent to Britain to be educated.   During
World War II, Kenya and Rhodesia took as many as they
could accommodate and a temporary school was set up
at Mbeya.   After World War II, the new settlers and
employees demanded local secondary education and paid
a per capita annual tax of £20 towards a secondary school.
One-fifth of the German reparations money was allocated
to build a first class grammar school near Iringa--

St. Michael's and St. George's. Tanganyika's Special
Representative to the U.N. in June 1957 promised that
it would become non-racial, fulfilled in 1960 when the
first Africans and Asians were enrolled. European enrollment dropped and the Property Fund was not available
after Independence. The Government took over the institution. The school closed in 1963, not due to failure in
integration of the student body, but for purely financial
reasons. Several international primary schools are still
operating for the expatriate community.

EUROPEANS. They had reached a total of 2570 by 1906.
Of the 2772 listed in the following year, 319 were given
as officials, 168 as soldiers and 303 as missionaries.
Of the total, 70 percent were Germans. Two hundred
Afrikaaners had reached Arusha by 1905 and were given
an average of 2500 acres per family. Settlers increased
in this decade so that by 1912, they had reached 758
among a total of 4744. Greek, Dutch and Danish were
the major groups of plantation owners. Although the
Europeans came from many countries, less than one percent of the land was occupied by settlers or developed by
companies. By 1930 the Europeans totalled approximately
8000. The number rose to 10,600 by 1948 or 0.1 percent
of the population, to 18,000 by 1952 and 20,600 in 1957.
At independence there were more than 23,000, the peak
figure. The number had dwindled to 17,500 by 1965 and
has never consisted of more than 0.1 percent of the total
population.

EVANGELICAL LUTHERAN CHURCH IN TANZANIA (ELCT).
Formed when the various Lutheran Church groups in Tanzania decided to unite in 1963. Bishop Stephano R. Moshi
held the top post until his death in 1976, having been re-
elected every four years. Bishop Sebastian Kolowa succeeded him. ELCT consists of the synods of the South,
Central, Eastern and Coast, Kenya, Arusha Region, Mbulu
and Ulanga Kilombero and the Diocese of the North,
Northwestern, Northeast and Pare.
      Every synod has its president at the head and each
diocese a bishop. These heads confer in Executive Committees and in Conference. ELCT is also a member of
the Lutheran World Federation and the World Council of
Churches. The ELCT prints a magazine called Uhuru na
Amani (Freedom and Peace), operates a radio station
"Voice of the Gospel," the Makumira Theological College,
a training seminary and a medical school as part of its

activities.   The Lutheran Church managed about one-tenth
of the medical services and one-sixth of the education
services until 1970 when the schools were nationalized.
In 1975 there were 380 native pastors, 47 missionaries,
2242 evangelists, 15 hospitals, 71 dispensaries and 1
leprosarium recorded (some figures were missing).   Their
membership had reached over 700,000 in 1975.

EVERY HOME EVANGELISM, TANZANIA (EHE).   Registered
officially on 16 September, 1970, for the purpose of dis-
tributing Bible literature.   The World Literature Crusade
in America supports this interdenominational branch of
CCT.   More than 3 million pieces of literature have been
distributed, 6000 Bibles and New Testaments given to
school children in the first five years of its existence.

EXECUTIVE COUNCIL.   Established on 31 August, 1920.
Its function was to advise the Governor on such questions
as the law prescribed should be dealt with by the Governor in Council and on such matters as he saw fit to sub-
mit to it.   The final decision remained in the hands of
the Governor; he could agree or disapprove the advice
of the Council.   The Council was first composed of ex
officio members only.   Later the Governor added unofficial members by appointment.   Ex officio members held
their seats by virtue of their position as heads of certain
important departments of the territorial government.
There were changes during 1954 in the unofficial member-
ship--3 Africans, 2 Europeans and 2 Asians were appointed who began to take on Ministerial duties.   In 1959
the Council became the Council of Ministers, including
five TANU members.

EXPORTS.   Agricultural products have always contributed the
largest amount of exports.   In the first half of 1958,
sisal was 27 percent, coffee 19 percent and diamonds 11
percent of the total exports.   The major agricultural
products made up 57 percent of the total in 1961.   Sisal
led as the number one export until 1966 when cotton took
first place.   The order of importance given in 1966 was
cotton, coffee, sisal, diamonds, cashews, cloves, canned
meats, oilseeds, tea and skins.   Export values for major crops are given as: coffee, 1 billion Shs. in 1975/76;
cotton, over Shs. 330 million in mid-1970's annually;
sisal, Shs. 463 million in peak year 1974; tea to Shs. 90
million by mid-1970's yearly; tobacco about Shs. 200 million
by 1975/76; and pyrethrum for Shs. 22.2 million yearly.
The total 1976 exports were valued at Shs. 4189 million.

-F-

FAMILY PLANNING ASSOCIATION OF TANZANIA (Swahili:
    UMATI). Founded in 1959 as the Family Planning Asso-
    ciation of Dar es Salaam and confined its services to
    within the city limits. Its name was changed to include
    all of Tanzania in 1966 and then in 1967 given a Swahili
    name, whose short is UMATI as it is known to most
    people. There are more than 54 branches and the Asso-
    ciation's membership exceeds 50,000. Its executive com-
    mittee consists of its national officers, branch chairmen
    and a representative from TANU, UWT, TAPA, and
    NUTA. UMATI works through the Regional Medical Of-
    ficers and maternal and child-welfare services conducted
    at hospitals. The Association is represented in the Na-
    tional Council for Social Welfare and in the National Cul-
    ture and Welfare Committee of TANU. The Swahili for
    UMATI is Chama cha Uzazi na Malezi Bora cha Tanzania.

FATUMA, QUEEN. Came to the throne in Zanzibar towards
    the close of the 17th century and was still Queen in 1711.
    She is said to have married Abdulla, 'king' of Utondwe,
    to whom she bore a son, Hassan. She remained consis-
    tently loyal to the Portuguese in a time when all other
    East African rulers had gone over to the rising power
    of Oman. She made efforts to smuggle food into Mom-
    basa. In an attempt to retaliate, the Arabs raided Zan-
    zibar. The Queen and her followers fled into the bush.
    When Fort Jesus fell to the Arabs in 1698, Queen Fatuma
    was left behind in Zanzibar by the Portuguese. The Arabs
    took her, her son, and two others as prisoners to Oman. She
    was allowed to return to Zanzibar in 1709. She died some-
    time between 1711 and 1728 and was succeeded by her son,
    Hassan, who is regarded as the founder of Zanzibar town.

FIAH, ERICA. A Ganda shopkeeper, led the African Com-
    mercial Organisation which was founded 1934 in Dar es
    Salaam. He founded a newspaper called Kwetu in 1937.
    He was the first African to express that effective im-
    provement required political power as well as economic
    and educational achievement. He abandoned the Associa-
    tion in 1939 and later interested himself in the affairs of
    the Dar es Salaam dockworkers.

FIPA (tribe). Of Bantu stock mixed with Hamitic blood. A
    large percentage of them are Christian. Their principal
    crop is finger millet. They are located between Lakes
    Tanganyika and Bukwa. They are a large tribe, believed

to have been more than 30,000 in 1910, reaching 80,000 by 1950 and 90,000 by 1960. They are matrilineal and traditionally emerged from Northeastern Zambia and Sukumaland. They had chiefs. Wheat, coffee, and fruits are among the other crops grown. Fish are obtained from the lakes.

FISH. In the middle and late 1950's Lake Tanganyika, Lake Rukwa and the territorial waters of Lake Victoria yielded an estimated 50,000 tons of fish annually. Most of the catch were dagaa and species of Tilapia and were consumed mainly within Tanganyika. There was a small amount of sun-dried dagaa and smoked Tilapia supplied to the Congo and Ruanda-Urundi. The total value of the catch was over £2 million.

By 1962 most of the deep water fish resources of Lakes Victoria and Tanganyika were still untouched. A 30,000 ton crop was projected from these lakes annually without overfishing. Marine fisheries in Zanzibar and Pemba by 1961 yielded about 2000 tons of fish valued between £100,000 and £150,000. The Nyegezi Fisheries Institute near Mwanza is expected to help improve this industry. Lake Nyasa brought in 6.6 million shillings from 5,209.5 tons of fish in 1974. This is a huge increase-- over Shs.3 million in 1973. The Nyanza Fishing and Processing Company opened a multi-million factory in 1976 to process fishmeal from the small Lake Victoria fish (haplochromis). At full capacity it can produce 3500 tons annually worth Shs.10.5 million.

FIVE-YEAR PLAN FOR ECONOMIC AND SOCIAL DEVELOPMENT, 1964-69. It had the additional advantage of the creation of the Education Planning Unit in 1963. The plan became the first coordinated and comprehensive one, being an integrated plan in which the people were involved and felt responsible for its implementation. This plan did not reject foreign aid that was available, neither did it depend on it so absolutely (56 percent local and 44 percent foreign resources) as the previous Three-Year Plan had. It was the first significant reference to a measure for self-reliance. At the plan's introduction, it was regarded as the first stage of a general attempt to reduce inequalities and expand opportunities for the population as a whole. It was a declaration of war against three enemies: proverty, ignorance and disease. The three major long-term objectives for 1980 were to raise the per capita income from Shs.386 per annum to Shs.900; to be fully

self-sufficient in trained manpower requirements; and to
raise the expectation of life from thirty-four and forty
years to fifty years.

The expansion of post-primary education held a
high priority especially higher school in secondary education.   Adult education and literacy were recognized as
economic functions.   Universal primary education was
set as a goal for 1989.

The Arusha Declaration was announced in 1967,
just in the middle of this Five-Year Plan.   Hence, re-
visions were made in the Plan's objectives and a greater
self-reliance program was implemented.

FLAMINGOES.   One of the largest congregations in East Africa is found at Lake Manyara.   At certain times of the
year they number so many that they form a solid line of
shimmering pink, stretching for several miles.

FLETCHER-COOKE, SIR JOHN.   Had a swift rise in the
Colonial Service and became the British Representative
on the Trusteeship Council at thirty-seven years of age,
and, as such was Tanganyika's Special Representative to
the U.N. in June 1957.   In 1959 he was made Tanganyika's Chief Secretary, was Minister for Constitutional Affairs and then Deputy Governor during Internal Self Rule.

FORESTRY.   Huge tracts of miombo woodland cover about
one-third of the country in the south and west-central
areas.   Tropical rainforests cover 0.5 percent of the
country.   Reservation of land for forestry dates back to
the years before World War I.   About 10-15 percent of
the land of Tanzania has been set aside for forest reserves.   Thirty thousand square miles are subjected to
planned management and are systematically harvested.
Forty-four thousand square miles are subjected to exploitation for the sawing of logs.   Production is estimated at
5 million cubic feet yearly.   The 1975 production of wood
is 160,000 cubic meters, but the needs are 190,000 cubic
meters yearly.   Tanzania exports mainly podo, mvule,
mninga and Grevillae Robusta (an excellent flooring material).   There is a great potential for exotic conifers.
There is cyprus in some rain forests.   In 1949 the Colonial Development Corporation set out to plant 30,000
acres of wattle, a type of acacia, in the Southern Highlands and by 1955 it had planted 33,000 acres.   The production of the tanning extract began in 1959 in a factory
near Njombe.

FRANCISCAN FRIARS. The first missionaries on Tanganyika soil in 1505. They met with failure due to the defeat of the Portuguese occupation at the hands of the Arabs in 1513. Their golden Monstrance for the Church of Our Lady of Belem is kept in the Museum of Ancient Art in Lisbon, Portugal.

FUNDIKIRA, CHIEF MGALULA II. By 1917 the Chief had established himself as one of the leading figures of Tanganyika. His palace outside Tabora became a shining example of Governor Cameron's policy of indirect rule. In 1929 he was accused of embezzlement and sentenced to imprisonment. The court of appeal quashed the sentence and sent him away from his people who were being concentrated into new settlements. Lack of tact in the Fundikira affair resulted in a serious reversal for the policy of indirect rule.

FUNDIKIRA, CHIEF ABDULLA III (1921-). Born near Tabora and educated locally, at Tanga S/S (1938-39), and at Makerere College (1940-44) where he received a Diploma in Agriculture and at Cambridge University in England in 1953. He became the first African Agricultural Officer in 1957 and was stationed at Newala. In August 1957 he was appointed Chief of Unyanyembe over about 150,000 subjects and held the position until 1962. He became a member of the Legislative Council in 1958 and was appointed the unofficial Minister for Lands and Surveys on 1 July, 1957. In 1960 the portfolio was called Lands, Surveys and Water. He moved on to the Ministry of Justice in 1961 but left the Cabinet in early 1963 in protest against land policy. Besides a number of chairmanships, he was Chairman of the Board of Directors of East African Airways from 1964 to 1973 when he retired. He is also a Muslim leader active in Islamic affairs.

FUNDIKIRA, CHIEF SAID (? -1858). Son of Chief Swetu of Unyanyembe, made a treaty with Sultan Said in 1839 which enabled the Sultan's subjects to travel across Unyamwezi to trade. He first learned of his selection as mtemi (chief) while serving as a carrier in a caravan. He built up a powerful chiefdom at the expense of his neighbors; he had enormous stores of ivory, 2000 head of cattle, and an unlimited number of slaves. His successor was Mwana Sele. The line of succession changed during his reign from matrilineal to patrilineal.

-G-

GAME RESERVES. Eight percent of Tanzania's land is set aside
for game reserves. The seventeen reserves, the year of
their gazetting and areas (all but #17. in sq. km.) are:

1. Selous	1951	51, 200	10. Ugalla	1965	4864
2. Rungwa	1951	8960	11. Rubondo	1965	410
3. Kizigo*			Island		
4. Maswa	1969	2176	12. Mkomazi	1951	3584
5. Ibanda	1972	205	13. Uwanda	1969	4740
6. Burigi	1972	2180	14. Ukwaja*		
7. Bihara-	1959	2180	15. Saadani	1969	256
mulo			16. Rumayika/	1965	161
8. Mt. Meru	1951	317	Uruganda		
9. Kiliman-	1959	890	17. Saanane	1964	38 ha.
jaro			Island		

(*means reserve proposed in 1976)

GENERAL ENTRANCE EXAMINATION. Organized for Std.
VIII by the Examinations Officer of the Ministry of Education and conducted on a regional basis. It was set
centrally in the English language and consisted of papers
for Maths, English and General Knowledge. The name
was changed to Primary School Leaving Examination in
1967 as the educational policy began to change regarding
the role of primary education.

GEORGES, PHILIP TELFORD. A West Indian born on 5
June, 1923, who was the Chief Justice of Tanzania 1965
to 1971. After an education locally, he attended McGill
University from 1942-47, the University of Toronto, Canada, 1943-47 where he received a B.A. (Honors) Law Degree and then went on to the Middle Temple, London, in
1949. He had a private practice in Trinidad from 1949-
62, then was appointed Judge of the Supreme Court in
1962. He was seconded to Tanganyika for the Chief Justice position in 1965 and held the job until he returned to
Trinidad in 1971. The University of Dar es Salaam conferred an honorary Doctorate of Law. He earned a Doctor of Law from the University of Toronto in 1969.

GERMAN EAST AFRICA. Tanzania's name from 1890-1918.

GERMAN EAST AFRICA COMPANY. Formed from the Society for German Colonisation in order to administer the
protectorates gained by the treaties signed in 1884 by
Karl Peters and native chiefs in the area between Rivers

Pangani and Rufiji.   The company was officially taken
over by the Emperor on 26 February, 1885.   By a treaty
of 20 December, 1885, Germany secured privileges at
Dar es Salaam and Pangani and the right to send certain
goods duty-free through the coastal strip belonging to the
Sultan of Zanzibar to the interior.   Peters' treaties continued to claim large areas--hence the Anglo-German
Agreement of 1886.   Germany had annexed the area
claimed by the treaties without consulting the Sultan.   The
take-over aroused widespread hostility and resentment
also among the natives in the areas, leading to revolts
which were costly and difficult to put down.   In 1888 the
German East Africa Co. had to ask for Imperial troops
to suppress a rising at the Coast led by Bushiri bin Salim al Harthi.   By 1890 the German government took
over control of the German East Africa Company's area.
See also SOCIETY FOR GERMAN COLONISATION.

GERMAN-EAST AFRICA INTERACTIONS.   By 1871 German
firms had secured/nearly a quarter of the Zanzibar Island
trade.   German explorers Wilhelm Peters and von der
Decken had already visited the interior and missionaries
Rebmann and Krapf had arrived.   In 1884 Karl Peters
signed treaties with the native chiefs and gained nominal
control of a large area near the coast.   The German
East Africa Company administered the territories until
the Emperor took charge of the Company and formed a
Colonial Office.   Germans introduced sisal, cotton, coffee,
and maize, and contributed much through agricultural research.   Dr. Koch discovered a remedy (atoxyl) for sleeping
sickness which helped to check this scourge of East Africa.
By 1914 the administration conducted most of its correspondence with the village headmen in Swahili.   Education had had
a better beginning than in neighboring countries.   The negative characteristics are given as: thorough exploitation of
the land; lack of close contact with the people.

GERMAN-PORTUGUESE AGREEMENT OF 1886.   Settled the
southern boundary on the coast to be the mouth of the
Ruvuma River.   The area south of the river was not
formally relinquished to the Portuguese by the Zanzibar
Government until after World War I.

GERMAN RULE, AFRICAN RESISTANCE TO   see   RESIS-
TANCE TO GERMAN RULE

GHENDEWA, CHIEF OF UGWENO (Pare).   Rebuilt a new

capital which was strongly fortified. He raised a standing army including a personal bodyguard. Ghendewa made
an alliance with Chagga Chief Rindi of Moshi. He invited
Chagga troops to assist him in subduing his Southern District. He had the qualities of a man who could have restored the power of Ugweno and maybe even enlarged his
own political influence. But he was concerned primarily
with trade and the alliance with Rindi did not give him a
great advantage. Instead the Chagga began then to raid
Ugweno also, took cattle and killed Ghendewa.

GOGO (tribe). There was little unity in this Central Tanganyika tribe before 1800. The arrival of the Masai and
their attacks caused them to unite in larger groups.
They copied the customs of the Masai. From 1830 regular caravans passed through Gogoland. Chiefs made them
pay Hongo (a tax) which was very profitable. The Gogo
have been attacked by the Hehe and Masai. Since this
Bantu group has adapted an economic way of life essentially similar to that of the pastoral Nilo-Hamites, they
have been able to survive in the arid plain of Central
Tanganyika. Their houses are flat-roofed, low and have
mud roofs. Cattle is a symbol of wealth. Thus overgrazing of land has been a problem. Cassava and grapes
have been introduced to this dry area. "Operation Dodoma" gathered them into Ujamaa villages in the early
1970's.

GOLD. Discovered in 1922 in the Mwanza and Musoma Districts and along the Lupa River near Lake Rukwa. Although gold was mined in many places, these deposits
were the most important producing areas. The 1938 output exceeded 100,000 ounces. The 1939 output was valued
at almost £1 million; gold exports were exceeded in value
only by sisal. In 1966 two of the three major gold mines
closed down. Lupa and Singida were almost exhausted by
1970. Two mines are scheduled to be operational by
1977; the Buck Reef in Geita and Lupa Goldfields. The
quantity of gold sold dropped considerably in 1966 and in
1974. Only 2400 grams were sold in 1975.

GOMBE NATIONAL PARK. Gazetted in 1968, it is located 15
miles north of Kigoma on the eastern shore of Lake Tanganyika. It was originally made a reserve and created
for the protection of one of the last troops of about 200
chimpanzees in Tanzania, and also the red colobus and
putty nose monkeys. It is the smallest of the national

parks with an area of 52 square kilometers only. Reserved mainly for research, it is not opened for tourists but special permission for day trips can be obtained. It gained international fame through a woman anthropologist, Baroness Hugo van Lawick, who made a comprehensive two-year study of the 60 to 80 strong troops of chimpanzees there.

GORDON, GEORGE BERNARD (1924-). Born in Brighton, United Kingdom. He joined the British army in 1942 and was seconded to the Kings' African Rifles (KAR) from 1944-46. He was appointed Administrative Officer of Tanganyika Civil Service in 1946, served as a District Commissioner 1949-52, a Community Development Officer 1953-55, Establishment Officer 1956-60, Chief Establishment Officer 1961-62, made Principal of the Civil Service Training Centre in 1963 and worked in administration in the Civil Service Establishment until the mid-1970's.

GOSPEL FURTHERING FELLOWSHIP. The head office is in Nairobi since 1935. The Tanzania office is at Bonga, Bahati. There are eight church buildings and a membership of 500. Hope Bible Institute is responsible for the Bible instruction in the one Bible School. They also operate a bookshop. This Fellowship joined CCT in 1960.

GRANTS-IN-AID. Begun to Voluntary Agency schools in 1927, they were extended to Asian schools in 1929. The schools were managed by the Voluntary Agencies (VA's) but capital grants were given by government for the initial buildings and equipment grants were reckoned on a pupil basis. Salaries of the teachers were paid by government as well. At any time the grant could be withheld if the agency did not comply with government standards. Schools were nationalized in 1970 which cancelled the grant-in-aid system. Doctors' and nurses' salaries were also paid by the government in many of the private hospitals in a similar aid program.

GRAPES. Introduced to the Dodoma area in 1957 by the Roman Catholic missionaries. By 1963 Brother Maggioni had a half acre under cultivation. Bihawana wine was first brewed in 1963. Isanga Prison followed and got 18 tons of grapes from a 10-acre plot in 1967. The Ujamaa villages and secondary schools began to plant vineyards also. In a good season 10,000 bottles of

Bihawana Wine can be made (1975 figure).

GREAT NORTH ROAD. Crosses Tanzania from the Zambia
    border to Namanga on the Kenya border. It is a difficult
    passage or impassable in some parts during the rainy
    season. The construction was completed between the
    northern and southern boundaries in 1932. The total
    length is more than 800 miles. In the southern part of
    the country it seems to follow fairly closely an Arab
    slave traders' route of the 1800's.

GREAT UHURU RAILWAY. Finished 23 October, 1975. It
    is 1162 miles (1859 km.) plus 133 km. track for sidings
    and sheds, has 300 bridges and 23 tunnels--the longest
    tunnel being 917 meters long and the longest bridge 427
    meters. It has a 1067 gauge allowing speed in excess
    of 100 km.p.h. In July 1976 there were 147 stations.
    Two express trains complete the journey in 35 hours by
    running at 40 m.p.h. or less and stop at 12 stations only
    while daily trains make the journey more slowly stopping
    at each place.

GROSS DOMESTIC PRODUCT (GDP). In 1961 £7.5 million
    was obtained from industry while £80 million came from
    the agriculture sector. By 1964 it was divided into the
    following factors: commercial agriculture including hunt-
    ing, fishing and forestry--46.7 percent of GDP; commer-
    cial sector including finance, insurance, real estate bus-
    iness services--22.1 percent; mining and quarrying sec-
    tor--2.5 percent; non-monetarized sector "subsistence"--
    33 percent; construction, public utilities, transport--6.9
    percent and manufacturing and industry--7.1 percent; the
    1964 GDP was Shs. 394 million. From 1960 to 1966 it
    increased more than 47 percent. It grew annually by 5
    percent in the First Five-Year Plan (1964-69) and 4.8
    percent in the Second Five-Year Plan (1969-74) and was
    raised to Shs. 900 million in 1974. From 1961 to 1974
    manufacturing and construction rose from 7 percent to
    17.5 percent of the GDP. In 1975 there was a 4.8 per-
    cent increase.

GROUNDNUT SCHEME. Begun in 1947 in Southeastern Tan-
    ganyika as a source of oil to relieve the shortage of mar-
    garine in England. The Overseas Food Corporation, the
    representative of England's Ministry of Food, moved into
    the 5000 square mile area with men, money and machines.
    The material was salvaged from Pacific Ocean beaches,

something too hard to maintain. The natural surroundings
were unsuitable--too dry and the soil hardened too quickly
for the heavy machinery. The Scheme was very poorly
planned; very little research on the local conditions had
been done. Rain was less than usual in 1947 and 1948
and the harvest was bad in 1949. The Scheme was abandoned in 1951 after $86.4 million had been spent on it,
$60 million of which was lost. Bad planning, ignorance
and lack of thorough preparation are the causes given for
the collapse of the Scheme.

GROUNDNUTS (peanuts). Probably introduced to Africa from
the Americas by the British or other European traders
during the 15th century. The Nyamwezi and Sukuma
tribes were reported as growing groundnuts from 1905-12.
An unsuccessful adventure with groundnuts was undertaken
in southeastern Tanganyika in 1947 with the hope of growing groundnuts as a source of oil on a 5000 square mile
area. Due to various causes it was abandoned in 1951 at
a great loss. See GROUNDNUT SCHEME.

-H-

HA (tribe). Located between Lakes Tanganyika and Victoria,
are a large tribe, were third largest in the 1948 census
with 286,000 members and 730,000 in the 1957 census.
The Tusi tribesmen entered their country 200 to 300 years
ago and became overlords of the Ha. In the 19th century
they made iron hoes and weapons. They are great wan-
derers providing emigrant labor as far away as Tanga
and Dar es Salaam on sisal and other estates. Some
settled down in the coastal areas and adapted the coastal
way of life. As a whole the Ha are among the most primitive, hanging to traditional ways. Witchcraft plays a
large role in their daily loves. The Ha are cattle keeping agriculturalists. Honey and tobacco are their products.

HADIMU (tribe). One of the native tribes to Zanzibar. The
name, meaning "slave," is unfounded, for the Hadimu
were neither conquered or enslaved by the Arabs. The
members are of a very mixed origin, consisting of immigrants from different parts of the mainland who have arrived in the island at very different dates. Their one
common link, giving them a sense of unity, was the fact
that they acknowledged the sovereignty of a single ruler,

the Jumbe or Mwenyi Mkuu. After Sultan Said moved his
capital to Zanzibar, the general trend of events was for
the Hadimu to remove out of the more fertile area in the
western portion of the island to the less fertile area in
the eastern and southern portions. When the Mwenyi
Mkuu removed from the town of Zanzibar, the exodus
tended to increase. The result was something like a native reserve where they could conduct their own affairs
while subject to poll tax and other demands. The dual
monarchy came to an end when the young son of the last
Mwenyi Mkuu died of smallpox while living in Zanzibar
town. Sultan Majid forced a union of the Tumbatu with
the Hadimu in 1865 and the Tumbatu followed the pattern
of the Hadimu although they did not accept the subordina-
tion very well. The magic of the Hadimu of Zanzibar is
characterized chiefly by the use of potent poisons and by
the fact that witch-doctors are credited with powers of
being able to keep leopards under control and to send
them at will to do harm.

HADZAPI (tribe). Also called Kindiga or Tindiga. They are
hunters and collectors in Central Tanzania around Lake
Eyasi. Their diet consists of wild berries, roots, fruit
of the baobab tree, honey and occasional game meat.
They are one of the smallest tribes who numbered only
600 in the 1957 census. However, they have maintained
their culture in spite of the agricultural tribes nearby and
even the efforts of government to help them settle down
as agriculturalists or pastoralists have been mainly ineffective. They have unusually long and powerful bows and
use poison on the tips of the arrows. They are a remnant from the Bushman of Southern Africa and speak a
click language closely related to the Bushmen dialects.

HAMED BIN MOHAMMED see TIPPU TIP

HAMED BIN THWAIN, SULTAN. A grandson of Sultan Said,
was placed by the British on the Zanzibar throne in 1893
in place of Khalid. He had accepted conditions which reduced the Sultanate to ceremonial functions and influence
in customary affairs only. So he began his reign as a
pliant and cooperative agent of the British. When Arthur
Hardinge was appointed Agent and Consul-General in May
1894, the Sultan accepted without protest the humanitarian
flavor which was introduced into the administration. In
June 1895 Hamed became bitter and distrustful when the
British Government decided to use the £200,000 of

Zanzibar Government money obtained from the Germans
for the mainland possessions, to pay most of the £250,000
due to the bankrupt Imperial British East Africa Company
as compensation for the loss of its charter.   So, while
Mathews and Hardinge were occupied with the Mazrui rebellion on Kenya mainland, Sultan Hamed built up his private bodyguard and had 1000 men by October 1895.   The
arrest by the British of one of his bodyguard at the palace brought matters to a head.   Fighting broke out on
17 December, 1895.   The landing of the naval forces and
threat of the marines overawed the Sultan and he agreed
to disband his bodyguard at the rate of 25 per month.
He died on 25 August, 1896, rather suddenly and not without some suspicion of poison.   He was a man of high
culture and literary taste and a profound student of Arabic
literature.   He seemed to have a liberal turn of mind.

HAMERTON TREATY.   Signed in 1845 by Col. Atkins Ham-
    erton, the British Consul, and Sultan Said in Zanzibar.
    It was aimed at restricting the slave trade entirely to
    Sultan Said's East Africa possessions, i. e. , no slaves
    were to be shipped from the Coast north of Mogadishu
    area.   Although the treaty was ineffective, it began to
    undermine the Sultan's power.

HAMOUD BIN MUHAMMED, SULTAN (1851-1902).   Selected
    by the British when they overthrew Khalid's seizure upon
    Hamid's death in 1896.   No large Arab faction had sup-
    ported his claim and he was totally dependent on British
    support.   He was an admirer of European ways and sent
    his only son to Harrow School in England.   His ambition
    was that his boy should succeed him even though Zanzi-
    bar custom laid greater claim to the Sultan's brother.
    He therefore paid the price of cooperation and henceforth
    the Sultan's sovereignty was no more than a legal fiction.
    The Sultan signed the Anti-Slavery decree on 5 April,
    1897.   He died in 1902 and was succeeded by his seven-
    teen-year-old son fresh from schooling in England.   Ha-
    moud was an intelligent and generous man, of fine phys-
    ique, with a courtly and charming presence.

HANCOCK, MARY E.   (1910-77).   Born in England in 1910
    and received her teacher's training there.   She arrived
    in Tanganyika on 11 July, 1941, and worked with the
    Ministry of Education from 1941 to 1964 as Head-mistress
    of various schools in the Southern Highlands and as an
    Education Officer from 1954-63.   She served in Lake and

Western Province and was the Assistant Provincial Education Officer in Musoma and Tabora. She left government service in 1963 and was in charge of the Women's
and Girl's Development Section of the Tanganyika Episcopal Secretariat from 1963 until the department closed.
She took out Tanzanian citizenship and lives at Lushoto.
She was a member of Parliament since 1970 and a member
of UWT.

HANGA, ABDULLA KASSIM (1932-69). Born in Zanzibar and
educated locally, then went on to Moscow to study economics. For a time he was married to a Russian woman.
On return he was Deputy General Secretary of the ASP
and opposed to the Government at independence; he was
one of ASP's strongest admirers of the more militant
UMMA Party. After the January 1964 revolution, he was
proclaimed Prime Minister but the post was abolished a
few hours later. He became the Vice President of the
new Republic. After the Union of Zanzibar and Tanganyika in April 1964, he was first appointed Minister of
State with the Union, then Minister of Industries, Resources and Power and lastly Minister of State in the
President's Office for Union Affairs. He became the
chief liaison officer between the Central Government and
the Island. He held this position until he was deprived
of office in 1967. He was arrested on 3 January, 1968,
put into detention in Zanzibar in 1969 and executed by
firing squad during the same year.

HASSAN BIN OMARI MAKUNGANYA (? - 1895). Led an attack on Kilwa in 1894. When the Germans destroyed his
fort, he fled inland and planned a second offensive but
was not successful. In October 1895 four companies were
sent against him. He escaped but was later captured in
Mavunjo along the Lindi road on 15 November, 1895. He
was hanged in Kivinje on a mango tree, henceforth used
for mass executions.

HASSAN BIN SULAIMAN I. He began building the Great
Mosque on Kilwa about A. D. 1270. Either he or his
successor, Hassan bin Sulaiman II, built a large palace.

HASSAN BIN SULAIMAN II. Ruled Kilwa from 1310 to 1333
and conquered Mafia Islands. He is credited with having
built the large and magnificent palace, Husuni Kubwa.

HAYA (tribe). The Bahima (Bantus) emigrated south into

northwestern Tanganyika and became strong, powerful chiefs and rulers. There were three kingdoms--Karagwe in the west, Ihangiro in the south and Greater Kyamtwara in the east. The Northern Chiefdom, Kizibo, was ruled by a section of the Bito. After a civil war, Greater Kyamtwara was split into four sections: Kianja and Bukara were ruled by Hinda while Bugabo and Kyamtwara were ruled by Nkengo.

When the Germans arrived in the eastern area, they found the Haya in conflict. Kayoza of Bugabo was stronger than Kahigi of Kianja or Mukotani of Kyamtwara. Therefore, Kahigi and Mukotani welcomed German support against him. Favor fell to Kahigi who manipulated with diplomatic skill; he offered services and unwavering support to the Germans. Mukotani was deposed in 1895 for allegedly stealing guns from the military station. Kianja gained sub-chiefdoms from Kyamtwara. The Bukara chief lost in the same way and Bukara was partitioned between Kianja and Kyamtwara. In 1905 the Germans made Mutatembwa's son, Mutahangarwa, who was educated in Roman Catholic schools, a superior chief with Kahigi. A relative of Mutahangarwa, Fransisho X. Lwamgira, became the German officer's confidential adviser on Haya affairs.

From 1853 to 1880 the chief of Karagwe in the west was Rumanika. He warmly received Speke. His rule was hard, but fair; there was not much intertribal fighting.

From the early chiefdoms, the Haya were hierarchically organized and highly developed. A research done in the 1950's revealed that there was an average of 3.4 persons per household and that around 30 percent of the children born died before the age of five.

The Haya live on some of the richest land in Tanzania. Coffee and bananas are grown for cash and food. The traditional houses were beehive-shaped huts with grass-thatched roofs. Grasses also made soft carpets for the floor and woven coverings for the kitchenware and fine drums. In 1964 Haya were considered to be 6 percent of the population of the country and contributed 7 percent to the leadership (elite) sample.

HEHE (tribe). The Hehe State was formed in response to the military revolution brought to the area by the Ngoni peoples moving northwards from Southern Africa in the 1840's. Up to 1850 there were nearly 30 separate groups. Muyugumba (from an Usagara family) and his son Mkwawa both united the clans of the Hehe people. From 1878-83

they had five years of war with the Ngoni. The Hehe
became dominant and confined the Ngoni to an area around
Lake Malawi. Muyugumba died in 1879 when he was
ruling the whole tribe. His rule was strongest nearby.
He had fought the Gogo and Sangu as well as the Ngoni.
          In June 1891 Emil von Zelewski, Commander of
the Defense Forces, set out on a punitive expedition
against the Hehe. Mkwawa interpreted that as an attack
and his forces ambushed the Germans on 16 August and
killed 290 German men, annihilating the force. The Hehe
captured three cannons and 300 rifles. The German officers sought revenge and in October 1894 Mkwawa was
severely defeated when the Hehe capital was taken. Captain Prince established a new military station at Iringa
in 1896 and, in a series of operations during 1897 and
1898, broke the power of the Hehe. Sudanese troops then
helped to guard Iringa. Mkwawa was hunted for four
years; he lived in the bush and finally committed suicide
to avoid capture. His skull was sent to Bremen, Germany where it was placed in a museum until it was returned to the Hehe in 1954. The Hehe and Kuria tribes
have proved the most adaptable to police work and made
up 50 percent of the police force in 1964.

HELIGOLAND TREATY   see   ANGLO-GERMAN AGREEMENT
     OF 1890

HIGH COURT OF TANZANIA.   The final arbiter in questions
     pertaining to validity of membership in the National As-
     sembly.   It is the superior court of record and the high-
     est court of appeal in constitutional matters.   The Presi-
     dent appoints the Chief Justice of the High Court and at
     least eight associate judges of the High Court after con-
     sultation with the Chief Justice.   In Zanzibar the High
     Court has general supervisory and review powers over all
     courts.

HIGHER EDUCATION.   Not offered in Tanganyika in pre-in-
     dependence days.   Students went to interterritorial insti-
     tutions in East Africa, the Royal Technical College and
     Makerere College or received scholarships to England
     and Ireland, the U. S. A. and India.   In 1959, 70 Africans
     held degrees and 44 had diplomas.   In 1960 it was es-
     timated that 600 Africans were taking post-secondary
     courses.   The first African woman was admitted to Ma-
     kerere in 1951.   It was 1956 when the first African wo-
     man graduated from a university.

University College, Dar es Salaam, opened on Lumumba Street in 1961 with a Faculty of Law. The University of East Africa was formed in 1963 and the University moved to "The Hill" in 1964 and opened new faculties year by year. It is estimated that in 1966/67
there were 552 Tanzanians studying at the University College, Dar es Salaam, 455 enrolled in sister institutions
and 818 Tanzanians abroad in post-secondary institutions.
Upon nationalization in 1970, the University College became the University of Dar es Salaam and President
Nyerere its Chancellor. Its enrollment in 1974 was 2260.
The 1966/77 figures in the Budget Speech reveal that
there were 2644 in the University of Dar es Salaam, 89
at Makerere, 125 in Nairobi and 907 teachers abroad.
Mature entry is favored at the University. Also, it is
considered to be a learning institution for workers. See
also UNIVERSITY COLLEGE OF DAR ES SALAAM; UNI-
VERSITY OF EAST AFRICA; and UNIVERSITY OF DAR
ES SALAAM.

HIGHLANDS. Northern Highlands: Mt. Kilimanjaro, Mt.
Meru, Winter Highlands and Usambaras. Southern Highlands: Kipengere Range east of Mbeya.

HILTON-YOUNG COMMISSION. A British Parliamentary Co-
mission, headed by Sir Edward Hilton-Young, came to
East Africa in 1927/28 to look into the possibilities of
an East African Federation in such areas as railways,
harbors, post, telegraphs, aviation, customs, defense and
research. Even though the Report said, "Not yet ripe,"
it suggested an eventual union between Kenya, Uganda and
Tanganyika.

HOLY GHOST FATHERS. A French group from Alsace arrived in Zanzibar in 1860 from Reunion (Bourbon). They
operated a hospital, orphanage, elementary and industrial
schools. Fr. Horner crossed on to the mainland in 1863
and by 1868 began a freed slave settlement at Bagamoyo.
They taught and cared for over 300 Africans from different parts of East Africa. By 1872 they had agricultural schemes with coffee, workshops, elementary schools
and a novitiate for African sisters. A terrible cyclone
laid most of these to ruins in 1872 and they had to be rebuilt. When members within a community married, they
settled in new villages farther inland. By 1885 there
were five of these villages, some over 100 miles away.
On 21 December, 1906, the Bagamoyo Vicariate

was created and grew so rapidly that by 1910 it was divided into Bagamoyo and Kilimanjaro. In 1934 the new
Prefecture Apostolic of Dodoma was detached and en-
trusted to the Passionists. In 1952 the Tanganyika Han-
deni District was given to the Prefecture of Tanga and
Rosminian Fathers. The Tanganyikan Hierarchy was es-
tablished in 1953. The Eastern Ecclesiastical Province
under the Metropolitan of Dar es Salaam contained the
Diocese of Morogoro (Bagamoyo) and Moshi (Kilimanjaro).
Bishop Joseph Kilasara of Moshi was consecrated in 1960.
In March 1953 the Moshi Diocese was divided and the
Diocese of Arusha was erected. Two major seminaries
Kibosho and Morogoro served these three diocese until
September 1963 when Morogoro was closed down.

HONEY. In Central Tanzania are many wooden cylinders
hanging on trees to get honey. Honey and beeswax
brought in Shs. 5. 7 million in foreign exchange in 1973.
An ultra-modern processing plant costing Shs. 1. 1 million
was built at Handeni in Tanga Region and began operation
by end of 1975.

HOROMBO, CHIEF see OROMBO

HUT TAX. The first taxation ordinance in 1897. The main
objective was to be educative; it was intended to oblige
Africans to accept paid labor and accustom themselves
to European administrative discipline. At first unpaid
labor on public works could be offered in lieu of paying
the hut tax, but later the need for current revenue soon
cancelled this arrangement. In 1905 Gotzen fixed the
minimum assessment at three rupees per hut. Some authorities believe that the way the authorities collected the
hut tax caused some of the grievances which led to the
Maji-Maji uprising.

-I-

IBN BATTUTA (1304-1378). Greatest of Muslim travellers
of the Middle Ages, he was born in Tangier. He was
an early historian and the only Muslim traveller of the
Middle Ages to give an eyewitness description of the
coastal towns. He visited Kilwa, Mombasa and Mogadishu
in 1331.

IMPERIAL BRITISH EAST AFRICA COMPANY. Founded in

1876 as the British East Africa Association. Mackinnon reconstructed the association and in 1888 it was given a royal charter and its new name. The purpose of the Society was to spread British influence in East Africa and was founded with the approval of the Sultan of Zanzibar. His possessions and the mainland and adjacent islands had been defined in the delimitation treaty. The IBEA Company received its charter from the British Government in 1888 and was authorized to act on the Government's behalf. IBEA went bankrupt in 1891 but was kept going by supporters until 1894 when the British Government bought it out and took over. It surrendered its charter in 1895.

INDIAN EDUCATION AUTHORITY. Created after World War II to care for Indian education in the territory, it had control of their non-native education tax funds and management of their schools. The body was abolished after independence when schools were integrated and a single advisory body was established in place of the four authorities.

INDIAN NATIONAL ASSOCIATION. Formed in Zanzibar in 1910. It was concerned with Indian commerce and finance and only political when touched. In 1934 they accused the Zanzibar Government of trying to drive Indians away from Zanzibar. They were joined by Indians in India in organizing the boycott of the clove trade in 1937.

INDIANS. Asians from the Indian sub-continent; hence Indian and Pakistanis. In 1833 the firm of Wat Bhima was appointed to the post of customs collectors for Zanzibar. The policy of political support for Indian merchants trading under the British flag and engaged in legitimate commerce had been initiated as early as 1811 with Captain Smee's visit to Zanzibar. The opening of the British Consulate in Zanzibar in 1841 reinforced this policy. By that time there had been 1000 British Indian subjects in Zanzibar and the number rose to around 6000 by 1860. Nearly all the foreign trade passed through their hands. About that time they moved on to towns on the coast and traded as retailers with locals and wholesalers with Zanzibar. They became the financiers of the caravans, providing credit and provisions--a vital function though an unpopular one.

On the mainland there were 6723 in 1910 and a

quarter of them lived in Dar es Salaam. The Europeans showed hostility to the Indians because they were British subjects, they were racial antagonists, and they were commercial competitors. In May 1906 legislation was drafted requiring that all accounts be kept in Swahili or in a European language. Governor Rechenberg defended the Indians. The Tanga Indian Association was established in 1914 with 16 members for allegedly apolitical ends.

There were around 10,000 Indians in Tanganyika when the Germans were deported during World War I. They gained economic opportunities and soon controlled more than 96 percent of the Dar es Salaam retail trade and bought some German sisal plantations which caused a protest from the South African community near Arusha and Moshi. They also entered other employment with 804 Indian staff employed by the Administration and 886 serving on the Railways in 1921. The Indian population was estimated to have reached 25,000 in 1931.

By 1939 the Indian economic interest was believed to be around £13 million sterling which included 17 percent of the non-African agricultural land, 90 percent of town properties, 80 percent of the cotton industry, 80 percent of the sisal industry, 50 percent of the import trade, 60 percent of the export trade and 80 percent of the transportation services.

Indians are famous for their goldsmithing. They have also contributed greatly in the medical services: 40 percent of the country doctors were in private practice in 1960 and most of them were Indians.

There are three main groups of Indians in Tanzania: 1) the Gujarati-speaking predominate and have a monopoly on trade (general shops). They are Hindus, Aga Khan followers, Shia and Ithna-Ashari sects. 2) Punjabi-speakers are Hindus, Moslems and Sikhs. 3) Roman Catholic Goans are about 90 percent of the Christian Asians. They are well-educated and Westernized.

In 1970 when major industries were nationalized and large housing and businesses were nationalized, the Indian community was affected the most. There has been some emigration to other lands, but many of them have taken out Tanzanian citizenship since independence.

INDIRECT RULE. The policy of administration introduced by Governor D. Cameron and by the Native Authority Ordinance enacted in 1926. The policy identified African leaders in each area and granted them executive, judicial and financial powers within their tribal boundaries. These

officers were backed by the authorities of the British
Colonial Government and its officers. The chief responsibilities of the African leaders were to collect taxes,
maintain law and order, maintain the local roads, and
keep a census of the people and livestock in their areas.
The policy was criticized for three reasons: traditional
local leaders were not recognized by all the people they
were supposed to govern; educated Africans believed indirect rule was a plot to keep them out of central government; and it hindered the growth of nationhood.

INDUSTRY. In 1964 the manufacturing industry was 7.1 percent of the G. D. P. Manufacturing is geared to serve the
consumer demands of the commercial sector (food, bev-
erages, cigarettes or simple inputs like paints, twine,
saw milling, etc.). Industry has been largely confined
to limited processing of agricultural and animal exports,
light industries deal mostly with consumer goods and
heavy industry has also begun. Mining is limited to industrial diamonds. Over 90,000 are employed in industry by 1976. Manufacturing contributed 10 percent to the
G. D. P. in 1976, mining and quarrying 1 percent and
commerce about 12 percent.

INSTITUTE OF ADULT EDUCATION. Began in 1963 although
from 1960 to 1962 Dr. A. T. C. Slae had begun the work
from Makerere College. The Institute was opened in the
same building earlier used by the University College,
Dar es Salaam and was under the auspices of that institution. The first director, Paul Bertelsen (1963-67) was
followed by Dorothy Thomas (1967-70). A Tanzanian,
Paul J. Mhaiki, succeeded her (July 1970 to June 1973)
until he was appointed Principal of Kivukoni College.
Fr. D. Mbunda was the fourth director.
    The Institute of Adult Education Decree of 1964
assigned more duties to the institution than providing extra-mural classes. It was also to become a center for
study and research as well as for training adult education
teachers and administrators. In 1967 when the Senate of
the University of East Africa started the Mature Entry
Age Scheme, the Institute was made directly responsible
for the examinations. A two-year Certificate Course in
Law was also offered in connection with the Faculty of
Law.
    In 1969 the Commission of Enquiry advocated that
adult education be extended to the rural areas. So the
Institute began a training program of one-year leading to

a diploma, a radio suite was completed in 1972 for training in radio programming, a research unit was added in
1970 and a vigorous national correspondence program was
introduced.   Third-year education students at the University of Dar es Salaam can also specialize in adult education.   Primers on development topics and national policies
have been written for newly literates.
        The largest section deals with the correspondence
courses.   These courses cover political education, book-
keeping, administration, Swahili, English and mathematics.
There are introductory courses and then Stage One (to
Form 2 level), Stage Two (to Form 4 level) and Stage
Three (to Form 6 level).   The courses for Universal
Primary Education of teachers were offered by this section.   These 13 different courses have been introduced
at the rate of 3 or 4 a year since 1972 and have had an
average yearly enrollment of about 5,000 or a total of
20,231.

INSTITUTE OF EDUCATION.   First attached to Mpwapwa
    Teachers Training Centre in cooperation with the Teacher
    Training Advisory Board.   It was given the task of syl-
    labus and examinations revision and also textbook writing.
    It was planned to move the Institute to the Dar es Salaam
    College of National Education when opened, but instead it
    became attached to the University College in 1965.   It is
    an organizational bridge between the teachers colleges
    and the university.   Some of the activities undertaken by
    the Institute have been courses for teachers and tutors
    all over the territory, educational research, maintainance
    of a science center, production of filmstrips for use in
    history and geography teaching in primary and secondary
    schools, the preparation of textbooks and aids in the
    Swahili language for primary education, subject curriculum
    revision, and coordination of the teacher training college
    programs.   The Institute became a   parastatal organiza-
    tion in 1976.

INTEGRATION COMMITTEE.   Set up in 1958 to examine the
    whole education, multiracial systems of education and
    make recommendations for integration into one system
    of education.   Their recommendations for integration were
    accepted by the government in its White Paper No. 1 of
    1960.   The Asian vernacular medium was dropped; titles
    referring to race or religion were abolished; English me-
    dium schools were required to introduce Swahili as a
    subject in the school; and the same examination for all

at end of the primary course, either in English or Swahili
editions. Eleven English medium schools were allowed
to remain.

INTERNATIONAL PRIMARY SCHOOL. In Dar es Salaam, it
was established as a private school in 1963 by the Governments of the United States and Great Britain in addition to other sources. The school was the first of its
kind in East Africa. It enrolls students from Tanzania
and other backgrounds.

IRAMBA (tribe). In the interior, the tribe was made up of
matrilineal clans forming separate territorial units and
for that reason had no common political head.

IRAQW (tribe). A people of whom comparatively little is
known and their ethnic and linguistic affinities are uncertain. It is possible that they may be the last survivors
of the "Azanian" peoples. They construct mainly the
sunken, flat-roofed dwelling known as tembe. It is a pit
covered with a flat roof of mud and dung, not thatch,
which is rarely above ground level. They live south and
west of Lake Eyasi. Iraqw are tall and light-skinned
with Semitic features. They are a proud, reserved people noted for their statuesque, immobile posture and a
sharply defined figure. They tend to be withdrawn, tend
their cattle and crops and only sell what is necessary to
purchase their few needs. Conversely, their land-reha-
bilitation and destocking program went into effect with the
assistance of local leadership, without any resentment
felt in other areas. They number more than 200,000.

IRINGA. A growing town in an agricultural area. It has an
altitude of 5000 feet and good climate, is situated along
the Dar es Salaam-Zambia road a distance of 250 miles
west of Dar es Salaam. In August 1896 Captain Prince
established a new military station at Iringa. By 1905 the
population was 2500, 22,000 in 1967, and 51,000 in 1977.
Maize is the main crop grown for food and cash and tea
is processed and packed at Iringa. TANCUT is the dia-
mond-cutting factory at Iringa.

IRON ORE. Ore and coal deposits are found in considerable
quantities close to each other. The Liganga deposit is
30 miles from the Ruhuhu River basin east of Lake Nyasa
where coal is found. The Liganga field is believed to
have more than 45 million tons of ore. Transportation

and high smelting costs have not made it economically or
technically feasible to exploit this resource yet.

ISIKE, CHIEF KIYUNGI (? -1893). Chief of the Nyamwezi,
he was installed in 1876 and had built a good army by
1885 and levied customs duty (hongo) from traders passing through his country. In 1886 a German, Gieseche,
was killed due to fraudulent trade transactions. Isike
confiscated his property and forced the White Fathers out
of Kipalapala in 1889, his hatred for Europeans growing.
On 1 August, 1890, Emin Pasha concluded a treaty with
the Tabora Arabs. Isike was forced to surrender two
cannons and to pay an indemnity of ivory. In 1892 the
Germans attacked Isike and his son. The German expedition was nearly annihilated in August 1892. Isike ordered all caravan routes through his country closed. The
Germans retaliated under von Prince and destroyed
Isike's fort in January 1893. Isike blew up himself and
his family to avoid capture by the Germans.

ISIMILA. Located south of Iringa, it is a hand-axe site for
archeologists. The abundance of implements at certain
places suggest these were camps near drinking places
where game would congregate certain times of the year.
Some of the finest hand-axes are over 15" long and weigh
over 9 lbs.

ISLAM. The one-quarter of the population adhering to Islam
is concentrated in the coastal regions and in towns of the
old trading routes. Islam became established along the
coast as early as the eighth century. Kilwa was a major
center of Islamic influence. Later Zanzibar became the
great Moslem stronghold. The Moslem community has
remained basically conservative in its approach to social
affairs in Tanzania. See also MOSLEMS.

IVORY. Tabora and Ujiji were the early trading centers for
Arab caravans dealing in slaves and ivory. Ivory was
in great demand in India for decorative purposes and
making into bangles for Hindu women. The sale of ivory
from elephants shot on control averaged over £70,000
annually from 1954-60. Ivory is often smuggled out by
poachers of wild animals.

-J-

JAMAL, AMIR HABIB (1922-   ). Born on 26 January, 1922,

at Mwanza into a business family, he schooled in Tanganyika and then went to India to train as a doctor. He
did not gain entrance into the Medical School and instead
studied politics and economics at Calcutta University until 1942. He returned to Tanganyika and entered the
family business in 1943. He was first elected to Legislative Council in 1958 and was appointed the unofficial
Minister for Urban Local Government and Works in 1959.
This quiet-spoken, thoughtful, pipe-smoker has held a
number of Ministerial portfolios and positions in the government since independence: 1960-64, Minister for Communications, Power and Works; 1964-65, Minister of
State, President's Office, Directorate of Development and
Planning; 1965-67, Minister for Finance; 1972-75, Minister for Commerce and Industries (reorganized STC and
NDC); 1975-77, Minister for Finance and Planning; and
in 1977, Minister for Communications and Transport.

JAMSID BIN ABDULLAH, SULTAN (1930-). He succeeded
his father Sultan Abdullah at thirty-three years of age
in 1963.   On 12 January, 1964, he fled during the Revolution to Mombasa, and not being received, went on to
Dar es Salaam. He later moved on to Britain.

JAPHET, NKURA KIRILO (1921-). Born in Meru, Arusha.
He was an African farmer, a trained teacher and medical assistant. He was Secretary of TAA, Arusha Branch,
at the time of the Meru Case. He formed the Meru Citizens' Union and it had 8000 paid-up members. The first
objective was to stop the evictions of Meru and eventually
to remove all European settlers. He lobbied to the U.N.
Visiting Mission of 1951. Before the report was published,
the Meru had been evicted--330 tax payers, 1000 men,
women and children. K. Japhet spoke to the Trusteeship
Council in New York during 1952. Governor Twining appeared on the Government side when the General Assembly case was heard that autumn. From 1954-58, Japhet
was the Provincial Chairman of TANU. He was also a
member of the Meru District Council from 1954-65. He
served as a Committee member of the Cooperative Union
of Tanzania and of the Cooperative Bank of Tanzania.
He lost his Parliamentary seat in the 1965 elections.

JOHNSTON, SIR HARRY H. A British naturalist, came to
Zanzibar in April 1884 with the aim of leading a scientific mission to Mt. Kilimanjaro. He examined animal
life and vegetation around the mountain from his base at

Moshi. He received the protection of the Chagga Chief
Mandara. Britain refused to acknowledge the treaties he
obtained from the chiefs in 1884; British policy was to
support the Sultan. However, by September 1886 Mackinnon confirmed Johnston's treaties. The friendship Johnston had with the local chiefs led to mistrust and he
later moved on to Taveta across the border in Kenya and
bought a small area of land from the local chiefs.

JUMA, WAZIRI (1931-   ). Born in Tanga and educated in
Tanga (1939-40), Zanzibar Teacher Training Centre (1949-
50) and Makerere College (1951-53) where he received a
teachers certificate. After teaching for three years, he
became an administrative officer (1957-63), was appointed
as Regional Commissioner for Mbeya Region in 1963 and
Arusha in 1965. After a year as Tanzania's Ambassador
to the People's Republic of China, he was TANU'S Secretary for Social Culture and Women's Affairs. In 1967 he
was Census Administrator. He worked for a number of
years in the Tazara Railway Service and in 1975 was appointed Ambassador to Sudan.

JUMBE. A recognized headman or leader of a clan or small
group of Africans in a village. A number of jumbes were
under the authority of an akida. The headman, or jumbe,
was given magisterial powers and had the responsibility
for law and order within the respective jurisdiction.

JUMBE, ABOUD MWINYI (1920-   ). Born on 14 June, 1920,
and educated locally in Zanzibar. He studied at Makerere
College for a diploma in education from 1943 to 1945.
He spent the following 14 years as a schoolmaster. In
1953 he was the leader of the Zanzibar National Union,
a shortlived multiracial national movement linking Arabs
and Africans in a common struggle. He resigned teaching in 1960 to join the Afro-Shirazi Party and was elected
as ASP member in both polls. He was appointed opposition Whip and attended constitutional talks in London in
1962 and 1963. He served as Minister for Home Affairs
after the January 1964 revolution in Zanzibar and Minister of Health and Social Insurance and Minister of State
in the First Vice President's office in the Union. On
12 April, 1972, he became the 1st Vice President of the
United Republic of Tanzania and Chairman of the Revolutionary Council.

-K-

KADUMA, IBRAHIM M. (1937-   ).   Born near Malangali in
    Iringa Region.   After completing his primary education
    locally, he studied at Malangali Secondary School and
    Tabora Secondary School.   He studied next at Makerere
    College from 1962-65 and received a B. Sc. in Economics.
    He worked in accounts and economics while training in
    York University, England (1965-66).   He completed his
    studies with a B. Phil. (Public Finance).   From January
    1967 to 22 June, 1969, he served as Director of External
    Finance and Technical Cooperation in the Treasury De-
    partment and the next year as Deputy Secretary, Treasury
    and Treasury Registrar.   For the next three years he
    was the Principal Secretary to the Ministry of Communi-
    cations, Transportation and Labour and the Ministry of
    Treasury.   From July 1973 to November 1975 he was the
    Director of the Institute of Development Studies, Univer-
    sity of Dar es Salaam.   From November 1975 until Fe-
    bruary 1977 he was appointed Minister of Foreign Af-
    fairs, and then became Vice-Chancellor of the University
    of Dar es Salaam.   He is an MP from Iringa and a mem-
    ber of many boards.

KAGURU (tribe).   They numbered 87,000 in 1957.   They re-
    side mainly in Kilosa and Mpwapwa areas.   They are ma-
    trilineal and conservative; few left their homeland in
    early years for even nearby job opportunities.   In the
    1820-70 period, there seems to have been a movement
    mountainwards due to raiding precipitated by Arab trade
    and slaving.   Erosion, isolation to modern conveniences
    and cooler climate encouraged an emigration or depopula-
    tion from the mountains in the 1880's.   Settlements were
    fairly large, owing to the need for defense from raiding.
    In the plateau the settlements are much smaller.   The
    main cash crops are maize, tobacco and sugar cane.
    Kaguru believe that most illness, death and sterility in
    humans and much livestock are caused by witches.   At
    various periods there have been widespread witchhunts,
    but more recently such activities and accusations are
    considered illegal.

KAHAMA, CLEMENT GEORGE (1929-   ).   Born on 30 No-
    vember, 1929, in Bukoba District.   He studied at Tabora
    Government Secondary School from 1948-1950 and then
    became an Administrative Assistant at the Tanganyika
    Medical Headquarters.   He was Secretary-Treasurer of

the Bukoba Cooperative Union, Ltd. in 1951, then went
abroad to Lughborough College for three years. He joined
the Bukoba Coffee Cooperative as Secretary-Treasurer
and then was its first General Manager from 1956-59.
He joined TANU and was elected to the Provincial Executive Committee and was a member of the Legislative
Council 1957-58. On 1 July, 1959, Kahama became the
unofficial Minister for Cooperatives and Community Development and in September 1959, the Minister for Home
Affairs in the new government until 1961. He held the
portfolios of Minister of Commerce and Industry and Minister for Communication and Works before he entered the
diplomatic service in 1965 as Ambassador to the Federal
Republic of Germany and later was East Africa's Ambassador to the EEC. In 1966 he began a long term of
service with the National Development Corporation, a post
he held until he became the Director of Capital Development for the building of the new capital city, Dodoma.

KAHIGI, CHIEF. Of Kianja in West Lake, he was an accom-
    modating leader to the Germans. He welcomed German
    support against his rivals. He offered services and un-
    wavering support to the Germans and in turn got favors
    from them. He adopted German military techniques,
    taught himself rudiments of literacy, and was capable of
    operating a system of tax collection. He was not sympa-
    thetic to missionaries and only Kahigi was permitted by
    the Germans to exclude them from his kingdom. Kahigi
    was an enthusiastic coffee grower. In 1905 the Germans
    made Mutatembwa's son (Roman Catholic educated) super-
    ior chief with Kahigi.

KAMALIZA, MICHAEL MARSHALL MOWGRAY (1929-   ).
    Born in Malawi and received a mission school education.
    He attained a diploma in Bookkeeping and Accounting.
    He was a union man and became treasurer of a union of
    labor in 1952. He helped Maynard Mpagala and Rashidi
    Kawawa to organize a trade union and staff conference
    which worked out a constitution for a national center,
    The Tanganyika Federation of Labour, formed 7 October,
    1955. He was the General Secretary of Transport and
    General Workers Union in 1957 and made President of
    the Tanganyika Federation of Labour (TFL) in 1960, a
    post he held until 1962. In 1963 he was appointed Min-
    ister of Labour. The following year all workers' unions
    were absorbed in NUTA (National Union of Tanganyika
    Workers) of which he was the General Secretary. He

continued in a dual capacity until 1967 when he was relieved of his ministerial duties since he could not do
both.   He carried on as Secretary General of NUTA until 1969.   In 1965 he had also become the Vice President
of the All Africa Trade Union Federation and the headquarters were transferred in December 1966 from Accra
to Dar es Salaam.   His vice presidency continued until
1969, the year he faced trial on charges of attempting
to overthrow the Government.   He was later released
from prison and, after a period of time, served as manager of a company in the northern part of Tanzania.

KAMBONA, OSCAR SALATHIEL (1928-   ).   Born in August
1928, a son of an Anglican priest of Nyasaland who settled in Tanganyika.   He attended a primary school near
Songea and then Liuli Mission School for a teacher training course.   He attended Tabora Government Secondary
School in 1945 on remission of fees.   Later he enrolled
in Dodoma Alliance Secondary School and his fees for the
three years were paid by Rt. Rev. Frank Q. Thorne of
Nyasaland.   In 1948 he went on to St. Paul's Teacher
Training Centre for two more years and returned to teach
at his alma mater at Dodoma.   In 1954 he volunteered
to be TANU's Organizing Secretary and was appointed and
carried the responsibility until 1966.   In 1955 he was offered a scholarship for four years of study in England
and read law in Middle Temple, London.
        On return to Tanganyika, he assumed a series of
ministerial posts: Minister of Education, Minister for
Home Affairs, and Minister for External Affairs and Defense.   In January 1964 he displayed great courage at his
post during the mutiny of Battalion I.   In April 1964 he
resigned the Defense Ministry for health reasons.
Nyerere took over the Ministry of External Affairs.   He
was also Chairman of the Dar es Salaam based African
Liberation Committee of the OAU.   Beginning 1965 he
was made Minister of Regional Administration and in 1967
appointed to the new Ministry of Local Government and
Rural Development.   He resigned from this post due to
ill health in 1967 and went into voluntary exile in June
1967.
        He has been charged with master-minding a plot
against the Government between July 1968 and September
1969.   In 1970 he was charged in absentia at the Dar es
Salaam treason trial.   On 9 December, 1971, the 10th
Anniversary of Tanganyika's independence, two planes
dropped leaflets over Dar es Salaam and more on 1 June,

1972. They challenged President Nyerere to face him in free elections and were signed by him as Leader of the Movement for Free and Popular Democracy. His brothers, Mattiya and Otini were detained in 1972 following a series of bomb blasts for which he was considered to be responsible. Kambona lived in England and made visits to Portugal and moved to Uganda in 1975 where he continues to reside.

KANDORO, SAADANI ABDU (1926-). Born in Ujiji, Kigoma on 8 December, 1926. He attended Ujiji, Iringa, and Mwanahala Government Schools and joined Bwiru Teachers Training Centre near Mwanza in 1944. Two years later he became the treasurer of the Uyumi Usagara Federation in Tabora. His political activities were banned when he was the Lake Province Secretary for TAA and was active in business. In 1958 he was elected a member of the Provincial Committee and served at Tabora and later Dodoma, coming on the Dar es Salaam as an Administrative Secretary, Branch affairs, later administrative Secretary of the Elders' Section and Assistant Publicity Secretary. He was appointed Area Commissioner of Mafia in 1962 and of Bagamoyo in 1964. In 1965 he became the chairman of TANU Disciplinary Committee. He is author of Mwito wa Uhuru (1961).

KAPUUFI, CHIEF (?-1891). Earlier known as Nandi, he reigned for 30 years and was the most rich and powerful of all the Fipa chiefs. He welcomed Arab traders to his court and obtained firearms in this manner.

KARA (tribe). Located in Lake Victoria, they are superior cultivators, keeping the land productive. They developed an intensive mixed crop-and-cattle farming system without European guidance. The system maintains the fertility of the inherently poor land under almost continuous cropping. The tribe is unusual in that they believed in individual ownership of land and regarded cattle as an integral part of a mixed-farming system and limited their numbers to fit the size of the holding and the fodder supply.

KARIMJEE, ABDULKARIM YUSUFALI ALIBHAI (1906-). Born in Zanzibar and is Muslim. He was educated in Zanzibar, India and Karachi, then was director of a number of commercial firms including the International Motor Mart Ltd. He was Mayor of Dar es Salaam 1951,

1953, 1954 and 1955 and Member of Legislative Council from 1949 to 1959, served as Deputy Speaker 1954-58 and Speaker from 1959-62. Some of the other responsibilities he held were: Chairman of University College, Dar es Salaam; Chairman of Tanganyika Library Services Board; Director of the National Bank of Commerce and National Development Corporation; and Vice-Chairman of the University of East Africa. He was conferred the Hon. LL. D. in August 1973 by the University of Dar es Salaam. He is a Member of Tanzania Sisal Authority and of Ngorongoro Conservation Authority and still in business in 1977.

KARUME, ABEID A. , SHEIKH (1905-1972). Born on 4 August, 1905, a distance of 7 miles from Zanzibar town. His father died when Abeid was only eight years of age. He reached the first year of secondary education and then during his 17 years as a sailor, travelled to Europe and Asia. He was also a boxer and footballer. In 1938 he led a small, but dynamic, labor movement for dockers and sailors known as the Syndicate. He entered politics in 1954 and was appointed councillor for the township of Zanzibar. He was later President of the island's African Association. The African Association united with the Shirazi Association in 1957 and formed the Afro-Shirazi Party (ASP) with Sheikh Karume as leader. In the caretaker government he was appointed Minister for Health and Administration. He assumed leadership of the Opposition in the National Assembly in 1963 and became leader of the Revolutionary Council and the new republic after 12 January, 1964. On the occasion of the Union of Zanzibar and Tanganyika on 26 April, 1964, he became President of the Zanzibar People's Republic and First Vice President of the United Republic of Tanzania. He was assassinated on 7 April, 1972.

KATAVI NATIONAL PARK. Originally a game reserve 37 km. away from Mpanda, was opened in 1974. It has an area of 2253 sq. km. and is famous for its large herds of buffaloes, hippos, elephants and some leopards.

KAWAWA, RASHIDI MFAUME (1928-   ). Born in Songea District, a member of the Ngoni tribe. His father was a game-ranger and his forebearers were elephant hunters. While studying at Dar es Salaam Junior Secondary School in Form II, he organized boys for a literacy campaign among the adults they knew. He later went on to Tabora Government Secondary School. He had no fees for

Makerere College and so was employed as a PWD clerk.
In 1951 he joined Tanganyika Government Social Development Department as Film Assistant. The only Tanganyika male star, he led in three popular films and proved
himself as a producer and scriptwriter. A financial
crisis occurred and the business closed down. He joined
the Tanganyika African Government Civil Service Association and became its Assistant General Secretary in 1952
and President in 1954. In 1953 he was sent to Urambo
in Kenya to organize the welfare of the hard-core Kikuyu
Mau Mau suspects. He resigned his job in 1955 and
formed the Tanganyika Federation of Labour. He was the
first General Secretary until 1959 and then President.
In 1956 he attended a Trade Union Course in London.
He won a seat in Legislative Council in 1958 and in September 1960 was appointed Minister for Local Government
and Housing. In April 1961 he became the Minister without Portfolio and then Prime Minister from January to
December 1962 when Nyerere resigned to go to the grass
roots of the Party. When the Republic was formed in
December 1962, he became its Vice President and leader
of the National Assembly. On the occasion of the Union
of Zanzibar and Tanganyika on 26 April, 1964, he was
made the 2nd Vice President and Minister for Defense
and National Service. He played a major part in starting
Ujamaa villages and in introducing National Service for
Youth and molding TPDF as a training institution for defense and socialism. He was reinstated as Prime Minister on 1972 and transferred to the Ministry of Defense
and National Service in February 1977.

KAYAMBA, MARTIN (1891-1939). The great-grandson of
    Kimweri ya Nyumbei, Chief of Usambara, started school
    in Zanzibar at the age of four and then went on to Mom-
    basa. He was the youngest schoolboy at St. Andrew's
    College, Kiungani in 1902. He read there until 1906.
    At fifteen years of age, he began travel and experience
    in Kenya and Uganda as a clerk and trader and was im-
    prisoned by the British. He married in 1908 and had a
    daughter and a son. In 1912 his wife and mother both
    died at Mombasa. So he returned to Zanzibar, took up
    teaching, failed and resigned. In February 1917 he be-
    came court interpreter in Tanga. At that time he re-
    married. In 1923 he was put in charge of the District
    Office under D.O. Philip Mitchell as Chief Clerk. He
    helped form the Tanganyika Territory African Civil Ser-
    vice Association on 22 March, 1922--a supratribal

association from which the leaders of TAA emerged. He
was a member of the Advisory Committee on African
Education, was one of the African representatives to London to the British Parliamentary Council in 1931, awarded
the M. B. E. in May 1932 and appointed Assistant Secretary in the Dar es Salaam Secretariat in December of that
year. In 1936 he decided to go to Europe for health reasons "for a change and education. " He returned in 1936
and in 1938 resigned from his Secretariat position. He
was a chicken farmer on retirement. He wrote a book
called African Problems.

KERERE (tribe). Of Lake Victoria area, it had a former feu-
dal landlord and tenant system. The introduction of cash
crops changed the system when the landlords began to
charge rent instead of gifts in kind. Also scarcity of
land outside the large estates, led small farmers to acquire land of their own. They are related to the Jita and
Sukuma tribes in vernacular language and in culture.

KHALID BIN BARGHASH, SULTAN (? -1927). Made an unsuccessful bid for the throne on the death of Sultan Ali
in 1893 and usurped it on Sultan Hamed's death in 1896.
Both times he was rejected by the British. The British
Navy bombarded the palace in 1896 and about 500 of his
defenders were killed or wounded. Their resistance collapsed quickly and Khalid fled to find refuge in the German consulate. On the capture of Dar es Salaam during
the World War I, he was exiled to St. Helena, on to Sey-
chelles in 1921 and then allowed to live in Mombasa where
he died in 1927.

KHALIFA BIN HARUB, SULTAN (1879-1960). A great grandson of Sultan Said bin Sultan and grandson of Sultan Thwain
of Muscat, reigned from 1911 to 1960 and was much be-
loved and respected by his subjects. He saw Zanzibar
grow into a modern state under British Protection with
formal transfer from the Foreign Office to the Central
Office on 1 July, 1913. His authority helped to maintain
stability and peaceful relations among the various communities in Zanzibar.

KHALIFA BIN SAID, SULTAN (1854-1890). A brother of Sultan Barghash and ruled from 1888-1890. Before his sul-
tanship, he had been imprisoned in a chamber beneath the
Palace by Sultan Barghash for six years because he was
suspected of intrigue. After that he resided in the country

in complete isolation. He carried his quiet, relaxed life-
style into his public life and was never feared nor respected by his subjects as former Sultans. He was considered to be of a weak disposition and abnormally ignor-
ant of affairs. He agreed with the English and Germans
in 1890 to concede the administration of the territory between the Umba and Ruvuma Rivers to them but retained
sovereignty. In 1890 the German Government paid 4 million marks to the Sultan for the final cession of the Tanganyika coast. He also handed over the northern strip
of the coast to the British East Africa Company which administered it in the name of the Sultan and paid an annual rent of £11,000. In the 1890 slave agreements, for-
eigners could intercept Arab dhows and children were
born free. He died of heat apoplexy at the age of thirty-
six.

KHERI, MWINYI (?-1885). Born in Bagamoyo area, he probably arrived in Ujiji during the mid-1840's and became
head of the resident Arab community after Muhammed bin
Sali's death. He married the daughter of the chief of
Ujiji. Arabs and Europeans recognized him as represent-
ing authority of the distant rulers of Zanzibar. He was
a merchant and head of the Arab community for several
decades, drawing his power from his standing as senior
member of the community as well as his personal fortune. In 1876 his wealth included 120 slaves, 80 guns
and 9 canoes, or, in Ujiji values, estimated at $18,000.
His real source of strength came from the relationship
he worked out with the Ha power structure of Bujiji. At
first he welcomed the London Missionary Society to the
area in 1878, but then was suspicious that they would
undermine his relations with the Ha rulers and refused
to give them land. By his peaceful delaying tactics, he
could avoid a British presence which might have hindered
his interests. The London Missionary Society quit Ujiji
in 1883 and in the Lake Tanganyika area five years later.
Kheri caused difficulties also for the White Fathers when
they settled in the area of his raids in 1879. He did,
however, give them more personal protection possibly because they were French and did not make official contact
with Zanzibar as the English missionaries had done.
Kheri remained governor until his death in 1885.

KIGOMA. A town on the eastern shore of Lake Tanganyika,
grew up mainly for its location as port and western railhead of the Central Line. It has small industry and

marine workshops. Kigoma and Ujiji are often called
"twin cities." Kigoma had over 8000 people in 1967 and
Ujiji had 13,000. In 1975 they had a combined total of
27,000 and in 1977 had 28,000.

KIIZA, KLEMENS. A Ziba aristocrat, he was educated by
a Roman Catholic mission. He served at Mutatembwa's
court, the mission and District Office in West Lake. In
1920 he founded the Bukoba Bahaya Union, a native trading company in Bukoba and pioneered modern politics in
the province. He criticized the Council of Chiefs and
advocated that educated men replace them. He went into
the coffee business. In 1928 he added a coffee hulling
machine, acquired land on which to erect a 22,000 Shs.
coffee-curing factory in 1931. During the depression, he
went heavily into debt. In 1936 he organized a Native
Growers Association partly to supply coffee to the factory.
He later clashed with the new government rules and he
lost his hulling license. He was forced to sell his factory to Asian creditors in 1946.

KILIMANJARO CHRISTIAN MEDICAL CENTRE (KCMC). The
idea of this teaching and consulting hospital developed
from the Tanganyika Government's approach to the Lutheran Church as they contacted the Lutheran World Federation and other agencies to sponsor the project. The
Good Samaritan Foundation was established in 1962 by the
founder and chairman, Bishop S. R. Moshi, under the
Christian Council of Tanzania. This agency was able
to receive the foreign funds for the erection of the buildings. The Tanzania Government meets the operational
costs. Services are free.

In 1965 construction for the Staff Quarters and
Nurses Hostel was begun; in 1968 the hospital building
construction work began and was completed in December
1970. Medical services were offered as of 1 January,
1971. President Nyerere officially opened the hospital
on 6 March, 1971. A Board of Governors consists of
equal representation from the Good Samaritan Foundation
and the Tanzania Government. The first Medical Superintendent was Dr. Otto Walter and the fourth and present
is Dr. John Lyimo, a Tanzania Senior Consultant Radio-
logist.

All patients are referrals from other hospitals.
By 1976 two of the consultants were Tanzanians and the
rest were expatriates. There are an average of 400 in-
patients per day, around 35,000 per year and approximately

60,000 outpatients yearly. The Nursing School, opened
in April 1971, has an intake of 30 per year. The African
Medical Research Foundation made the Flying Doctor Service available by 1972 and developed a consultant service
to other hospitals. A radio connection to other hospitals
is maintained. In addition to nurses training, KCMC
trains interns from the University of Dar es Salaam Faculty of Medicine, medical assistants, dressers, a labor-
atory auxiliary, a radiographic auxiliary, medical record-
ers and up-grading medical assistants for ophthalmolo-
gists. By 1976 the hospital had plans for expanding their
Ear-Nose-Throat unit and adding a wing of 50 beds for
eye treatment.

KILIMANJARO NATIONAL PARK. Gazetted in 1973. It has
an area of 756 sq. km. and contains the most beautiful
and highest mountain in Africa, reaching an altitude of
19,340 feet. It is a scenic park rather than game park,
although it does have elephants, buffaloes, klip springers
and rhinoceros. A Norwegian team is laying out roads
and replacing the old huts for climbers.

KILIMANJARO NATIVE COOPERATIVE UNION LTD. (KNCU).
This Union was the reorganized structure of the Kilimanjaro Native Planters Association after the Cooperative
Societies Ordinance had been enacted in 1932. The
KNCU was registered on 29 December, 1933, with 11 cooperative societies and 16,800 members. That same
year the coffee collected and sold amounted to 896 tons
and was valued at Shs. 1,300 per ton. The main purpose
of the KNCU was to market their coffee and to raise the
yield and quality. The KNCU building was erected in
1953. Their school trained inspectors, instructors, nur-
sery men and growers. The hostel was opened in 1956,
the College of Commerce (now Moshi Cooperative College)
began in the KNCU building in 1961. It has now moved
to new premises. It also had a printing press, a library
of 6000 books, restaurant, laundry and a ginnery.
     The number of affiliated societies in the KNCU
raised to over 50 and members to more than 118,000 in
the mid-1970's.
     In 1966 the KNCU decided to diversify its crops
and functions. Coffee remains the primary crop, but
maize, beans, oilseeds, hides and skins, cotton, pyrethrum, rice and cashews are also marketed. Along with
increases in marketing, the wholesale distribution of consumer's goods and hardware was added to its functions

in the same year.   Another function was added in 1974,
the Transport Wing.

When fifty farms were nationalized in Kilimanjaro
in 1973, forty-four were given to cooperative, two to Kilimanjaro Development Corporation and four with a total
of 8,040 S. were given to KNCU.

KNCU has included many services to its members
and community.   Over 1000 good grade cattle worth £1.5
million have been imported as loans to farmers.   The
KNCU has aided many primary schools, given Shs. 50,000
each to ten private secondary schools, built Lyamungu
Secondary School and handed it over to the Government
to operate in January 1962, operates Moshi Cooperative
College with secondary and post secondary courses in
commerce, domestic and retail sciences, and provides
in-service training for its staff.   With the Government's
new marketing policies of 1976, the KNCU was reorganized
in the Regional Trading Corporation, Tanganyika Coffee
Board, National Milling Corporation, etc.

KILIMANJARO NATIVE PLANTERS' ASSOCIATION (KNPP).
Formed in 1925 when 12 coffee societies joined.   In 1928
it opposed a government proposal to register all Chagga
land holdings.   The Government suggested KNPA be
merged with the native treasury and the Association refused.   In 1929 the Association asked for representation
in the Legislative Council when they feared amalgamation
with Kenya.   During the Depression its finances collapsed.
In 1932 the Cooperative Societies Ordinance was passed
in the Legislative Council.   By the following year, the
KNPP had been decentralized into eleven local cooperative
societies which were united in the Kilimanjaro Native Cooperative Union and registered on 29 December, 1933.

KILWA.   Located on the coast approximately 150 miles or
250 km. south of Dar es Salaam and was at one time the
greatest of the mercantile towns of East Africa covering
an area of 102 acres.   It was referred to in Milton's
Paradise Lost under the Portuguese name Quiloa.   The
founding of Kilwa has been ascribed to the 10th century
(Arab version) and the 11th century (Portuguese version),
so there are conflicting dates in the early history of Kilwa.   There is common agreement that Shirazis had come
from Persia and the first ruler was Sultan Ali bin Husain who reigned for 40 years.   He was nicknamed "Nguo
Nyingi" (many clothes).   The old settlers were later able
to drive out the Shirazis and appointed a puppet ruler of

their own. The rightful ruler Hassan bin Suleiman I,
finally returned and the usurper was killed. (See pages
x and xi for the list of rulers and lengths of rule.)

     Kilwa's greatness was established in the 13th cen-
tury under new Shirazi rulers who probably came from
the Banadir coast. Hasan bin Ali was called the founder
of Kilwa. He ruled over Zanzibar, Pemba and a large
part of the mainland. Some historians call him Ali bin
Hassan and others Hassan bin Daudi. During his 70
years as Sultan, he transformed Kilwa from a small
trading post into a powerful island fortress as he gained
mastery of the gold trade previously controlled by Mogadishu. The dhows from Sofala stopped for water and
food or were intercepted by the Sultan and made to pay
taxes. Kilwa began minting its own coins. Cowrie shells
were used for bartering. Hassan bin Talut (1277-94),
his successor as Sultan, introduced copper coins.

     By the time Ibn Battuta visited Kilwa in 1332, Ma-
fia Island had also been added to the kingdom. Sultan
Daudi bin Suleman (c1333-56) was known as the "Master
of the Princes." Kilwa declined after his leadership.
There was a temporary revival during the 15th century
but it declined again by 1490 as a result of competition
from Mombasa. There were 14 Sultans between 1442 and
1498. The offices of Qadhi and Amir were granted to
new arrivals from Persia. This led to divisions which
assisted Portugal in their conquest of Kilwa and later
weakened efforts to set up a stable regime.

     In 1500 Pedro Alvaris Cabral, discoverer of Bra-
zil, visited Kilwa. The following year John de Nova
visited with a fleet. In 1502 Vasco da Gama sailed into
the harbor, landed with a large force of soldiers, seized
the palace, imprisoned the Sultan Ibrahim and only released him after he had acknowledged the rule of the King
of Portugal. The island was forced to pay an annual tribute. The Sultan did not, however, comply after that.

     On 23 July, 1505, Francisco d'Almeida found the
residents had fled before him before he landed. So his
men stripped the town and burned it. By 1506 Portugal
had claimed control over the entire coast and over trade
on the Indian Ocean. The town did not recover commer-
cially or culturally because the trade ties that had been
cut by the Portuguese had not been reestablished. A
marauding band of some 5000 Zimba warriors destroyed
Kilwa in 1587 and continued northward destroying as they
went.

In 1724 Kilwa gained freedom from Mozambique
with the aid of Europeans. Nearer the end of the 18th
century the economy revived as Kilwa was the principal
center of the East Africa slave trade. In 1776 the treaty
between Sultan Hasan bin Ibrahim and M. Morice, a
Frenchman, held the Sultan to a contract for 100 years
in which he agreed to supply Morice with 1000 slaves
annually. The Yao kept the slave supply coming from
their own or other tribesmen. Zanzibar, the center of
Arab slave trade, also got most of its slaves from Kilwa.

Saif bin Ahmed took Kilwa in 1784 but the Imam
of Oman recaptured it. They were then subject to the
Zanzibar Governor of the Sultan of Muscat. Trade lapsed
in the middle of the 19th century. In 1846 Sultan Said
dismissed the governor and none replaced him. The town
fell to ruins.

KIMWERI THE GREAT (?-1869). A strong and fair paramount chief in the first half of the 19th century. He
ruled over Vuga Kingdom in the northern area of the
Usambara. By 1850 his kingdom stretched from Kilimanjaro to the coast and was 140 by 60 miles. The resul-
tant conflicting claims to the coastal areas by the Sultan
and Kimweri were settled with Tanga and remaining
coastal areas under the Sultan and Kimweri providing administrators with the Sultan's approval over the rest.
This arrangement lasted until 1852 or 1853 when Kimweri's power began to decline and, after his death, the
Sultan claimed all the coastal lands.

Kimweri had succeeded his father Kinyasi at the
Kilindi capital Vuga. He consolidated the system of government with the king becoming ruler in fact as well as
in theory. The subordinate chiefdoms were all ruled by
Kimweri's brothers and cousins. He replaced them with
his sons, the mothers being from commoner clans. He
had districts with governors, prime ministers and com-
manders of the army. He levied tribute, often cloth payment, all the way from the hills of South Pare to Pangani on the coast. He had one weakness; he tried to prevent other chiefs from trading in ivory and slaves and
obtain gunpowder. According to historical traditions,
Kimweri's most important weapon in fighting back was
control of the rain. He is believed to have had magical
powers and hurled famine at his enemies.

After his death in 1869, his kingdom broke up.
The Sultan claimed his coastal lands. His grandson
Shekuwavu succeeded him and Semboja, his son with a

chiefdom Mazinde on the main trade route in the west, sought help from Taita, Kenya and Shekuwavu was killed. Then Semboja and Kibanga, a grandson in the east, held a long war of succession. Semboja took over Vuga but the center of power moved to Mazinde. Kibanga allied himself with the Germans, sold them all the land they wanted and secured the recognition of Kinyasi, his candidate for the Kilindi throne.

KINDIGA. See HADZAPI for this tribe called Kindiga or Tindiga or Hadzapi.

KINYASI, CHIEF. Of Vuga, Usambara ruled in the 1870's until he abdicated in 1903. He was chief of Kilindi and an ally of the Germans. He provided services for the settlers and planters in the area, but abdicated rather than supply labor by force or be assassinated. He had lost the majority of his inhabitants over the years; it was estimated that they had numbered 3000 when he became ruler. On his abdication, the Kilindi administration broke down. Kinyasi became the akida of Mlalo during indirect rule. During this time he became an adherent of Islam. He met much opposition from Semboja's lineage and retreated to inactivity. He seemed to be timid and still suffering from the fears which led to his earlier abdication.

KIPANDE. A ticket system by which the employees of a plantation were paid on a piecework basis. The employees could work as they pleased, provided they accomplished a standard of 30 days work within a six-week period. Under this system the employees could choose the circumstances under which they would work. The adoption of a minimum wage legislation led to a serious dispute over the conversion of the kipande system to a monthly wage system. These disagreements led to a series of wild-cat strikes by plantation workers. The government banned two leading officers of TFL.

KIRK, SIR JOHN. Began life in Zanzibar as a doctor at the British Army in 1866. He soon began to spend time on political matters and became Sultan Barghash's chief adviser and supporter. He also aided many travellers and missionaries. He was British Consul and then appointed Consul General of Zanzibar in 1873 and established himself as an unofficial prime minister to the Sultan. In 1863 Dr. Kirk with Sir Bartle Frere forced Sultan

Barghash to declare slave trade illegal. Kirk left Zanzibar in July 1886 after 16 years in the Consulate.

KISABENGO. The first real chief in Uluguru, he was a Zigua who made himself leader of a group of runaway slaves around 1850. The Sultan of Zanzibar was angry with him, so he moved west to the country of the Luguru people. He raided the surrounding country for slaves and imposed heavy tolls on caravans passing through from Tabora and on their return from the coast. Zimbamwene, his town, was situated near the present site of Morogoro. In 1871 Stanley admired the high stone walls, watch tower, and carved wooden gates which had been damaged by floods. Kingo, his descendant, occupied Simbamwene yet by 1890.

KISENGE, ELIAS (1923-   ). Born in Usangi, Pare. He attended Tabora Government Secondary School and then entered government service and 1938-48 he worked for the provincial administration in various towns of the Northern Province. Concurrently he was Provincial Secretary of TAGSA (Tanganyika African Government Servants Association) and a keen member of TAA. In 1948 he transferred to Same as chief clerk of the local council and as secretary of the Pare Tribal Association. At the end of 1948 he transferred to the Treasury at Dar es Salaam and in the next year became TAGSA's Organising Secretary. He was transferred to the Southern Province when "strike talk" was heard, but he got back to Dar es Salaam and Same. In 1954 he resigned from both the Pare Council and Association and became District Secretary of TANU without a salary. In April 1956 he moved to Tanga as TANU Provincial Secretary and set up a Youth League, called TANU Volunteer Corps. In October 1956 he held the office of Deputy Organising Secretary of TANU in Kambona's absence. He gained the full title in 1957 and continued in this position until 1960. Kisenge entered Legislative Council as a member in 1960. In the new government he has continued to be politically active. He has been a Junior Minister in the Vice President's and President's Office, Deputy Chairman of Tanganyika Licensing Authority and in the Civil Service Commission. Upon leaving politics, he became General Manager of Tanganyika African Motors Transport with its head office in Tanga.

KISUMO, PETER (1935-   ). Born in Pare District and

educated locally. He became Local Secretary of the
Trades Union Movement in 1959, and was appointed General Secretary in 1961. He was Regional Commissioner
for Kilimanjaro Region, Singida and Kigoma, then Minister for Local Government and Rural Development from
June 1967-69 when he became Minister for Regional Administration and Rural Development. He again filled Regional Commissioner offices in Kilimanjaro and Mwanza
in the mid-1970's. He resigned in January 1977, should-
ering the blame for conditions which existed under his
jurisdiction in Mwanza.

KIUNGANI see ST. ANDREW'S COLLEGE

KIVUKONI IDEOLOGICAL COLLEGE. Part of the national
    party TANU, it is located near the harbor in Dar es
    Salaam. During the annual conference of TANU at Ta-
    bora in 1958, a decision was made to establish a college
    for adults of both sexes with courses and training leading
    to better understanding of the problems and potentialities
    of the country. It was founded with funds raised in Tan-
    ganyika. The College offers short and long courses for
    leaders and workers, ranging from 1-2 week seminars,
    3-month courses and a 9-month course. Students have
    been regional officers, party leaders, university graduates,
    headmasters of secondary schools and primary school
    teachers. Kivukoni aims at training students for respon-
    sibility regardless of the educational standard reached,
    i. e. , the training of administrators for Government and
    Party organization. From 1961 when the school opened
    with 39 students and 3 full-time staff members, the Col-
    lege has held courses in residence, but from 1974 Kivu-
    koni has started up-country zonal colleges as a joint ven-
    ture with the cooperative movement. The Principal in
    office end-1976 was Paul J. Mhaiki.

KIWANGA, CHIEF. A Hehe ruler of the Bena in the upper
    Kilombero Valley. He is considered to have been the
    most powerful ruler in that valley. He helped the Ger-
    mans against the Hehe and expanded his territory. He
    once offered a small child to Captain Prince. When he
    heard of Maji-Maji he executed all available hongo and
    hastened his forces to Mahenge where he helped to re-
    store German control of the Kilombero Valley. In the
    same process, he himself was killed by rebels. He was
    succeeded by his son, the favorite Salimbango, who was
    only eleven years old and the regency was held by one
    faction of the chiefdom.

KLERRUU, WILBERT (1932-71).   Educated in Tanganyika and
then went on to the University of California, where he
graduated with a Ph. D. in Political Science.   On return
to Tanzania, he served as Assistant Publicity Secretary
in 1962 and then Publicity Secretary.   From 1964-67 he
was TANU National Executive Secretary.   He served as
Regional Commissioner of Mtwara Region and then in
Iringa, where he was shot while visiting Ndelela Ujamaa
Village.   He is survived by a wife and three children.

KOMBO, SHEIKH THABIT (1904-   ).   A Shirazi of Zanzibar
with little formal education beyond study of the Koran.
He worked on local ships (1920-25) and as a railway engineer (1926-29), and then ran a shop for a Shirazi cooperative in Zanzibar town.   He was a member of the
Clove Growers' Association (1939-53) and awarded the
Coronation Medal in 1953.   His efforts as leader of the
Shirazi Association led to cooperation between his association and the African Association in the 1957 elections.
Soon afterward they merged to be the Afro-Shirazi Party
(ASP) with Kombo as Secretary General, a post he held
as long as ASP existed as a party.   ASP was defeated
with the 1963 elections but returned to power after January 1964 revolution and merged with UMMA.   All other
parties were banned.   In 1965 Kombo was considered second to Karume.   In 1967 Sheikh Kombo was appointed
Zanzibar Minister for Trade and Industry.   In 1975 he
became ASP Chairman for Commerce and Industries.   He
was active in the discussions in 1976 for the merger of
TANU and ASP.

KRAPF, JOHANN LUDWIG (1810-81).   Born in Derendingen,
Germany on 11 January, 1810.   In 1837 he went as a
missionary under the Church Missionary Society to Ethiopia for six years.   In May 1844 he arrived with his
wife at Mombasa.   She died a few weeks later.   He travelled from the CMS Mission at Mombasa to the Usambara Mountains and found Chief Kimweri friendly to missions.   He was joined by Rebmann, Ernhardt and others
and made journeys into the interior; they explored Mt.
Kilimanjaro, Mt. Meru and the Usambara areas in 1848
and went on to Kilwa.   In 1853 Krapf was in ill health
and did not rejoin Mombasa Mission.   He returned to
Kimweri and began a mission at Tongwe.   The first mission in the interior lasted only a few months; his ill
health forced him to give up.   The reports and rudimen-
tary maps of the explorers were very useful for

subsequent exploration.   The 1855 map drawn by Krapf
and his friend was called the "Slug Map."   It joined
Lakes Victoria, Tanganyika and Nyasa all in one.   While
in East Africa Krapf had published a first Swahili grammar, began translation of the New Testament, and collected the material for his Swahili Dictionary.   He died
in Germany on 26 November, 1881.

KUNAMBI, BERNADETTE NEMPHOMBE (1934-   ).   The wife
of the former Chief of the Luguru, she was born near
Morogoro, educated locally, and took a teacher training
course in 1951-52 after completing secondary education.
She taught in various primary schools from 1953-60.
Kunambi conducted volunteer literacy classes 1961-62 and
then became the Chief Commissioner of the Tanganyika
Girl Guides Association in 1963.   She held a variety of
posts, including YWCA National General Secretary, Assistant Secretary of the Community Development Trust
Fund, Town Councillor of Morogoro, Chairman of the
Tanganyika Council of Women and Chairman of the Hospital Advisory Committee at Morogoro.   She was a member of Parliament and was appointed Area Commissioner
for Ilala District when Dar es Salaam became a Region
mid-1970's.   She and her husband are both active in Roman Catholic organizations.

KUNAMBI, CHIEF PATRICK.   Also known as Sultan of the
Luguru, he is one of the few members of his tribe who
has had the benefits of higher education.   He was educated at local mission schools and then at Makerere College.   He was assistant headmaster of a secondary school
near Morogoro when he was appointed Deputy Sultan of
the Luguru in 1955.   Kunambi has a strong feeling for
traditionalism but he would also like to see the Luguru
make greater advances in the modern world.   In 1955 he
was appointed to the Tanganyika Legislative Council.   He
also assisted in drafting TANU's constitution and was a
member of TANU's Organizing Committee.   In 1958 he
contested for the Eastern Province Legislative Council
seat under UTP and lost to Nyerere 1:3.5.   His relationships with TANU members cooled off and he left
TANU, but continued as Deputy Sultan of the Luguru.

KURIA (tribe).   Located in Northwest Tanzania on the east
side of Lake Victoria in Tarime or North Mara District
of Mara Region.   They have proved very adaptable to
police work and, in 1964, along with the Hehe, made up

50 percent of the police force. They are agriculturalists
with cattle. Cattle are valued very highly and a must for
the brideprice.

KWAVI (tribe). Sometimes called BARAGUYU or LIOKOPI.
They are the "agricultural Masai." When the Masai expanded in the Rift Valley between 1650 and 1700, they
retained their identity and much of their culture.

KWERE (tribe). Numbered 40,000 in 1957. Most reside in
the Coast Region or eastern Morogoro and in the rolling,
open bush. They are hoe-cultivators, cultivation often
being done in terms of small holes rather than in an entirely hoed field. Kwere are also skilled and artistic
carvers and make various ingenious animal traps. They
are a matrilineal society with no centralized authority.

KYARUZI, VEDAST K. (1921-   ). Born on 21 February,
1921, north of Bukoba. After a local education, he
studied medicine and was the house physician to the Sewa
Haji Hospital in Dar es Salaam in 1944. He qualified in
Medicine at Makerere College in 1948 and was a licensed
practitioner in 1949. He transferred in 1951 from the
Sewa Haji Hospital to the Morogoro Prison Hospital. He
was a member of the Action Group and Chairman of TAA
in 1950. At Independence he was made the Permanent
Head of the Foreign Affairs Ministry, leaving that in 1963
to become the Permanent Representative of Tanganyika
to the U.N. In the 1970's he served in Nigeria under
the World Health Organisation.

-L-

LABOUR BOARD. A Labour Board was set up in 1922 to
deal with questions of rates of pay for government laborers throughout the territory. Fixed rates of pay for un-
skilled employees had been set up earlier and it was
thought the rates might need to be revised from time to
time. In 1926 Tanganyika was the first British depen-
dency to establish a Labour Department. It was abolished
for economic reasons during the Depression. In 1938 a
Labour Advisory Board was created to regulate pay and
conditions of labor. It was set up under the Chief Inspector of Labour.

LAIBON (laiboni, pl.). The intermediary between his people

and the spirit world. He supposedly could make the rain
fall and provide in other ways for the prosperity of his
fellow tribesmen. He could make medicine that would
protect the warriors and ensure the success of their raid.
The war captains of the Masai had to seek their leader's
permission before embarking on any major raids. Office
of senior Laibon was hereditary; all important Laiboni
throughout Masailand came from the same sub-clan and
therefore, had connections. Although they exercised great
political power, they never compared to the office of territorial chief. Supet (c. 1788 birth) was believed to be
the greatest laibon in the history of the Masai. He ad-
vised and directed the Purko during the early Masai wars.

LAKE MANYARA NATIONAL PARK. Gazetted in 1960. The
    name 'Manyara' comes from a plant that the Masai use
    for making a living stockade around their kraals and which
    is more durable than anything made out of thorn branches.
    It is small--123 sq. mi. or 350 sq. km. of land located in
    the Rift Valley about 75 miles Southwest of Arusha. The
    Germans wrote about the amount of big game and aroused
    the interest of hunters around 1910. It was made a game
    reserve in 1957. Lake Manyara is well-known for its
    vast flamingo congregations; there are so many certain
    times of the year that they seem to form a solid line of
    shimmering pink stretching for several miles. There are
    more than 350 species of birds including egrets, ibises,
    storks and kingfishers. The park is also famous for its
    great herds of buffalo and for its tree climbing lions which
    lay out on acacia tree limbs 10 to 20 ft. above the ground.
    The elephant population exceeds five per square kilometer.
    Buffalo herds, Klipspringer and redbuck, giraffes, hip-
    popotamus and rhinoceros can all be seen.

LAKE NYASA. The third largest lake bordering the country.
    Stanley saw it on his first journey and found Livingstone
    there on his second trip. There has been a minor ter-
    ritorial dispute over Lake Nyasa with Tanzania claiming
    that the boundary is midway and Malawi claiming it runs
    near the eastern side. The lake covers an area of 360
    miles by 15-50 miles wide or 11,000 square miles
    (2150 in Tanzania) and a catchment area of nearly 50,000
    square miles. Nyasa is subject to very considerable
    changes of level; since 1900 it has fluctuated more than
    twenty feet causing a commercial problem. Its deepest
    point is 2316 feet. It is known to have at least 200
    species of fish. The fish caught in 1975 weighed a total

of 35,000 tons and were valued at Shs. 60 million. In
March 1976 two passenger ships began services on the
lake, the MV Mbeya and MV Iringa. The harbors on the
Tanzania shorelines are quite poor.

LAKE TANGANYIKA. The second deepest lake in the world
with depths recorded to be over 4700 feet and 4758 feet
at its deepest point. Its area is approximately 400 miles
by 56 miles and Tanzania claims 5150 square miles of it.
The coast is precipitous and its harbors are few and
poor. The Malagarasi River which drains the western
part of the Central Plateau, empties into it. The salt in
the River causes the waters of Lake Tanganyika to be
brackish.

      Around 1820 an Arab caravan crossed Lake Tan-
ganyika. In 1857 it was discovered by Burton and Speke.
The German Administration reached Lake Tanganyika with
the Railway line in 1914 and Kigoma became the main
town as a port and railway station. East African Harbours Corporation operates shipping services on the Lake,
the main movement between Kigoma and Burundi and
Zaïre.

LAKE VICTORIA. Formerly called Lake Nyanza. Its waters
are shared with Kenya and Uganda. It covers a rough
circle with about 220 miles in diameter and has a super-
ficial area of 27,000 square miles the size of Scotland
or three times the size of Massachusetts (43,450 square
miles belong to Tanzania). It is the largest lake in Africa and third largest in the world. It is the second largest fresh water lake in the world. The inflow from rainfall is estimated at 98 billion cubic meters and from tri-
butaries at 16 billion cu. m. The outflow due to evaporation is 93 billion cu. m. and into the Victoria Nile is 21
billion cu. m. It is a comparatively shallow lake with
its deepest point being 230 feet. The deep water fish resources are almost untouched.

      Lake Victoria is located in the Central Plateau and
has an elevation of 3390 feet (1133 meters) above sea
level. It modifies the climate for 50 miles inland, causing a higher rainfall and less diurnal and annual ranges
of temperature. The gradual slope of the lake shores
permits an agricultural development not possible along
the steep embankments of the Lakes Tanganyika and
Nyasa. The soils of the Lake Victoria Basin and its islands are adequate for intensive cultivation. Hence, a
denser population with agricultural development, cooperative

systems and manufacturing of dairy cattle products.
Lake Victoria has rail, road and shipping services
and its dhows, tugs and steamers do the largest shipping
business of Africa's lakes.   Train ferry services were
begun in 1966.   Trade and transportation had a setback
whenever the East African Community member states
quarrelled between themselves.   Marine Research and
training of fishermen is also located near Mwanza.

LAMECK, LUCY SELLINA (1931-).   The first Tanzanian
woman to become a Junior Minister, was born at Moshi
on 15 July, 1931.   After a local education she trained
as a nurse in Tanga 1949-50 and then left nursing in 1953
to become a secretary in the KNCU at Moshi.   She
studied abroad in Ruskin College at Oxford University from
1957-59 in economics, history and political science.   On
her return she was elected a member of Parliament and
continued as an MP right through the 1960's and 1970's.
She became the Organising Secretary of TANU's Women's
Section in 1960 and in the 1960's held the Junior Minister
position for Community Development and Cooperatives,
for Commerce and Industries and of Health.   She was a
member of TANU Central Committee and National Executive from 1961-65.   Her most recent post is with the
Ministry of Cooperatives and Community Development.

LAND ORDINANCE OF 1923.   Granted much ex-settler land
to African farmers.   Instead of granting leases for a
period of one year, it permitted leases of up to 99 years.
No new grants of freehold could be given and no more
than 5000 acres could be leased to a non-African unless
approved by the Colonial Secretary.

LAND POLICIES.   Native Reserves were set up in 1895.   All
tribes were to have four times the cultivated crop areas.
The rest would be government land and could be given to
settlers or sold.   Up to 1914 less than 1 percent of the
total area of the country was given to Europeans, but consisted of the best land.   Governors Rechenberg and Schnee
held differing views about the settler ownership.   African
ownership of land was protected.   Settler land could be
allocated only on one-year leases.
Article 6 of the British Mandate for East Africa
stipulated that the laws, customs, rights and interests
of the African population should be consulted in all matters concerning land allocation and that there should be
no transfers of land except between Africans without official consent.

The Land Ordinance of 1923 made all land public, but recognized existing rights and titles. It forbade new grants of freehold, granted leases up to 99 years, and set 5000 acres as a limit for lease of land to non-Africans unless approved by the Colonial Secretary. Certain heavily populated areas were closed to non-Africans.

In 1959 non-Africans controlled 1.6 percent of the total land area. In 1960 the land given back to Africans was more than that allotted to non-Africans during the same year.

On the mainland about 80 percent of the land was held in the 1960's by individuals or by groups under customary rules of tenure in accordance with traditional or tribal rights; approximately 10 percent of the total acreage was held by plantation farmers under leasehold. Land held under a right of occupancy was held from the government under certain terms. The terms apply to commercial and residential land in urban areas as well as rural agricultural and pastoral lands. The Land Regulations of 1948 with an extension by an act of 1961 described the agricultural rights. Communal ownership by tribe, neighborhood or clan was common among herders and farmers.

The government reserves the right to take or resume possession of any land which it may acquire for the public interest. Developed land receives a compensation. Land has been redistributed during the process of moving into Ujamaa villages. About 10 percent is set aside for conservation, 10 percent for forest reserves and eight national parks making about 25 percent set aside for these purposes.

Land in Zanzibar was held as domain by the Sultan who favored Omani Arabs with land rights. After the 1964 Revolution, large holdings were given to collectives in which the squatters could participate. Others were distributed to orphans, widows, needy or landless persons.

LANGUAGES. 1) Bantu--belong to the Congo-Kordofaman language family. 2) Nilo-Hamitic-Iraqw, Gorowa, Burungi--Nilo-Saharan language family. 3) Nilotic--Masai. 4) Khoisan--Kindiga and Sandawe--click. 5) English--joint legal status until 1967, remained as language of commerce and higher education. 6) Asian languages-- Gujerati, Punjabi, Kindustani, Konkani. See also SWAHILI.

LEAD. Mined at Mpanda, 200 miles southwest of Tabora.
     It is mixed with ores of copper, silver and gold. A rail-
     way branch line connects Mpanda with the Central Line.
     At the end of the 1950's the mining of lead was valued at
     approximately one million English pounds. Lead mining
     ceased around 1960.

LEAKEY, LOUIS S. B. (1904-). Born in Kenya and took
     part in several historic expeditions of the African jungle
     in the 1920's. His wife found Zinj anthropus or "Nut-
     cracker Man" at Olduvai Gorge in 1959. Zinj was found
     in direct association with stone tools of the Oldowan cul-
     ture. Leakey believed him to be "near man, slightly off
     the human line" and forced to extinction. The second
     find was a creature believed to have had a brain and hands
     capable of making tools and to be a direct ancestor of
     man. He was called "Homo habilis" or "Handy Man."
     In 1965 Leakey was conferred with an honorary degree
     of Doctor of Science at the University of Dar es Salaam.
     He suffered a mild heart attack on a plane in 1970, the
     year he became the Director of the National Centre of
     Pre-History in Nairobi.

LEGISLATIVE COUNCIL. Established in 1926 by Governor
     Cameron with 13 government officials and 10 or less
     others. The unofficial members in 1926 consisted of five
     Europeans and two Asians. In 1938 three Indians were ap-
     pointed to LEGCO as unofficial members. The first Afri-
     can members were appointed in November 1945; they were
     Chief David Makwaia and Chief Abdiel Shangali. A third
     African was added in 1946. In June 1947 Adam Sapi was
     appointed and followed in April 1948 by Juma Mwindadi.
     The Africans did not have an easy time; Europeans were
     courteous but did not accept them as social equals. Other
     Africans were suspicious and saw them as European pup-
     pets. In 1953 the constitution was mended to provide for
     a Speaker over the LEGCO, a function the Governor had
     held up to this time. The first elections to the LEGCO
     were held in 1955. LEGCO consisted of the Speaker, 31
     ex officio and nominated members and 30 representative
     members (10 European, 10 Asian and 10 Africans). There
     were 9 elected unofficial members of each race and 1
     nominated of each race.
          In 1960 there were 71 LEGCO seats of which 21
     were non-Africans. TANU won 70 of the seats and
     Nyerere formed a government. In May 1961 LEGCO was
     changed to the National Assembly.

The Legislative Council in Zanzibar was also
formed in 1926. See also NATIONAL ASSEMBLY.

LEIPZIG MISSION. These Lutheran missionaries came to
Machame near Moshi in 1893. From there they reached
out to Old Moshi, Mamba, Shighatini, Mwika, Meru and
Gonja. Chiefs Shangali, Marealle, Rindi and Kuimbere
were friendly to them. A seminary for teachers and
pastors was opened at Old Moshi in 1902. Churches,
schools, dispensaries and a hospital were built. By the
end of World War I, Christians numbered around 10,000,
by 1939 there were 39,000, by 1952 a total of 90,000 and
by 1958, only 65 years since the beginning of this Diocese, there were 120,000. The first native pastors were
ordained in 1934. Stefano Moshi became Asst. Bishop in
1940. In 1942 the church began to work side by side with
the Mission and by 1958 "Mission" was swallowed by the
church structure. At that time Rev. Moshi was made the
Diocese head and in 1964 he was consecrated Bishop of
the Diocese. This Diocese has since been reshaped so
that two more parts have been formed. The Synod of
Arusha Region was made in 1973 and its leader is Rev.
M. Kilevo. The Diocese of Pare was created in March
1975 with Rev. E. E. Mshana as its Bishop. There are
more than 280,000 Christians and 630 worship centers,
160 African pastors and 620 evangelists, 3 Bible Schools,
5 hospitals, 20 dispensaries and one medical school.
        In 1911 another group of the Leipzig Missionaries
went to Iramba. Many were baptized. After World War
I, the German missionaries were not permitted to return
and Augustana Mission from U.S.A. carried on the work.

LETTOW-VORBECK, GENERAL PAUL VON. The German
Commander-in-Chief in Tanganyika during World War I,
knew he could not win the war in East Africa against the
British superior forces, so his aim was to keep British
troops occupied as long as possible. Lettow-Vorbeck
withdrew his troops, as slowly as possible, never facing
a decisive battle and destroying crops and railways as he
went. In November 1918 when peace was declared in
Europe, Lettow-Vorbeck, still undefeated, laid down his
arms. He had been successful in his policy of keeping
a superior enemy force occupied for four years.

LIFE EXPECTANCY. Between 35 and 40 years at independence on the mainland and 40-45 in Zanzibar. The Five-
Year Plan of 1964-69 set a goal at 50 years by 1980. By

1971 it was estimated to be 41 years and 47 by 1977.

LINDI. Originally an open area for cultivating millet and rice
and hunting wild animals in the forest. The town developed
as a port for slave trade. The first Sultan was Kitenga.
In May 1890 General Wissman seized Kilwa and Lindi and
put them under German rule. The population has steadily been rising: 1905--3,500; 1945--8,600; 1959--10,000;
1967--13,351; 1977--17,000. Lindi is now an important
market town for sisal, rice, cassava, copra, and cashew
nuts.

LITERACY. In 1950, 5-10 percent of the population were
considered literate. The figure rose to 10-15 percent
Swahili literates in 1965 and 1 percent English on the
mainland. The same year Zanzibar was recorded as 30
percent literate. 1970 was proclaimed Adult Education
Year and approximately 20-25 percent were literate then.
By the end of 1974, 50 percent had become literate. On
12 August, 1975, four million sat for a literacy examination and 2.5 million (54 percent) passed well; 17 percent
reached Stage I and 37 percent Stage II attained; 10 percent could not be placed in Stage I, II, III or IV. (Stages
I and II are functional literates.) In 1975, five and a
quarter million had joined adult education classes or 94
percent of the recorded illiterates. The 1975 literacy
figure was 61 percent. See also ADULT EDUCATION.

LIVINGSTONE, DR. DAVID (1813-73). Born at Blantyre,
Scotland. After journeying in South and Central Africa,
he came for his last journey in 1866. He believed the
Nile was connected with Lake Tanganyika or the Lualaba
River. In April 1866, he set off along the Ruvuma River
and travelled around Lake Nyasa. Bad weather and
shortage of supplies delayed him; he reached Ujiji in
February 1869. After a rest of some time, he tried to
explore the Lualaba River, but was prevented by Arab
slavers. He returned to Ujiji in October 1871. The
following month he was discovered there by H. M. Stanley. Stanley left Livingstone at Tabora when he returned
in March 1872. Livingstone left Tabora in August to explore the Lualaba further. He met his death at Lake
Rangweulu in May 1873. His followers returned his body
to the East African coast. Burial was made in Westmin-
ister Abbey later. Livingstone's writings played a major
part in ending the slave trade due to his eye witness accounts. They also influenced the opening of Protestant
missions in Central Africa.

LIWALI. A headman usually an Arab, appointed by the Government to deal with the affairs of the Muhammadan community.

LOCAL EDUCATION AUTHORITIES (LEAs). Formed during
the Three-Year Plan in effect from 1961-64. The Education Act of 1961 established them. The Central Government delegated authority to the LEAs for administration
of the primary schools in their areas. The LEAs paid
teachers' salaries and provided equipment or money to
buy supplies for the primary schools.

LOCAL GOVERNMENT ORDINANCE OF 1953. Provided for
the gradual removal of the traditional authorities and for
elected councils to replace them. The Ordinance provided for both local and county councils. It included a
provision enabling the local government bodies to achieve
an autonomous status known as Town Councils. By the
end of 1957 there were approximately 2500 rural councils
of all types.

LOCALISATION POLICY. The change of name from Africanization for the process in which citizens of any ethnic group
were given responsibilities in administration in lieu of
expatriates. See also AFRICANIZATION.

LONDON MISSIONARY SOCIETY. Decided to carry on what
they considered the explorer David Livingstone's unfinished
work. In 1878 E. G. Hore and J. B. Thomson arrived
at Ujiji. Mwinyi Kheri did not interfere in their spiritual
work but would not let them have land. However, when
they launched a steamer in 1883, they left the missionaries in peace. Lack of success caused the London Missionary Society to end their work in Ujiji in 1883 and at
Mtowa in 1885. They transferred their activities to Ka-
vala Island, offshore from Mtowa, where they remained
until 1888. The Society was later known as the Congregational Council for World Missions.

LUGURU (tribe). One of the largest tribes in Eastern Tanzania. They live in the Uluguru Mts. and were not a
single tribe; the people who now call themselves by that
name are the products of the migration and assimilation
of people from several different tribes. It is believed
that their ancestors came to the mountains some 300
years ago. Caravans of slave traders and explorers
passed through their country. They were long famous

for rainmakers who provided services to many neighboring peoples.   The Holy Ghost Fathers reached the Luguru
tribe very early and made a great impact.   The Luguru
of the mountains are mostly Roman Catholics and the low-
landers tend to be Moslem.   These agricultural people
are reluctant to leave their traditional lands and hence
have a very high rate of population density which reaches
800 per square mile in a core-area of about 1000 square
miles in size.   They seldom migrate thus causing the
overpopulation problem.   They are hoe cultivators with
rice, maize and sorghum as staple crops and a matrilineal descent society often following matrilineal rules of
inheritance.   Moslem and Christian Luguru generally follow patrilineal rules that create misunderstandings at
times.   For years attempts to introduce cattle had failed
due to the tsetse fly.   They have a good system of terracing on the hills.   In 1957 they numbered over 200,000.

LUGUSHA, HAROUN MSABILA (c. 1920-   ).   The 26th chief
of the 20,000 Sikonge near Tabora.   He attended Tabora
Government Secondary School 1936-36 and then went on
to Makerere College where he received a diploma in Agriculture in 1943.   He was nominated to the Legislative
Council in 1953.   In 1957 he was appointed Assistant
Minister for Local Government and Administration.   He
did not support TANU and was a signer of the UTP mani-
festo.   As Deputy Speaker of the Legislative Council, he
had to resign other offices including his membership in
the Executive Council as of 1958.   In 1959 he was made
Chairman of the Wanyamwezi Federation Council.   He became the Chairman of the Tanganyika Agriculture Corporation in 1961.   In January 1964 he was removed and
sent into enforced exile where he was detained until 1967.
He is a holder of a M.B.E.   He returned home later to
Sikonge.

LUKINDO, JOSEPH (1918-   ).   The first African Postmaster
in the colonial days and the first African Head Postmaster in Dar es Salaam after independence, appointed in
May 1964.   Lukindo was born in Korogwe area on 16
September, 1918.   His father was a Jumbe in the Chief's
court.   He attended Minaki Secondary School from 1936-
38 completing Std. X, then took a teaching course while
studying Std. XI.   He joined the Post Office Training
School as a Postal Clerk and Telegraphic Trainee and
served in a number of northeastern post offices until
1943.   He became an instructor at the Central Training

School in Dar es Salaam and transferred to Nairobi when
the school was moved to a cooler climate in 1949. Many
transfers in Post Offices in Tanganyika followed. After
a 4-year course in London, he was appointed Principal
Administrative Officer, a post he held until his retirement in August 1972. He retired to his home community
as a farmer.

LUKUMBUZYA, CHIEF MWINAMIA MICHAEL (1930-). The
Ukerewe child chief who went to primary school with bodyguards who protected him against possible assassinations
and did his chores as well as suffered his punishments.
When he was sent to Tabora Boys School, Mr. Blumer,
the Head, sent his bodyguards home and he had to rough
it. He also studied at Makerere. Although he was made
Chief of Ukerewe in 1939, he only assumed his duties as
chief after completion of his studies in 1954. At independence he opted to enter government service and has
been the Principal Secretary of the Foreign Ministry,
Tanzania's High Commissioner to New Delhi, Ambassador
to the U.S.A. and Stockholm and was appointed to Ottawa
in 1976.

LUO or LWOO (tribe). Belong to the Nilotic group. They
numbered 82,900 in 1957 and live just over the border
from Kenya in Mara Region. They are successful farmers and are found all over Tanzania as semi-skilled
workmen or in marketing. The main body of the tribe
is found in Kenya.

LUSINDE, JOB MALECELA (1930-). Born on 8 October,
1930, a son of Rev. Petro Lusinde Malecela, a CMS
priest near Dodoma. He was educated locally at Dodoma
and then at Tabora Government Secondary School. After
receiving his Diploma in Education from Makerere College in 1953, he stayed on at the Demonstration School
at Makerere College for a five year teaching career and
then at Dodoma as a secondary school teacher. He then
went into politics with five years of practical experience
in local government as executive officer and Town Council
Chairman (the first Tanzanian to hold the post). His politics and his contemporary Oscar Kambona have often
appeared further left than the governments as a whole.
He was elected Deputy Provincial TANU Secretary in the
Central Province. Since independence, he has held a
number of responsible positions in the government: Minister of Local Government and Regional Administration;

Minister for Home Affairs; and many years in the Ministry of Communications, Transportation and Labour. As such he was responsible for building the Great Uhuru Railway. In 1975, he opened a new Ministry of Works. He was also Chairman of TAPA many years. In 1976 he was appointed to China as an Ambassador of Tanzania.

LUTHERAN CHURCH. The Evangelical Lutheran Church of Tanzania (ELCT) had its beginning in many different Lutheran societies in Europe and America. The following have been considered in separate entries: BERLIN MISSION; BERLIN EVANGELICAL MISSIONARY SOCIETY FOR EAST AFRICA; BETHEL MISSION; LEIPZIG MISSION; AUGUSTANA MISSION; SWEDISH LUTHERAN MISSION; NORWEGIAN LUTHERAN MISSION.
   In 1938 at the outbreak of World War II the various Lutheran Missions joined to form the Missions Church Federation (MCF). Under this united front they began a Pastoral Training at Mlalo, a medical training center, Ilboru Secondary School and Vuga Press along with other undertakings. During World War II the Lutheran World Federation sent Americans and Swedes to take over responsibilities where German missionaries had been forced to leave. A number of German missionaries returned later and blended into the work as they found it. Lutheran Missionary Societies had changed into churches by independence so another great step was taken when, in 1963, the churches united to form the Evangelical Lutheran Church in Tanzania with headquarters at Arusha. See ELCT for more details.

LWAMUGIRA, FRANCISCO XAVIER (1875-1950). Born in West Lake, he was brought up in Mutatembwa's court. He took casual lessons in reading and writing with Bible classes. Lwamugira developed good relationships with the German rulers and later with the British. He became secretary general to the Council of Chiefs; was Government Interpreter 1901-13; Ruga Ruga instructor and commander, 1903-16; compiled the first of many local histories in 1906; in 1931 he was one of the African representatives to London before a Joint Committee of the British Parliament on Closer Union in East Africa; was secretary to local councils and retired in 1947.

-M-

MACKINNON, WILLIAM. A British businessman and a shipowner running steamship services in the Indian Ocean for more than twenty years. He believed that Sultan Majid's territory could be developed with British capital and experience. He helped Majid to begin the building of Dar es Salaam and make roads on the mainland. His motives appear to be mixed--philanthropic, religious and commercial. He was not a good administrator or leader and left this to his officials such as Mackenzie and Lugard. In 1872 the British-India Company began mail service between Zanzibar and Aden. That same year he tried unsuccessfully to form a company to lease and develop the mainland. Mackinnon frequently urged Britain to intervene. He formed the British East African Association to trade in the interior (later known as the Imperial British East Africa Company in 1888).

MAFIA. An island group off the mouth of the Rufiji River, is one of the most pleasant places of East Africa. It is 27 miles by 9 miles. Mafia was conquered by the son of the first Sultan of Kilwa who later succeeded him. Relations have always been close with Kilwa. There are more coins of Kilwa found on Mafia than on Kilwa. Mafia was probably more important than Kilwa in the early days of the Shirazis. It was an important site in the 12th century to the end of the 14th century and was deserted soon afterwards. The Portuguese had an agent at Mafia and a small blockhouse. The inhabitants were known as Wambwera and were related to people of the opposite district headquarters--Kilindoni. Mafia was ceded to Germany in 1890, placed in the hands of the Zanzibar Government in 1916 and transferred to the Government of the Tanganyika Territory in 1922. Chole was the German administrative headquarters on the island. The British moved it because it has a bad harbor.

The African population is heterogenous due to immigrations from the Middle East, the Indian sub-continent and the African mainland. The island is mainly coral overlaid with soil on which scrub bushes grow. The coconut plantations are important.

MAIZE. Probably introduced from America in the 15th century by the Portuguese or European traders. The quantity harvested each year fluctuates very much in accordance with the amount of or lack of rainfall received. The 1960 harvest figure of 77,946 metric tons rose to 193,204 metric tons in 1970, giving an increase of 148 percent. The National Milling Company bought 91,000 tons in 1975/76 from the farmers. Over 200,000 tons were imported in 1973-75 years when Tanzania's harvest was poor. Maize-meal supplies most of Tanzanians with their daily diet of food.

MAJID, SULTAN (? - 1870).   Ruled Zanzibar from 1856 to 1870. He tried to decrease the unlawful export of slaves to Arabia by stopping dhows going there during the rains, but he wasn't very successful. In 1862 in the discussions with the French versus the British, it was agreed that Zanzibar should remain independent and no country would start a colony on the coast. In the 1860's William Mackinnon helped the Sultan to develop roads. The building of Dar es Salaam was begun in 1866.

MAJI-MAJI REBELLION.   Preceded in late 1904 among the Matumbi and Ngindo tribes by a movement called Jujila or Jwiyila.   They made pilgrimages to Ngalambe for military training, received medicine and returned home. They were ordered to work for the Germans until Kinjikitile Ngwale, the medicine man sent by God to save the people from German oppression, made war on the Germans. The tribes became impatient and uprooted some cotton in Jumbe's plantation.
     Maji-Maji originated in July 1905 in the Matumbi Hills northwest of Kilwa and spread.   The tribes taking part in Maji-Maji Rebellion were: Ngoni, Bunga, Mwera, Sagara, Zaramo, Matumbi, Kitchi, Ikemba, and Bena and a number of the leaders were of the Pogoro tribe.   They were not joined by the Hehe, Chagga and Nyamwezi. The Maji-Maji Rebellion covered an area from Dar es Salaam to Kilosa, then to the northern tip of the Lake Nalawi.
     Cotton may have been a grievance as many of the Southeastern tribes had to work 28 days a year on a headman's plot and their subsistence farming suffered. Another source of conflict may have been the scarcity of land.   Still another authority says it was not so much the hut tax or forced labor as the way in which local officials collected it and sent the natives to work.
     Maji-Maji acquired an ideological content and needed commitment to the native doctor Ngwale.   The "Maji," a corn, water and sorghum seed mixture, was supposed to create an immunity to bullets.   Their great belief in the medicine man's "maji" helped them to face

bullets without flinching.

The Maji-Maji Rebellion found the government un-
prepared and much damage was done until the government
reinforcement arrived.   It is believed that about 120,000
people died as a result of the uprising.   The rebellion
was suppressed by the spring of 1906 except in the southern area.   The Ngindo were the last ones to be brought
under control in January 1907.

MAKAME, SHEIKH HASNU (1920-   ).   Born in Zanzibar in
1920 and educated at Dole Secondary School, Dole Teacher
Training College and at Exeter University where he received a Diploma in Public Administration.   After three
years of teaching, he joined Government Service in 1948.
He was Mudirial Officer, Zanzibar from 1948 to 1953,
Labour Officer from 1957-60, a member of Parliament
from 1961 and Treasurer of ASP later.   In 1964 he was
the Permanent Representative to the U.N. and Ambassador for Zanzibar to the U.S.A. and Minister for Finance
and Development.   After the 1964 merger he was Minister of State for External Affairs, then appointed as Minister for Communication in the Union government.   Later
he became Minister of Health, Minister of State in the
President's Office (Foreign Affairs) and then in 1967 became Minister for Information and Tourism.   When the
Information Ministry was removed in 1970, he remained
with National Resources and Tourism until 1975.   That
year he was made Minister of State in the President's
Office for Capital Development.

MAKERERE UNIVERSITY COLLEGE.   Founded in Uganda in
1922 as a college with vocational rather than academic
emphasis.   In the 1930's the first Tanganyikan Africans
entered Makerere for a full medical course.   Only 10
had become fully qualified by 1952.   In 1954 each of the
113 students cost the Tanganyikan Treasury £740.   Bursaries of about £220 a year were awarded.   Until 1958,
Tanganyika students' upkeep cost at Makerere was £47,520
of which the administration paid £47,000.   This is the
reason for the limited members.

Tanganyika could not fill its quota because secondary schools were too low and too few as feeders.   Before 1959 Tanganyikans had to enroll for a preparatory
course before entering Makerere University College because there were no higher school certificate courses
here.   After a two-year preliminary course, students
could go on to an additional two years of teacher training

and a post graduate course leading to a diploma in education. Makerere was linked to Dar es Salaam and Nairobi Colleges by an act of EACSO in 1962.

MAKONDE (tribe). Of southeastern Tanzania, they number
around 500,000. They are an agricultural people with
millet as their main crop and livestock of less importance.
They are famous for their fine carvings of wooden masks
and human figures. They are known for their elaborate
body tattooing done mostly in geometrical patterns of the
face, chest or back. The lip plug was once popular as
an ornament among women. They are a matrilineal tribe.
      In the 18th and 19th centuries the Makonde were
crucial to the East African Slave trade as a source of
slaves on the Arab caravan routes to Lake Nyasa. They
remained aloof during the Maji-Maji uprising. In 1917
the German forces made a last stand near Newala before
fleeing across the Ruvuma River into Mozambique. During the British era there was a great exportation of human resources to find a method for paying taxes. However, the educated found little industrial, missionary and
government employment. In 1947 the Groundnut Scheme
shattered the leeway generally given to administrators in
the vast estates north in Nachingwea but had a direct impact, both negative and positive, on the Makonde economy
as well as the social order. The labor recruitment of
the Makonde introduced them to new skills, new forms of
wealth, theft, prostitution, etc. and the influx of Europeans, Asians and Arabs through their towns. Just at the
stage of depression of the "white man's madness," four
years after the introduction of the Groundnut scheme and
its failure, TANU came upon the scene. Therefore,
TANU made good inroads in that area.
      Makonde carving originated in Mozambique and is
done in ebony. They also carve balsawood face masks
used in initiation rites.

MAKWAIA, CHIEF (?-1945). Of Usiha Chiefdom in Shinyanga, he travelled to London in 1931 to testify at hearings
on the question of closer union for the East African territories. Elected by a joint meeting of the Sukuma and
Nyamwezi chiefs, he was most representative of the African witnesses selected by the Tanganyika Administration.
He spoke no English and relied on a Sukuma interpreter.

MAKWAIA, CHIEF DAVID KIDAHA. Of Usiha in Sukumaland,
he was the son of an accommodating leader to the Germans.

He was educated at Tabora Government Secondary School
and Makerere College and was a leading member of the
aristocrats at Makerere known as the "Hamlet of Tanganyika. " He interrupted his studies when his father
died to become chief, but later received a scholarship to
study at Oxford. He was the first Sukuma chief to send
a wife and daughter to Tabora Girls School.

As a Roman Catholic, he used David rather than
Kidaha as his name. Deeply conscientious, he felt it
was wrong for a Roman Catholic to be chief of a predominantly Moslem tribe. So he resigned and was succeeded by his brother Hussein.

Makwaia was appointed a member of Legislative
Council in November 1945 and the first African appointed
to the Executive Council. He became an Assistant Minister on 1 July, 1957. He did not support TANU and
joined the People's Democratic Party in 1962. He was
placed under restriction October 1962 at Tunduru and
welcomed back from deportation in March 1963. He joined
TANU for the first time in January 1964.

MALANGALI SCHOOL. A central school built by Mumford in
1927 as an experiment. It was built on the theory that
building a school just ahead of the African way of life
would make the transition easier for its pupils. Rather
than beginning with something modified from European
practices, the base had genuine African foundations. The
endeavor was controversial and expired upon the departure
of Mumford in 1931.

MALARIA. A disease spread by the anopheles mosquito and
is the greatest single cause of illness and mortality.
Less than 10 percent of the population lives in a very
dry and high area where malaria is not endemic.

MALECELA, CIGWIYEMISI SAMUEL JOHN (1934-). Born
near Dodoma on 20 April, 1934. After a secondary education at a local mission school from 1947-52, he went
on to St. Andrew's College at Minaki, then to Bombay
University where he obtained a Bachelor of Commerce
Degree in 1959. He went on to Cambridge to study administration after one year of government service in 1960.
In 1962-63 he was Tanganyika's Consul to the U.S.A. and
3rd Secretary to the newly independent country's U.N.
Mission. His U.N. service was interrupted one year to
become the Regional Commissioner of Lake Region in
1963 and then he returned as Chief of the U.N. Mission.

He moved on as Tanzania's Ambassador to Ethiopia in
1968.   In 1969 he began some years of service in the
East African offices as Minister for Communications, Research and Social Services and later Minister for Finance
and Administration in the East African Community in
Arusha.   He has also held Chairmanship in West Lake
Cotton Advisory Committee and the Lint and Seed Marketing Board.   From 1972 to 1975 he served as Tanzania's
Minister for Foreign Affairs and in November 1975 was
transferred as Minister of Agriculture.

MANDARA, CHIEF   see   RINDI

MANG'ENYA, CHIEF ERASTO A.M. (1915-).   Born in Tanga Region.   After completing primary education in 1931,
he joined Minaki Teacher Training Centre in 1933, went
on to Uganda and obtained a Diploma in Education in 1937.
He began to teach in secondary schools in 1938.   He
opted for government service when his Chieftainship ended
in 1960 and has held a variety of posts--Parliamentary
Secretary for Communication, Power and Works, for External Affairs, Ambassador to the U.N.   Minister for
Community Development and National Culture, Chairman
of the Permanent Commission of Enquiry and Speaker of
the National Assembly since 1974.   He has been cited as
a man of much ability, energy and humanity and, as such,
was very advantageous to the Permanent Commission of
Enquiry in its first years.

MANGI.   Another local name given to a Chief.

MANIOC   see   CASSAVA

MANNING, JULIE CATHERINE.   Born in Morogoro, a daughter of an Assistant Medical Officer.   She was educated in
a local primary school, at Loleza Middle School and Tabora Girls Secondary School.   Her sister was the first
Tanganyikan woman to take a medical assistant course
in 1959.   Julie was the first Tanganyikan woman to study
in the Faculty of Law in the Dar es Salaam University
College from 1961-64 and received a LL. B. (London).
She became a State Attorney in 1964, went for a Legal
Officer Course in London in 1965 and became the Local
Government Legal Adviser in 1966.   She worked in the
Attorney-General Chambers and was the Senior Parlia-
mentary Draftsman in 1972.   In 1975 she was made the
Minister for Justice, one of the first two women ministers

appointed at that time.

MAREALLE, MANGI TOM. A grandson of the leading Chief
    Marealle, was Paramount Chief of the Chagga from 1952
    to 1960. He holds a social science diploma from the Uni-
    veristy College of Aberystwith in Wales and worked in the
    Social Welfare Department in Dar es Salaam, then became
    a secretary of TAA. He was installed Paramount Chief
    of the Chagga in an elaborate ceremony in 1952. The
    following year he made a great hit in both high society
    and in television while attending Queen Elizabeth's Coron-
    ation in England. He began to alienate himself from the
    younger, educated Chagga; he was not able to resolve
    Chagga traditions, Chagga modernism and Tanganyika na-
    tionalism all in himself. As a chief he had made great
    strides in education and economic development. In June
    1957 he attended the U.N. Trusteeship Council and re-
    ported with Fletcher-Cooke, Cohen and Nyerere. He
    voiced the African point of view and asked for independence
    in 15 years. In October 1959 when another plebiscite was
    held, he was sacked from Paramountcy Chief and swept
    from office. He later became a U.N. official in Rawal-
    pindi and continued with the U.N. in various places.

MAREALLE, CHIEF NDAROGHUO KILAMIA (c. 1836-1906). He
    was the first chief to build a storeyed house and to speak
    fluent Swahili. After Rindi's death in 1891, Marcealle of
    Marangu became the powerhead of the Chagga at the base
    of Mt. Kilimanjaro. He was clever, cruel and ambitious,
    defeated Moshi by military might and emerged as the
    leading German ally on Mt. Kilimanjaro. He provided the
    Germans with auxiliary warriors for campaigns, maintained
    a personal friendship with Captain Johannes, the local
    commander, and his mastery of intrigue played on the
    German insecurity.
        In 1892 Marealle "framed" the new chief Meli of
    Moshi, and in 1897 was responsible for the poisoning of
    Sina. In 1900 he engineered a plot linking both Kibosho
    and Moshi Chiefs with unrest among the Arusha and Ma-
    sai. Both were hanged with 17 leading men from several
    chiefdoms. So Marealle took over on the southeast slopes
    of Mt. Kilimanjaro and held concessions to land rights
    and economic opportunities with license to plunder women
    and cattle from Rombo.
        After 1901 his power waned as the new Commander
    Merker resented the privileges formerly granted. The
    Chief of Rombo hatched a counter plot accusing Marealle

of conspiring with the Masai.   Marealle fled to Kenya in
1904, alarmed by the combination of forces.   When he
returned in 1905, he was restored as Chief of Marangu.
He was chief from 1880 until his death.   When he died
in 1906, he was survived by 7 sons and 6 daughters.
He had had 60 wives but many of them did not bear children.

MAREALLE, CHIEF PETRO ITOSI (1906-   ).   Born on 13
June, 1906, a son of Chief Ndaroghuo Marealle.   Petro
went to a bush school until World War I disrupted his
education as the school closed down.   So he herded goats
and cattle.   He had a private teacher.   In 1925 he attended the government school at Tanga, but due to the
hot weather, transferred to Old Moshi Government Central School.   He passed his exam in 1929 and was employed as clerk at Old Moshi Central School.   In 1932
he took over the chieftainship from his brother who abdicated.   In 1946 he was elected Divisional Chief.   When
the chieftainship was abolished, he was appointed Executive Officer at Kilimanjaro District Council in 1961.   He
was the Acting President of the Chagga in 1962, then appointed Chairman of the Local Government Service Commission, added Chairmanship of the Civil Service Commission in 1967 while also heading the Local Government,
a post he held until 1974.   He is author of a book Maisha
ya Mchagga Hapa Duniani na Ahera (The Life of a Chagga
in This World and the Next) and two pamphlets, Chagga
Concept of Truth and Problems of Babies.

MARUMA, CHIEF JOHN NDASIKOI (1914-   ).   Born in Kili-
manjaro Region and attended Old Moshi Central School,
King's College at Budo, Uganda and Makerere University
College.   He received a diploma in education from the
Institute of Education, London University, in 1950.   He
was then made the Divisional Chief for Rombo, a post
he held until independence when he became the Executive
Officer for the Chagga Council.   He was awarded the
M. B. E.   He has also been Chairman of the Council of
KNCU College of Commerce from 1955 to 1960 and Chair-
man of Transportation Licensing Authority from 1963.
He later retired to private business in Dar es Salaam.

MARYKNOLL FATHERS.   Arrived in 1950 from America.
Musoma and North Mara became a Prefecture Apostolic
under their care.   It became a Diocese in 1957.   Maswa,
another area for which they were responsible, became

a Diocese in 1956 and its name changed to that of Shinyanga because it included Shinyanga, Maswa and three
chiefdoms of Mwanza District. They amalgamated with
other orders to form the present Tanzania Episcopal
Conference (TEC).

MASAI (tribe). A Nilo-Hamitic speaking group who had settled in the Rift Valley plateau area by 1800. They occupy
a large grassland area of Northcentral Tanzania and
Southcentral Kenya where less than 30" of rain falls
yearly. They are pastoralists and some semi-agricultur-
alists. Their social unity is based on age groups, a
person going through 5 or 6 phases in life, from the
moran (warrior) to the elder. The laibon was their spiritual leader. This patrilineal society was truly pastoral,
not attempting to create any organized state. They had
two abiding passions--cattle and war. God, they believed, had created cattle for their exclusive benefit. So
they made raids to regain their property. The size of
a man's herd was the indication of his wealth. Their
food was cattle blood and milk.
        The Masai are particularly known for their per-
sonal adornment. Both men and women wear large metal
hoops in the upper part of the ears and heavy bells in the
ear lobes. Younger men are known for their elaborate
hair arrangement made with a mixture of cattle manure
and red clay. Women customarily wear elaborate collars
of beadwork.
        Since 1 January, 1968, the government has forbid-
den the Masai to appear in public places in their traditional dress because they were becoming a "showpiece"
for tourists and delayed development. In the 1970's the
Masai began to settle down from a nomadic life and mix
some agriculture with their pastoralism. There are
more than 60,000 in Tanzania and slightly more in Kenya.
See also LAIBON.

MASHOMBO OF MSHEWA. Of South Pare, he was the economic if not political power of a great area by 1870. He
had been a trader in Taita across the border in Kenya
and acquired a technique for divining sorceries used in
ordinary court cases and in cases of sorcery. Instead
of punishing sorcerers, he employed them in his private
army. His army of witches was strengthened by mer-
cenaries from Taita. He died in the early 1870's. He
is noted as a uniting force when forces of disunity were
so powerful.

MASWANYA, SAIDI ALI (1923-   ).   Born during June 1923 in
    Tabora District.   After attending Tabora Government Se-
    condary School, he served in the Uganda Police Force
    from 1942-49 and then in the Tanganyika Police Force
    from 1949-53.   He then became active in politics and was
    the District Secretary of TANU at Shinyanga in 1956 and
    then held several regional TANU posts in West Lake.
    He rose to Deputy Organizing Secretary-General at the
    Headquarters in 1959.   In 1960 he was Deputy Mayor of
    Dar es Salaam.   Since independence he has been a mem-
    ber of the Executive Committee and held many govern-
    ment positions--Parliamentary Secretary to the Minister
    for Commerce and Industry (1961), Minister without Port-
    folio (1962), moved to Health (1963), then Agriculture
    (1964), Lands, Settlement and Water Development (1965/
    66), Home Affairs (1967-69).   He has also been President
    of Tanzania S. P. C. A.   His most recent appointment on
    26 October, 1975, was Executive Chairman of Tanzania
    Tobacco Authority.

MAYAGILO, JUSTIN DOTTO (1923-   ).   Born in Shinyanga
    District and educated locally.   He joined the KAR as a
    trainee bandsman on 1 January, 1937.   As an entertain-
    ment for war-weary troops, he travelled with the brass
    band to many countries during World War II.   At war end
    he participated in the Victory Parade held in Great Brit-
    ain.   He married in 1941 and has six children.   After
    World War II he resigned from KAR and tried to settle
    back home.   In November 1946 he left home to join the
    Police Force and was instructed to form its own band.
    Under Bandmaster Singh, he trained the "green hands"
    and became interested in conducting.   When he was trans-
    ferred to Mwadui in 1960, he became Bandmaster.   By
    1963 he was in charge of the band in Dar es Salaam.
    He led the Police Band to Nairobi, the East African Com-
    munity inauguration and Expo 70 in Japan.   He has been
    promoted and is the Director of Music in the Police Force
    and was Assistant Superintendent of Police from 1964.

MBEGA, CHIEF.   During the mid-18th century he invaded
    Usambara from the Nguru (Nguu) hills to the South and
    gained political power with the support of the discontented
    Shambaa.   He married at least one wife from all major
    Shambaa clans.   His sons became district governors.
    Bughe, Mbega's son, ruled in the last decade of the 18th
    century.   Mbega, also called Shebughe, built a military
    force and started to expand the kingdom but was killed.

His grandfather was said to have been an Arab. Mbega
acquired a packet of magic which allowed the control of
clouds and of rain as well as control over animals and
means of foretelling some future events. He hunted pigs
and made friends everywhere when he killed off the men-
aces and divided food among the natives.

MBEYA. Formed as a town in the Southern Highlands in
1935 for European agriculture and settlement. Situated
on the Tanzania-Zambia Road, it has developed into a
thriving trade town with a good climate and many agricultural products. Its population by 1967 exceeded 12,000,
and in 1977 reached 22,000.

MBUGU (tribe). Non-Bantu emigrants who arrived in the 17th
century. They settled on the Pare Mountains and were a
Cushitic-speaking people. They have since been Bantuized
and absorbed by the Pare.

MBUGWE (tribe). A matrilineal tribe in Central Tanzania
around Lake Manyara. They are the exception among
their neighbors in that they had developed a chiefdom
structure to aid in defense against the Masai raiders.
They are agriculturalists and herders of stock. They
have low, mud-roofed houses (tembe).

MBUNGA (tribe). The northermost tribe to have been sub-
jugated by the Zulu. They claim to be descendants of
the Zulu-Ngoni with their original home in Tanganyika to
have been Songea. They live in Ulanga and made warlike
incursions into the north up to Morogoro and were paci-
fied by the German administration. They are rice farmers.

McGAIRL, JAMES LLOYD. A Scot who did more for Afri-
cans in urban areas than any other European. As a
Community Development Officer in the 1950's, he started
activities in the Arnautoglu Community Centre in Dar es
Salaam. Prominent Africans flocked to him, including
R. Kawawa, D. Phomeah, O. Kambona and Z. Mtemvu.
Upon leaving service with the Community Development
Department of Tanganyika, he became the Personnel and
Training Officer for the Williamson Diamonds Ltd. at
Mwadui in 1963.

MCHAURU, THECLA. Her father was a liwali in Masai District. She became a Makonde female leader and ran a

nursing program in the district. In 1955 and 1956 she
and her husband, Frederick Mchauru, proved a very effective team working in Community Development. She
established mid-wives' programs, organized more than
600 women into clubs and taught nutrition, child rearing
and home management. Her husband organized villages
into progressive societies for self-help. She served as
Secretary General of UWT. On 20 February, 1976, she
was appointed a member of the Permanent Commission
of Enquiry.

MEDICAL SERVICES. The Medical Department was opened
   on 1 April, 1891, with five doctors and fourteen workers.
   In 1893 the Sewa Haji Hospital in Dar es Salaam began
   operation. Before World War I the Medical Department
   of German East Africa had been staffed professionally
   by German nationals and the few mission hospitals by
   German and Britains. There were 12 general hospitals,
   a sanitorium, a mental hospital and leprosy segregation
   camps. During World War I they were replaced by medical officers of the Royal Army Medical Corps, the Indian Medical Service, the East and West Africa Medical
   Service and the Nyasa-Rhodesia Force.
        The tribal medicine men use traditional methods
   of medical and psychological diagnosis and cure. They
   have always had a big business.
        The first military and civilian medical services
   organized by the British was at first regional. The first
   Chief Medical Officer was Dr. John B. Davey. In 1919
   the Urban Sanitary Inspector Course began. In 1921 there
   were 15 medical officers and 21 subassistant Surgeons,
   31 registered medical practitioners (26 in government
   service, 3 private, 1 in CMS and 1 in Church of Scotland). In 1926 the dressers courses began. Dodoma
   Mental Hospital (Mirembe) opened in 1927. In 1943 the
   first African nurse graduated.
        It was discovered during World War II that one-
   third of the army recruits were unfit for army service
   and another third were unfit for active duty. By 1952
   only ten Tanzanians had fully qualified at Makerere Medical College. In 1960 Muhimbili Hospital in Dar es Salaam
   began operating.
        At independence the central government, local au-
   thorities, missionary societies and industries maintained
   a total of nearly 19,000 hospital and dispensary beds.
   The hospitals admitted over 300,000 patients in 1961 and
   initial consultation or treatments were given to over 10

million outpatients and over 300,000 expectant mothers
and children at hospitals, dispensaries and special clinics.
About one out of six children born were delivered in the
presence of a medical attendant.   Between 4,000 and
5,000 leprosy patients resided in leprosariums.
       By 1967 about 20 missionary societies provided
for over 40 percent of the hospital and dispensary beds
and 33 percent or more of the maternal and child care
services.   About 60 percent of these societies received
financial grants from the government under the grant-in-
aid program begun in the late 1930's.   The Tanzania
Christian Medical Association and the Chief Medical Officer nominated the Consultation Committee which coordinated the Voluntary Agency and Government Services.   The
doctor-patient ratio in 1967 was given as 1:200 in Dar es
Salaam with 15 percent of all government hospital beds
and 1:31,000 up-country.
       In 1974 there were 744 doctors in Tanzania.   Of
these, 34 were from Cuba, 60 from China and 310 were
Tanzanians.   Curative medical emphasis changed to preventive medicine and environmental health measures.   In
July 1976 there were 18,460 hospital beds, 149 rural medical centers, 1986 dispensaries and two consultant hospitals, Kilimanjaro Christian Medical Centre at Moshi and
one at Mwanza.   The aim in December 1976 was to provide 25 new rural health centers and 100 new dispensaries
every year.   At the same time Government announced its
intention to ban all private medical services and make all
medical services free to the public.

MELI, CHIEF.   Son of Mandara or Chief Rindi of the Chagga,
    repulsed the German expedition of authority in June 1892
    and was defeated in August 1893.   He was chief from
    1891 to 1900 and was hung by the German authority from
    a tree outside the boma.   He had refused to share the
    chiefdom with his brothers, Kirita and Salema.   So their
    mother poisoned Kirita and had him strangled in his sleep
    to avoid clashes between the brothers.   On his last
    breath, Kirita cursed Meli and blessed Salema.   As it
    turned out, Meli and his sons had a short rule and Sale-
    ma took over.

MENNONITE MISSION.   Bishop E. W. Stauffer was the first
    Mennonite missionary from the U.S.A.   He arrived in
    1934 and consulted with Pastor E. Sywulka of the African
    Island Mission near Mwanza, then began work in Mara
    Region.   The missionaries operated a hospital, several

dispensaries, a print shop, Bible School and primary
and middle schools.   Their six stations were scattered
throughout Mara Region.   The first African pastors were
ordained in 1950.   By 1958 Mennonite Mission began
handing over to Tanganyika Mennonite Church and the process was completed in 1960.   See also TANZANIA MEN-
NONITE CHURCH.

MERERE I, CHIEF TOWELA MAHAMBA. Of the Sangu, he
was grandson of Chief Mui' Gumbi and had been given
one of Munyigamba's daughters as a wife.   Around 1875
when she became blinded by smallpox, Merere insulted
Munyigamba by returning her to him.   He responded by
attacking Merere and he and his subjects fled to Ukimbu.
They had returned by 1877.   Mkwawa was given two
daughters by Merere as his wives but the two men never
made peace.   Merere formed temporary alliances with
others, Mkwawa and Nyungu ya Mawe.   Merere was defeated by the Hehe.   His son, Merere II Mugandilwa assisted the Germans in their wars against the Hehe.

MERERE II, CHIEF MUGANDILWA OR PAMBALU (?-1893).
Assisted the Germans in their wars against the Hehe.
Tom von Prince appointed Merere of Usangu to rule Uhehe
but the plan was abandoned.   Merere raided and plundered a number of neighboring chiefdoms.   He died in
1893.

MERERE IV (?-1906). A chief of the Bena of Usangu, was
the strongest ruler in Iringa District and had a strong
boma near Mbeya.   Around 1860 he started a school for
young boys at his capital.   By 1870 he had a large chiefdom, but it was eroded by Mkwawa until 1891.   Merere
IV prevaricated until the German troops compelled his
loyalty.   He then helped the Germans against the Hehe
and thus his territory expanded.   He fortified his capital
and fought against the Ngoni.   Twice he was persuaded
to supply auxiliary warriors only by the approach of German forces.   It is believed that he died of poison in 1906.

MERERE V. Of the Bena, he has been described as "vain,
lazy, extravagant, and a stupid tyrant who fleeced his
subjects in the most unworthy manner. " He has also
been called the best-hated man in the whole country.   He
was deported in October 1910 to Mafia Island for misgov-
ernment.   Mtengula, his half-brother, succeeded him.

MERINYO, JOSEPH. An early Chagga leader from the Moshi chiefdom, served as an interpreter in the Boma for Charles Dundas. He was an educated man and coffee farmer and was the Interregnum ruler of the Kombe clan (Machame) from 1917 to 1918. He was President of the Kilimanjaro Native Planters Association formed in 1925 and an organizer with Petro Njau of the Kilimanjaro Chagga Citizens Union in the 1940s.

MERU CASE. Acted as a catalyst in the early 1950's. It enabled a Tanganyikan as an inhabitant of the Trust Territory, to speak up before the U.N. Reallocation of land required the Meru tribe to move out of the Sanya Corridor Farm 31. About 78,000 acres of alienated land were to be turned into a ranching and dairying area with compulsory dipping of livestock and hopefully become the source of a meat industry. One thousand people (330 taxpayers) were evicted and moved 35 miles away, their 492 huts and storehouses were burned, 400 cattle and 1200 sheep were impounded and 12 arrests made. The evicted families disliked the land and returned to other tribal lands. Kirillo Japhet took the matter before the U.N. Later the government tried to make amends by allowing the Meru to graze their cattle in the Sanya Corridor, provided they used the cattle dips and there was no danger of infection. Settlers had 99-year leases on the farms and the Meru could not resettle. Then the settlers had bad luck: their cattle died, crops failed, families became ill--and they decided to move off. They blamed the witch doctors. The Meru Citizens Union was formed in 1948. Since independence the Meru have repurchased Farm 31 with Compensation Money.

MGONJA, CHEDIEL YOHANA (1934-). Born on 31 December, 1934, at Vudee in the Northern Highlands. After completing secondary education at Ilboru Secondary School in 1952, he went to Tabora Government Secondary School for his Higher School Certificate course. He went on to Makekere College for a B.A. and then studied administration and international relations at Cambridge University after having a brief career in local government as District Officer at Tanga and Arusha in the interim period. Coming back from England in 1961, he joined the Ministry of External Affairs and was transferred to Tanzania's Mission to the U.N. He returned in 1964 and was a Senior Secretary in the Foreign Ministry. He was made a member of Legislative Council in 1965. He

transferred to the Ministry of Community Development
and National Culture in 1967, then Minister of State for
Foreign Affairs and became the Minister for National
Education in November 1968.   During his stay here he
rapidly Tanzanianized the Ministry, got the adult literacy
program off onto a national scale and oversaw the first
Form IV and Form VI papers marked in Tanzania in
1971.   In 1972 he was appointed the Mtwara Regional
Commissioner in a move to decentralize power, giving
more authority to the regions, and in 1977 he became
RC of Tabora.

MHANDO, BEATRICE (1943-   ).   Born in Morogoro Region
and educated locally completing secondary education at
Morogoro in 1961.   She received a Diploma in Home
Economics in Holland in 1966 and was posted as the Acting Principal of the Buhare Home Economics Centre near
Musoma.   She married in 1968.   After some time in a
Regional Development Office and as Regional UWT Secretary of Tanga, she was appointed on 20 February, 1976,
as Secretary General of UWT.

MHANDO, STEPHEN.   Dr. Kyaruzi's helper when he took
over TAA.   He replaced Kambona as Organising Secretary of TANU in 1955 when Kambona went to England.
An extremist, his ambition soon drove him to overreach
himself.   At the end of 1956 he went to India to secure
scholarships for Tanganyika students.   He proceeded on
to Burma where he spent so much money that TANU
sacked him.   Returning to Dar es Salaam, he took up
journalism.   He also taught Swahili in East Germany for
awhile.   By 1965 he was back again and a member of the
University College of Dar es Salaam.   Several years
later he was appointed a Minister of State (Foreign Affairs)
in the President's Office.   He is a member of Parliament.

MICA.   The chief mineral produced in the German era.   Tanzania has been the chief producer of mica in the British
dependencies.   Much of it is sheet mica of the highest
quality.   The main producing areas are the Uluguru Mountains, Bagamoyo, Korogwe, Mpwapwa, Morogoro, Mbeya,
Kigoma and Mpanda.   The annual export value at the end
of the 1950's was approximately £70,000.   In 1966 they
mined 537 tons and predicted an annual future average
of 100 tons a year.   There has been a drop in price and
in production.   In 1973, 16 tons were sold at Shs. 533,340;
1974 only 9 tons worth Shs. 227,340; and in 1975 only 6.9
tons were mined.

MIDDLE SCHOOLS.   Developed in the later 1950's and contained Std. V to Std. VIII.   Most of them were boarding
schools as they drew their pupils from a large area of
feeder primary schools.   True to their name, they provided the link between primary and further education in
secondary institutions or training courses.

MIGEYO, ALI (c. 1896-   ).   Born in West Lake around 1896.
In 1935 he turned politician and spread TAA and the Bahaya Union in villages.   He represented West Lake in the
TAA meeting held in Mwanza in 1950.   He was jailed
from 1954 to 1957 and again 1964 to 1965.   He was a
member of the National Executive Committee in 1958 and
the TANU District Chairman for West Lake 1961-64.   He
was appointed in October 1965 to Parliament and later
retired to farming.

MIHAYO, ARCHBISHOP MARCUS (1907-   ).   Born at Kahema
and attended Junior Seminary at Itaga and Senior Seminary at Kipalapala, completing in 1930.   His ordination
to priesthood occurred in 1940.   He was then a seminary
teacher until 1943, a Curate at Lukula, and then a parish
priest until 1960.   At that time he was consecrated Archbishop of Tabora.   He served as Chairman of the Tanzania Episcopal Conference from 1965-68 and was a representative to the Synod of Bishops in Rome during 1967.

MIKINDANI.   A coastal town in the former Southern Province
and was a slave trading town.   At one time it was the
district headquarters for Mtwara, but is now a trading
center only.   Sometimes it is called a "twin town" with
Mtwara.

MIKUMI NATIONAL PARK.   Located 180 miles west of Dar
es Salaam along the tarmac road leading to Iringa, Mbeya
and Zambia.   It was previously a controlled hunting area
and gazetted in 1964.   It has an area of 500 square miles
(3230 sq. km.) and is the second smallest national park,
but contains a cross-section of almost all the game found
in Tanzania--small elephants, lions, rhinos, hippos and
large buffalo herds.   The Uhuru Railway line to Zambia
marks the new Southern park boundary.   Weekend excur-
sions are taken out of Dar es Salaam.

MILLET (SORGHUM).   Grown mostly as subsistence farming for food and brewing of beer.   It has high protein
value and stores well.   It was estimated that 15,000 tons

were grown in 1960 and 22,000 in 1970. In the 1975/76
season National Milling Corporation purchased 2900 metric
tons of Sorghum; 1198 metric tons of Finger Millet and
1103 metric tons of Bullrush Millet from the farmers.

MINERALS. Many have played a significant role in Tanza-
    nia's exports. The diamond mines, which supplied 90
    percent of Tanzania's mineral exports, were headed to-
    wards exhaustion in the 1970's. The 1949 mineral value
    was set at £2.6 million while the 1959 figure was £6.99
    million. See DIAMONDS, GOLD, COAL, IRON, MICA,
    LEAD, PHOSPHATES, SALT, TUNGSTEN, and TIN under
    their own headings. In addition, pyrochore, the source
    of columbium, is mined at Panda Hill near Mbeya,
    meershaum clay near the Kenya border produces pipes
    for export, Kaolin production near Dar es Salaam was
    1,003.5 metric tons in 1975/76; calcite was 5390 metric
    tons; Gypsum 12,839 metric tons; lime 472.75 metric
    tons; Art Stones 31.9 metric tons and Amethystine Quartz
    70.08 metric tons. There is also commercially exploit-
    able soda in Lake Natron. The total mineral value in
    the mid-1970's was Shs.150 million annually.

MIRAMBO, CHIEF (c.1840-1884). A chief of the Nyamwezi
    of Urambo who was thin, approximately six feet tall and
    very active. Mirambo was captured by the Tura (a
    group of the Ngoni) and learned their military methods.
    In the 1860's he used a small group of warriors to gain
    control of the chiefdoms surrounding his own, Uyowa.
    By 1870 he took the best boys from defeated groups who
    were twenty years of age and gave them hard training.
    He taught them to use guns and travel fast with little
    food. He had up to 5000 of them in his army which he
    called the "Ruga Ruga." Between 1870 and his death he
    led expeditions far afield and gained control of the trade
    routes and most of the Unyamwezi country. After con-
    tinuous conflict with the Arabs of Tabora, he defeated
    them in a battle in 1876 and peace prevailed. He made
    them pay tribute to him when using his route. By 1884
    he also obtained tribute from minor chiefs over most of
    the area between the southern shores of Lake Victoria
    and Lake Rukwa and dominated the trade routes from
    Tabora to Uganda, Ujiji and Ufipa. Mirambo was anxious
    to have the goodwill of the British Consul in Zanzibar.
    He also welcomed European missionaries for the external
    contacts they provided for his people. He was a great
    organizer, but failed to train a successor, so after his

death in 1884 the kingdom broke up into separate chiefdoms.

MISSIONS CHURCH FEDERATION (MCF). In 1938 the Lutheran churches of the South, Eastern and Coast, Usambara,
Uchagga, Central and Bukoba areas joined in a search
for greater unity. This enabled them to open the theological training school at Mlalo, the medical school at
Bumbuli, the Ilboru Secondary School near Arusha, and
the Vuga Printing Press. During World War II when the
German missionaries had to evacuate, MCF requested
the Lutheran World Federation for missionaries to fill
the need. The MCF was replaced by the Evangelical
Lutheran Church of Tanzania (ELCT) in 1963.

MKELLO, VICTOR. President of Tanganyika Federation of
Labour and General Secretary of Tanganyika Plantation
Workers' Union in 1963. He was considered a black
chauvinist and placed in preventive detention at Sumbawanga
in that year. He had been appointed a member of the
National Assembly in May 1962, but the appointment was
revoked in 1964. He was freed in July 1966 and, after
some years, came back into active political life and was
an Area Commissioner in the Iringa Region during the
mid-1970's and in the Tabora Region later.

MKWAWA, CHIEF (?-1898). Came to power after his
father's successful chieftainship in which he had united
the 30 Hehe groups into one. When the Germans began
their rule in German East Africa, Mkwawa tried diplomacy and peaceful means to resist them. He tried to
get allies but failed. When he sent an unarmed envoy
with gifts to the commander of the German defense
forces, Emil von Zelewski, in 1891, the Commander and
his men killed the envoy. So Mkwawa's men ambushed
the Germans, killed Zelewski and around 300 others.
For three years there was quiet in the land and Mkwawa
built a wall. It was 8 miles long, 12 feet high and 4
inches thick and surrounded his fort at Kalenga near
Iringa. He brought young boys from all over the chiefdom to be taught, always having 200 to 300 soldiers
ready at the fort. Chief Mkwawa controlled the ivory
trade himself which he sent yearly to Bagamoyo for exchange in cloth, beads and guns. He had 30 sub-chiefs.
        In 1894 another German expedition was sent
against Mkwawa and Mkwawa was badly beaten. He escaped and continued his guerrilla warfare. The German

Governor offered 5000 rupees for his head. In a series
of operations which took place in 1897-1898, the Hehe
were decisively defeated. As Sergeant Merckel approached
Mkwawa's hut in June 1898, Mkwawa who was sick and
alone with two pages, shot himself and one page to avoid
capture. His head was sent to Germany. The Treaty of
Versailles provided for its return. It was finally brought
in 1955.

MOMELA LAKES. (Later part of Arusha National Park.)
They are between Mt. Meru and Mt. Kilimanjaro and
were preserved as a game sanctuary since German times.
They were gazetted as a national park in 1962. The area
includes five large lakes with a wealth of bird life and
heavy concentrations of rhinoceros, elephants, buffaloes,
bushbuck, waterbuck, and others. They are adjacent to
Ngurdoto Crater.

MORAVIAN CHURCH. The first Moravian missionaries came
from Germany in 1891 and lived in Southern Tanganyika
near Mt. Rungwe. Although several of the first missionaries died from fever, the rest pursued their purpose
courageously. By 1899 they had 19 missionaries, more
than 5 stations and 100 Christians. Moravians from Denmark and the U.S.A. replaced the Germans in World War
I. When Bishop O. Gemeseus had to return to Germany
during World War II, the church was cared for by the
Western Tanganyika Bishops, a pattern continuing to the
present time. Pastor A. Jongo is in charge of this
Southern group.
        Another group of Moravians from England, the Lon-
don Missionary Society, arrived at Tabora on 26 December, 1897. They opened stations around Tabora and in
Iramba. The opening of the Central Railway Line through
Tabora increased the population of the town and area.
N. H. Gaarde was made the first Bishop in 1936. On
his way back to Denmark he died in the Red Sea. So in
1946 Bishop Ibsen was called to fill the vacancy. The
first African Bishop, T. Kisanji, was consecrated to the
office in 1966 when Bishop Ibsen returned to Europe.
        The Southern and Western groups have a "Joint
Board," theological college at Chunya, a Bible School at
Sikonge and a magazine called Ushinde (Victory).

MORESBY TREATY. Signed by Capt. Fairfax Moresby, sent
by the Governor of Mauritius, and Seyyid Said on 21 September, 1822. It made it illegal to sell slaves from East

Africa outside Sultan Said's dominions. The treaty out-
lawed the sale of slaves to Christian merchants, but not
to Moslems. It permitted Britain to capture Arab slave
ships trading in non-Moslem states. The treaty also recognized the Sultan's claims to the East African coast
from Cape Delgado south to the Horn. This anti-slavery
treaty was very difficult to enforce.

MOROGORO.   Kisabengo, a Zigua from the coast near Bagamoyo, got into trouble with the Sultan of Zanzibar. So
he fled to the Uluguru Mountains, conquered the northern
area and built a fortified town named Simbamwene at the
present site of Morogoro town. The settlement was engaged in servicing the many caravans which journeyed
through the area. High winds and hard rains destroyed
much of the town and wall, according to Stanley's description on his return journey through Morogoro. The Central Railway Line reached Morogoro in 1907.

   Morogoro is situated in a good agricultural region;
the Faculty of Agriculture of the University of Dar es
Salaam is located there. It is the center of a network
of highways as well as Central Line station. A cotton
ginnery, rice and flour mills, sorting sheds for mica,
cotton and sisal fields grace its horizons. The town has
a steady population growth: 8000 in 1945; 15,000 in 1959;
25,000 in 1967; and 44,000 in 1977.

MOSHI.   A town situated at the foothills of Mt. Kilimanjaro,
it has an altitude of 2900 feet. It is a station on the
railway from Dar es Salaam to Arusha and has good
road connections to all major towns. It has an automatic
telex exchange and an international airport service. Due
to its climatic advantages, it has developed well agricul-
turally and industrially. The town had a population of
14,000 in 1959 and in addition to the chief product, coffee,
there were sawmills, a textile factory, large soap works,
a canning factory, sweet factory, and out of town about 14
miles a sugar refinery.

   The population increased to 27,000 by the 1967
census. There were 4500 Asians who were mostly all in
the township and around 1500 Europeans who made up 7
percent of the total Tanzania European group. The majority were in agriculture. They were a varied ethnic
group, many transient but British and Greeks more permanent. It was these groups who were affected by nationalization of farms in 1970. The main African group
around Moshi are the Chagga who totalled around 340,000
in 1967.

Coffee, the principal source of income, earned
£14 million in 1966. A research sub-station is located
here. KNCU (q. v.) has developed services to the community. Moshi town continues to grow, reaching 53,000
by 1977.

MOSHI, BISHOP STEFANO REUBEN (1906-1976). Born on
the slopes of Mt. Kilimanjaro on 6 May, 1906. His
father was a Leipzig Mission evangelist. After a local
education, he trained as a teacher and taught at Marangu
Teacher Training College for 25 years and served also
as Principal. He studied at the Lwandai Theological College from 1947-49 and at the Lutheran Bible Institute at
Minneapolis, U. S. A. from 1952-53. He left teaching in
1955 and entered administration of the former Lutheran
Church of Northern Tanganyika (later Northern Diocese)
and became its Head in 1958. From 1961-63 he was the
elected President of the former Federation of Lutheran
Churches of Tanganyika and was the first leader of the
Evangelical Lutheran Church in Tanganyika (ELCT) when
it was formed in 1964. That same year he was consecrated Bishop of the Northern Diocese. He held both
1964 posts until his death in 1976 along with a number of
other leadership roles. He joined the Christian Council
of Tanganyika as a member in 1960 and was the first
African Chairman of CCT when elected in 1965. In 1960
he became the President of the YMCA (Tanganyika) at its
formation; was a member of the Chagga Council 1959-61
and elected Vice President of the Lutheran World Federation in 1963. In 1970 he was awarded with two Doctor-
ates of Divinity. He died on 14 August, 1976.

MOSLEMS. Greatest concentration is in Zanzibar, Pemba
and Mafia Islands and inland where the Arab traders
made contacts. About one-fourth of the population is
Moslem. The majority of the African and Arab Moslems
are Sunnites. Indian and Pakistani Moslems are generally
members of one of the Shia sects. The Moslem community has remained basically conservative in its approach
to social affairs in Tanzania. The Khoja Ismailis have
been leaders and are strong supporters of social advancement as instructed by the Aga Khan, their spiritual leader.
Moslem holidays are nationally celebrated.

MT. KILIMANJARO. Situated about 3° south or 207 miles
south of the equator and the highest point in Africa, is
made up of two peaks, Kibo (19,321 feet) and Mawenzi

(17,500 feet) united by a saddle. The snowline is at
19,000 feet and there are glaciers at its summit. Sul-
phur emanation has been known since 1932 on Kibo Summit. Mt. Kilimanjaro is a volcanic mountain with a large
eruption 1940/41 and small eruptions in 1954 and in January 1955. The Eastern Rift of the Rift Valley extends
to the mountain.

The mountain has a cold, dry alpine climate, low
humidity, little precipitation and considerable extremes
in temperature. The southern slopes face the prevailing
winds from the Indian Ocean and get more than 45 inches
of rainfall yearly. The northern slopes receive less than
30 inches annually. The tropical forest lies between 5600
and 9500 feet. A network of irrigation channels on the
southern face bring water from the forest belt to the
Chagga garden plots on the slopes just below the rain forest.
The population density on the lower slopes has reached
800 per square mile. Cattle are tended inside and the
women climb the mountain to cut the tall grasses to feed
the cattle. Coffee and bananas are the main crops grown
at the foot of the mountain.

The mountain served a great religious purpose in
the Chagga native religion and reports say that human
sacrifices were offered up on the mountain. Mountain
climbing is very popular for tourists. The first successful foreign ascent of the mountain was made by a Leipzig
scientist, Professor Meyer, in 1889. Tours can be arranged with a few hotels for a five-day climb with guides,
porters, etc. or climbers can go on their own.

MT. MERU. The second highest peak in Tanzania with its
peak reaching an altitude of 14,979 feet. It is a volcanic
mountain and has greater steepness than Mt. Kilimanjaro.
Its physical features are much like Mt. Kilimanjaro but
the tropical rain forest ranges from 4600 to 6000 feet.
The southern slopes face the prevailing winds from the
Indian Ocean and receive more than 40 inches of rainfall
yearly while the northern slopes receive less than 30
inches annually.

MOYO, HASSAN NASSOR (1933-   ). Born in Zanzibar. After
completing primary education, he was a carpenter and
rose in the trade union movement to Secretary General
of Zanzibar and Pemba Federation of Labour, a post he
held for six years. He was a member of the ASP National Executive Committee. After the April 1964 merger, he was appointed Justice Minister of the Union

Government, but the folio was later abolished. He then
became Zanzibar's Minister for Agriculture and Land Reform. He went for political studies in the Soviet Union.
In the mid-1970's he was a Minister of State in the First
Vice President's office, and in February 1977 he was appointed Minister for Home Affairs.

MRANGA. Of Ugweno, he was a foremost Tanganyika reformer of the 16th century who seized power from the
former clan of blacksmiths. He undermined their power
and centralized it by taking over the system of initiation
for young men and made it an educational as well as a
political institution. He created a large bureaucracy with
a minister in each and even appointed a minister to su-
pervise and coordinate the agricultural work. He created
a hierarchy of councils and appointed members of his
family as district governors.

MSUYA, CLEOPA DAVID (1931-). Born on 4 January,
1931, in Pare District. He attended Old Moshi Secondary
School (1944-49) and Tabora Government Secondary School
(1950-51), and then attended Makerere College where he
studied geography, history and political education and received his B.A. in 1955. He was a Community Development Officer and rose to Acting Deputy Commissioner
by 1961 and Commissioner for Community Development
by 1962. He was the Permanent Secretary for the Ministry of Community Development and National Culture
(1964-65), Principal Secretary for the Ministry of Lands,
Settlement and Water Development (1965-67), then to the
Ministry of Economic Affairs and Development Planning
(1967-70), joined the Treasury in 1970 and was appointed
Minister for Finance in 1975. His portfolio was changed
to Minister for Industries in November 1975.

MTEI, EDWIN ISAAC MBILIEWI (1932-). Born on 12 July,
1932, near Moshi. He was educated at Old Moshi and
Tabora Secondary Schools and at Makerere University
College from 1953-57 and was awarded a B.A. (Hons.)
degree in political science and history. From 1957-59
he was a managerial trainee with East Africa Tobacco
Company. He entered government service in 1959. His
first post, Assistant Secretary, Chief Establishment Office, concerned Africanization and training in the Civil
Service. He was seconded to the East African Common
Services Organisation (EACSO) and held a series of high
appointments, most of them financial, until 1964. He

returned as Permanent Secretary to the Treasury and
was made Governor of the Bank of Tanzania in 1966. He
directed Tanzania's break with the 40-year-old East African Currency Board in June 1966. He also helped with
the nationalization of commercial banks in 1967. At the
same time he was honorary treasurer of Dar es Salaam
University College (1966-70) and Chairman of the University Grants Committee with effect from 1970. He transferred from the Bank of Tanzania in 1974 when he was
appointed the Secretary General of the East African Economic Community. In February 1977, he was appointed
Minister for Finance and Planning.

MTEMVU, SHEIKH ZUBERI M. M. (1928-). Born on 20
December, 1928, and first attended an African Muslim
School, then primary school, Dodoma and Tabora Secondary Schools up to Std. XI. He was a Sub-Inspector of
the Tanganyika Police Force, a Social Development Department Worker, taught literacy in Tanga and Community Development Assistant at Tanga to 1956. Then he
was the Acting Organising Secretary General of TANU.
He resigned from TANU after the Tabora TANU meeting
in January 1958 had decided to participate in the elections.
TANU sacked him from TANU membership on 31 January,
1958. He formed a racialist party, Tanganyika African
Congress, but the May registration was refused. Then
he formed the African National Congress and polled only
53 votes as the only opponent of Nyerere. The ANC
policies were: Africa for the Africans only; a rapid civil
service Africanization; self-government for indigenous
Africans only; and a racial stand on citizenship for non-
Africans. In 1961 he visited China and other communist
countries. In 1963 when Tanganyika became a one-party
state, he joined TANU. By 1966 he was Assistant Secretary to the Village Settlement, Water Development and Irrigation Divisions of the Ministry of Lands, having served
in administrative positions in the President's office and
Minister of Agriculture before that, then continued on in
the Ministry of Health, Cooperative Division of Agriculture
and when Dar es Salaam became a Region, he worked in
a District Office.

MTWARA. Near the Mozambique border, this town has a
natural harbor with a spacious and sheltered bay. It was
once intended as the major port to handle the produce of
the Groundnut Scheme and construction began in 1948.
The Scheme failed. Mtwara was made a town by ordinance

in 1949. The port was officially opened in 1954 and
has shipping services along the coast. In 1959 there
were 10,000 residents. Mtwara owes its existence to
the Railway built for the Overseas Food Corporation.
A cashew nut factory began operating in 1968. Its yearly
capacity is 30,000 tons of processed nuts. The 1967
census reported over 13,000 inhabitants. At times its
census is linked with Mikindani.

MUHAJI, OMARI AHMED (1922-   ).   Born in Kondoa.   He
    trained as a teacher in Mpwapwa Teachers Training Cen-
    tre in 1940 and served as a primary and middle school
    teacher for nine years.   He then served five years as
    an African School Supervisor and District Education Of-
    ficer, then as Secretary-General of the East African
    Muslim Society for four years.   In 1967 he was appointed
    to Junior Minister positions, was later Secretary of
    TANU in Mwanza and Tanga, and lastly Minister of Home
    Affairs from 1973-75.   He retired from public office in
    1975, but remained a member of Parliament and a na-
    tional leader for TAPA.

MUHIMBILI HOSPITAL.   In 1893 an Indian Sewa Haji gave
    money to build a hospital for Germans to be treated.
    The Sewa Haji Hospital was opened in Dar es Salaam in
    January 1897.   In 1920 the British added new buildings.
    The Sewa Haji Hospital had 40 beds and 36 cots in 1955.
    The following year the new set of buildings on a plot a bit
    farther away were dedicated on Princess Margaret's visit
    and the hospital was then called Princess Margaret Hos-
    pital.   At independence the 762-bed hospital received a
    a new name--Muhimbili Hospital.   By 1967 it had be-
    come an 800-bed teaching and consulting hospital.   The
    first six graduates of the School of Medicine completed
    their course one year after the school became a Faculty
    of the University College in 1968.   Other training facili-
    ties were expanded.   The new maternity building opened
    in December 1973.   In 1975 there were over 1200 beds
    and 24 wards in the hospital and 40 to 50 operations
    daily.   On 16 January, 1976 the Minister of Health an-
    nounced that the Hospital would become parastatal.   This
    meant that it would offer free medical treatment and be
    independent except for financing by the Ministry.   In 1976
    there was a doctor for 8 beds (1:50 other places), 1
    nurse for 8 and 1 nursing assistant for 2.6 beds.

MUHSIN, SHEIKH ALI   see   BARWANI

MUMFORD, WILLIAM BRYANT (1900-1951). Came to Tanganyika in 1923 from Cambridge University where he had
an M.A. in anthropology. He was an Education Officer
in Bukoba from 1923 to 1925 and served as headmaster
of the Bukoba Central School. He was secretary of the
Education Conference held in 1925 in Dar es Salaam.
Through a grant from the Rockefeller Foundation, he
travelled for two years in Britain, Canada and the U.S.A.,
discussing problems of African education with anthropolo-
gists, psychologists and educationists. From a Canadian
university he received a Ph.D. degree in 1930 on the
subject of the Malangali experiment. He aimed at developing an educational system which met the needs of the
African in Africa. Malangali School was designed to assist in the general problem of social adjustment. He had
the support of the Director of Education, but he was absent for long periods of time and his assistant was unable
to practice exactly what Mumford had in mind. This
caused varied attitudes to develop among the students.
Mumford went on leave to the U.S.A. in 1933 and resigned from service the following year. His original,
imaginative and significant contribution ended with his
departure. He was Head of the Colonial Department of
the Institute of Education at the University of London in
1940. He died on 28 January, 1951.

MUNANKA, ISAAC MULLER BHOKE (1927-   ). Born in
North Mara and also attended Tabora Secondary School.
He was first employed as a government clerk (1948-52).
Munanka was a Vice President of TAA, joined TANU at
its inception in 1954 and served as its National Treasurer
for a number of years. At TANU's National Conference
at Tabora in January 1958, he was one of the chief op-
ponents of Nyerere, favoring a boycott of the elections
and a call for a general strike. Public disorders in the
Lake Province caused the British to ban branches of
TANU for which he was responsible. Since independence
he has been politically active, holding various positions
in the government. He has been a Minister of State in
the President's Office and in the Vice President's Office
and headed the Central Establishment Division, being responsible for the Civil Service organization and training.
He lost his Parliamentary seat in 1970. He also served
as secretary of PAFMECA and several other public organizations. He is a personal assistant in the President's
Office.

MUNYIGUMBA, CHIEF (Binini) (?-1879). Also MUYUGUM-
BA. His family had come from Usagara and became
chiefs through marriage. Muyugumba united the Hehe
tribe around 1950; they had been about 30 separate groups.
This unity was strong enough to successfully compete with
other African tribes like the Ngoni. They defeated the
Bena (1874-75) and the Segu (1877). Between 1878 and
1881 they fought against the Gwangwara, but neither side
could win and peace was made in 1881 by the new Chief
Mkwawa, who had come to power in 1879. After Munyigumba's death, his son Mkwawa led the Hehe's stubborn
resistance against the Germans.

MURRAY, WILLIAM DAVID FRASER (1919-). A Scottish
barrister and idealist, he served with the KAR in Burma
and lost an arm. He was an advocate in Tanganyika.
He also served as Vice Chairman of the Council of the
University College, Dar es Salaam and Director of the
East African Airways Corporation. His wife Moira became secretary of Tanganyika Council of Women, founded
by Lady Twining in 1953.

MUSEUMS. All top posts in the Tanganyika National Museum
were localized by 1973. The National Museum supports
ethnographic and archeological fieldwork. It has a large
collection of African art and traditional handicrafts and
is the repository of the famous fossil man, Zinjanthropus. A second museum is located several miles out of
Dar es Salaam and is a village museum where various
tribal-type houses have been constructed. Craftsmen
demonstrate their skills and tribal dancing groups perform
sometimes for tourists. A total of over 120,000 visit
the two museums in a year.

MUSOMA RESOLUTION. Enacted in November 1974, it called
for Universal Primary Education in 1977; forbad direct
entry into the University from 1975 on. Entry thereafter into the university required work experience
and applications accompanied by recommendations from
a) employer, b) work fellows, and c) TANU branch leaders. A statement in October 1976 modified the Resolution
saying girls may now enter the University after serving
National Service without a period of two years in work.

MUTAHANGARWA, JOSEPH (1905-). Born in Bukoba and
attended a dispenser's course at Sewa Haji Hospital in
Dar es Salaam, he then began dispensing medicine in 1925

at Bukoba. He later became an instructor at Sewa Haji
Hospital and Tabora.   In 1933 he was sent to Uganda for
advanced training and was the first man to qualify in
medicine at Makerere College from Tanganyika.   He
qualified in 1940.   On 14 January, 1942, he performed
the first all-African major operation at Sewa Haji Hospital.   He retired from government service in 1951 and
practiced on the border between Uganda and Tanzania for
years afterward.

* MUTATEMBWA, CHIEF.   When the Germans arrived in West
Lake in 1890, they found the successor states from the
Civil War in Greater Kyamtwara in a power struggle.
The struggle was increased by the support of the Buganda
via Kiziba, a nearby chiefdom, led by Mutatembwa.
Mutatembwa unwisely relied upon the Buganda and defied
the Germans and ended in defeats.   Mutatembwa perse-
cuted the local CMS leaders who arrived and aimed at
establishing a wholly-African church.   The Kiziba began
to see the value of education and supported mission.
This in turn helped to gain the favor of the Government
by the end of the 1890s and so he became a chief in 1903.
In 1905 Gotzen visited Buhaya and proclaimed Mutatembwa
"Superior Chief" alongside Kahigi.   His son Mutanangarwa
succeeded him.

MUYUGUMBA, CHIEF   see   MUNYIGUMBA

MWAHAWANGU, CHIEF.   Of the Sangu, he fled when his people were attacked by the Ufipa Ngoni in the 1840s.   After
about ten years he returned, united all the Sangu people
and made a strong fighting force.   His successor, Merere,
was able to dominate the Southern Highlands in the 1860s
and 1870s.

MWAKAWAGO, DAUDI NGELANTWA (1939-   ).   Born in Iringa
District on 19 September, 1939. He studied at Malangali
and Tabora Secondary Schools and then specialized in social sciences and history at Makerere University.   At
Manchester University he received a Diploma in Adult
Education.   On returning to Tanzania, he taught from
1965-70 at Kivukoni College and then served as its principal from 1971-72.   He was appointed Minister for Information and Broadcasting in 1972 and transferred to
the Principalship of Kivukoni College in February 1977.

MWANA MWEMA.   The Queen in Zanzibar who broke faith

with the Portuguese in 1652 when the Omani Arabs sacked
the Portuguese settlement in Zanzibar. The Queen's
towns were destroyed.

MWANZA. Has always been one of the five largest towns in
Tanzania. In the 1950s it had not reached 20,000 yet,
but its position as railhead of a branch railway line from
Tabora and main Tanzania port on Lake Victoria, has
given it many advantages and it has been a very fast-
growing town in population, factories and trade. Its population had reached 35,000 by 1967 and 63,000 by 1977.
Mwanza handles trade from Musoma and Bukoba as well
as Uganda and Kenya when relationships with those countries permit smooth trade. Ferries for railway cars provided additional services as of 1966. Mwanza is the center for the nearby Geita Goldfields and Mwadui diamond
mines as well as a good agricultural area. It is the headquarters of the East African Inland Marine Services. A
new, large hospital on Buganda Hill is a consultant hospital. Mwanza has an international exchange system. Its
industries are many, including cotton ginning, flour- and
oil-milling, soap manufacturing, textile milling and boat
repairing.

MWAPACHA, HAMZA. Nyerere's closest friend at Makerere
College. They founded the Tanganyika African Welfare
Association known as TAWA. At Vedast Kyaruzi's advice,
they dropped their own creation and transferred their activities to TAA. Mwapachu trained as a social worker
in Britain. Steeped in Moslem discipline, he provided the
solid facts on which Tanganyika's constitution was formed.
Mwapacha became a Welfare Officer in Dar es Salaam.

MWENE SELE, CHIEF. Chief Fundikira's successor of the
Nyamwezi. He was friendly with the Arabs and provided
food, ivory, porters, hospitality and trading information
in return for a share of profits. However, he grew to
dislike the behavior of the Zanzibaris and the dominance
of trade they gained during the 1850s, so he turned
against them. They supported a rival Mkasiwa, who became a puppet ruler at Unyanyembe.

MWENYI MKUU. The "ruler" of the Hadimu tribe in Zanzibar and was the descendant of the old "kings" of Zanzibar
referred to by the Portuguese, and by Sir James Lancas-
ter when he came to Zanzibar in 1591. The last Mwenyi
Mkuu, the Lord of Dunga, is believed to have been of

Persian descent. It is almost certain he lived from 1785
to 1865. The Mwenyi Mkuu had been transferred from
Zanzibar town to the eastern part of the island by the
Oman Arabs. Mwenyi Mkuu had charge of local jurisdiction of the Hadimu and collected the hut tax from his subjects and divided the proceeds equally with the Arab Sultan at Zanzibar town. His will and word were law and
he held absolute power of life and death over his own
people. He was believed to have supernatural powers.
The whole native population regarded him and his abode
with superstitious dread. It was considered sacrilegious
for anyone to be higher than he, so everyone met him on
their knees with covered heads. Mwenyi Mkuu, the last
of the "kings" of Zanzibar died in 1865, and his son
lacked any special influence or character and died in 1873,
terminating the office.

MWINYI, ALI HASSAN (1925-). Born in Kisarawe District
and educated in Zanzibar's primary and secondary schools,
then in a teacher training center. He then studied at the
Institute of Education of the University of Durham for
further professional training. He returned and taught in
Zanzibar's primary schools and teachers colleges from
1945-61. He then studied in Britain for two years for
a diploma in education. In 1964 he was appointed Principal Secretary to the Ministry of Education in Zanzibar.
He has held a number of chairmanships for various boards
and official bodies including The East African Currency
Board (Zanzibar), Film Censorship Board, Editorial
Board of Zanzibar Government Progress Reports and National Swahili Council in Dar es Salaam. He has also
been a member of the College Council of the University
of East Africa and Printing Press Corporation Board of
Zanzibar. In 1969 he was appointed to Minister of State
in the President's Office, in 1972 to Minister of Health
and transferred to the Ministry of Home Affairs in 1975.
He resigned in January 1977 due to situations in his
ministry.

MWONGOZO see TANU GUIDELINES

MZIZIMA. Name that was given to Dar es Salaam, meaning
"healthy town." It is the traditional, local name.

MZUMBE. An area near Morogoro town which has been an
institutional area; in 1953, a Central School was established for the training of Native Authority staff. A

Secondary School and Institute of Development Management are the present centers for learning.

- N -

NAMFUA, JACOB (1937-1973). Born in Kilimanjaro District
and was educated to a secondary level, then went on to
Mbagathi Posts and Telegraphic Training School in Uganda. He later attended Labour College in Kampala from
1958 to 1959, then to the U. S. A. in 1962 for further
studies, in Britain from 1964-67 studying economics,
politics and philosophy and received a B. A. (Hons.) Degree at Oxford. He was the Secretary General of the
Tanganyika African Postal Union from 1958-60, Secretary
General and Treasurer of TFL 1960-61, a nominated
member of the Legislative Council in 1960, Principal
Secretary to the Ministry for Economic Affairs and Development Planning, Minister for Information and Broadcasting and lastly Regional Commissioner for Kilimanjaro
Region when decentralization of power sent some ministers to the regions. Namfua met his death in a tragic
accident at Same on 30 May, 1973.

NATIONAL ASSEMBLY OF THE PARLIAMENT. Preceded by
the Legislative Council formed in 1926. On 1 May, 1961,
the body was renamed Tanganyika Parliament. At Independence it was redesignated National Assembly. It is
composed of 120 members (107 until 1970 additions), 22
ex-officio members (the Regional Commissioners), 15
National members elected by statutory bodies, 10 members appointed by the President, a maximum of 32 members of the Zanzibar Revolutionary Council and no more
than 20 other Zanzibaris appointed by the President in
agreement with his First Vice President (The President
of Zanzibar). The total assembly may reach 204 members. There is an elected Speaker who cannot hold any
other office. Unless dissolved by the President, elected
members of the National Assembly serve a 5-year term.
A quorum of at least one-fourth must be maintained at
all times for the National Assembly to meet. In the
case of a tie when voting, the Speaker or the Deputy
Speaker casts the deciding vote. This is the only voting
privilege given to the presiding officer. The Constitution
provides for six standing committees of the National Assembly: Finance and Economic, Political Affairs, Public
Accounts, Social Services, Standing Orders and General

Purpose. The National Assembly passes bills and sends them to the President for assent or confirmation. He has the power to veto.

NATIONAL BANK OF COMMERCE (NBC). All nine commercial banks were nationalized on the mainland in 1967 and now function as branches of the National Bank of Commerce under the direction of the central bank, The Bank of Tanzania. The central bank issues and controls currency. NBC in February 1976 had 85 branches and 303 sub-branches. NBC also has a joint insurance scheme with the National Insurance Corporation whereby the money is banked (saved) and at the same time the depositor is insured.

NATIONAL CENTRAL LIBRARY. Opened on 9 December, 1967. Its main functions are housing the Administrative Headquarters of the Tanzania Library Services and reserve of stock of books; acting as a national deposit library; providing a public library for the residents of Dar es Salaam; and coordinating school libraries throughout the mainland.

NATIONAL CONFERENCE. It was TANU's highest organ with more than 400 members who were party officers from national, regional and district offices, district delegates and delegates from TANU's departments and affiliated organizations, plus National Assembly members and specially nominated delegates. It was the highest policy making body and its executive committee was the supreme policy making body. The National Conference of TANU could revoke any lower-level decision of its officers, expel members and amend its own constitution by a two-thirds majority.

NATIONAL DEVELOPMENT CORPORATION (NDC). The National Development Corporation Act was passed in the National Assembly on 5 June, 1962, and the Tanganyika Development Corporation was established in 1963 to foster industrial development. Its successor, the National Development Corporation, was formed January 1965. It became the agent for government to control major shares in seven firms in 1967: Tanzania Breweries, 60 percent; Kilimanjaro Breweries, 60 percent; British American Tobacco, 60 percent; Tanganyika Metal Box Co., 50 percent; Tanganyika Extract Co., 49 percent; Tanganyika Portland Cement Co., 50 percent; and Tanzania Shoe Co.

(BATA), 60 percent. It owned Lake Manyara Hotel and purchased the New Africa Hotel. In 1969, the NDC was reorganized. It had 22 subsidiaries in 1971. It is responsible for public investment, initiation and management in the manufacturing, processing and mining industries.

NATIONAL EXECUTIVE COMMITTEE (NEC). The supreme policy making body of the party and government and was the highest executive Committee of TANU. It was composed of 18 members who were high-level party members, professionals and government leaders including Cabinet ministers, the secretaries general of NUTA and CUT (ex officio members). The NEC met every three months while the National Conference met biannually. The NEC approved nominations of candidates for the 15 institutionally sponsored members of the National Assembly and approved or selected nominees for constituency elections.

NATIONAL PROVIDENT FUND (NPF). Begun 1 October, 1964, with an aim to providing retirement pensions for all public and private wage earners over 55 years. Those employed on contract by firms with over 10 employees benefitted from the NPF to which the employer and employees both contributed at the rate of 5 percent of the wages payable. Fund benefits included retirement, illness and survivors' pensions. It was an important source of long-term finance to the government as most of its money was invested in government securities.

NATIONAL SERVICE. Established in 1963 on a voluntary basis. The National Service Act of 1966 made it compulsory for secondary, technical college and university graduates. Some youths continued to volunteer. The Act was protested by the university students in October 1966. About 400 students were summarily dismissed. Most of them were reinstated after a year. National Service required a two-year period. Until 1975 the basic training was for three months and then trainees could volunteer to join the army or police force or enter village development programs. During that one and a half years they received a basic allowance and were paid 40 percent of the wage they would have received had they been outside the National Service program. In 1975 the time spent at the camps was extended from six months to one year. This year was taken before entering training courses or the university if ex-Form VI or after a training course if ex-Form IV. All discharged national servicemen are subject to recall for periodic military training and compose a sizeable reserve force.

NATIONAL UNION OF TANZANIA WORKERS (NUTA). Tanganyika had 39 unions with a membership of 65,000 in 1960. The Tanganyika Federation of Labour was dissolved and leaders were detained when they threatened to call a general strike in support of the mutineers in January 1964. NUTA replaced the TFL. It is an affiliate of TANU: its Secretary-General and Deputy Secretary General are appointed by the President. They represent NUTA on the National Executive Committee of TANU as ex-officio members. From its formation, Michael Kamaliza was the Secretary General of NUTA and the Minister for Labour until 1967 when he was relieved of his ministerial duties due to many demands in both positions. The creation of the Federation of Tanganyika Employers in 1965 provided for a clearing house and coordinator of policy vis-a-vis NUTA. NUTA represents all wage earners and has a number of branches.

NATIONALIZATION see NATIONAL BANK OF COMMERCE; NATIONAL DEVELOPMENT CORPORATION; MOSHI; EDUCATION SECRETARIES GENERAL

NATIVE AUTHORITY ORDINANCE OF 1923. Strengthened the local authority of administrative officers, chiefs and headmen by conferring upon them the power to issue orders and regulations for matters regarding the maintenance of order and prevention of crime. The second duty was to administer justice, a function performed through the Native Courts.

NATIVE AUTHORITY ORDINANCE OF 1926. A revision of the 1923 ordinance. It divided Tanganyika into eleven provinces. Its main functions were maintaining order and collecting hut and poll taxes.

NDAMBA (tribe). Have inhabited the plains of the Kilombero Valley longer than any of their neighbors. They had a firmly organized patriarchal order, which broke down when the Mafiki invaded from the South. They were later pushed farther up the river by the warring Hehe, Ngoni and Bena. They are the foremost fishermen in the area. They plant rice and frequently build their houses on poles. Their last tribal chief died in 1944.

NEW, CHARLES (1840-1875).   Born in London during January
1840 and became a missionary under the United Methodist
Free Church in 1863 near Mombasa.   In 1871 he made a
journey to Mt. Kilimanjaro and was the first European to
climb to the snowline on the top of the mountain.   Until
1872 he worked among the Nyika peoples and made journeys to the Galla and Chagga.   In 1874 he returned from
England to East Africa.   He died in February 1875 while
returning from a visit to Mandara, the Chagga chief.

NGONI (tribe).   An offshoot of the Zulu tribe who moved out
of Natal to escape the rule of the Zulu chief Chaka around
1824.   As they moved northwards from South Africa, the
main body reached the northeastern corner of Lake Nyasa by 1840.   In 1860 one group settled in what is Songea
while others moved off in several directions.   The decentralized tribal groups which they met were either incorporated with the Ngoni or they united against the Ngoni.   Later the Ngoni allied with the traders and in a short
time the area was depopulated.   They did not have any
time to cultivate, so they attacked others to steal food and
cattle.   In 1866 they fought against Kilwa Kivinje and won.
Generally the effect of the arrival of the Ngoni in Southern Tanganyika was to bring war to an area that had been
peaceful.
         The Northern group first clashed with the Sangu
people on the western edge of the Iringa Plateau.   They
fought five years (1878-82) against the Hehe and were then
confined to an area east of Lake Malawi.   In 1882 they
destroyed a mission station at Masasi.   In 1897 the Germans established a garrison at Songea without meeting
resistance from the Ngoni.   They are a patrilineal society.   They had a centralized pattern of political organization with a paramount chief and sub-chiefs under him.
They kept cattle until 1945 in the Ulanga District when
the tsetse fly caused their extinction.   They are hoe cultivators.

NGORONGORO CRATER.   Sometimes called "Africa's Garden
of Eden, " it is found within the Ngorongoro Conservation
Area.   The giant crater is the second largest in the world
with a diameter of 11 miles or 16 kilometers, which
makes it the earth's largest intact crater.   The floor area
is 102 square miles, depth is 2000 feet (600 meters),
average height of rim is approximately 7600 feet and
floor 5600 feet.   It was first incorporated with the Serengeti National Park but was later separated.   Ngorongoro

Crater has fantastic scenic grandeur, and one of the
heaviest concentrations of wildlife in Africa with over
30,000 animals. Wildebeests vary in number from 7500
to 10,000. The African (major) species not found are
giraffe, kudu, sable, roan and crocodile. It also has
prolific floral life. The Conservation Area is 60 to 70
miles wide and has an area of 3200 square miles. It
has multiple land use: grazing of cattle, wildlife conservation and forestry. The more than 8000 Masai living in the area are being educated to appreciate the value
of its wildlife. This is a popular tourist site.

NGULU (tribe). Numbering 53,000 in 1957, they live in the
fertile and precipitous Ngulu Mountains and their foothills
in northwest Morogoro Region and in southwest Handeni
of Arusha Region. Traditionally the Ngulu had no central
political authority; each small area with its dominant
matrilineage stood independent of each other except for
social ties between them. Many Ngulu responded enthu-
siastically to the Arab caravans and began to trade, some
taking arms to hunt down captives to sell. They bought
and sold their neighbors into slavery to caravans. A
weak chief at Maskati in South-central Ungulu was recognized by most of the surrounding areas. The Germans tried
to utilize him and later administered through akidas. The
commonest tradition is that the Ngulu is a branch of the
Zigua who were so frequently raided that they escaped to
the mountainous areas. Ngulus consult diviners in cases
of misfortune and illness.

NGURDOTO CRATER. Lies under Mt. Meru about 10 miles
north off the Arusha-Moshi Road. It was gazetted as a
National Park in 1961. It is a connoisseur's park with
a crater floor of grass about one and a half miles wide
and a few hundred feet below the rim. No visitors are
allowed to descend in it. Momela National Park, adjacent to the western side, became a National Park in 1962.
The crater later merged with Momela to become part of
Arusha National Park in 1970.

NJAU, ELIMO (1932-   ). Born at Marangu near Moshi in
1932 and attended Old Moshi and Tabora Secondary
Schools. He studied in the School of Fine Art in Makerere University College in 1953 and was awarded the Fine
Art Diploma and Education Diploma in 1957. For a
while he was Art Master of Makerere Demonstration
School. He since founded Kibo Art Gallery on Mt. Kili-

manjaro which exhibits works of many East African ar-
tists. Njau was awarded a British Council scholarship
to study the works of art in the major art galleries in
Britain. He held an exhibition of his own work in the
Commonwealth Institute of London. Njau is a most gifted
painter by virtue of his imaginative powers combined with
forceful technique and a very personal style. He does
many mural paintings and African landscapes.

NORWEGIAN LUTHERAN MISSION. In 1950 this mission took
over from the Swedish missionaries at Mbulu. At that
time there were 170 Christians and 150 catechists. New
stations were built at Kansay in 1951, Hydom in 1953,
Mbulu in 1955, in addition to Dongobesh. As the church
increased, new centers of worship were opened up. The
fear of hospitals decreased as the years went by. The
Synod is called Mbulu and Pastor Bartholomayo Yonathan
is in charge. By 1976 there were 10,000 members, 12
pastors and 66 evangelists.

NSEKELA, AMON J. (1930-). Born on 4 January, 1930, near
Rungwe and attended secondary schools at Malangali and
Tabora, then went on to Makerere, taught several years,
then got an M.A. in History and Political Science at the
University of Pacific, California. He holds a diploma in
education also. Then he began a series of government
jobs--Administrative Officer, Establishment Office, Principal and Permanent Secretaryship to a variety of ministries, Chairman and Managing Director of the National
Bank of Commerce, 1967-68, Chairman of the National
Insurance Corporation of Tanzania, Ltd. 1966-68, Direct-
or of East African Airways from 1968, Director of Tanganyika and Italian Petroleum Co., Ltd. He also wrote
a history of Tanzania in Swahili. In 1974 he was appointed High Commissioner to Britain.

NTARI, CHIEFTESS THERESA. Born at Kasulu near Kigoma
and received a secondary education at Tabora Girls Secondary School. At seventeen she succeeded her father to
be chief of Kasulu and she administered for 17 years.
She was Mwami (Chief) from 1946-63. She was elected
President of the Chief's Convention, 1957-61, and was a
member of Legislative Council, later National Assembly,
from 1958. She was Parliamentary Secretary to the
Minister of Community Development and National Culture
in 1962 and to the Ministry of National Cultural and Youth
in 1963. She then retired into private life in Dar es

Salaam.   In the 1970's she took up a job with the East
African Community at Arusha.

NYAKYUSA (tribe).   They were, in 1948, the ninth largest
    tribe in Tanganyika with 192,000 members.   They orig-
    inated in the Livingstone Mts. of Rungwe District.
    Their agriculture is highly developed and intensive with
    a variety of crops--bananas, finger millet, maize, cas-
    sava, sweet potatoes, groundnuts and two major crops,
    coffee and rice.   The cultivation was traditionally done
    by men and boys.   As the men seek employment outside,
    women take over.   Cattle of a short-horned, humped type
    are fairly numerous and highly prized.   They are among
    the best known of the African peoples in the literature of
    social anthropology.   They have two interesting indigenous
    social organizations: a residential pattern of age-vil-
    lages; and a rapid proliferation of independent chiefdoms
    as these are divided regularly in each generation.   They
    differ from other Bantus in that their village is organized
    by a system of age sets rather than kinsmen and by a
    system of inheritance in which property passes from
    brother to brother rather than father to son.

NYAMWEZI (tribe).   The "people of the Moon" near Tabora
    are one of the largest tribes in Tanzania, sometimes
    considered to be the second.   They moved into Central
    and Northern Tanganyika from the Northeast probably
    before A.D. 1350.   Around 1700 to 1800 the Nyamwezi
    became an important trading people.   Whole clans would
    travel with their cattle as far west as the Congo forest
    to collect copper, wax, ivory, and slaves.   They then
    travelled to the coast to exchange them for cloth, metal
    tools, pots and cowries.   By 1839 Sultan Said made a
    treaty with the Nyamwezi Chief Fundikira, which enabled
    his subjects to travel across Unyamwezi to trade.
    Mwene Sela (Fundikira's successor) was friendly with the
    Arabs.   The Nyamwezi provided food, ivory, porters,
    hospitality and trading information in return for a share
    of profits.   But Mwene Sela grew to dislike the Zanzi-
    baris and their dominance of the trade they gained in the
    1850's.   He turned against them, so they supported a
    rival, Mkasiwa who became a puppet ruler at Unyanyem-
    be.   Around 1860 Mene Sela fought the Arabs for 4-5
    years.   From 1871-1884 Mirambo and Nyungu ya Mawe
    successfully resisted the Zanzibaris and regained control
    of the trade routes west and south of Tabora.   The
    Arabs still controlled Unyanyembe and the new ruler

Isike, but their power was weakened and never recovered.
After Mirambo's death in 1884, his kingdom broke up into small groups again as he had not trained an heir or
built a proper system of government.   Nyungu ya Mawe
died the same year and was succeeded by his daughter.
The Nyamwezi made wood sculptures in the form of abstract statuettes of ancestors for use in their religious
rituals.   A considerable number of Nyamwezi are mobile
due to the tsetse fly-infested area in which they live and
herd their cattle.   Group cooperation is very important
especially in the millet growing area where cultivating
and threshing were done together.   They are both farmers and herders.   As a whole, they are hard-working,
law abiding and very likeable traditionalists.   In 1948
the census count was 363,000.

NYERERE, JOSEPH KIZURIRA (1934-).   Born near Musoma
and is a brother of President Nyerere.   He was educated
at St. Mary's Secondary School, Tabora (1950-53) and at
St. Francis College, Dar es Salaam (1954).   He was
TANU's District Secretary at Musoma in 1955 and then
moved to TANU Headquarters (1955-57).   He was Adult
Mass Education Organiser and Chairman of TANU Youth
League (1957-59).   He has been a member of National
Assembly since 1960, a member of the Central Committee of TANU and National Executive of TANU.   He was
Junior Minister in the Ministry of Culture and Youth and
of Information and Tourism, was Regional Commissioner
of Mwanza (1964-67), and Secretary General of the TANU
Youth League.   The most recent position is membership
in the East African Legislative Council with the appointment made in 1976.

NYERERE, JULIUS KAMBARAGE (1922-).   Born in March
1922 at Butiama, a small village near Lake Victoria.
He was named after a rain spirit because it was raining.
He is the son of Chief Nyerere Burito of the Zanaki tribe
and his 18th wife Mugaya.   At eight he entered Musoma
Middle School and at twelve entered Tabora Government
School and was made a prefect.   As a prefect, privileges
included a double ration, something he agitated against.
From 1943-45 he was at Makerere University College
where he received a diploma in education.   As a star
debater, he introduced international affairs into the discussions.   While still at Makerere, he began TAWA
(Tanganyika African Welfare Association), but later decided to work through TAA.   Being a Catholic, he was

given a teaching position at St. Mary's Mission School,
Tabora, where he taught history and biology to the top
forms for three years.   In 1949 he was Tanganyika's
first student to enroll in a British University and received
a B.A. at Edinburgh.   He was the first Tanzanian to be
awarded a M.A. (1952).   It seems as though the foundations of his political philosophy were laid while at Edinburgh.

He returned to Tanzania and became History Master at St. Francis College, Pugu, near Dar es Salaam.
He married Maria Gabriel on 24 January, 1953.   During
that same year he became President of TAA.   On May
12, 1954, he was appointed a temporary member of the
Legislative Council to replace David Makwaia serving on
the Royal Commission for Land and Population Problems.
When TANU was formed on 7 July, 1954, he was made
its first President.   On 22 March, 1955, he resigned as
a history teacher at St. Francis.   The Maryknoll Fathers
gave him a job translating the Catechism and Gospel into
Zanaki, to write a Zanaki grammar and to teach Fr. Wil-
le the Zanaki language.   In the autumn of 1955, he completed the job and returned to Dar es Salaam.   Maria ran
a small shop for finances while he gave his time to political activities.

During 1955 he took TANU demands to the U. N.
Nyerere returned to the U. S. A. in 1956, lectured in colleges and secured scholarships for Tanzanians.   He also
appeared on television.   On 20 December, 1956, he ad-
dressed the Fourth Committee at the U. N.   After his
U. N. speech, Governor Twining instructed the Secretariat
to correct the misrepresentations in Nyerere's Speech to
the 4th Committee and to place a ban on his open-air
meetings because of the inflammatory statements he was
making.   The pamphlet was printed in April 1956.   So
Nyerere went to the villagers in Tanzania and talked to
the elders for four months.   Sauti ya Tanu (Voice of TA-
NU) was printed irregularly.   In February 1957 he made
a third visit to the U. N.   He was also nominated a member of Legislative Council in 1957, but he resigned later
in protest at lack of progress.   Nyerere was made Chairman of Tanganyika's Elected Members Organisation.
From July-August 1958 he was tried for libel (he denies
writing the article in the Party paper) and ordered to pay
a fine or go to jail.   Governor Turnbull had dissuaded
him and he paid the fine.   In 1959 he visited the U. S. A.
and Canada as a State Guest for five days.   He advocated
the establishment of an East African Federation and was

prepared to postpone Tanganyika's independence if it
could be formed.

When Tanganyika received its preliminary responsible Self-Government in October 1960, he was its Chief
Minister.   In May 1961 full self-government was attained.
Soon after Independence (9 December, 1961) he resigned
as Prime Minister and was out from January to December 1962 building up the Party, leaving the government
administration to Rashidi Kawawa.   In December 1962
Tanganyika became a Republic with J. K. Nyerere as its
first President.   On 14 January, 1963, he announced a
One-Party system of government to be introduced.   It
came into effect in 1965.   He has been elected president
in 1962 on a 98 percent majority vote, in 1965, 1970 and
1975.   Very few "No's" are stated each time.

He broke off diplomatic relations with Great Britain from 1965-68 due to Great Britain's failure to act in
the Rhodesian crisis over UDI.   When the university students demonstrated against the National Service Act in
1966, he slashed all middle- and high-level government
salaries including his own of £3,000 a year to narrow
the yawning salary-basic wage gap.   In 1967 he authored
the Arusha Declaration.   It is said that he wrote it out
by hand during the Arusha Conference.   He has been the
philosopher and main policy maker for TANU, humbly
explaining through discussions or speeches and literally
taking part in the Self-Help schemes and Self-Reliance
activities in Ujamaa villages.   He is called Mwalimu
(teacher) by the citizens.   He has written many articles
and books and his speeches are compiled into several
books.   Nyerere was awarded an honorary degree as
Doctor of Law from Duquesne University, U.S.A., in
1960, a second one from Edinburgh University, Scotland
later and in 1966 an honorary degree of Doctor of Philosophy from the University of Cairo.   He became the
Chancellor of the University of East Africa and Fellow
of Makerere College in 1963 and Visitor of University
College, Dar es Salaam.   He translated Shakespeare's
Julius Caesar into Swahili.

NYERERE, MARIA (GABRIEL).   A daughter of Gabriel and
    Anna Magige and wife of President Julius K. Nyerere.
    She is a Simbiti from Kinesi in North Mara near Musoma.
    She studied at the White Sisters Girls' School at Sumve
    near Mwanza for eight years and obtained a teaching cer-
    tificate, becoming the first woman teacher of her tribe.
    She also studied at St. Joseph's Convent, Dar es Salaam,

to perfect her English and general education.   She was
married on 24 January, 1953, at Musoma after a six-
years' engagement to Julius Nyerere.   She has been a
leader in encouraging women to take a more active role
in development projects and social services.

NYIHA (tribe).   They consider the Mbozi District in Mbeya
Region to be their place of origin.   They numbered over
25,000 in 1931, 54,000 in 1948 and 56,000 in 1957.
They are patrilineal by descent and were traditionally
hunters.   They now cultivate and keep cattle.

NYIKA PLATEAU.   Covers two-thirds of Tanganyika and lies
1000 to 3000 feet above sea level.   It is narrow, little
more than 50 miles wide at Tanga Region, but widens in
the Southern part of Tanganyika where it reaches almost
to the shore of Lake Nyasa.   It has many old hard crys-
talline rocks.

NYIRENDA, MATTHEW.   Born in Nyasaland and recruited as
a dispenser in 1926.   He built up the general and TB
services of Mwika Dispensary and was awarded the British Empire medal in 1948.   He was on leave pending
retirement in 1955 when he suffered a stroke and died
of heart failure in the Moshi Hospital soon afterward.
His son, Second Lieutenant Alexander Nyirenda was the
first African (Tanzanian) commissioned from Sandhurst.
He joined the Tanganyika Rifles in 1961 and hoisted the
new flag and lit a torch on Mt. Kilimanjaro on 9 December, 1961.

NYUMBA YA MUNGU DAM.   Situated on the Pangani River
30 miles south of Moshi.   The 140 ft. high by 1300 ft.
long edifice was completed in December 1966.   Its purpose was to control river floods and to make more water
available for irrigation and power.   The 8000 kilowatt
hydro-electric power station began operation in early
1966.

NYUNGU YA MAWE (?-1884).   A member of the Nyamwezi
chiefly family.   He fled in 1865 after the death of Mwana
Sele.   He made his capital at Kiwale and in 1870 dominated most of the Kimbu country.   Between 1870 and
1880 his warriors campaigned successfully over most of
the country east and south of Tabora.   He subdued most
of the Kimbu chiefdoms with the Rugaruga.   He developed
a more durable administration system than Mirambo; he

created a special class of territorial governors (vatwale) over the conquered areas who had no local ties (similar to akidas) and who owed allegiance to him.   He was ruthless, a brilliant general and clever administrator. When he died in 1884, he was succeeded by a daughter.

- O -

OKELLO, JOHN (1937-   ).   "Field Marshall" of the Zanzibar Revolution, he was born near Lira in Lango District of Northern Uganda on 6 October, 1937, and a bricklayer by profession.   He came to Zanzibar in 1959 and worked in Pemba for several years as a mason, painter and occasional laborer.   He gravitated towards the ASP and by 1961 was the secretary of the ASP Youth wing for Pemba.   He moved to Zanzibar Island in early 1963.   He shot suddenly into the world political limelight as a result of the vital part he played in overthrowing the Government of His Majesty the Sultan of Zanzibar: He commanded the "freedom fighters."   In March 1964 he was prohibited from returning to Zanzibar and expelled from Tanganyika and Kenya.   He returned to Uganda and has since served a number of jail sentences in Kenya and breaches of security regulations in Uganda.

OLDUVAI GORGE.   Located due north of the tip of Lake Eyasi and is a tourist attraction.   In 1911 Professor Kattwinkel of Berlin discovered Olduvai Gorge when it was in German East Africa.   His discovery was in a sense accidental.   He had been sent from the Berlin Museum to collect insects.   One day, when he was chasing a rare butterfly across the southeast corner of the Serengeti Plains, he almost fell to his death over a 300-ft. cliff.   He did not get his butterfly, but he found fossil bones sticking out of the rock face as he climbed over the cliff edge.   He took some specimens back to his friends whom he thought would be interested in seeing them.   Kattwinkel's accidental discovery of Olduvai Gorge led to important work carried on there before World War I by a Professor Hans Rech who handed it over much later to L. S. B. Leakey.

      Before 1959 a piece of upper jaw containing two teeth from the Laetolil beds in Northern Tanganyika and two large milk teeth were seen at Olduvai Gorge.   In July 1959 Mrs. Leakey discovered a skull (Zinjanthropus) in the lowest bed of Olduvai Gorge, Bed I, which was

named "Nutcracker Man" because of the enormous size
of his molars. Zinj is the ancient name given to East
Africa. The skull was associated with a living floor
which contained numerous waste flakes knocked off in
making Oldowan choppers, a broken hammer stone and
fragments of bones of small animals and birds which
formed part of the diet of Zinjanthropus.

Eighteen months later Leakey reported the discovery of the remains of a juvenile creature even older
than Zinjanthropus as well as fragments of an adult.
The child was no more than twelve years old at death;
this was represented by a clavicle, bones of the foot
and hand, a lower jaw and two parietal bones. The
parietals are larger than those of the adult Zinjanthropus, suggesting that this hominid had a bigger brain. In
July 1961 Drs. J. F. Everden and G. H. Curtis of the
University of California established the date for the Zinjanthropus level to be 1, 750,000 years. Evidence from
Olduvai shows that the prey of these hunters were of
huge proportions. There is no evidence that Zinjanthropus killed those animals. In 1961 Leakey found a skull-
cap of an individual from Bed II at Olduvai. It has
enormous brow-ridges and is very like Pithecanthropus
of Java and Peking.

OLE SAIBUL, SOLOMON ALEXANDER (1935-). Born in
    Arusha area and educated at Ilboru Secondary School
    (1953-54), Tabora Senior Secondary School (1955-56),
    Makerere University College (1957-61) and Exeter Uni-
    versity (1961-63). He has worked with the Ministry of
    Lands, Forest and Wild Life since 1963, rising to Con-
    servator at Ngorongoro Crater (1965). In November
    1975 he was appointed Minister for Natural Resources
    and Tourism.

OMARI, DUNSTAN ALFRED (1922-). Born on 2 August,
    1922, at Newala and educated in St. Joseph's Secondary
    School, Masasi and St. Andrew's College, Minaki. He
    received a diploma in education at Makerere College in
    1945 and taught at St. Joseph's and Tanga Secondary
    Schools (1946-49). He then went to the University of
    Wales for a B.A. in Economics at Aberystwyth in 1953.
    He returned to Tanzania and rejoined the civil service
    as an education officer (broadcasting) in the Social Wel-
    fare Department. He was the first African to be ap-
    pointed District Officer in Tanganyika (1955), also the
    first District Commissioner (1958-61). In 1960 he was

awarded the M. B. E.   He served as High Commissioner
for Tanganyika to London (1961-62), Permanent Secretary
in the President's Office (1966) and head of Tanganyika
Civil Service and Secretary to the Cabinet.   In 1964 he
was appointed Secretary General of EACSO and later for
the East African Community in 1967.   He went to live in
Nairobi in 1968, was company director of 20 or more
companies and a management consultant.

ORMSBY-GORE COMMISSION.   A British Parliamentary
Commission, visited East Africa in 1924 to consider and
report on, among other things, "measures to be taken to
accelerate the general economic development of the East
African dependencies, and the means of securing closer
coordination of policy on such matters as transportation,
cotton-growing, control of human, animal and plant dis-
eases. " It recommended regular, periodic conferences
of relevant Governments and of officials to deal with matters of common interest; a complete customs union of the
three countries; uniformity of commercial law on companies, bankruptcy, patents, designs and trademarks;
creation of a central research institute at Amani to serve
all three countries; and operation of the Voi/Kahe Railway
Line by the Uganda R. R.

OROMBO (sometimes called Horombo).   A tall, young Chagga
man with no hereditary claim to leadership (it is widely
believed that he was of Masai origin), but rose to power
around 1800 through trade with Pare iron.   He built a
large "empire" (two-thirds of Chagga land) with his capital at Keni--all built with slave labor.   This was the
earliest Chagga empire.   He led raids for cattle and
slaves.   He never kept slaves long; he brought them to
work for him for a time and then they returned to their
homes and he brought another supply.   He had 37 wives
from all over his kingdom.   In each conquered area he
appointed a local leader to be in charge as his righthand
man. He was killed in a campaign against some Masai.
After his death his empire collapsed and reverted back
to small, local units.

- P -

PALLOTTINE FATHERS.   Began to work in the Prefecture
Apostolic of Mbulu by 1943.   The greater part of the
new Prefecture had hitherto been attached to the Vicar-

iate Apostolic of Tabora. The eastern part had been a section of the Vicariate of Kilimanjaro. They amalgamated with other orders to form the present Tanzanian Episcopal Conference (TEC).

PANGANI. A seacoast town nearer to Tanga than Bagamoyo. It had 3200 inhabitants by 1905 and has been greatly influenced by the Arab-Swahili culture. It was once a flourishing center for the export of slaves, but now relies on the copra industry for most of its trade.

PANGANI RIVER. In Northeastern Tanzania, it has been developed for hydroelectric power and supplies Arusha, Moshi, Tanga, Morogoro and Dar es Salaam. It rises in the Mt. Kilimanjaro snows and flows to the Indian Ocean between the Masai Steppe and the Pare and Usambara Mountain Ranges. A 21,000-kilowatt Hale hydroelectric power station is located on the River southwest of Tanga and a 17,500-kilowatt Grand Pangani Falls power station is located immediately south of it. North of the Hale scheme is a 8000-kilowatt hydroelectric power station at Nyumba ya Mungu.

PARE or ASU (tribe). A Bantu tribe numbering more than 150,000, they are found in the highlands of northeastern Tanzania. Pare were considered separate from the Gweno people in the description Krapf gave of the area and it seems that, until the beginning of the 19th century, they were two separate communities which grew closer and closer during the second half of the 18th century with the peopling of Middle Pare. The division between the two communities formed a natural geographical demarcation boundary. Sometime around A.D. 1500 the Wasuya clan successfully organized a revolution and overthrew the smiths, the Washana. During the crisis a people called Wabwamba moved into South Pare. Later others came from the Taita Hills, Nguu Mts., Usambara, and Masai Steppes. New settlers from Zigua country as well as Pare from North and South Pare, filled the Middle Belt. Caravan routes passed through Pareland. Wagweno sold ivory and made raids for captives to be sold as slaves. Rindi of Moshi, after an alliance with Ghendewa of North Pare, finally raided Pare and Mashombo raided South Pare. German authority reached the Pare in 1891.

PASSIONIST FATHERS. The Prefecture of Dodoma was erected in 1935 and given to these missionaries from Northern

Italy.   It became a Vicariate in 1951 and a diocese in
1953.   The northern part of the Diocese was detached
from the Vicariate of Kilimanjaro; the Central and Western parts from Bagamoyo and the Southern part from
Iringa.   They later amalgamated with other orders to
form the present Tanzania Episcopal Conference (TEC).

PEACE CORPS.   Came from the U.S.A. as teachers first
in 1963 and taught in the upper primary school classes.
A great demand was for vocational and agricultural education teachers.   Teachers were not replaced after a
two-year assignment.   A few volunteers remained on
road construction, but the positions as a whole were
filled with locals.

PEANUTS   see   GROUNDNUTS

PEMBA ISLAND.   The Sultan's "other" island with Zanzibar,
it is smaller than Zanzibar, being 42 miles at its longest and 14 miles at its widest.   It has an area of 380
square miles, is fertile and has a varied topography with
small, steep hills and valleys.   It produces 85 percent
of the cloves of Zanzibar Islands.   It receives more than
80" of rainfall on its western coastline.   The Arab name
for Pemba is "al Khudhra" (the green island).   The
Queen of Pemba and her son, the King of Otongo, are
mentioned in the second Cabreira expedition.   Persian
settlers are believed to have arrived about the 10th century.   They made a strong impact as a unifying force
among formerly separate villages.   Early references to
Pemba mention it as a place of provision for large ships
to Mombasa and Malindi in 1506 and that it had 4 or 5
quarrelling kings.   The Portuguese subdued it in 1510.
Pemba supplied grain and timber to Mombasa.   The Portuguese and local relationships were hostile.   The Turkish
raid killed or drove out the Portuguese by 1585.   Cabreira
"plagued" the people of Pemba in 1634 at twenty-seven
years of age.   The new Sultan of Mombasa claimed the
island in 1605 and took it by force the following year.
His successor Hasan was recognized as ruler of Pemba
and paid an annual tribute of rice to the Captain of Mombasa.   The Mazrui Governor revived the lordship and
exercised authority in the 18th century, but shared the
customs with the Sultan of Pate.   The 1728 treaty between
the Portuguese and Pate gave Pate claim to part of the
island.   Pemba was taken from the Mazrui's in 1822 by
Sultan Said's Governor of Zanzibar.

The Arab authority developed by agreement rather than by force. Arab-African relationships have been more amicable than on Zanzibar Island. The clove and coconut plantations were held both by Arab and Shirazi families. Squatters were permitted to settle on the land but could claim no land right. The 1967 census gave a total population of 164,243.

PEOPLE'S CONVENTION PARTY (PCP). Formed at Mwanza in 1962 in opposition to "radical" legislation. It opposed government land bills and played upon the fears of the African farmers that their land could be confiscated. Samson Masalla was the PCP president. The PCP was refused registration by the Regional Commissioner in Mwanza. Since chiefs had lost their traditional power, it had caught the interest of several of them for a while.

PEOPLE'S DEMOCRATIC PARTY (PDP). Formed in 1962 under the leadership of C. K. Tumbo. Tumbo believed in a more Africanization policy. On other social issues, the party was rather conservative as it attempted to play to specific grievances. Tumbo was appointed High Commissioner to London and the Party went into oblivion within a year of its creation and some of its founders were appropriated by the People's Convention Party.

PEOPLE'S LIBERATION ARMY (PLA). Formed in Zanzibar after the Revolution of 12 January, 1964. Those insurgents in the Revolution formed its nucleus and others joined them. After the Union of Zanzibar and Tanganyika on 26 April, 1964, the PLA united with the Tanganyika Rifles to form the TPDF.

PEOPLE'S REPUBLIC OF ZANZIBAR. Had a short life, from 12 January, 1964, after the Revolution until 26 April, 1964, when it united with the mainland to form the People's Republic of Tanzania.

PER CAPITA INCOME. Annual income estimated to be, in 1976, $137 or over 700 shillings.

PERIODICALS AND NEWSPAPERS. The following are some that have been and are being printed in Tanzania and East Africa:
1. Dar es Salaam Times, 1919-26; Tanganyika Times, 1926-30; Tanganyika Standard and Tanganyika Weekly Standard, 1930-72; Daily News and Sunday

News, 1972- , Dar es Salaam.
2. Amtlicher Anzeiger fur deutsch-Ostafrika, Dar es
   Salaam, 1900-16.
3. Das Hochland, 1930-37.
4. Deutsch-Ostafrikanische Rundschau, Dar es Salaam,
   1908-12.
5. Deutsch-Ostafrikanische Zeitung, Dar es Salaam,
   1899-1914.
6. Der Pflanzer, Tanga, 1905-10; Dar es Salaam, 1911-
   14.
7. Tanga Post and East Coast Advertiser, 1919-25.
8. Usambara-Post, Tanga, 1904-14.
9. Zanzibar Official Gazette, from 1914.
10. Tanganyika Official Gazette, from 1919; UR of Tanzania Gazette.
11. East African Economic Review--semi-annual.
12. East Africa Journal from 1964.
13. East Africa Medical Journal.
14. Mbioni (Kivukoni College monthly).
15. Tanzania News and Review from 1936.
16. Tanzania Trade and Industry.
17. Uchumi from 1970 (Economics).
18. Zamani from 1967 (History).

PERIPLUS OF THE ERYTHRAEAN SEA. A trader's handbook
   to the commerce of the Indian Ocean written in the first
   or early third century A.D.   The author was an Alexan-
   drian Greek.   The island of Menouthias was probably
   Zanzibar; Rhapta called after the sewn boats; and the
   Swahili Mtepe was possibly the area of Kisiju south of
   Dar es Salaam where an allegedly Roman head was found.

PERMANENT COMMISSION OF ENQUIRY. Established by the
   constitution and has the power to enquire into the conduct
   of the holder of any office in the government and governmental organizations. It is intended to protect the individual rights of citizens and to consider allegations of mis-
   conduct. The Court system is under the supervision of
   this commission and headed by the Chief Justice. The
   Commission determines policy, regulates judicial practices and controls magisterial appointments. It is subject
   to the direct control of the President, but otherwise un-
   challenged and is guaranteed independence from political
   control.

PETER, DR. KARL. The President of the Gesselschaft für
   Deutsche Kolonisation (Society for German Colonization)

founded in 1884, landed secretly in Zanzibar with two
other friends on November 1884.   They proceeded to the
mainland and obtained treaties with chiefs in the area
between Rivers Pangani and Rufiji.   Large tracts of land
were handed over "for all time" in exchange for a few
trinkets.   He returned to Europe with the treaties where
they were confirmed by Bismarck and officially annexed
without reference to the Sultan.   The rights of the Society were ceded to the new German East Africa Company
also headed by Peters.   By 1891 Peters was a Reich
Commissioner in the Colonial Service.   He became cruel
and ordered the hanging of a native servant called Malruk
for petty theft.   He was nicknamed "Mkono wa damu"
(The man with the blood-stained hands).   Peters was also
found guilty of dereliction of duty on various occasions
and of "conduct unworthy of his official position. "   In
1893 he was dismissed from the Colonial Service and deprived of his title and pension.   He also had to pay for
the costs of the hearings.

PHILIP COMMISSION.   Created in mid-1965 under the leadership of a Danish economist, Kjeld Philip.   Its responsibility was to examine the existing and long-range problems
of economic unity in East Africa.   They did a comprehensive study and their suggestions were embodied in the
Treaty for East African Cooperation which the Heads of
the East African States signed in June 1967.

PHOSPHATE.   Found in Minjingu Hill east of Lake Manyara.
It was formed from bird guano dropped on an island when
the lake was larger.   The high quality phosphate totals
ten metric tons.

POGORO (tribe).   They inhabit the hilly country in the Ulanga
District. Their economy is based on agriculture, but they also used to keep cattle.   They were reputed for their
rain-making ceremonies and their divination.   They are
organized into a number of small chiefdoms.

POLICE.   A centrally controlled force including men and
women charged with law enforcement.   Some of the older
members are veterans of the colonial service while younger members are graduates of the police colleges.   The
Tanzania Police numbered 8250 in the 1967 census.   The
force is proportionately small, one policeman to 1, 500
citizens for every 72 square miles.   The Women Police
have mainly administrative and secretarial functions.   The

Hehe and Kuria have adapted well to police work and
make up almost 50 percent of the force.   Besides their
regular duties, the police have detachments to patrol
railroads and harbors, the Women's Police Division and
the Dog Section.   The Mounted Police Unit was formed
in 1966 and has six horses which are used to control
crowds.   The Criminal Investigation Department (CID)
plays a very important part in the force.   At the end of
1971 there were 50 Tanzanian technicians and 352 radio
operators in the Signals Branch.   The Police Marine
Unit opened in 1965.   The Police Air-Wing was organized
in 1971 and was primarily concerned with tracking cattle
rustlers.   Since 1969 the Police Training School at Moshi
offers training to prison and immigration officers as well
as police and came under the Ministry of Home Affairs.
The Police College at Dar es Salaam opened during 1961
and accommodates 60 officers at a time.   Police are regarded as potential reserves for national emergencies and
are active in politics, a right granted in 1964.   The Inspector General of Police was a member of the TANU
Central Committee.

POLYGAMY.   The practice of a married person having more
than one partner.   The type commonly practiced in Tanzania is polygyny--the man with more than one wife.
See POLYGYNY.

POLYGYNY.   The marriage situation of a man who has more
than one wife.   It is common in Tanzania and legally accepted.   A polygynous family may live in one, two or
more households, depending on whether the wives live and
work together or have separate houses and fields.   Each
wife is entitled to a house or hut and shamba (plot of
ground).   The first wife generally holds a special position
and is consulted about each new wife.   She can refuse the
marriage and her husband will forget the idea.   Younger
wives can be ordered about by her and some wait on her,
treating her like a mother.   There is little difference in
the status among co-wives (excluding the senior wife) and
they often show jealousy among themselves.   If they do
not live in a large communal, the husband circulates
among the number of villages, spending time with each
wife separately.   The Moslem religion permits some polygamy and a number of the African independent churches
sanction it.   Most of the Roman Catholic and Protestant
churches are not in favor of it.

Population Composition   164

POPULATION COMPOSITION. The composition of the population was created by the following migrations: 1) Original
peoples (Bushmanoid race) are considered to have been a
type of the Bushman of South Africa. Remnants speak
the Khoisan language and are hunters on grasslands. The
Hadzapi and Sandawe are remnants. 2) The "ancient Azanians" were Caucasoids who arrived around 1000 B. C.
Sometimes they are called "Southern Cushites." They introduced domestic cattle and possibly cereal cultivation.
They populated the adjoining areas of Kenya highlands in
Northern Tanzania. Some of the traces they left are:
stone burial chambers; hut circles; terraced fields; roads
and irrigation works; tall, bearded, red-skinned people;
and the Iraqw of Northern Tanzania as living descendants
whose language is identified as Cushitic. The Greek
treatise Periplus (1st c. A. D.) covered the area as far
south on the coast as Zanzibar and no mention was made
of black people. 3) The Bantu, of Negroid stock, came
around A. D. 1000. 4) The Nilo-Hamites from the North
arrived after A. D. 1000. They are more recently called
Cushitic. They controlled the highland area in Kenya
down to Iringa. 5) Nilotes (Luo) after A. D. 1600. They
were numerous enough to preserve a language, but not
sufficient to form a substantial state. 6) In the 18th century, the Sukuma and Nyamwezi moved eastward in Tanzania. See also BANTU.

POPULATION STATISTICS. Census totals: In 1905 the population of the mainland was estimated at 4,000,000. The
1914 Zanzibar total was 197,199 with 114,000 on Zanzibar
Island and 83,130 on Pemba Island. On the mainland:

Year	Africans	Indians	Arabs	Europeans	Others
*1921	4,107,000	9,441	4,041	2,447	1,539
†1948	-	-	-	-	-
°1957	8,942,000	84,100	23,300	23,100	4,300
**1967	12,178,000	122,000	-	12,200	-
†††1976	-	-	-	-	-

Totals:
*4,124,447; †7,477,677; °9,076,000; **12,200,000; ††13,063,220

The total given for Tanzania in its entirety for 1977 is
15,252,000.

Rate of growth: The population growth rate for
Tanganyikan Africans is as follows: 1931-48, 1 percent;

1948-47, 1.75 percent; 1957-65, 2 percent; 1966, 2.25 percent; 1964-69, 2.3 percent; 1974, 2.7 percent.

Mortality rate: (See also LIFE EXPECTANCY.) In 1920, 300 children out of 1000 live births in Tanganyika died before reaching adulthood; in 1948, 220 out of 1000; in 1958, 190 (T) plus 160 (Z) per thousand; and in 1975, 152 per thousand. More than 40 percent of the population are under fifteen years of age.

Density per square mile: Tanzania ranges from 3 to 800 people per square mile. The following chart shows the breakdown of population density.

Year	Tanganyika	Zanzibar
1958	10 per sq. mile	24 per sq. mile
1964	25.8	293
1967	34.8	347.1

Urban population: In 1950-52, 3.3 percent of Tanganyika's and 27 percent of Zanzibar's population lived in urban areas. In 1967, the percentage had risen to 4.8 (T) and 50 percent (Z). Towns have over 60 percent of the non-African population. Over half of the population lives on one-sixth of the land area.

PORTUGUESE. The arrival of the Portuguese at Zanzibar in the 16th century had minimal influence on the course of Tanzania's history. However, they did make the following contributions: 1) They added a number of words to the Swahili language; 2) their links with India brought many traders and craftsmen; and 3) they introduced new crops, mainly from the Americas: maize, groundnuts, cassava, sweet potatoes, pineapples, pawpaws and guavas. The ill effects of their control resulted when they plundered and disrupted trade on the coast, exacted heavy taxes, and accumulated personal loot.

POSTAL SERVICE. In 1933 Tanganyika joined the customs union originally established by Kenya and Uganda in 1923 and postal services were amalgamated. East African Postal Services and Communications operates under the East African Community. In Tanzania there are over 100 branches of the Savings Bank operated by the Postal Service. The growth rate of the postal services (from 184 post offices in 1963 to 267 in 1966) exceeded the growth rate of the population, reflecting rural development and a growth in the rate of literacy. Services ex-

ceeded 300 post offices as Ujamaa villages were established.

PRATT, ROBERT CRANFORD (1926-). Born in Canada in
1926 and attended McGill University and was a Rhodes
Scholar at Balliol College, Oxford in 1950-52. After a
lectureship in Political Science at Makerere University
College (1954-56) and an assistant professorship at Mc-
Gill University (1956-58), he took two extensive field
research trips to East and Central Africa with the Institute of Commonwealth Studies at Oxford. He is the
writer of Buganda and British Overrule and co-author of
A New Deal in Central Africa. He was appointed Principal of University College, Dar es Salaam in 1961 when
it opened its first faculty, the Faculty of Law. He was
succeeded by Dr. W. K. Chagula.

PRESBYTERIAN CHURCH. Came to Dar es Salaam in 1950
and has since begun in Tanga as well. There are three
worship centers and about 500 members. The Church
took over from the mission in 1956. It has been a member of CCT since 1973. Rev. George Cooper is the
Chairman and James Msikinya is Church Secretary.
Their pastoral training is done in St. Paul's College,
Limuru, Kenya.

PRESIDENT OF THE UNITED REPUBLIC OF TANZANIA.
The Head of State and Commander in Chief of the Armed
Forces. He has initial veto power over all legislation.
He appoints the cabinet ministers, Chief Justice and other
members of the High Court, officers in the judicial system and up to 10 members in the National Assembly. He
has the power to make or abolish offices and to terminate
appointments.

PRIMARY EDUCATION. In Tanganyika it had been the responsibility of government and voluntary agencies from the
German era to 1970 when all schools were nationalized.
In 1945 only 7.5 percent of Tanganyika's children attended
school, but by 1958 it had reached 24.1 percent. It rose
to 50 percent and held there during the 1960's as the
number of school places increased with the rate of population increase. With the stress and expansion of primary
education again in the 1970's, the figure rose to 60 percent in 1975. Universal primary education was targeted
for 1977. In the 1960's about 10-13 percent of primary
school "graduates" found places in the secondary schools

and the majority of the rest were just squeezed out of
the system.   In 1975, 6.4 percent of the primary school
leavers had joined secondary schools, so primary education has taken on a new aim--to prepare a complete education for life rather than preparatory for further formal
education.   A work-study education emphasis began with
the Arusha Declaration in 1967.
    Primary education consisted of Standards I to IV
for many years with an examination at the end of Std. IV
to serve as a base for selections to Std. V in the Middle
School.   Middle Schools were often boarding schools and
contained Std. V to VIII   Std. VIII was dropped at the end
of 1966 and primary education changed to Std. I to VII as
the primary schools added Std. V, then VI and VII as they
could build the classrooms and teachers could be provided.
For a picture of the expansion of primary education, the
following chart is added:

YEAR	SCHOOLS	PUPILS
1903	35	1,559
1911	-	35,511
1960	3270	450,000
1967	-	825,000
1971	4133	902,609
1974	-	2,183,070

In 1976 more than 156,000 students finished Std. VII and
more than one-third of them, or 56,000, were girls.
    In Zanzibar, they set up their Education Depart-
ment in 1907.   In 1910 there were 141 children in primary schools and 194 in eight District Schools.   By 1951
there were 13 grant-aided schools catering mainly to Indians, 35 primary schools with 4608 boys and 7 primary
schools with 1053 girls.
    Of the primary education on the mainland, 85
percent was in the hands of missions in 1945.   By independence about two-thirds of the schools were operated
by missions.   Therefore, time elapsed until 1970 when
the Tanzania Government could take over, or "nationalize"
the schools.   In 1967 the government had decreed that the
heads of all primary schools be Tanzanian citizens.
Std. VIII examinations had been written in English, so the
medium of instruction had shifted from Swahili to English
sometime during Std. VI.   From 1 January, 1968, the
language medium was to be Swahili for all subjects on all
levels of the primary school except in a few selected
schools which remained English medium schools.   English
was then taught only as a subject.

PRIMARY SCHOOL LEAVING EXAMINATION.   Called the
General Entrance Examination until 1966.   The name was
changed due to the function which it was to fulfill; it was
no longer an evaluation to select 13 percent of the
Std. VIII leavers who could find vacancies to enter Form 1
in secondary school.   It was to be considered as a method
of evaluating a successful completion of the primary
school course for all Std. VII pupils.   In 1968 examinations
were set in Swahili and English versions as the language
medium was changing and thereafter they were all set in
Swahili.

PRISONS SERVICE.   On the mainland it is under the Commissioner of Prisons as an agency of the Police Force.
There are around 50 prisons of 4 types on the mainland:
remand prisons, minimum security prison farms, the
prison for the mentally ill, and the maximum security
prison.   Most of the buildings were constructed by the
Germans before 1918.   Most offer vocational training
courses in an attempt to provide prisoners with a skill
marketable on their release.   Prison farms often supply
enough to meet feeding costs and basic maintenance work.
Detention facilities adjoin major police stations at regional
capitals and are sufficient for temporary detention.   Parole is granted for good behavior and character development.   A member of the CID section in the local area
supervises his parole period.
          In Zanzibar, vocational training and prison farms
provide work for the prisoners and defray the expenses
of the service.   The Social Insurance Department assists
discharged prisoners to reestablish themselves in society.

PROPERTY TAX.   Imposed in urban areas.   There are three
types of property taxes: a site rate or general rate on
the "unimproved value of land" held by the government
leasehold or long-term right of occupancy within its jurisdiction; the urban house tax levied against buildings and
houses on land not subject to the site tax; and the monies
paid in by the central government in lieu of the site tax
on property which the government controlled and by EACSO
on property which it had used.

PYRETHRUM.   First experimented with in Tanzania in 1932
at Ihemo Experimental Station, then Dabaga and Mufindi.
Tanzania is the second largest world producer after Kenya.
Tanzania's flowers have a large quantity of oil in the dry
flowers, averaging 1. 3 percent.   In Tanzania almost the

only processing done by 1961 was drying and pressing the
flower into bales.   By 1967 all the production was processed at Arusha, and the U. S. A. , the principal consumer,
was taking over 60 percent of the production.   Production
rose from 275 tons of dried flowers in 1953 to 1700 tons
in 1962, 4400 tons in 1966, and 5000 tons in 1967.   Then
pyrethrum fell off drastically from the 1966/67 season
due to the production of chlorinated hydrocarbon insecti-
cides.   However, the chemicals were found to be harmful
to man and animals, so pyrethrum stood a chance again.
In 1974/75 there were 4741 tons of dry flowers exported,
an increase of 1500 of 1973/74.   Pyrethrum is grown in
the Southern and Northern Highlands at Iringa, Njombe,
Mbeya, Arusha, Moshi and Mbulu.

- R -

RADIO TANZANIA.   Estimated to have a radio audience of
over four million or one-third of the total population.
Tanganyika Broadcasting Corporation began in 1951 as
the "Voice of Dar es Salaam. "   It became an independent
corporation in 1956 and in the same year a new 20-kilo-
watt transmitter permitted broadcasting to be heard all
over Tanzania.   The Corporation was dissolved on 1 July,
1965, and incorporated in the Ministry of Information and
Tourism as a Division--Radio Tanzania--under a Director.
Its services include: Swahili; English; Education (School
broadcasts began in 1954); External; and Commercial (begun in 1965).   One shortwave transmitter in Dar es Salaam broadcasts to southern Africa at 100 kilowatts.   The
Voice of Tanzania, Zanzibar, monitors separate programs.
In January 1973 a color television service, the first in
Black Africa, was begun in Zanzibar.

RADIO VOICE OF THE GOSPEL (Swahili: REDIO SAUTI YA
INJILI).   The present Lutheran Radio Centre at Moshi
had its beginning in July 1961 when F. E. Baglo, a Canadian, arrived at Mwika Bible School to take up the Directorship of a radio broadcasting program.   The following year the preparations for building and programming
were underway and the first program was heard on the
air in February 1963.   The Studio buildings were inaugurated in March 1963.   It has grown from a staff of 5 to
23.   Bishop Daniel Magogo is its fourth and present director.   The Moshi Centre prepared the tapes of the Swahili
programs for ten hours per week aired from Addis Ababa
until the Ethiopian station was nationalized in 1977.

RAILWAYS. Tanzania has around 2700 miles of track. The
Tanga Line was begun by the Germans in 1893, the Central Line was begun in Dar es Salaam in 1905 and completed in 1911. The TANZAM (Great Uhuru) Railway was
completed in 1976. In 1973 the Tanga Line was linked to
the main Kenya line. The East African Railways and
Harbours was a service within the East African Community and broke up into national railways in 1976. A train
ferry service was inaugurated on Lake Victoria in 1966.
See also CENTRAL LINE OF TANGANYIKA; TANGA
LINE; GREAT UHURU RAILWAY; and EAST AFRICAN
RAILWAYS AND HARBOURS.

RAINFALL. East Africa lives up to its rainfall expectation
about once in every three years. It varies from place
to place and time to time and generally is less than expected for its altitude. Rainfall is affected by the monsoon
rains and by the position of the sun. Its extent is con-
ditioned by the land relief and the position of the lakes.
Two percent of the region receives 2 inches per month
and 16 percent of the mainland can expect less than 20
inches in 4 out of 5 years. Three percent of the mainland can expect, with 90 percent probability, rainfall
greater than 50 inches (1,250mm.) per year. Twenty-
one percent can expect, with 90 percent probability,
rainfall greater than 30 inches (750 mm.). In other
words, one-third receives sufficient rainfall for intensive
agriculture, one-third receives enough for the growth of
bush and grass. The rest are in between. The Central
third of the country is rather dry; nine months of the
year evaporation exceeds rainfall. Although flooding is
quite common along the coast, most of the country is
semiarid.
        Altitude plays a large role in determining rainfall
patterns. The highland areas and Lake Region area have
two rainy seasons and two dry seasons; November to
December and March to May, are the light and heavy rainy
seasons respectively. In other areas the two rainy seasons merge into one: December to May. Areas with
more rainfall support a greater population.

RAISMAN COMMISSION. Formed in 1961, it tried to deal
with the imbalance of inter-East Africa trade; they introduced a measure of fiscal compensation from Kenya to
the other two countries. The Commission's recommendations led to the formation of a distributable pool of revenue made up of 40 percent of the corporation tax and

6 percent of the customs duty revenue collected by the three countries.

RAMAGE COMMITTEE. Appointed in 1958 to decide on further constitutional changes.

REBMANN, YOHANNES. A missionary from the Church Missionary Society at Mombasa, the first Christian mission there. He arrived in Chaggaland in 1848 and explored Kilimanjaro and Usambara areas.

RECHENBERG, ALBERT FREIHUR von (1862-1935). The first civilian governor, was born in Madrid and spent much of his youth in Russia. Educated at a Jewish Academy, he acquired a doctorate in law and a reserve commission. He served as Provincial Magistrate in Tanga from 1893 and in Zanzibar Consulate from 1896. After serving posts in Moscow and Russia from 1900-1906, he returned as Governor of German East Africa. He was a linguist, speaking Swahili, Arabic and Gujerati. An aristocrat, arrogant and sardonic, sharp-tongued, he made many enemies of the settlers and appeared to be a lonely bachelor or lacking talent for popularity. But he showed expertise as an able administrator. While German Governors were generally pictured as energetic expansionists, urging right-wing policies against left-wing opposition, Rechenberg had progressive views and advocated policies with left-wing support against right-wing opposition. He supported a dual mandate--for the sake of Europe and of Africa, opposed corporal punishment except that due to the course of law, promoted extension in the native health and education services and fostered scientific advance in tropical agriculture to benefit native cultivators. He reformed the local administration by incorporating more Africans in the work of the government and opposed settlers who wanted plantation agriculture to be the basis of the colony's economy. He would not force Africans to work for the settlers and allowed settlers no say in government. He even closed down newspapers putting forth the settlers' views. His governorship from 1906-1911 was considered a success and trade tripled between 1905-1912. He left East Africa in 1911 and concentrated on Eastern Europe.

REDIO SAUTI YA INJILI   see   RADIO VOICE OF THE GOSPEL

REFUGEES.   They have come to Tanzania from a number of
neighboring countries and South Africa.   About 15, 000
Tutsi from Rwanda arrived in 1961, around 100, 000 Mo-
zambicans were here by 1965 and several hundred from
the Congo.   The United Nations High Commissioner for
Refugees has aided in their welfare.   The African-Amer-
ican Institute established a residential secondary school
for 200-300 refugees from Southern Africa.   It was named
the Kurasini International Education Centre and provided
secondary education and commercial training.   During the
1976 Sabasaba Celebrations, the President of Mozambique
handed the vacated school over to the Tanzania Government.

REGIONAL COMMISSIONER.   The TANU Party Secretary as
well as the administrative head in the Region.   In the
colonial days the Provincial Commissioner filled the post.

REGIONAL EDUCATION OFFICER.   A liaison officer with
other officials of other ministries and translates to the
Regional Commissioner the educational policy decisions
he receives from above.   The REO represents the Ministry of National Education in the field and is responsible
for education in his area.   Since secondary schools and
teacher training colleges were directly responsible to an
official in the Ministry, relationships between REO's and
the Principals/Headmasters in his area were not always
clear.

REGIONS.   From the eight provinces, seventeen regions were
cut out in 1963:   Arusha, Coast, Dodoma, Iringa, Kigo-
ma, Kilimanjaro, Mara, Mbeya, Morogoro, Mtwara,
Mwanza, Ruvuma, Shinyanga, Singida, Tabora, Tanga,
West Lake.   Three more have been cut out since then:
Rukwa, Dar es Salaam, and Lindi.

RELIGION.   By 1967 about half of the people adhered to various tribal religions and the rest of the population was divided quite equally between Islam and Christianity.   The
Tanzania Episcopal Conference combines the Roman Catholic groups into one.   The majority of the Protestant
groups are members of the Christian Council of Tanzania.
Asians are Moslems, Hindus, Sikhs and Buddhists.   The
Indian and Pakistani Moslems belong to one of the Shia
groups while African and Arab Moslems are mainly Sunnites.

REPUBLIC OF TANGANYIKA, THE. Formed in December
1962, one year after Tanganyika's independence and adopted a constitution relevant to a republic. It ceased to exist when it united with the People's Republic of Zanzibar
on 26 April, 1964, and took the title of the Republic of
Tanzania.

REPUBLIC OF TANZANIA, THE. Formed on 26 April, 1964,
when the People's Republic of Zanzibar and the Republic
of Tanganyika joined. Each former country remained with
its own local structures in a number of areas and, in others, joined for Union matters of administration. Each
country retained its single party, ASP and TANU, until
1977.

RESISTANCE TO GERMAN RULE. 1888-89: Eastern Coastal
area led by Bushiri; 1891-92: Around Bagamoyo and Zaramo country; 1892: Chagga of Moshi led by Meli; 1892-
93: Nyamwezi under Isike around Tabora; 1894-98: Hehe
under Mkwawa near Iringa; Also Gogo, Yao, Chief Taga-
ralla of Ujiji and three chiefs of Bukoba led some resistance; 1905-07: Maji-Maji Rebellion.

REVOLUTIONARY COUNCIL OF ZANZIBAR. Installed as the
government body in January 1964 after the successful
revolution and overthrow of the Government. The 32
Council members are ASP leaders and referred to as the
legislative body. The cabinet is formed from the Council,
so the Council has both executive and legislative powers.
Land is vested in the Revolutionary Council. It may provide up to 32 members for the National Assembly. Its
president is the Head of State in Zanzibar.

RHAPTA. The first town to be mentioned in any book and
its location is not clearly known. It is believed to be up
Pangani River or on the Rufiji delta. Around A. D. 110
the Periplus of the Erythrean Sea mentions Rhapta as a
place somewhere on the Tanganyika coast. It had organized trade, ivory export and iron weapons and implements
imported. Arab merchants were settling near the Rhapta
savages, intermarrying with them and speaking their language.
        The Geography of Ptolemy written between the
second and fourth centuries describes Rhapta as a metro-
polis. It was the most important pre-Islamic trading
town on the African coast. It was then a center for an
export trade in ivory to be significant later on.

RICE.   Grown mostly for subsistence.   The 1960 production
of 34, 859 tons increased by 195 percent to the 1970 production of 102, 223 tons.   It was necessary to import rice
in the early 1970's and a campaign of "Kufa na Kupona"
(Life or Death) raised the production along with favorable
rainfall in 1975 and 1976, and a good harvest was realized.   The National Milling Corporation marketed 100,000
tons in 1975/76.

RIFT VALLEY.   The Rift Valley located in Tanzania contains
both the lowest depth (in Lake Tanganyika) found in Africa
as well as the highest point (Mt. Kilimanjaro) in Africa.
The Rift Valley runs through Central Tanzania and the
heart of the Southern Highlands.   It ploughs through a
volcanic area and large areas are broken by gorges.
There is a strong bifurcation in the South.   The Western
Rift with its lakes forms the border of Tanzania with
Burundi, Rwanda and Uganda and sets off the western
edge of the Central Plateau and Lake Victoria Basin.
The Eastern Rift with its lakes and mountains divides the
Central Plateau from the Eastern Plateau.   It is a series
of isolated mountains and mountain chains interspersed
with lakes and craters.   The Rift Valley demarcates the
rolling plains with a series of immense faults creating
both depressions and mountains.   The mountains rise
sheer and rugged.

RINDI, CHIEF.   Of Moshi, he was also called Mandara but
he preferred Rindi (Loud overshadowing all lands).   This
one-eyed chief began to rule around 1860 but fled into
exile during the 1860's and was replaced by his brother
Kitori.   He returned and ruled from 1870 to his death in
1891.   The English traveller Johnston stayed with him in
1884.   In 1885 he signed a treaty with the Society for
German Colonisation and allowed the Church Missionary
Society to build a mission.   He became a good friend of
Dr. Juhlke and offered a blood pact to him, presenting
a daughter in marriage.   His good behavior towards Dr.
Juhlke had three results: Kilimanjaro remained in Tan-
ganyika in the 1886 delimitation treaty; German agents
were posted to Moshi; and Germans came in conflict with
Sina at Kibosho.
        Rindi used great diplomacy with Europeans and
other chiefs.   The Europeans thought he was "Paramount
Chief" but less in power.   So he was able to unite the
Germans to destroy Sina's prominence.   He engineered
complicated alliances with the Arusha against Chief Sina

of Kibosho who held power at Kilimanjaro.   Sometimes
he won, sometimes he did not over other chiefs.   Rindi
had ruled the greater part of the mountain right down to
Same but, as he grew older, Sina became stronger as
well as Marealle.
      Rindi traded with Swahili ivory traders and en-
couraged them to use Moshi as a base.   He learned Swahili, employed a Swahili clerk and corresponded with the
Sultan, Queen of England and Kaiser Wilhelm II.   He died
in 1891.

RIVERS.   Great Ruaha is the greatest tributary of the Rufiji
      River and drains the Usagara Mts.   Grummeti flows
      from Eastern Mara Region to Lake Victoria.   Kagera
      flows into Lake Victoria near Bukoba, is navigable 90
      miles from the mouth.   Malagarasi flows into Lake Tan-
      ganyika near Kigoma.   Mara borders South Mara and Ta-
      rime Districts and flows into Lake Victoria.   Mkomazi
      in the Masai Steppe is bounded by the Pare and Usambara
      mountain ranges.   Pangani rises in Mt. Kilimanjaro, Pare
      and Usambara Mts. and flows into the Indian Ocean south
      of Tanga.   Rufiji enters the Indian Ocean south of Dar es
      Salaam.   Its headwaters are the Kilombero rising in the
      Southern Highlands.   Ruhuhu drains the Ungoni Highlands
      into Lake Nyasa.   Rungwe drains the Lake Rukwa basin
      in the north.   Ruvu begins in the Uluguru Mts. and has
      its mouth near Bagamoyo.   Ruvuma is on the border of
      Mozambique and Tanzania and empties into the Indian
      Ocean.   Wami rises south of Kilosa and empties into the
      coast opposite Zanzibar.   It has irrigation potential.

RIVERS-SMITH, STANLEY (1877-1965).   After two years with
      the Egyptian Civil Service, he became the Director of
      Education in Zanzibar, a position he held from 1907 to
      1920.   Bishop Frank Weston of the UMCA was the driving
      force behind the development of St. Andrew's College
      which was transferred to Tanganyika in the mid-1920's
      where it grew to be one of the outstanding schools for
      Africans.   Rivers-Smith was appointed the first Director
      of Education in Tanganyika in 1920.   He left the position
      and Tanganyika service in 1931.   He wrote the book Afya.

ROADS.   In 1877 Mackinnon began a Dar es Salaam-Lake Ny-
      asa road and completed 70 miles of it.   The mileage of
      roads "passable to light motor traffic in the dry season"
      increased from 2650 miles in 1921 to 12,000 in 1938.
      The Usangi-Ugweno-Mwanza Road began as early as 1921

and was opened to traffic in 1936. In 1940 there were
19,000 miles of passable roads. Only the Great North
Road was passable during the rainy season. This road
passes through the major towns--Mbeya, Iringa, Dodoma
and Arusha--on its way from Zambia to Kenya. Two
roads from Uganda join in West Lake and connect to the
Great North Road at Mbeya. The major road from Dar
es Salaam to Iringa connects to it also. After World
War II the British spent more than £4 million on Tanganyika's road system. By 1958 Tanganyika had about
26,000 miles of road with 4000 of these ranked as major
roads and 500 miles were hard-topped. The Moshi-
Arusha Road was one of the best in Africa. At the end
of ten years of independence the central government reported 1550 miles of bituminized roads, 595 miles of engineered gravel major roads, 8405 miles of other earth
roads and 5880 miles of regional roads taken over. The
major roads form a network of trunk routes running from
North to South or East to West. In addition to trunk
routes, a series of roads link major population centers.

ROBERT, SHAABAN (1909-1962). One of East Africa's most
distinguished writers was born near Tanga in January
1909 and educated in Dar es Salaam. He spent all his
life on or near the coast, much of it in the British Government service. He was a creative writer and wrote in
a number of different forms: short story, political al-
legory, simple autobiography, essay, translation, traditional poem and novel. He introduced essay into Swahili
literature and served as Chairman of the Swahili Committee in Dar es Salaam. He was a fervent Moslem and
African patriot, protesting subjugation to European colonialism, was moralistic but his writings showed a deep
and gifted mind and passionate soul. His first works
were Pambo la Lugha (The Embellishment of Language)
and his self-portrait Maisha Yangu (My Life). Possibly
his finest work is Kusadikika, Nchi iliyo Angani (Faith
for the Country of the Sun). His novel, Siku ya Watenzi
Wote, was written shortly before his death. He is considered the most distinguished of all East African writers
and was honored with the KBE and won the Margaret
Wrong Medal and Prize. He died in June 1962.

ROCK PAINTINGS. Less well known than those of South Africa, Rhodesia and the Sahara, but are often of high
quality. The earliest paintings probably date back to the
later Stone Age times. Most are centered on Kondoa

with around half of them between Dodoma and Arusha.
Up to 1000 sites have been discovered. At least sixteen
styles of the Stone Age times are said to be distinguished.
The earliest paintings are invisible unless the silica film
which covers them is sprayed with water.   Then it be-
comes temporarily transparent.   The subjects are very
commonly herbivorous--antelopes, elephants, giraffes,
rhinos, ostriches.   The animals are naturalistic and very
well drawn in some styles while others are crude and
stylized.   The animals are usually single figures super-
imposed one on top of the other, though occasionally arranged in groups of friezes. Although animals are the most
common subjects there are many lively groups of people.
The latest paintings show a degeneration, the outlines being thick and the attitude of the animals stiff.

ROMAN CATHOLICS.   They consist of two archdioceses with
    Archbishop Cardinal Rugambwa and Rev. Mark Mihayo at
    Dar es Salaam and Tabora respectively.

Date of Entry	Order	Place
1868	Holy Ghost Fathers	Bagamoyo, also Dar es Salaam
1878	White Fathers	Tabora
1888	Benedictine Mission	Dar es Salaam, Pugu, Lindi, Tosamaganga
1919	Consolata Sisters	Iringa
1921	Capuchin Sisters	Dar es Salaam
1932	Passionist Fathers	Dodoma
1943	Pallottine Fathers	Mbulu
1945	Rosminian Fathers	Singachini
1946	Maryknoll Fathers	Musoma
1953	Maryknoll Fathers	Shinyanga
1963	Salvatorian Fathers	Ndanda

In 1953 the hierarchy of Tanganyika was formally established and dioceses were erected. The Tanganyika Catholic
Welfare Organization was created in 1957 and was the
forerunner of the Tanganyika Episcopal Conference in
1962 which was renamed in 1964 to Tanzania Episcopal
Conference.   The first major seminary was Rubya in
Bukoba, founded in 1911.   The church has operated many
schools, hospitals, social services and printing presses.
In 1968, primary schools numbered 1378, secondary
schools numbered 44 and there were 25 hospitals.   The
total membership was estimated at 2,878,600 in 1976.

See also TANZANIA EPISCOPAL CONFERENCE; various orders; and CARDINAL RUGAMBWA.

ROSMINIAN FATHERS.   An order from Ireland, it entered the newly erected Prefecture of Tanga in 1950.   It had previously formed part of the Vicarate of Kilimanjaro where they first entered at Singachini in 1945.   It became a Diocese in 1958.   They amalgamated with other orders to form the now known Tanzania Episcopal Conference.

RUAHA NATIONAL PARK.   Gazetted in 1964, it is the second largest national park and covers an area of 12,950 sq. km.   Previous to this it was the southern half of the large 7500 square mile Rungwa Game Reserve.   It is famous for its greater kudu and many elephants.   Lion and leopard are frequently heard but seldom seen.   Giraffes, buffaloes, rhinos, dik-diks, warthogs and game birds can also be seen.

RUBBER.   From 1906 to 1912 during the governorship of Rechenberg, rubber was introduced and a rapid expansion of rubber production took place.   Rubber prices slumped in 1913 and the crop was largely abandoned.

RUFIJI RIVER.   Tanzania's largest river, it drains the Southern Highlands and most of Southern Tanzania.   The basin covers nearly one-fourth of the country's total area which is the most extensive and productive piece of lowland in Tanzania.   It is navigable for 61 miles.   Very much of the fertile land near the mouth has not been utilized due to the severe flooding of the river at certain times of the year.   It is a very small stream and gets dry other times.   The Rufiji is one of the largest rivers in Africa with an average discharge of 43,050 cubic feet per second (1,133 cu. m./sec.).   It has major potential for irrigation and hydroelectric power development.

RUGAMBWA, CARDINAL LAURIAN (1912-   ).   Born at Bukongo in Northwestern Tanzania on 12 July, 1912.   He was converted to Christianity at nine years of age with his parents and two brothers.   He comes from noble ancestry on both sides of the family--father of Basita tribe and mother a Bayinga.   After attending a White Fathers Mission School, he entered Junior Seminary at Rubya in Bukoba in 1927 and then attended Senior Seminary at Katigondo in Uganda until 1943.   He was then ordained a priest in 1943 and sent to Rome to study canon law from

1948-51. His doctoral thesis was on social and educational work in East Africa. In 1952 he was consecrated the
first Bishop of the new diocese of Rutabo. He was the
first Negro to enter the Roman Catholic College of Cardi-
nals on 31 March, 1960, and the first African Cardinal.
He became the Bishop of Bukoba in August 1960 and en-
throned as Archbishop during 1969 for the Diocese with
headquarters in Dar es Salaam.

RUGA RUGA. The army of young warriors under Mirambo
and Nyunga ya Mawe of the Nyamwezi in the 1870's and
1880's.

RUHINDA, CHIEF. About 1500-1600 when Bunyoro-Kitara
collapsed, the Chwezi maintained control of Ankole in
Uganda. Ruhinda established the rule of his clan (the
Hinda) there. He later conquered Bukoba and Karagwe
in Tanzania, and Burundi and established sub-dynasties
there. When he died, these became independent kingdoms.

RUMANIKA I, CHIEF ORUGUNDU (?-1880). Chief at Karagwe warmly received Speke. He succeeded his father as
chief in 1853 after an Indian trader induced the King of
Buganda with large presents to send troops to defeat
Rwegira, the rival claimant. At each new moon 35
drums were placed in a row to call people to come and
swear loyalty to their Chief Rumanika. Speke and Grant
reached his court in October 1861. His reign was characterized by further expansion of the Arab/Swahili trade,
struggle and feuds between him and his brother Rwegira
over the question of succession, and a series of wars.
He became increasingly dependent on Buganda. He died
around 1880.

RUPIA, JOHN. Born in Shinyanga. He was one of the founders of TANU and served as its Vice President from 1956
to 1960. He was also its National Treasurer for a time.
He lost his National Assembly seat when he stood for the
Shinyanga constituency in the 1965 elections; he had moved
to Dar es Salaam quite a number of years before that.
He was a member of TANU's Central Committee and
named a trustee of TANU.

- S -

SAFWA (tribe). Located east of Mbeya, they are split into a

number of small chiefdoms. In 1910 they were over
9000, in 1931 they were 24,000; in 1948, 50,000 and in
1957, 63,000. They lack traditional history and it is
believed fire and agriculture were introduced around
1900. They have a deep-seated belief in witchcraft and
sorcery.

SAGARA (tribe). Early historical material dealt with Kaguru
misnamed Sagara or with detribalized settlements along
the important trade routes between Morogoro and Mpwapwa. The Sagara proper are located near Kilosa in the
mountains north of it and in the large area to its south.
In 1957 the tribe numbered 32,000. The Sagara claim to
have migrated north through the Ruaha Valley led by a
Bena called Kidanamhale. They are a matrilineal tribe.
During the era of Indirect Rule, the Sagara had two
chiefs and a number of headmen although they did not
have centralized authority traditionally. The establishment of sisal estates in Usagara has brought in many
outside influences.

SAID BIN SULTAN, SULTAN (c. 1791-1856). Born at Semail
in Muscat, Oman, he became Sultan at his father's death
in 1804 at around fifteen years of age. Said ruled jointly
with an elder brother and his cousin, Bedr bin Saif, was
regent. He was not confirmed as absolute ruler until he
murdered Bedr in July 1806 and his brother had died.
From 1806 to 1817 he established his reign in Oman and,
with British help, rid the coastal waters of pirates. He
instructed his governor in Zanzibar to invade Pemba,
which was then conquered in 1822. In 1828 he visited
East Africa and subsequently made frequent visits to Zanzibar and had a large palace built there in 1832. He led
an expedition to Mombasa and subjected it finally in 1837.
He was shrewd, energetic and ambitious and established
an impressive sphere of influence, developing a commercial rather than territorial empire. He did not rule as
a king: each town on the coast had a governor (wali) and
a few of his soldiers. If customs duties were collected
correctly, each governor could do as he pleased. He
held a baraza and judged cases brought to him. He started the growing of clove trees on Zanzibar and encouraged
Indians to settle there as traders and money-lenders.
He welcomed European and American traders, signed a
trade treaty with the U.S.A. in 1833 and with Britain in
1839. About 1835 he began to send caravans into the interior under his protection and in 1839 made a treaty with

the Nyamwezi chief for his subjects to get free right of
passage. He became wealthy from trade in slaves, gold,
ivory and cloves. America opened a Consulate in Zanzibar in 1837, he moved his capital there in 1840 and then
Britain and France sent their first representatives in
1841. The Hamburg firm opened a branch in 1849. He
was tactful and diplomatic, preferring to negotiate rather
than to fight. He was noted for his generosity and tole-
rance. He died in 1856 at sea while returning from
Oman. His power died with him as Oman and Zanzibar
were then separated.

SAIDI, AUGUSTINE (1929-). Born in Kilimanjaro and educated at St. Mary's Secondary School, Tabora (1950) and
Alligarh Muslim University in India, receiving a B.A.,
LL.B. and M.A. He then became an advocate in Tanganyika, was a Resident Magistrate, Senior Resident
Magistrate, Puisne Judge (1964), Acting Chief Justice,
Zanzibar (1965-66) and appointed Chief Justice in Tanzania in 1971 after having served as a Judge in Tanzania again. His Chief Justice position was given to Francis Nyalali in February 1977.

SAIF BIN AHMAD AL-BUSAIDI. In 1784, he attempted to
make a separate sultanate of Kilwa and Zanzibar and
failed. Imam reestablished his control of the coast.

ST. ANDREW'S COLLEGE. Opened in 1869 at Kiungani as
a primary school for ex-slaves in Zanzibar. In the late
1870's there were 88 students. In 1884 the institution
was changed to a teacher training center for teachers and
pastors. After 1896 the enrollment slowly dropped and
in 1906, a crisis year, there were 45 students. The
college moved to the mainland in 1925. Two of the alum-
ni, Cecil Majaliwa, the first priest, and Hugh Peter Kayamba, a teacher, received secondary education in England before World War II. By 1909 Masasi archdeaconry
employed some 60 teachers and clergy trained at St. Andrew's College and by 1914 Bonde had received 80 teachers and clergy.

ST. MICHAEL'S AND ST. GEORGE'S. Opened in 1959 to
provide junior and senior secondary education for Euro-
peon children. It is located near Iringa. In 1960 it became educationally integrated into a multi-racial dimen-
sion. Twenty-one Africans and twenty Asians were admitted after interviews and testing. The group met high

academic and sports standards. They followed the customs and standards of European education. The European
enrollment dropped as expatriates left the country after
independence. The Property Fund was not available. So
the Government took over the operation of the school and
failed to meet costs. It closed in 1963 for financial
reasons. In 1964 it reopened as Mkwawa High School.

SALT. The Vinza of Western Tanzania produced salt from
brine springs which was used in traditional trade. Salt
was used as currency. Until the present the main source
of salt is the brine springs at Uvinza on Lake Tanganyika.
There is a minor source on the coast which is exploited
by solar units. The production increased slightly during
the first years of independence. The installation of a
vacuum plant raised the annual production to 40,000 tons
which is sufficient to meet internal demands as well as
to export. In 1975, 45,000 tons were sold of the 1,003.5
million tons mined, raising Shs. 3.8 million from foreign
trade and Shs. 9.5 million in internal trade.

SALUM, SALIM AHMED. Zanzibari born, he was the first
Tanzanian to hold a town clerk post when he was appointed Dodoma Town Clerk. He is a Permanent Representative at the U.N. for Tanzania and headed the OAU Liberation Committee. In 1973 he was awarded "The World
Diplomatic Award" in recognition of his services to humanity through the U.N.

SALVATION ARMY. After a beginning in Kenya in 1921 and
Uganda in 1931, the Salvation Army entered Tanganyika
in 1933 under the leadership of Colonel F. G. Dare.
From the first station at Tabora, the church spread to
Moshi, Chunya, Tarime and Mbeya and on to include 31
places in Tanzania. Their members in Tanzania total
3436 and the main office is in Dar es Salaam. They operate a guest house and a school for unfortunate children
and care for orphans.

SALVATORIANS. Arrived in 1955 in what is now the diocese
of Nachingwea. Bishop Coty was consecrated in Rome in
1963. They amalgamated with other orders to form the
present Tanzania Episcopal Conference (TEC).

SAMBAA or SHAMBALA (tribe). Had for generations been
ruled by the Kilindi. They live in the Usambara Mts.

SANDAWE (tribe).   A remnant tribe of the early peoples of
     Tanganyika before the arrival of the Bantus.   The San-
     dawe were formerly hunters and gatherers but took up
     agriculture after the arrival of the Europeans.   Some al-
     so herd cattle.   The Sandawe have been receptive to out-
     side cultural influences.   They numbered 30, 000 at inde-
     pendence.

SAPI, CHIEF ADAM (1920-   ).   Grandson of the great Chief
     Mkwawa was born at Iringa in 1920 and attended Malanga-
     li Secondary School and Tabora Government Secondary
     School.   He was the Paramount Hehe Chief from 1940-62.
     He succeeded to the chiefdom when he was a student at
     Makerere College.   He was appointed a member of Legis-
     lative Council in 1947 and elected Chairman of the Chiefs'
     Convention in May 1957.   It met two or three times a
     year until 1961.   Adam Sapi was made Speaker of the
     National Assembly in 1962, a position he held until 1974.
     He holds the Order of the British Empire.   In 1965 he
     was appointed Chairman of the Board of Trustees of Tan-
     ganyika's National Parks and held many chairmanships
     for a number of years.   In the mid-1970's he was Minis-
     ter of State for Capital Development and Chairman of the
     Board of Directors of Tanzania Wildlife Corporation.

SARAKIKYA, MARISHO SAM HAGAI (1934-   ).   Born at Meru
     in 1934 and studied at Old Moshi and Tabora Secondary
     Schools until 1957.   He entered the Military Academy at
     Sandhurst, England as a member of the KAR and then
     the Tanganyika King's African Rifles in 1958 as a private.
     He was commissioned in 1961 at Sandhurst.   He is self-ef-
     facing to the point of shyness but is a smart, efficient sol-
     dier.   He was promoted to Brigadier and Chief of the TPDF
     soon after January 1964 when he was still a Captain.   He had
     remained loyal at Tabora during the mutiny.   He rose to Ma-
     jor General in 1969 and was also Chairman of Tanzania's
     Olympic Committee.   He is a mountain climber having
     climbed Mt. Kilimanjaro 17 times and Mt. Meru 30 times.
     In 1974 he was appointed Minister of the newly created Min-
     istry of National Culture and Youth.   He is a member of the
     Executive Committee of the Amateur International Boxing
     Association and President of the Tanzania Red Cross.   He
     was appointed High Commissioner to Nigeria in August 1977.

SARWATT, S. E. (1930-   ).   Born in Mbulu District and re-
     ceived his secondary education at Old Moshi Secondary
     School.   Following that he joined the then Mbulu Central

Treasury and rose to the position of Treasurer by 1951.
He was appointed top administrator of Mbulu District in
1953, a position he held until 1960. He is a member of
Parliament since 1958 and joined the Central Legislative
Assembly in 1965. He was Deputy Speaker of the National Assembly from 1964 until 1968 when he was appointed Chairman of East Africa Legislative Assembly, a position he was still holding by 1977. Sarwatt is also
Vice-Chairman of the Tanzania Tourist Corporation and
a member of NAFCO (National Agriculture and Food Corporation) Board. He was Chairman of the Governing
Council of the Morogoro Agricultural College till it became a Faculty of Agriculture with the University of Dar
es Salaam. He represented the Ministry of Agriculture
(Tanzania) on the East African National Resources Research until 1968. He was the first Chairman of the
Tanzania Wheat Board.

SCHELE, GOVERNOR. Appointed Governor of German East
Africa in September 1893 and soon sent expeditions to
deal with the hostile tribes under Bwana Heri and Mkwawa. Schele returned to Germany in January 1895 and was
succeeded by Governor Wissman.

SCHNEE, HEINRICH, GOVERNOR. Took over from Governor
Rechenberg in July 1912. Although he had neither hind-
sight nor foresight, he was competent, well-intentioned
and humane, and effected a real improvement in relations
between the administration and the settlers by adopting a
more friendly policy to settlers than his predecessor.
He restricted the immigration of Indians and their right
to acquire township land. He restrained the competitive-
ness of labor recruiting at the cost of longer contracts.
He facilitated land alienation by easing the terms of leasehold contracts and fixing lower prices than set earlier.
The first district councils with unofficial European majorities were elected in 1913. Municipalities were formed
in 1914 under complete European representation and control. He remained Governor until 1916 when the British
overran Dar es Salaam.

SCRIPTURE UNION. The Tanzania branch was opened in
1958 under the CCT. The first job of the secretary was
to prepare the literature in Swahili. After several years
the work increased and a Committee was elected to im-
plement the work. Scripture Union is known as Umoja
wa Kujisomea Biblia in Tanzania and is a member of CCT
since 1962.

SECONDARY EDUCATION.   Until the conversion of Tabora
Central School into a Junior Secondary School by adding
Grades IX and X in 1933, no secondary education facilities existed in the territory.   Prior to this a few students had been sent to Uganda to join their Junior Secondary Schools with the hope of entering Makerere later.
From 1933 to 1938 four mission and three government
secondary schools added Grades IX and X.   More Junior
Secondary Schools were opened in 1942.   A territorial
examination was introduced at the end of Std. X in 1947.
There were 19 Secondary Schools in 1957 of which three
had Std. XI and XII also (Forms 1-4).   By 1960 the number was 28, of which 15 were full secondary schools
    The Three Year Plan of 1961-64 boosted secondary
education by allocating one-third of the total plan expenditure on education to secondary schools.   The Territorial
Examination for Std. X was also abolished to meet more
quickly manpower needs.   Only 2.1 percent of the secondary school age population was attending secondary school.
The number of School Certificate graduates rose from
1202 in 1960 to 3275 in 1964 and Higher School graduates
from 110 in 1960 to 620 in 1964.   Much progress was
made in the number of schools and pupils since independence as well.
    In 1967 all Headmasters were replaced with a Tan-
zanian citizen as a government policy.   The School Certificate exams were localized to an East African edition
and then to the national level by 1970.   Zanzibar had one
secondary school by 1951 with 389 pupils.

SEGEJU (tribe).   Migrated from Kenya into the area NE of
Tanga.   The original immigrants consisted of a war party
who were cut off from their fellows by the flooding of the
Umba River.   They decided to settle in the Digo country.
They were only men, so they married with the local Digo
and Shiraz.   They are patriarchal.

SELF-HELP SCHEMES.   Initiated after independence and volunteer labor on community projects saved hundreds of
thousands of shillings.   During 1962-63, the following
figures were given: 10, 000 kilometers of country road
built; 368 schools; 267 community centers; 166 dispensaries; 515 wells; 415 irrigation canals and 108 small dams.
The value for these self-help projects was given at
£500,000.   Self-help activities became the basis for the
self-reliance activities later on and for the Second Five-
Year Plan.

SELOUS GAME RESERVE.   Gazetted in 1951, it is the largest
(51,200 square miles) in Tanzania and of East Africa's
game reserves.   Its name honors the great explorer,
elephant hunter, soldier and great naturalist.   The Reserve has more than 15,000 square miles of brachuotegia
country in the Rufiji River Basin southwest of Morogoro.
There are estimated to be around 35,000 elephants and a
concentration of lions.   It has been preserved as a natural reserve rather than a national park.   The Tanzania
Wildlife Safaris Ltd. control safaris to this area.   It arranged for its first safaris in 1963 and then the first full
season in 1964.

SEMBOJA (? -1895).   Chief at Mazinde and son of Kimweri
the Great.   He allied with Taita and killed Shekulwavu,
a grandson who succeeded Kimweri.   The Usambara kingdom's center of power moved from Vuga to Mazinde on
the main trade route.   Shekulwavu's brothers conquered
the eastern part of the kingdom.   Semboja was sympathetic with Abushiri and opposed the end of the slave
trade.   In support of the Abushiri rebellion, Semboja confiscated 250 loads from Meyer and Baumann, two German
explorers.   Baumann was influential and from then on the
Germans believed Semboja to be an unfriendly bandit.
Semboja died in March 1895 by a natural cause.

SEPEKU, ARCHBISHOP JOHN (1907-).   Born in Tanga and
trained as a teacher.   After teaching in primary schools
in Tanga and Coast Region, he finished secondary school
and a teacher training course for Grade I at Minaki.   He
then joined Magila Seminary in 1935 and was ordained
deacon in 1948 upon completion of the course and ordained priest in 1940.   He returned to Tanga to be the
Archdeacon from 1960-63.   He became the Assistant
Bishop of Dar es Salaam in 1963 and Bishop in 1965.
He was the first Tanzanian Anglican Archbishop at his
1970 consecration.   He also supervises the 410-acre
farm of the church at Mtoni area.

SERENGETI NATIONAL PARK.   Tanzania's largest National
Park, located east of Lake Victoria, is one of the most
popular in wild life attractions in East Africa with more
than 3.5 million animals.   In the early 1920's the first
professional safaris started to open up the area.   In 1929
the Central part of the park was made a full game reserve.   The whole of Serengeti was made a closed reserve in 1950.   Gazetted in 1951, it was the first nat-

ional park under the National Park Board.   It included
Ngorongoro Crater but was separated in 1959.
        The park, with over 5600 square miles (14,763
sq. km.) contains a large concentration of varied wildlife
(not less than 170 species of animals) and attracts more
tourists than it can accommodate.   It is particularly
famous for its more than 2000 lions, more than 3 million
large animals and more than a half million gazelles.
Migrations occur in May or June and over 1.3 million
wildebeests and 200,000 zebras move across the plain as
a cloud or heavy line.   Giraffe, buffalo, lion, cheetah,
ostriches and hyena are also in large numbers.   The
Serengeti Research Institute at Seronera is the most advanced center for the study of ecology in Africa.   It was
established in 1966 by the Trustees of the National Parks
to conserve wildlife.

SESAME.   Grown for local consumption and for export.   Mt-
    wara is by far the greatest producer, supplying 80 per-
    cent of the crop marketed.   In 1972, the peak year,
    10,000 tons were exported.   Although 1973 and 1974 were
    poor agricultural years, they still averaged 3000 tons
    each year for export with a value over Shs. 12 million.
    The 1975/76 figures rose to 6000 tons.

SETTLERS.   Settlers were officially encouraged in order to
    help pay for the cost of administration and railway con-
    struction.   In 1898 the first Germans settled at Usam-
    bara.   More Germans entered Meru in 1905.   By that
    time there were 180 white farmers.   In 1907 other Ger-
    mans settled at Kilimanjaro.   By 1913 there were esti-
    mated to be 992 white farmers and sisal was the impor-
    tant crop.   Coffee and rubber had also been planted.
    Much of the land had been taken from the Masai.   The
    settlers wanted a greater voice in the government and
    there was a confrontation between Gov. Rechenberg and
    the settler leader Paul Rohrback.   Gov. Schnee, who
    succeeded Gov. Rechenberg, improved the system of la-
    bor recruitment and allowed the settlers to be represented
    on the Advisory Council in 1913.   German settlers were
    deported after World War I and over 6000 English settlers
    came in the 1920's.   By 1925 the German settlers were
    allowed to return.   The two largest groups of settlers
    were Greek and German.   They settled mainly on the
    Northern Highlands and Southern Highlands.

SEVENTH DAY ADVENTIST CHURCH (SDA).   The first mis-

sionaries came from Germany in 1903 and began their
work in Pare. Soon afterward they also began stations
all along the East Coast of Lake Victoria from Mwanza
to the Kenya line. The first missionaries there, W.
Ehlers and A. C. Enns, were sent by the SDA World
Council with headquarters in U.S.A. Another area, Morogoro, was opened later.

Besides building worship centers throughout Tanzania, the SDA's have an 80-bed hospital, 23 dispensaries, a secondary school, a seminary at Arusha, a print
shop at Morogoro and a Bible Correspondence department.
The headquarters offices are at Busegwe in Mara Region.
Rev. L. C. Robinson is church Chairman and Rev. Salz-
mann is Secretary-Treasurer. Four of the five dioceses
have African pastors in charge and all have African Assistant Chairmen and treasurers. There are about
33,000 SDA Christians, 206 churches, 46 pastors and 192
colporteur/evangelists.

SEWA HAJI HOSPITAL   see   MUHIMBILI HOSPITAL

SEWA HAJI PAROO (1851-1897). Born in 1851, a son of an
Ismail Khoja businessman. He was one of the wealthiest
Indian merchants at Bagamoyo and employed up to 4000
porters for his caravans to Dar es Salaam, Tabora, Ujiji
and Mwanza. Besides carrying on a profitable trade of
his own, he also equipped the caravans of explorers. He
assisted the Roman Catholics in freeing young women
slaves who were lepers and putting them into camps. In
1895 the Aga Khan conferred the title Alijah on him. His
numerous donations to the German East African government and the Roman Catholic missions gained him a visit
to Berlin for the Order of the Imperial Eagle at the hands
of the Kaiser. He died in 1897 while on a visit to Zanzibar.

SEYYID. Another name for the Sultan. See references to
the Sultans by their names.

SHABA, AUSTIN KAPERE EDWARD (1925-). Born at Sumbawanga in 1925 and attended Tabora Government Secondary School from 1939-44 and then trained as a medical
assistant at the Dar es Salaam Medical School from
1945-47. He served as an assistant in charge of a hospital in the Southern Highlands, then as a Senior Medical
Assistant 1953-57 and as a district officer in several
places 1957-60. His work earned him the British Empire

Medal. He made a number of journeys abroad. He became a member of Parliament in 1960 and held portfolios
with Local Government, Health and Labour and then was
Ambassador in Tanganyika's Mission to the U.N. 1962-63.
He returned to Tanzania as Minister of Local Government
and Housing and then for Health and Housing until 1968
when he resigned on 7 October, 1968, because he was no
Tanzanian citizen. He took out citizenship papers 10 days
later. In 1976 he was the Chairman of Tanzania Sisal
Authority at Tanga.

SHAIDI, MSANGI NARUNDU ELANGWA (1915-). The first
   African to become Commissioner of Police in the colonial
   administration, he was born in Pare District at Vudee on
   21 January, 1915, and attended Central School in Lushoto
   District for four years after a primary education. In
   1934 he got a job as clerk with the Moshi Trading Company and went on to storekeeper and salesman. After
   two months of service in 1936 with the Pare Native
   Treasury, he took a six-month course in the Dar es
   Salaam Training School for police. His first posting at
   Tabora was followed by many others in Tanganyika.
   While in Dar es Salaam in 1952, he got a scholarship for
   a six-month course in the U.K. On return, he was given
   the rank of Asst. Superintendent of Police. After another
   course in the U.K. in 1961, he was promoted to Deputy
   Commissioner of Police. After independence he was
   Tanzania's first full Commissioner of Police. In the
   Union, he was the Inspector General of Police. Since
   1972 he has been working with the Agricultural and Industrial Supplies Co., Ltd.

SHAMBALA (tribe). Also known as SAMBAA tribe. Their
   chiefdom developed as a result of northern influences.
   They have consistently resisted government efforts to resettle them in fertile lowlands.

SHAMTE, SHEIKH MOHAMMED. He came from a well-to-do
   Shirazi family, owned a large clove plantation in Pemba,
   taught and served as superintendent of primary schools
   in Pemba for 25 years before entering politics, and was
   the chief spokesman of the Zanzibar Government Party
   at the London Conference in 1962. He had formed a
   government with the combined ZNP and ZPPP in 1961
   and was the Chief Minister. At Independence in 1963 he
   became the Prime Minister but ZNP was in power. He
   was overthrown with his government in the revolution of
   1964 in Zanzibar.

SHANGALI, CHIEF.   Of Machame, he assumed chiefdomship
in 1890 by vassalage to Mangi Sina. He was polite and
friendly.   He later panicked, became fearful, and abdicated in 1901.   Shangali was reinstated as chief in 1918
as a temporary measure to pave the way for his son Abdiel who ruled Machame from 1923-46.

SHANGALI, CHIEF ABDIEL (1903-1976).   Born at Machame
and attended Tanga Government Secondary School from
1921-24.   He was called back during Std. X to become
Machame chief at twenty years of age.   He was Machame
Chief until 1946 when he became Divisional Chief until
1961.   He was the most powerful chief and his reign
marks the ascendancy of the Machame.   Machame was
the first center of Lutheran activities on Mt. Kilimanjaro; school attendance exceeded any other chiefdom; he
owned lucrative coffee plantations; and he advocated tribal
modernization through education and communal agriculture.
He had little education but he taught himself English.   He
was awarded the King's Medal in 1934 and the Coronation
Medal in 1937.   In 1943 he was one of the Chiefs to visit
the East African troops in the Middle East.   That same
year he became a member of Makerere College Assembly.
He was Chairman of the Chagga Local Executive Committee on African Education in 1944.   In 1945 he was the
first African to be nominated as an unofficial member of
the Legislative Council and in 1948 the first African to
be appointed to the Central Legislative Assembly.   He received the British Empire Medal in 1949.   Since independence he has had varied jobs including Executive
Chairman of Tanganyika National Tourist Board.

SHANGALI, CHIEF GILEAD ABDIEL.   Born at Kilimanjaro
and studied at Old Moshi and Tabora Secondary Schools.
He became chief in 1952 after leaving Tabora and continued until 1962.   He earned a Diploma in Public and
Social Administration from South Devon Technical College
1959-61, then became an administrative officer at Tanga
Regional Headquarters in 1962, went on to Tabora and
took various administrative jobs on a district level.

SHANKLAND, BERT (1932-   ).   Born in Scotland and came
to Tanganyika in 1957 as a service engineer for Riddock
Motors.   He has carried on in the automobile industry.
He is nationally famous for his safari appearances and
medals won: The East African Safari--won 1966, 1967;
Tanzania 1000--won seven times; Ethiopia Highlands--

3, 800 km. in 1970, 3rd place; and REC rally in Britain
with two victories.

SHIHATA. Created by an act of Parliament in October 1976
to be the official Tanzania News Agency. The aim is to
provide machinery for effective co-ordination of the activities of all public institutions engaged in the collection
and dissemination of news and news material, and to
facilitate optimum use of human and material resources
available in Tanzania for the purposes of newspaper information and broadcasting services.

SHIPPING. On 3 July, 1890, the first regular steamship
service was opened between Germany and East Africa
when the Reichstag, a 2300 ton ship, sailed from Hamburg. By now cargo and passenger vessels from all
over the world call in at Dar es Salaam. The dhow-har-
bor at Dar es Salaam has monsoonal traffic from Arabia,
the Persian Gulf or India. Shipping between Zanzibar,
Pemba, Mafia and the mainland is mostly privately operated. The East African Railways and Harbours, which
operated the shipping services on Lake Victoria and Lake
Tanganyika, separated with the East African Harbours
Corporation established at Dar es Salaam. The year
1966 stands out as a special year in shipping services
development: a train ferry service was begun on Lake
Victoria; Tanzania, Kenya, Uganda, and Zambia with a
private company established the East African National
Shipping Line as a cargo service to Europe and began
operations the following year with its first ships; and the
Chinese-Tanzania Joint Shipping Company was created to
bolster trade with the Far East.

SHIRAZ ASSOCIATION. Formed in Pemba in 1939, began
mainly for the protection of squatters and laborers, and
in Pemba also for the Shiraz Clove Growers. It was an
incipient trade union and grew in response to the Arab
Association activities. It played little part in politics until about 1957. The African Association (formed in 1934
in Zanzibar) and the Shiraz Association of Zanzibar merged
on 5 February, 1957, and were called the Afro-Shiraz
Union. The Pemba branch did not send representatives to
the meeting as they were pro-Arab and slightly anti-main-
land African.

SHIRAZI. The oldest inhabitants on the islands of the coast.
They most likely came in the 13th century via Somalia

from a place called Shiraz in Persia. Others came from the mainland and mingled with the peoples from Persian Gulf resulting in a mixture of African and non-African. They consider themselves African. Ex-slaves and descendants of slaves consider themselves Shiraz. Traditionally, they consist of three tribes--the Hadimu, Tumbatu and Pemba. There is a certain unity among them especially regarding Shirazi vis-a-vis non-Shirazi. Shirazi are all Muslims and follow the rites of the Shafi'i (Sunni) school of law. Shirazi considered Arabs as upstarts and usurpers; Omani Arabs were given land and political power by the Sultan. Arabs regarded Shirazi as inferior racially and culturally; the locals have greater antiquity and are less wealthy. Shirazi are peasant farmers and fishermen and have closer economic ties with the mainland although they considered mainlanders inferior. Arabs used slaves from the mainland; they did not enslave the Shirazi whose rulers at least kept slaves themselves. In Pemba there are Shirazi as well as Arab plantations of cloves even though they are smaller. Relationships are less strained on Pemba and more intermarriage occurs.

SIJAONA, LAWI NANGWANDA (1928-). Born in the Southeastern corner of Tanzania in the Newala District. He attended Minaki Secondary School from 1947-51 and then began a career on the staff of a local magazine as editor. He moved to local government as a clerk to the Newala Local Council in 1955 and was the first African Chairman of Lindi Town Council and in Tanganyika as a whole. In 1961 he joined the central government and was Parliamentary Secretary to the Ministry of Local Government and to the Treasury and then was Minister of National Culture and Youth from 1962-64. He transferred to Lands, Settlement and Water Development and Ministry of Home Affairs where he was responsible for police, prisons, immigration and citizenship. He represented Tanzania with neighboring states, Malawi and Burundi, as Minister of State in the 2nd Vice President's Office. From 1968 to 1971 he served as Minister for Health and Housing and Social Welfare and was also Chairman of TANU Youth League concurrent with that. In February 1972 he began a series of Regional Commissioner posts, serving at West Lake, Mwanza and Kilimanjaro.

SIKHS. They have shown themselves generally willing to

travel away from their home-territory.   In Tanzania
their reputation rests on their skills as masons and car-
penters.   Sikhs form a distinctive community.   They
have a simple and organized body of canonical literature,
a collection of sacred poetry written by their leaders
(gurus).   They stress more congregational worship and
domestic worship is less common.   Women are more
often present in the congregations than in the Hindu services.

SIKI, CHIEF see ISIKE, CHIEF.

SIMBA SPORTS CLUB.   Split off New Youngs in 1937 and
    called themselves "Stanley" and "Eagle of Night" first
    and then settled on the name Sunderland, which they held
    until 1971.   It was replaced by Simba when the new
    building was dedicated.   It was the first club to build a
    house like this.   In 1938 they won the Harvey Cup.
    Their popularity increased greatly from 1944-46.   In
    1965 and 1966 they were the champions of Dar es Salaam.
    In 1973 they won the National Cup and the East African
    Cup.   The latter was won again in 1974.   In 1976 they
    won over Moreto for the 1977 title.

SINA, CHIEF OF KIBOSHO (? -1897).   Held military power
    during the second half of the 19th century, beginning his
    rule in the early 1870's.   He encouraged cultivation and
    fostered trade.   His rival was Rindi of Moshi, so he
    built up a large army at his capital and fort.   He had
    his own blacksmiths and brought most of the territory
    conquered under his administration.   He had been the
    greatest peace-time chief.   The Germans had more pow-
    erful weapons.   When he was defeated, the Germans
    guaranteed peace on two conditions: he was to give his
    two districts to Rindi; and he had to release the Chief of
    Uru from his imprisonment.   He died in 1897, probably
    from poisoning.

SISAL.   Tanzania produces around 75 percent of the world
    production of sisal.   It was the first export and contrib-
    uted about one-third of the value of the country's total
    exports until 1964.   Falling world prices in the world's
    market due to synthetic fibres has been the cause of de-
    crease in production.   Sisal was introduced in Tanga
    District in 1892 by Dr. Hindorf with 62 bulbils obtained
    from Florida.   By 1905 it was the main cash crop in
    German East Africa.   The main growing areas are out

of Tanga, Dar es Salaam and Lindi and along the railway
lines.

Plants grow best with 40 inches of rainfall, but
in suitable soil can grow in 10 inches to 15 inches also.
The plants resemble giant pineapples and have a spike
which shoots up to six feet.   New leaves grow and older
leaves fan out and fall outwards.   When these old ones
mature and are approximately five inches wide and weigh
up to two and a half pounds, they are cut and taken for
processing, often by diesel locomotives on a light railway.   This had required two to four years of growth.
There is no definite harvesting season but a plant's outer
leaves are not taken off oftener than once a year.   Cut-
ting continues from five to seven years.   New plants are
formed on the tall pole or stem; they are blown down by
the wind and take root.   A plantation is also renewed by
suckers, a process in which the old plant and weak suckers are removed.

The greater use of sisal is binder twine and baler
twine.   Only approximately four percent by weight of the
sisal leaves is recovered as fibre.   Other by-products:
wax for use in polish; cortisone, a drug used in treating
rheumatism; pulp used as cattle food; and sodium pectate
for use in food processing and in the textile industry.

Production figures are as follows: 1913, 20,834
tons; 1929, 45,728 tons; 1951, 145,220 tons; 1958,
198,000 tons; 1966, 221,000 tons; 1975, 127,840 tons;
and 1976, 130,000 tons.   These are export figures mainly and there is much used locally in crafts and simple
domestic uses.   By 1951 Tanganyika had produced nearly
26 percent of the world's production of hard fibres and
41 percent of the total sisal produced.   Production began
to fall in 1971.   The 98,467 tons exported in 1975 brought
Shs. 362 million.   About 50 plantations were nationalized
in October 1967.   At the same time, between 50 and 60
percent of the sisal producing companies were also nationalized and the Tanzania Sisal Corporation was created.
Its activities were taken over by the Tanzania Sisal Authority in August, 1977.   Over 50 percent of all Tanzania
sisal is exported and marketed through the Tanzania Sisal
Marketing Association (TASMA).

In 1964 sisal baler twine and rope production began in Tanzania and three factories were producing about
10,000 tons of twine for export in 1966.   In 1976 80,000
tons were exported.   By 1980 all sisal processing is
hoped to be done at Tanga.   Decrease in prices has led
the Tanzania Sisal Corporation to attempt to diversify the

estates into maize, tea, sunflower and coconuts, but
cattle is the greatest alternative.

SLAVE TRADE.   Negro slaves were exported to Persia as
    early as the seventh century.   Slaves were taken to Ara-
    bia and India, where some were used as soldiers.
    About A.D. 760, four hundred soldiers from East Africa
    were in Bagdad.   About A.D. 900, a Chinese book refers
    to an African slave living in China.   By 1200 many Afri-
    can slaves in China were employed as door-keepers.   In
    1450 the approximately 4000 African soldiers in India
    were so powerful that they killed the Indian kings and
    ruled there until defeated by the Asians.   In 1776 Sultan
    Hasan bin Ibrahim signed a treaty with M. Morice, a
    Frenchman, to provide him with 1000 slaves annually for
    100 years.   There was a great need for labor on French
    sugar plantations on Reunion and Mauritius Islands.
    Slaves were brought to the coast by people living a little
    way inland, such as the Yao.   Warriors of the Yao tribe
    in Southern Tanganyika became secret collectors of boys
    and girls in their own district.   Around 1812 there were
    10,000 slaves sold a year at Kilwa.   The year before,
    the Zanzibar Slave Market had opened.   Eighteenth cen-
    tury slaves went to England and to America.   In 1744
    slaves were exchanged for sugar in Brazil.   Arab and
    Swahili slave caravans did not start to travel until the
    1830's.   Slaves were treated with extreme cruelty on the
    journey.   They had to carry heavy loads while chained or
    roped together.   Frequently two slaves were tied to a
    "goree" stick.   They were whipped to make them move
    and slaves too weak to go were killed.   Sometimes as
    many as two-thirds of the slaves in a caravan did not
    reach the coast.
        Kilwa was the mainland center of the slave trade.
    From Kilwa slaves were taken by French ships to Ile de
    France and Bourbon, by dhows to other coastal ports,
    mainly Zanzibar, and by dhows to the Muslim lands of
    Arabia, Persia and India.   The increasing wealth brought
    to Zanzibar and Kilwa caused the rulers of Oman to con-
    trol these places carefully.   Slaves were sold for Shs. 20
    to Shs. 50 in Zanzibar and Shs. 120 in Arabia.   By 1839
    40,000-45,000 slaves were sold annually in Zanzibar,
    half of them to Arabia, Egypt, the Persian Gulf and Por-
    tugal and half for local plantations.   It is said that four
    out of five slaves passing through Tabora died before
    reaching Arabia.
        In 1822 the Moresby Treaty prohibited Arabs to

sell slaves to Christian countries or non-Muslim traders.
The treaty was easily evaded. In 1839 a further extension was made to the Moresby Treaty. The Hamerton
Treaty of 1945 prohibited shipping of slaves from the
Coast. Even though the treaty was ineffective, it began
to undermine the Sultan's power. In 1872 Sultan Barghash
signed a treaty with the British government under a threat
of a naval blockade. This treaty was ineffective. That
same year the Zanzibar Slave Market was closed. It was
in 1890 that the Brussels Act abolished slavery with effect from 1892. By 1894 Sultan Hamoud signed a treaty
abolishing slavery itself in Zanzibar and Pemba. Slavery
was introduced in Legislature in 1909 and permitted slave
owners to free their slaves. In 1906 any child born after
1906 was considered free. No compensation was given
after 1909 when complete and final abolition was given.
The Slavery Decree of 31 December, 1911, also prohibited compensation. The laws for the abolition of slavery,
brought in 24 December, 1904, in German East Africa,
legislated for the freedom of all children born to house
slaves after 31 December, 1905. The British abolished
slavery on the mainland in 1922.

SMUTS, GENERAL JAN CHRISTIAN. The British general in
World War I who led the Allied forces from Kenya into
the German territory in March 1916. They came along
the Kilimanjaro front and by September 1916 had taken
six-sevenths of the German area and nine-tenths of its
population. General von Lettow-Vorbeck was pushed into
the Portuguese territory to the south in November 1917.

SOCIETY FOR GERMAN COLONISATION (Gesellschaft für
Deutsche Kolonisation). Founded in 1844 with Karl Peters
as its president. The Society sent Peters, Juhlke and
Count Pfeil to East Africa. They obtained treaties with
native chiefs in the area between Rivers Pangani and
Rufiji, gaining nominal control over 60,000 square miles.
The large tracts of land had been handed over "for all
time" in exchange for a few trinkets. On Karl Peter's
return to Germany in February 1885, the German Government recognized the treaties and granted a charter to
the Society for these possessions. Karl Peters then
formed the German East Africa Company to administer
the "protectorates."

SODEN, GOVERNOR JULIUS VON (1891-93 Gov.). The first
governor, founded the government system in Tanganyika

in 1891 and had a very clear idea about what form education should take. It was to be completely free from
Christian influences and the medium of instruction was to
be Swahili. The qualifications he required for the first
German education officer were agnosticism and a thorough
knowledge of Swahili. He was prepared, however, to pay
Muslim teachers, who visited government schools to give
religious instruction. The attempt to link Koranic
schools to government schools was not accepted by the
missionaries and Muslim-Government relationships in
education were embittered thereafter. He also tried to
overawe the indigenous peoples by establishing armed
posts in the interior even at the cost of weakening his
hold over the coastal districts.

SOILS. With few exceptions, soils are very poor and deficient
in humus. They are easily eroded and quickly leached.
The most fertile soils are located in the volcanic areas
around the mountains Meru and Kilimanjaro. The Western
Rift has a variety of moderately fertile soils. They are
limited mostly by low moisture-holding capacity and the
steepness of the local terrain.
      In the valley bottoms are the mbugas, dark heavy
clays of fairly high fertility. They are difficult to work
with hand tools, a factor limiting full utility. Other al-
luvial soils are limited due to saline or alkaline qualities
and the unevenness in texture of the mixture of heavy
clays interspersed with poor sandy soil requiring large
amounts of water.
      The soils of the Central Plateau vary from yel-
lowish and sandy to dark-brown clays. They have low to
moderate fertility. The more clayey soils are difficult
to handle when wet. South of Lake Victoria some mbugas
are found. The soils of the Lake Victoria Basin and its
islands are adequate for intensive cultivation. They are
sandy with limestone and coral outcrops in the south and
dry, well-drained yellow to red soils in the west.
      The soils of the Eastern Rift and Mountains are
very heterogeneous. Those under 5,000 ft. tend to bake
and crack deeply in the dry season and have poor drainage in the wet season. They are moderately fertile.
Between 5,000 and 14,000 ft. they tend to be highly acidic
and not very fertile. Above 5,000 ft. the soils of volcanic origin are highly fertile, acidic to neutral, deep and
well-drained. The steepness of the terrain and dispersion
limits the use of these soils.
      The Eastern Plateau soils have moderate fertility

and the utility is limited by the low level and irregularity
of precipitation in the area.   The yellow to red soils of
the hilly areas are better, but have an erosion problem.
In the flatter areas, good, fertile brown clayey soils
exist, but the poor drainage in the wet season limits
their exploitation.
        Coastal soils are light and sandy, have poor mois-
ture holding capacity, are extremely alkaline and a hard
subsoil hinders drainage.   There are patches of fertile
soils in the valleys and deltas of coastal rivers and on
the western side of the islands.   The islands are mainly
coral overlain with soil.   Several valleys contain a sticky
soil called Namo on which rice is grown.

SOKOINE, EDWARD MORINGE (1938-   ).   An appointed
    'Haigwanani' or leader of the Masai in Kisongo, he was
    born near Arusha in 1938 and educated at Umbwe Sec-
    ondary School and Mzumbe Local Government Training
    School.   After completing at Mzumbe in 1963, he attend-
    ed a seminar on administration and finance in West Ger-
    many.   He worked for the Masai District Council as its
    Executive Officer in 1965 and became a member of Par-
    liament the same year.   He was appointed Parliamentary
    Secretary to the Ministry of Commerce, Transportation
    and Labour in 1967, was Chairman of the Transport Li-
    censing Authority from 1967-70, and Minister of State in
    the Vice President's Office from 1970-72.   During that
    time he developed the National Service for Youth and
    molded TPDF for military and socialist training to re-
    cruits.   In February 1972 he was appointed Minister of
    Defence and National Service, a post he held until Feb-
    ruary 1977 when he was promoted to the office of Prime
    Minister.

SONJO (tribe).   Located in the midst of the Masai, who speak
    a Nilo-Hamitic language, is this small Bantu-speaking
    Sonjo island community.   They have an irrigation system
    borrowed from earlier inhabitants.   Sonjo mythology re-
    fers to a culture hero named Khambageu who appeared
    first in a former village known as Tinaga.   He did mira-
    culous acts and brought in a "golden age" of the Sonjo.
    The people at Tinaga treated him badly and he retaliated.
    Many people died and the survivors left the village in two
    groups; the one group was unable to speak the Sonjo lan-
    guage and moved west of the Serengeti Plains and formed
    the Ikoma tribe while the other group joined some Sonjo
    at Kheri.   Khambegeu joined the village of Soyetu for a

long and successful stay. Later he moved on to Belwa
and then Rokhari where he died.

SOUTHERN HIGHLANDS. A relatively dense population area
conducive to agriculture and industry. Almost 80 percent of the pyrethrum grown in Tanzania is grown in the
Iringa, Njombe and Mbeya area of the Southern Highlands. Corn, wheat, and coffee are also grown. Some
settlers are located in these Highlands.

SOUTHERN PROVINCE LINE OF TANGANYIKA RAILWAY.
Built for the project of the Overseas Food Corporation
known as the Groundnut Scheme. The first section from
Mkwaya at the head of Lindi Creek to Ruo and Nyaching-
wea was opened in 1949. The second section was opened
in 1954 when Mtwara port was linked with Ruo. The
third, and last, section was opened in 1958 from Chilin-
gula to Masasi to assist the production of cashewnuts.
The Tanganyika Agricultural Corporation took over the
planted and plowed-up lands, still optimistic about a
Southern route. The Railway was removed when the
scheme did not succeed.

SPEKE, JOHN HANNING (1827-1864). The discoverer of the
Nile Source, he was a fair-haired, heavy man. He was
born in Somersetshire on 4 May, 1827, and entered the
Bengal Army in India in 1844. He joined Burton on a
journey to Somaliland and then arrived with R. Burton in
Zanzibar in 1856 with the aim of exploring the inland.
They set off in June 1857 on an Arab route from Bagamoyo to Kazeh. He suffered an eye problem. In the
course of their journey Speke saw Lake Victoria and
guessed the river north of it was the Nile. He named
the lake "Victoria Nyanza." He reached Lake Tanganyika
in February 1858. He then returned with Burton to England. Speke arranged another expedition with James
Grant under the Royal Geographic Society and the British
Government. He led a caravan of 217 people inland in
September 1860. Speke became involved in an Arab-African warfare along the slave route to Kazeh and went on
to Buganda and Khartoum. In 1863 after the Speke-Grant
expedition, he wrote his Journal of the Discovery of the
Source of the Nile. On 15 September, 1864, a day before a meeting of the British Association at Bath, at
which Burton and Speke were to discuss their opposing
conclusions about the source of the Nile, Speke accident-
ally shot himself while out partridge hunting.

SPISS, BISHOP CASSIAN (? - 1905). Travelling with two lay
brothers and two sisters of the Benedictine Order during
September 1905 from Kilwa on Songea Caravan Route to
the Mission station at Peramiho, he was deserted by
his porters. At Liwale he was surrounded by rebels and
killed.

STANLEY, HENRY MORTON (1841-1904). Born on 29 June,
1841, at Denbigh, North Wales he was baptized John Row-
lands. At sixteen he went to America as a cabin boy on
a ship. Not long afterwards he was adopted by a merchant named Henry Morton Stanley and took his new father's name. He served in the Civil War on the southern
side. Later he became a correspondent for the New York
Herald. As such, he set out to find Livingstone in 1871.
He was a forceful man; he set himself a task and he allowed nothing to delay his fulfilling of that task. In November 1871, when he finally found Livingstone at Ujiji,
Stanley voiced the famous words--"Dr. Livingstone, I
presume?" On 17 November, 1874, he set out from Bagamoyo and reached Lake Victoria in 104 days. He set
out to travel around the lake by canoe to settle the European disputes about it. It took eight weeks to go around
it. He proved Victoria Nyanza to be one large inland
sea. Stanley then went on via Uganda to the mouth of the
Congo River. He visited Kabaka, Mirambo and Rumanika
between 1874 and 1877 to pave the way for Christian missions. He also travelled around Lake Tanganyika to prove
it has no connection with the Nile system. He crossed
Africa from west to east in 1887-89 with the Emin Pasha
Relief Expedition. His attitude towards human as well as
natural obstacles earned him the nickname of "The Smash-
er of Rocks. " He died in London on 10 May, 1904.

STATE FARMS. During the late 1960's the following State
Farms programs were noted:

Crop	No. of farms	Total acreage
Wheat	10	100, 000
Rice	4	13, 000
Vine	1	1, 000
Dairy	2	?
Ranches	9	-
Oilseeds	1	4, 000
Coconut	2	6, 000
Total	29	124, 000

During nationalization, State Farms were handed over
mainly to cooperative adventures. Of the 57, 9 are owned
by Tanzania Cotton Authority; 4 owned by Tanzania Tea
Authority; 1 by the Tobacco Authority of Tanzania; 4 by
General Agricultural Products Export Corporation; 14 by
Tanzania Sisal Corporation; 24 by NAFCO (National Food
Corporation); and 2 by the Ministry of Agriculture.

STATE TRADING CORPORATION (STC). When businesses
were nationalized in 1967, several large private import-
export houses together with two government owned retail
and wholesale companies (COSATA and INTRATA) formed
the nucleus of the STC, the authorized body for external
and wholesale trade. To a large extent the STC was expected to build on the work of INTRATA (The International
Trading and Credit Company of Tanganyika) and its management was retained to manage the new STC. It was
disbanded in 1973 and replaced by the Board of Internal
Trade supervising 20 regional trading companies and six
national import organizations.

STEERE, DR. BISHOP. A founder of the Anglican Church in
Zanzibar and Tanganyika in the UMCA. In 1876 he went
south with a number of Yao who had been slaves. They
got as far as Masasi but could not find their homes, so
they established a mission there. He built the Cathedral
and started a printing press. Bishop Steere's books in
Swahili are standard works. He produced a handbook of
the Swahili language in 1865.

STIRLING, LEADER DOMINIC (1906-). Qualified as a doctor in England and came to Tanganyika as a mission doctor in 1935. He built a hospital at Lulindi (Masasi) and
ran it for 18 years. His second hospital was built at
Mnero (Nachingwea). This he ran for 15 years. He finally took over the new hospital at Kibosho on the slopes
of Mt. Kilimanjaro and operated it for five years. He
has a special interest in training schools for nurses and
rural medical aids. He retired in 1969 to part time
work in hospitals at Lushoto and Bumbuli in Usambara
but he gave that up when political activities increased.
He was first elected to Legislative Council in 1959 and
has been active in TANU and LEGCO since. He served
as Chairman of the Tanzania Christian Medical Association
and as Chief Scout of Tanzania. In November 1975 he was
appointed Minister of Health.

SUGAR. Introduced in the lowland area of Moshi District, by
    1938 it had an output of 5,000 tons. Sugar was grown on
    plantations which operate their own factories. Production
    was as follows: 29,000 in 1961; 70,000 in 1966; 90,000
    in 1971; 115,000 in 1973/74; and 190,000 tons in 1976.
    By 1966 two large and three smaller factories were in
    operation and a sixth one was in construction. The two
    main producers were the Tanganyika Planting Company
    and the Kilombero Sugar Company together producing 85
    percent of the tonnage. Tanzania has a large, local con-
    sumption but still exported 30,614.6 tons out of the 1975
    production.

SUKUMA (tribe). South of Lake Victoria, it is the largest
    tribe in Tanzania with over 1.5 million, but it only con-
    sists of one-tenth of the total population. It is three
    times the size of any other tribe. The Sukuma are cul-
    turally and linguistically related to many of the western
    Tanzania tribes, especially the Nyamwezi just south of
    them. Politically, the Sukuma have been highly developed,
    loosely knit chiefdoms, more than 30 independent groups
    for more than 200 years, each with a ruler called the
    Ntemi. The Ntemi were of immigrant origin whose func-
    tions were primarily ritual and judicial. In 1932 the
    leaders of the 51 chiefdoms met at Mwanza as a step to-
    wards federal union. The Sukuma Federation was formed
    in October 1946 and 7 federations of chiefs were esta-
    blished. Their headquarters were located at Malya,
    Maswa District. The Sukuma Federal Council was ga-
    zetted as a Supreme Native Authority and dealt with mat-
    ters of policy and local legislation and controlled the
    amalgamated treasury of the chiefs.
        The Sukuma, a patrilineal society, are mainly sub-
    sistence agriculturalists and cattle raisers. Cattle is
    used for the brideprice instead of the traditional hoes.
    The soil is poor, rainfall is uncertain (less than 30 in-
    ches per year) and famine is not unknown. Rice and cot-
    ton are the cash crops. The cooperative movement de-
    veloped before 1950 and grew to marketing cotton, owning
    ginneries and rice mills. Millet, sorghum and maize are
    the other chief crops. Gold-mining at Geita and diamond
    mining at Shinyanga are wealth producing areas in the
    Sukuma tribal area.

SULAIMAN AL-HASAN BIN DAUDI. Reigned at Kilwa from
    1170 to 1188. With his father's help he gained the mas-
    tery of the gold trade. He conquered as far north as

Pemba Island and first founded Kilwa citadel building it
with stone and lime and embellishing it with towers.

SULTAN.   A ruler sometimes called Seyyid or Sayyid.   See
the lists of Sultans for Kilwa and for Zanzibar on pages
x-xii. See also each important sultan under his own personal entry.

SUNDAY NEWS.   Carries a fuller coverage of news than the
Daily News.   Feature articles and photos of weddings and
special occasions make it more attractive.

SUNFLOWER SEEDS.   An increase of over 100 percent took
place from 1960 to 1970 with the production being 6000
metric tons and 13,000 tons respectively.   The regional
collections have been over 7000 tons annually in the
1970's and the export value in 1975 of the 3313 tons was
Shs. 6.8 million.

SUSI.   A faithful companion of Livingstone on his journeys
who helped to carry his body back 1400 miles to the
East African coast.   After Susi's return from England,
he was for many years a UMCA caravan leader and was
baptized David.   He died in 1891, after being nursed
through a long illness by missionaries.

SWAHILI (language).   The name is derived from the Arabic
sahil (coast).   The Swahili language began to develop into its present form in the 13th century.   Bantu in structure, its vocabulary has been derived from many tongues
of traders--Arabs, Persians, Portuguese, Turkish and
Indians--and from English as well.   Swahili was the common language of the coast for years even though Arabic
was the official written language.   Many island and coastal inhabitants speak Swahili as their native tongue, others
as a lingua franca or the official language.   In 1927 the
governments of Uganda, Kenya and Tanganyika decided to
promote Swahili as a common "African" language throughout the whole of East Africa.   Critics of this policy also
suspected that an introduction of Swahili was connected
with the move towards a closer union of the three territories.   On 21 February, 1964, in Zanzibar, Swahili was
given the status of official language, but on the mainland,
Swahili shared with English the status of official language
until 1967 when Swahili only was maintained.

SWAHILI (people).   They do not actually constitute a separate

ethnic group but embrace the strongly Arabized and detribalized people along the coast and in the off-lying islands who derive from many tribes and often incorporate
significant elements of diverse alien stocks. They are
essentially Bantu people, a mixture of Persian Arab and
African Moslems through intermarriage. In religion,
dress and social intercourse, the details of their daily
life are modelled upon Arabs. The name is derived from
the Arabic sahil (coast). They total around one million.

SWAI, ASANTERABI Z. (1925-). A schoolmaster and business man, he was born near Machame at the foothills of
Mt. Kilimanjaro and was locally educated before he went
in 1944 to study maths and sciences at Makerere College.
He also studied at the University of Bombay, Delhi and
Pittsburgh. He joined the Institute of Education in 1946
and then taught in Dar es Salaam from 1947-50. He obtained a Diploma in Education at Makerere before teaching
in a secondary school at Dodoma. In 1951 he was the
Vice Principal of KNCU School at Lyamungu. The assistant warden at Makerere (1952), taught at Arusha (1953),
General Manager of the Meru Cooperative Union (1958)
and Chairman of TANU's Economic and Social Development Committee (1960) and Provincial Chairman. He became the National Treasurer of TANU. After independence he held many government posts: Minister for Commerce and Industry, Minister for Health and Labour,
Minister without portfolio, represented Tanganyika at the
U.N., first Minister for Development and Planning,
Minister of Industries, Mineral Resources and Power,
Minister of State in the President's Office, Minister for
Economic Affairs and Development, then in 1967 Minister
for East African Affairs. As such, he was Tanzania's
Minister to the East Africa Community. In 1976 he was
at the U.N.

SWEDISH MISSION. The Lutheran Swedish missionaries were
invited to Mbulu in 1939 by Chief Gitagano who had been
hospitalized at Singida. They carried on medical and
educational work and by 1950 the Norwegian Lutheran
Mission took over the 170 Christians and 150 catechists.
This was the beginning of what is now known as the Synod
of Mbulu. There are about 10,000 Christians and 60 worship centers, 9 African pastors and 31 evangelists, 1
Bible School, 1 hospital and 2 dispensaries.
        Other Swedish missionaries aided the Bethel Mis-
sion in Bukoba. See BETHEL MISSION.

SWYNNERTON, CHARLES FRANCIS (1877-1936). A naturalist interested in botany, he was appointed Director of Game Preservation in Tanganyika in 1919 at forty-two years of age. He had formerly worked in Rhodesia. Swynnerton drew up most of the game laws still in force after independence and also served as consultant to other East Africa governments. He undertook the study and control of the tsetse fly, publishing his standard work Tsetse Flies of East Africa in 1936. That same year on his way to Dar es Salaam to receive the CMG, he met with a fatal air accident and was buried near Old Shinyanga.

SYKES, ABDUL WALID (1924-1968). A son of Kleist Sykes, he joined the KAR at eighteen and served abroad. In 1948 he became the Secretary of the Dock-workers Union. He served as TAA's Eastern Province Secretary and, in 1953, as President of TAA. He was the first Tanzanian appointed to a senior post in the Prison's Department when he was appointed Assistant Superintendent.

SYKES, ALLY KLEIST (1926-). A son of Kleist Sykes, was TANU's first secretary in 1954 and designed the TANU card with green and black. He was General Secretary of TAGSA (Tanganyika African Government Servants Association). He was one of the two TANU members first to be detained at Salisbury on their way home from a political meeting in Lusaka. He is head of K. Sykes and Sons business in Dar es Salaam.

SYKES, KLEIST (1894-1949). Born at Pangani, he enlisted as a soldier in the signals section at the age of twelve. After World War I he was employed by the railways department. He was secretary of the Workers Union at the railways. He helped to form TAA and in 1929 was its first secretary. He also served as secretary of the Moslem Association. Upon his retirement from the Railway service in 1942, he founded the K. Sykes and Sons business. He was a member of the Dar es Salaam Township Authority in 1944.

SYMES, SIR STEWARD. A former Resident and Commander-in-Chief in Aden, he was Governor of Tanganyika from 23 May, 1931, to 18 February, 1934. He introduced a program of retrenchment and began a long term scheme to increase Tanganyika's prosperity by means of a productivity drive.

- T -

TABORA.   Earlier called Kazeh, it is situated in the Nyamwezi tribal area.   The first Arabs reached Tabora around
1825 after a four-month journey.   Around 1840 there were
25 Arabs living around Tabora and the location became a
sort of depot at a place where caravan routes from the
Lakes met.   By 1958 the town had a population of 15,000.
Shortage of water hinders its development.   The Central
Railway Line provided the main transportation for years
through Tabora.   By 1967 the population had risen to
21,000 and had become an important trading center for
agricultural produce--tobacco, groundnuts, grains and
pulses.   Besides the famous Tabora Government Secondary School where many government officials studied, Tabora has the Railway Apprentices School, Warder's
Training School, Secretarial College, and a blind and
deaf school.   In 1977 the population reached 29,000.

TABORA SCHOOL.   Opened in 1925 as a Central School and
for the first ten years received only sons of chiefs and
headmen.   Until its conversion to a Junior Secondary
School in 1933 by adding Grades IX and X, no secondary
education facilities existed in Tanganyika.   The school
trained clerks for Government service and commercial
firms.   Many of the leaders of Tanganyika after independence were 'old boys' of Tabora, having read there
when it went up to Std. XII.

TANDAU, ALFRED CYRIL (1936-   ).   Born at Mbinga on
6 January, 1936, and entered medical training in Dar es
Salaam in 1955 after completing his secondary education
at Old Moshi Secondary School.   Tandau attended Kasubi
College in Uganda 1955-56 and served as Assistant Cooperative Inspector at Songea in 1957 and on to a Lab
Technician on Training at Arusha for the East Africa
High Commission.   From 1957-59 he was a bank clerk.
He joined the Transport and General Workers Union in
1959 as a Branch Secretary at Arusha and transferred
to Dar es Salaam as its Financial Secretary.   He became
the Deputy General Secretary of TFL at twenty-six years
of age in 1962 and of NUTA in 1964.   In March 1968 he
was appointed General Manager of Friendship Textile
Mills and Secretary General of NUTA in 1969.   Tandau
was part of the All African Trade Union Federation
(AATUF), a post still held to the end of 1976, with
Headquarters in Dar es Salaam, and was its Treasurer

from 1966-71 and elected Agricultural Secretary General
in February 1971. In February 1972 he was appointed
Minister of Labour, in November 1975 was Minister of
Communication and Transport, and in February 1977 appointed Minister for Works.

TANGA. Established by the Persian traders in the 14th cen-
    tury and experienced a great development under the Ger-
    mans. The railway opened up the town to a wealthy
    hinterland and developed the sisal industry. The Tanga
    Line connects to the Dar es Salaam-Moshi/Arusha line.
    By 1905 there was a population of 5600 and by 1957 it
    was the second largest town with a population of 38,000.
    It held this position and had 61,000 people by 1967. In
    the 1950's Tanga had a RR schooner service with Dar es
    Salaam. All the sisal crop is exported at Tanga. It has
    a large, safe, natural harbor with 1200 feet of lighterage
    quays and five anchorages. It has a cranage capacity of
    74 tons. Tanga has an ample supply of power on the
    Pangani River 35 miles away. Industries besides sisal
    and timber, the main ones, are soap-making, oil milling,
    vehicle repair and woodworking. It has a 410-bed hos-
    pital and trains medical assistants. In 1975 the popula-
    tion had risen to 89,000 and by 1977 was 98,000.

TANGA LINE. Begun by a private company in 1893 and
    failed due to lack of funds. The government took it over
    and reached Korogwe by 1902. It took 12 years to build
    the Tanga-Korogwe-Mombo part. They reached Moshi by
    February 1912. The link with the Mombasa line, from
    Kahe Junction to Voi, was built by the British to further
    their 1915-16 German East Africa Campaign. For years
    this part of the line carried most of the coffee from
    Moshi-Arusha. The Moshi-Arusha extension was opened
    in 1929. A short, narrow gauge branch line from Ten-
    geru to Sigi was a useful link between the Usambara
    Railway line and Amani Institute. The line from Tanga
    to Moshi is 219 miles and to Arusha is 273 miles (352
    km.).

TANGANYIKA. The mainland of the United Republic of Tan-
    zania. The word "nyika" means "thorny bushland" or
    "wasteland." It was first a part of German East Africa,
    then known as Tanganyika after World War I when Britain
    held a mandate of the territory. The name "Tanganyika"
    was adopted by the British on 1 February, 1920. After
    World War II it was known as Tanganyika Territory and

was a trust territory of the U. N. Tanganyika was granted
independence on 9 December, 1961, and the word Territory was dropped from its name. On 26 April, 1964,
Zanzibar joined with Tanganyika to form Tanzania.
        Tanganyika is situated 1° S to nearly 12° S and from
29° E to 40° E. Altitude conquers latitude. At the coast
the mean temperature is 25. 5° C or 78° F. It covers an
area of 363, 000 square miles including about 20, 000
square miles of water surface. It is larger than Nigeria
and almost the size of Ethiopia and covers an area greater than Belgium, France, Switzerland and Italy combined.

TANGANYIKA AFRICAN ASSOCIATION (TAA). Began in the
    end of the 1920's and at first it seemed to have no politi-
    cal ambitions. It was formed by ex-secondary school
    students who were denied posts of any importance. At
    first it functioned mainly as a mutual benefit organization
    for urban Africans. It had 120 members. TAA held its
    first territorial conference in 1942. At its third one in
    1945 at Dodoma, TAA called for universal brotherhood;
    took a stand against the concept of Tanganyika as an area
    of white settlement especially rejecting white domination
    of political and economic power; complained that educa-
    tional opportunities for Africans were unsatisfactory; pro-
    posed education for both sexes be made compulsory; sug-
    gested Negroes from America and Africans from South
    Africa be recruited as teachers; called for the establish-
    ment and recognition of trade unions; and, did not attack
    the then existing government. After World War II, TAA
    became increasingly political. It developed to a national
    movement effected through tribal unions. The early TAA
    members had been junior government officials and teach-
    ers, but by 1948 traders and African farmers joined as
    well as government and native authority employees. TAA
    had many branches in the Lake, Northern, Eastern and
    Tanga provinces, and an annual subscription of six shil-
    lings. In 1948 there were 39 branches and 1780 mem-
    bers. After elections in 1950, TAA selected six Moslem
    old men (shiekhs) to be their advisers, hence to get re-
    spect and a hearing with Sir Charles, etc. They met with
    Drydale and wife, Minister of State for Colonial Affairs,
    who visited Africa and refused to lunch wherever Africans
    were not invited. By 1953 J. K. Nyerere was elected as
    TAA's President. On 7 July, 1954, drastic changes were
    made, including the name change to TANU.

TANGANYIKA AFRICAN NATIONAL UNION. Born on 7th July,

1954, after a four-day annual meeting soon after the
death of its forerunner TAA (Tanganyika African Association). The meeting was attended by 17 delegates: D.
Aziz, L. Bagoha, K. Gabara, A. Iranga, S. Kandoro,
J. Kassella, J. Kimalendo, N. K. Japhet Kirilo, S. Kit-
wana, G. Kunambi, C. Milinga, G. Pacha, J. Rupia,
S. Tewa Said, A. Sykes. A draft was drawn up, aimed
at transforming TAA from a social organization into a
political union. It was tabled and adopted and had 12 objectives. It aimed at uniting all nationalists in the country and opposing tribalism in the interests of building up
a nation-wide organization. It sought to achieve political,
economic and social advance for Africans. It worked for
self-government and independence and pledged to African
rule.
      In 1955 TANU asked for three Dar es Salaam
Legislative Council members to be elected and for more
African members. By 1956 TANU asked for all Representative Members to be elected by universal adult suf-
frage and demanded that half of the Executive and Legislative Council members be African. In 1956 TANU Conference made a small concession by agreeing that persons of mixed African and other blood be admitted, this
being a response to the UTP, a multi-racial party.
      The year 1958 was a year of great activity due to
the first general elections. All of TANU-backed candidates in the September 1958 elections were NOT defeated.
TANU mushroomed to a membership of 100,000 and 30-
some branches by 1956. The membership was between
150,000 and 200,000 in 1959. It brought the country to
independence in seven years.
      The National Executive Committee of the National
Conference was the supreme policy making body. Under
it and responsible to it was the Central Committee which
carried out the administrative duties. Under the National
level was the Regional divisions with the Regional Commissioner as the Party Secretary, then the District Branch
with the Area Commissioner as its Secretary, then the
Branch and cell divisions at the bottom. TANU's affili-
ates included members of NUTA, COSATA, and TAPA.
Departments within TANU which were the best known were
the Elder's Section, Union of Women of Tanzania and TYL.
      In 1963 membership in the Party was opened to all
citizens living in Tanzania. TANU's basic tenents were:
that the state should control the means of production and
that the society should not become economically stratified.
In 1976 a 20-man TANU and ASP Commission met to lay

the foundation for a merger and new party.   They amalgamated on 5 February, 1977.

TANGANYIKA AFRICAN NATIONAL UNION GUIDELINES:
(MWONGOZO) were drawn up in February 1971.   They
put a great deal of emphasis on building the country and
defending it.   They call for a leadership which is of the
people in economic as well as political matters.   They
call for new attitudes and practices in order to facilitate
public decision-making.   The Guidelines call for great
changes, possibly greater than of the Arusha Declaration.
They call for an understanding, both by management and
the people, of socialist and democratic activities.

TANGANYIKA AFRICAN NATIONAL UNION YOUTH LEAGUE
(TYL).   A department within TANU for the youth.   One
member from each region attends the National Conference
as an ex officio member.   Its members are considered
reserves for military emergencies, and, after the army
mutiny of January 1964, formed a great majority of the
new army.   TYL members, very politically aware, have
been troublesome at times during their history, but des-
pite sporadic attempts to governmentalize it by incorporating it into the Ministry of Culture and Youth, the TYL
held its own identity.   TANU Youth League has branches
in schools to link the life of the scholar with that of the
people.

TANGANYIKA AFRICAN PARENTS' ASSOCIATION (TAPA).
TAPA began in 1955 as DAPA in Dar es Salaam and
APA in Tanga and was formed on a national scale in
1957.   TANU had opened 233 schools and handed them
over with their 15,000 pupils to TAPA in 1956.   TAPA's
purpose was to organize some kind of formal or informal
instruction to meet the demands for primary education
which existing institutions could not satisfy; it was the
education wing of TANU.   Before independence TAPA ran
schools of dubious legality, recruiting whatever teachers
it could find from dropouts in the educational system.
After independence TAPA gained a new respectability
when it was recognized as a voluntary agency and had its
own Education Secretary General.   By 1970 government
nationalized 123 of TAPA's primary schools and they remained with 322 registered and 213 unregistered schools.
TAPA has been very active opening new schools and the
1976 figures were:

	PRIMARY SCHOOLS	TECHNICAL EDUCATION	SECONDARY EDUCATION	TOTALS
Schools	1,520	18	5	1,543
Pupils	156,441	1,438	891	158,770
Teachers	2,471	97	38	2,606

TAPA had a program in the 1970's for the training of its teachers and 229 of the primary school teachers were trained by 1976. The post-primary technical schools had 4-year courses, each specializing in several of ten professional options, masonry and carpentry being a requirement for each school due to the greater need for these skilled artisans in the nation.

From 1955 to 1976 TAPA had four chairmen, Clement Ntamila being the first and J. M. Lucinde, the fourth, having served the longest (1963-1976). The fifth and latest General Secretary, E. M. Waryoba, began his work in 1973. TAPA was an affiliate of TANU and had representatives on the National Executive Council of TANU. When TANU and ASP merged, this affiliate had to make some changes as well.

TANGANYIKA AGRICULTURAL CORPORATION (TAC).
Formed in 1953 to promote a healthy, prosperous, yeomen farmers class, firmly established on the land, appreciable of its fruits, jealous of its inherent wealth, and dedicated to maintaining the family unit on it. The settlement schemes under TAC were not very successful in creating a class of this type.

TANGANYIKA BROADCASTING CORPORATION. Formed in 1956 but changed to Radio Tanzania in 1965. It was an independent statutory body partly financed by government grants and partly by radio licenses and commercial advertisements. See also RADIO OF TANZANIA.

TANGANYIKA CHRISTIAN REFUGEE SERVICE. A branch of the Christian Council of Tanzania (CCT) which provides food and clothing to persons in special need. Farmers receive seeds to help them become self-supporting, students are sponsored in schools and colleges. Victims of serious floods are given assistance and flour mills, etc. are provided to settling refugees.

TANGANYIKA EDUCATION CONFERENCE OF 1925.   The
    first territorial education conference, it brought together
    approximately fifty administrators, missionaries, repre-
    sentatives of the Indian Association, the Chamber of
    Commerce, the British and Foreign Bible Society, the
    Planters Association and the editor of the Dar es Salaam
    Times.   The Conference was considered a success as it
    laid the groundwork for a partnership control over educa-
    tion in the territory between government and missions.
    In 1926 a Central Tanganyika Advisory Committee on Af-
    rican Education was formed and the machinery was set
    up for putting into operation the changes agreed upon at
    the Conference.

TANGANYIKA ELECTED MEMBERS ORGANISATION.   Formed
    in 1959 with Julius Nyerere as Chairman.   This group
    was composed of people who were elected to the Legisla-
    tive Council.

TANGANYIKA EPISCOPAL CONFERENCE (TEC).   The merger
    of all Catholic orders with Headquarters in Dar es Salaam.
    As early as 1938, an Education Secretary General had
    been appointed.   The Secretariat was first formed in 1954
    and called the Tanganyika Catholic Welfare Organisation.
    It had a secretary-general, a treasurer and five depart-
    ments: Education Dept.; Land and Finance (Welfare)
    Dept.; Lay Apostolate and Pastoral Dept.; Medical-Social
    Dept.; and Publicity Department.   The Tanganyika Epis-
    copal Conference was established and registered in 1957,
    renamed in 1962 and given its present name, Tanzania
    Episcopal Conference in 1964.   Archbishop Maranta was
    the first Chairman serving from 1956-64.   In 1962 Rev.
    Father Joseph Sipende was appointed the first African
    Education Secretary General.   The education system un-
    der his jurisdiction was as follows:

TYPE OF SCHOOL	NUMBER	TOTAL PUPILS
Primary Schools (I-VI)	1,116	168,923
Upper Primary Schools (V-VIII)	129	17,953
Secondary Schools	14	2,611
Teacher Training-Grade C	11	718
Grade B	2	116
Grade A	1	40
Boys' Trade Schools	12	499
Homecraft and Domestic Science	37	1,862
Co-ed Primary Schools	3	1,440
Co-ed Secondary Schools	1	348
Bush Schools (Part II)	1,580	65,105

From 1961 the Vatican Radio had Swahili broadcasts. There were 4 Senior Seminaries in 1962, 23 hospitals, 8 TB units, 5 training schools, 68 dispensaries, 74 bedded dispensaries, 64 maternities and 7 leprosariums. There were 300 priests ordained between 1917 and 1963, 89 brothers and 1491 sisters in Tanzania and 8 Bishops (including Cardinal Rugambwa). TEC operated 7 bookshops and 4 printing presses. See TANZANIA EPISCOPAL CONFERENCE for more recent information.

TANGANYIKA FEDERATION OF LABOUR (TFL). Registered in 1955 with 17 registered trade unions affiliated to it. There had only been five trade unions by 1947. By 1958 sisal workers formed the National Plantation Workers' Union with a membership of 30,000. During a general strike in Dar es Salaam when Asian and European supervisors manned the transportation system, TANU supported an effective boycott by African customers. The most important manifestation of common interest between TANU and TFL was a limited overlap of leadership. Rashidi Kawawa, general secretary of TFL until 1959 and later president, joined the TANU Central Committee in 1959 and was Vice President of TANU in 1960. In 1960 Kawawa was succeeded as president of TFL by Michael Kamaliza. The community of interest between TANU and TFL began to show rifts.

Some of the most important goals of the trade union movement were fundamentally inconsistent with those of a party which expected to operate a responsible government in a developing nation. TANU and TFL both sought Africanization in managerial positions. However, after independence when TANU was seeking to fill key positions with qualified employees, the rate of Africanization decreased and it came under fire from TFL. TFL also felt betrayed by TANU when it supported the managerial position in a strike at the diamond mine. These disagreements led to factionalism within the TFL--anti-government versus pro-government. Kamaliza, the pro-government leader, was appointed Minister for Health and Labour. He saw no difference between the goals of labor and those of government and introduced legislation to accomplish these goals: The Trade Unions Ordinance (Amendment) of 1962; the Trade Disputes (Settlement) Act of 1962; and the Civil Servants (Negotiating Machinery) Act of 1962. The legislation was passed. Unions were required to be under the TFL and the right to strike was restricted. When the TFL threatened to order a general

strike in support of the mutineers in January 1964, the
government dissolved the federation and detained 200 of
its leaders and active members. A legislative act replaced TFL with NUTA (National Union of Tanganyika
Workers) and appointed its executive.

TANGANYIKA LIBRARY SERVICES BOARD. Established under an Act in July 1963, was properly constituted in
November 1963 and assumed full responsibility on 1
April, 1964. The East African Literature Bureau was
the pioneer of the public library movement in East Africa and the Director and the TLS Board inherited 11 members of the staff, 50,000 books, Shs.8,259 and equipment
from the EALB. The first great task of TLS Board was
to prepare a library development plan acceptable to the
government to be incorporated in the 1964-1969 Five Year
Plan. They estimated library services in a total of 17
main centers throughout the country. By December 1967
the National Central Library was formally opened. Four
branches up-country were in operation by 1969--Mwanza,
Iringa, Bukoba and Tanga. Training of professional librarians began in 1964 and had trained 10 by 1969.
Moshi and Arusha were the next branch libraries to operate during the 2nd Five Year Plan.

Mobile Libraries began operating from Tanga,
Mwanza and Kibaha and a fourth one was added at Moshi
in 1972. Mobile Libraries were emphasized in order to
ensure that the new literates do not lapse into illiteracy
again. In 1970 the Board approved the formation of a
Special and Government Libraries Advisory Committee to
advise the Board on the development and coordination of
Special and Government libraries with other types of libraries.

The first attempt to aid School Libraries was made
in 1965 when the Children's and School Librarian of Tanganyika Library Services was commissioned by the Board
to undertake a survey of the School Libraries and prepare
a report on their improvement and development. In 1968
a UNESCO expert was seconded to TLS and three model
libraries were established at Mazengo S/S, Mzumbe S/S
and Kihesa S/S, teacher librarians' courses were set up
and in 1971 the first School Mobile Van started serving
School Libraries in Iringa, Dodoma and Morogoro Regions. The same year the Advisory Committee on School
libraries was established by the Board.

In June 1971 the TLS in collaboration with the
Ministry of National Education inaugurated the Library

Assistants course. There were then 7 branches and 2
sub-branches and the number increased until 1976 when
there were 11 branches and 3 sub-branches.
    Other methods used to reach the isolated public
are: Loan collections (184 centers), Static Centers,
Postal Library Service (membership of 2097 with 400
active members). See also TANZANIA LIBRARY SER-
VICE.

TANGANYIKA MISSIONARY COUNCIL. Formed in the early
    days of the Mandate and revised in 1934. It represented
    the Protestant Church agencies to government and com-
    municated back to the missions policies and regulations
    decided upon by the government. In 1938 a few Africans
    were invited to sit on the Council as representatives with-
    out voting powers. Members of the Council represented
    UMCA, CMS, Moravian, Berlin Mission, Bethel Mission
    and Leipzig Mission. In 1948 the Council was revised to
    form the Christian Council of Tanganyika (CCT).

TANGANYIKA NATIONAL SOCIETY (TNS). On 5 December,
    1955, the TNS Manifesto appeared in the Tanganyika
    Standard. It was the first multi-racial society in Tan-
    ganyika as opposed to the racial nationalism of TANU.
    The name never carried and it was changed to the United
    Tanganyika Party (UTP).

TANGANYIKA RIFLES. At Independence two Battalions of
    the KAR were transferred to the new government and
    called Tanganyika Rifles.   By early 1964 they numbered
    around 2000.   The one battalion stationed at Dar es
    Salaam staged a mutiny on 19 January, 1964, demanding
    higher pay and the discharge of their British officers to
    permit Africanization of the army.   Lesser disturbances
    were felt at Tabora and Nachingwea.   After the union of
    Zanzibar and Tanganyika, the Tanzania People's Defence
    Forces were formed.   The army up to 1964 was non-
    political.

TANGANYIKA STANDARD. Begun 1 January, 1930, in full-
    page format and normally six pages in length covering
    both international and local news, editorials, sports and
    other feature articles, and classified advertisement.
    "Letters to the Editor" contained criticism of and com-
    plaints about the government or voiced views on social
    and political problems.   Its name was changed to Daily
    News in 1972.   It had already been nationalized for over
    a year.   See also DAILY NEWS and PERIODICALS.

TANGANYIKA TERRITORY AFRICAN CIVIL SERVICE ASSO-
CIATION (TTACSA). Founded by Martin Kayamba while
in Tanga in March 1922. The Association later moved
to Dar es Salaam and some of its members took part in
the founding of TAA in 1928 and 1929. The Association
was a club for clerks and teachers, with newspapers and
a football team, and encouraged by the government. It
was not a mass nationalist movement, but it linked educated men with members of Tanga's coastal society, mix-
ing peoples of various religions and races into a friendly
associative group. TTACSA was later renamed Tanganyika African Government Servants' Association in 1943.

TANZAM RAILWAY see GREAT UHURU RAILWAY

TANZANIA EPISCOPAL CONFERENCE (TEC). The organization of Archbishops, and Bishops of Tanzania which aims
at adopting the most suitable means of promoting interests and the welfare of the total Catholic Church in Tanzania. See TANGANYIKA EPISCOPAL CHURCH for its
activities before 1964 when the name was changed. Before 1970 when the schools were nationalized, TEC operated 1378 Primary Schools, 44 Secondary Schools, 8
Teacher Training Colleges, 2 Commercial Schools, 15
Trade Schools, 48 Handcraft and Domestic Science centers, a school for the deaf and dumb and a School for
the Blind. Catholic Relief Services helped to provide
lunches in day primary schools, secondary schools and
hospitals. In the same year TEC had 25 hospitals, 75
dispensaries, 74 maternity clinics, 11 medical training
schools, and 17 TB units or small hospitals.
    Mwenge, Kiongozi and Ecclesia are their widely
circulated magazines. The first chairman of TEC was
Archbishop Maranta. There were 15 minor and 4 major
seminaries and 10 catechist training schools.

	1968		1976	
Members	2.2 million		2.9 million	

	African	Missionaries	African	Missionaries
Bishops	-	-	21	4
Fathers	401	877	625	790
Brothers	75	324	136	239
Sisters	1,408	773	2,234	589

TANZANIA LIBRARY SERVICE BOARD. Preceded by the
Tanganyika Library Services Board. The name was

changed in a 1975 Tanzania Library Services Board Act.
The main objective of the Act was to reorganize TLS
Board so as to confer upon it wider functions: documentation; training of librarians; control and supervision over
public libraries; promotion of literacy campaigns; stimu-
lation of the public interest in Tanzania literature; and
allied functions in relation to libraries and literature. It
is responsible for compiling the Tanzania National Bibliography whose yearly lists of local publications are acquired through legal deposit. The library contains over
one million copies of books and other library materials
on various subjects. There are 40 trained librarians,
all natives, 11 regional libraries, sub-branches with four
others in the building in 1975/76, 4 Mobile Libraries,
School Mobile Library operating in four regions, Nation-
wide postal service, a book box exchange service with
more than 150 centers in various institutions and a training program.

TANZANIA MENNONITE CHURCH (TMC, Swahili, KMT).
When the name was officially changed into Swahili in
January 1970, TMC was changed to KMT (Kanisa la Mennonite Tanzania). TMC began under Mennonite Mission
and became independent in 1960. At that time the stations were only in Mara Region, but now they have spread
to Dar es Salaam, Mwanza, Biharamulo, Arusha and into
Kenya.
    Before nationalization of schools, TMC was man-
ager for 45 Primary Schools and a member of the Alliance of Lake Churches operating Katoke Teachers
Training Centre, and Musoma Alliance Secondary School.
There were 18 pastors, 5 deacons and one bishop with
around 11,000 Christians by 1976. The Church operates
a hospital at Shirati and 5 dispensaries, a theological college and Bible School, Domestic Science courses for women, a hostel, print shop and bookstore. KMT has been
a member of CCT since 1967 and takes an active part in
its refugee service. Bishop Zedekea Kisare is the Chairman of the Executive Committee.

TANZANIA NATIONAL UNION OF TEACHERS (TNUT). Acted
as a subsidiary watchdog. It was incorporated later into
NUTA, the National Union of Tanzania Workers, a general trade union tied more tightly to TANU and government.

TANZANIA PEOPLE'S DEFENCE FORCES (TPDF). Formed

from the Tanganyika Rifles and the People's Liberation
Army of Zanzibar after the Union was created between
the two countries.   Even then the Tanganyikan battalions
were almost disbanded.   Members of the new army were
required to be members of TANU and were granted full
political rights.   The President of the country is the
Commander-in-Chief of the TPDF.   Under the terms of
an agreement in 1964 with Canada, the Canadian Armed
Forces Advisory and Training Team, Tanzania, provided
a 5-year training and organizational program for the
TPDF.   The Tanzanian Military Academy (TMA) was established for the army.   China has paid a large part in
the training during the 1970's.   The rank structure of
the TPDF is identical with that of the British throughout
the enlisted and commissioned ranks.   The Army Act of
1966 revised the system of military justice.   A manual
for courts martial similar to the U.S. Uniform Code of
Military Justice was adopted.   The TPDF are active in
self-reliance programs and in nation building activities.
See also ARMY; TANGANYIKA RIFLES.

TANZANIA POLICE   see   POLICE

TARANGIRE NATIONAL PARK.   The third largest in the
country, it was established in 1970 and has an area of
2600 sq. kms.   It is located 112 km. from Arusha.   It
is a sanctuary for the fast diminishing black rhinoceros.
It is also famous for fringed-eared oryx and lesser kudu.

TAXES.   Included are personal tax, local tax, property tax,
pay-as-you-earn system, income tax, import and excise
duties, export tax and corporation taxes as well as license fees.   Taxes are levied in a manner that the high
wage earner carries the heavier burden and the low wage
earner is benefitted, in other words, the gap of salary
range is closed by gradation.

TEA.   Mainly grown in Tukuyu, Mufindi, Mbeya, Usambara
Mts. and West Lake.   Small holdings of estates began
early in the 20th century in the Usambara Mts. in 1934
and expanded even to Mufindi in the Southern Highlands
in the 1930's.   By 1934 they had produced 23,000 kg.
During that year 2900 acres were allotted to Tanganyika
under the International Tea Restriction Scheme and these
acres were soon fully planted.   In 1938 an additional
2050 acres were allotted to Tanganyika.   By 1966 over
25,000 acres were in tea cultivation and 99 percent of

the 1966 yield (36,300 metric tons) was grown on plantations. A new factory to process tea was established in
Bukoba and it began operating in 1967. Exports of tea
rose from 3.6 tons in 1961/62 to 4.4 in 1964 and 6.2 in
1966. The Tanganyika Tea Authority was formed by the
government in 1969 to carry out the tea small holder expansion programs. TTA controls all aspects of the tea
in Tanzania--with a comprehensive marketing organization but the main thrust is towards production and processing. In 1976 there were more than 18,000 tons produced, 13 million kg. of Made Tea. Seventy-five percent
of it is exported.

TEACHER TRAINING. During the German era teachers were
trained at the Tanga School. A number of missions
opened teacher training in their Central Schools in 1925
and ran courses of 3 months to 1 year duration. For
Grade I level, St. Andrew's College and the Mpwapwa
Teacher Training Institute were opened in 1925 by the
UMCA and the government respectively. After the Depression, the entry requirements for Grade I and II
teacher training were increased by two years, i.e.,
Grade I to Std. X and Grade II to Std. VI. As the Middle
Schools increased and replaced the District Schools, candidates for Grade II training were selected from Std. VIII
graduates.
　　　　There were 14 VA and 2 government colleges in
1946. Government opened these immediately after World
War II--one in an abandoned Polish refugee camp and
one in a derelict Army transit center. By 1957 there
were 21 VA's and 5 government institutions. Government
had about one-fourth of the number of colleges and one-
third the number of students.
　　　　New categories of teacher training appeared after
Independence: Grade A, Grade B and Grade C and Education Officers. Teacher training centers were also consolidated with 240 to 280 pupils each and decreased in
number--22 to 11. The Institute of Education was founded in 1965 as a coordinating and advisory institution for
all agencies engaged in the training of teachers. Diploma
in Education courses opened for Form VI leavers in 1965.
　　　　Tanzania had hired very few untrained teachers until the end of the 1960's. But, with universal primary
education (UPE) stepped up to 1977, it became necessary
to shorten the Grade C courses, to multiply the number
of lower calibre cadre and experiment with a student
teacher training through correspondence, radio and select-

ed head-teachers as agents of the colleges in the field.
This program began in July 1976. A number of new
colleges (16) were opened in 1976 also. In 1975 there
were 25,413 teachers in Primary Education (17,461 men
and 7952 women); 2121 teachers in Secondary Education
(1501 men and 620 women); and 527 in teacher training
(397 men and 130 women)

TEACHER TRAINING ADVISORY BOARD. Preceded by the
    African Teachers Examination. The name changed in
    1958 and its functions included the revision of syllabuses,
    textbook production, as well as examinations. The
    Board advised through the Asst. Chief Education Officer,
    Teacher Training, in the Ministry and its members con-
    sisted of TTC tutors, representatives of Teachers' Unions,
    East African Literature Bureau, etc. It held its last
    meeting in 1965 and handed over the torch to the Institute
    of Education, its successor.

TECHNICAL EDUCATION. The two trade schools, Moshi
    and Ifunda, were upgraded to technical secondary schools
    in 1966 and 1964 respectively. The Dar es Salaam Col-
    lege was opened in 1958. A number of technical schools
    on a post-primary level were opened in many districts in
    the 1970's. Construction was begun in Aug. 1975 for a
    second technical college near Arusha. Phase one will
    take 250 students. Upon completion the college is ex-
    pected to enroll 480 students. Courses are for Form IV
    leavers leading to a Diploma in 3 years in either electri-
    cal, mechanical or civil engineering. There is also
    technical college in Zanzibar for post-primary students.

TEMPERATURES. Throughout the country, the temperature
    is generally lower than that of lower lying countries in
    similar latitudes. Tanzania has a range from a high of
    mid-90° F. on the coast to permanent freezing on the top
    of Mt. Kilimanjaro. On the plateau, temperatures are
    between 75° and 85° F. in the daytime and fall to 50° F.
    at night. On the mountain slopes it might fall to 30° F.
    The mean daily maximums range between 72° and 90° F.
    The mean temperature in Dar es Salaam is 25.7° C. with
    a range of an August mean of 66° F. and a March mean
    of 88° F.

TEN-YEAR PLAN FOR TANGANYIKA. Published in 1946
    when colonialization took on a new purpose--development
    for development's sake. This plan emphasized communi-

cations and education and, in particular, primary education, although secondary education was not forgotten. Its
target was to get 36 percent of the school age children
into school. There was an emphasis on technical education, especially for returning soldiers.

THOMSON, JOSEPH (1858-1895). A Scottish geologist born
on 14 February, 1858, he made his first journey to Africa at the age of twenty as a geologist to Keith Johnston's
expedition to explore the territory between the East Coast
and the Central Lakes. His leader died of dysentery only a month after leaving Dar es Salaam and Thomson ably
led the expedition to its objectives returning in 1880. Two
years later he returned to Tanganyika to lead an exploration of the Ruvuma River (1882), through Masailand (1883-
84) and three others in Africa later. The purpose of the
Royal Geographic Society's journey through Masailand was
to try to discover a short route to the northern end of the
lake Victoria Nyanza through the country of the Masai.
Thomson never fully recovered from the hardships of his
Masailand journey and died in London on 2 August 1895 at
an age of thirty-seven years.

THREE-YEAR PLAN OF TANGANYIKA (1961-1964)   see
DEVELOPMENT PLAN FOR TANGANYIKA 1961/62-1963/
64.

TIBANDEBAGE, ANDREW KAJUNGU (1921-   ).   Born in 1921
at Kashesho in West Lake. After a secondary education
at St. Mary's Secondary School at Tabora, he studied at
Makerere where he earned a Diploma in Education in
1944. He was a friend of President Nyerere at Tabora
and at Makerere. He was a teacher in Karagwe and a
Provincial Chairman of TANU in the Western Province
and a member of the first TANU National Executive Committee. He took a one-year course at the Institute of
Education, University of London in 1956/57. He ended
his teaching career when he joined Tanganyika's Foreign
Service in 1961 and was attached to the foreign offices at
Ankara, Turkey and Bonn, Germany. He returned to
Tanzania in 1967 as the Principal Secretary of the Ministry of Information and Tourism. His last foreign duty
was Ambassador to the Congo (Kinshasa). He retired in
1976.

TIN. Tin has been mined in the northwestern part of the
country in Karagwe District and with the Ruanda-Urundi

border. The production doubled between 1960 and 1966
but by 1967 the outlook was uncertain. Mining of tin has
been sporadic as it is extracted by private firms. In
1974 68.4 metric tons were sold for Shs.1.1 million but
in 1975 only 10.5 tons were sold for Shs.0.2 million.

TIPPU TIP (HAMED BIN MOHAMMED) (c.1830-1905). An
Afro-Arab born in Zanzibar, he was the son of a trader
with plantations around Tabora. He began his career by
working for his father and then for a friend. Tippu Tip
had a tall, bearded, dignified bearing and was more African than Arab. He was always immaculately dressed.
He was social and friendly, at ease with Africans, Arabs
or Europeans. Although he had a reputation of being a
fearless military leader, he also used persuasion and
diplomacy. He saw that European intervention could not
be resisted for long and so tried to come to terms with
it. In 1865 he reached the Ruemba area on the eastern
shore of Lake Tanganyika and seized the local chief's
supply of ivory and thus made a fortune. He installed
his brother there. He then moved around the southern
end of Lake Tanganyika and on to the Congo and became
a ruler and trader there. In 1883 Tippu Tip established
himself at Stanley Falls and made alliances with Mirambo
of Nyamwezi and Rumaliza of Ujiji to safeguard his caravans going to the East Coast. In 1890 he returned to
Zanzibar and died there in 1905. He spent his last
years as an important person in the Council of the Island.

TITI, BIBI MOHAMMED (1927-   ). The first woman to obtain a TANU card in 1954. She was born in Dar es Salaam and attended Uhuru Girls School from 1935-38. She
was a daughter of a small trader, married, had several
children, and ran a musical group called Bomba. In
1950, Bibi Titi developed the Haya and Asian women sew-
ing parties into indoctrination classes and sent her
trainees to various parts of Dar es Salaam and the Eastern Province to waken the women. By the time of the
first TANU Conference in 1955, the Women's Section had
5000 members with their own leaders. She was a member of the Executive Committee of TANU and Administrative Secretary and President of TANU's Women's Section.
By the end of 1955, TANU had more women members
than male members. Bibi Titi learned English at British
expense in order to become a Legislative Council member, a position she filled in 1960. She swayed crowds
by her dramatic presentation. Her husband left her be-

cause she was absent a lot.   She remarried in 1963, the
Head of TBC.
    When UWT (Umoja wa Wanawake wa Tanzania) was
formed in 1962, she was its President.   She was also
Junior Minister in the Ministry of Community Development
and Culture for awhile.   She gave up her UWT presidency
and membership in the TANU Central Committee in 1967
because of back trouble.   She was detained in 1969, faced
charges in 1970 in the treason trial masterminded by O.
Kambona, sent to prison, but later pardoned by President
Kyerere and permitted to live a normal life in the local
community.

TOBACCO.   Grown near Tabora, Iringa, Ruvuma and Mbeya.
    Before 1962 over 80 percent of the tobacco was produced
    on European plantations near Iringa.   During the 1950's
    and early 1960's four societies of tobacco growers near
    Songea formed a union to market their crops.   Between
    1962 and 1966 the production more than doubled, not due
    to the European plantations, but to the many local Afri-
    can farmers growing it.   The Tanganyika Tobacco Board
    was established in 1968.   Production shot up fast, from
    2700 metric tons in 1961 to 21,400 tons in 1970.   On the
    1 July, 1972, the Tanzania Tobacco Authority was offi-
    cially incepted with the mandate to promote the considera-
    tion, preparation, implementation and authorization of to-
    bacco research programs.   Approximately 70 percent of
    the total crop goes to outside markets.   In 1973/74 the
    foreign sales amounted to Shs.193 million.   There are
    two main brands of tobacco grown--Virginia Flue-cured
    and Fire-cured tobacco.   The 1975 production figure
    registers a drop in production, standing at 18,060 tons
    with exports valued at over Shs.82 million.   There was
    15 million kgm. of tobacco processed in 1975 and 19
    million in 1976.

TONGONI.   A northern coastal town, it was the center of the
    old state of Mtangata.   Excavations and clearance of the
    mosque done by the Department of Antiquities in 1958,
    revealed a settlement during the 13th or 14th century and
    a reoccupation in the 18th or 19th century.   The ruler of
    Mtangata was normally hostile to Mombasa and friendly
    to the Portuguese.   In 1631 the Portuguese settlers were
    murdered at the instigation of Dom Jeronimo.   There was
    a ruler still as late as 1728.   Later a shift in the popula-
    tion caused a break with tradition and a desertion of Ton-
    goni.

TOURISM.   Tanzania is the only country in the world which
has set aside almost a quarter of its land for National
Parks, game and forest reserves.   Whereas there was
only one national park at independence, there were eight
in 1974.   In 1966 there were 45,000 foreign visitors
bringing Shs. 60 million.   In 1973 there were 75,199 East
African tourists and 125,643 others who brought Shs.130
million in foreign exchange.   As accommodations at hotels expand and transportation improves, the number of
visitors increases.   There were 210,000 tourists registered in 1975 earning Shs. 83.1 million.   The new 400-
bed Mt. Meru Hotel in Arusha opened in mid-1976.   A
large expansion program has been launched in accommodations on Mt. Kilimanjaro also.   In 1976, tourism accounted for 5.9 percent of the national export.   There
were 279,060 tourists in 1976.   A College of African
Wildlife Management near Moshi operates a two-year course.

TOWN COUNCILS.   By 1967 thirteen town councils were responsible to the Minister for Local Government and Rural
Development.   A few government officers (medical, engineering, etc.) sat on the Council as ex officio members.   Town Councils received grants from the Central
Government and the other half of moneys came from property taxation and licenses.   The 1965 budget of recur-
rent expenditure was as follows: 6 percent for traffic,
fire and lighting services; 23 percent for public health;
24 percent for primary education; 6 percent to market
maintenance; 17 percent for roads and works; 20 percent
for administration; and 4 percent to capital accounts.

TRADE.   By the 1830's Arabs were already sending caravans
from Zanzibar into the interior of East Africa for ivory
and slaves.   Their routes were as follows:
        a) Southern route: from ports on Southern Tangan-
yika coast, especially Kilwa, inland through Yao, Makua
and Makonde country to Lake Malawi.
        b) The Central route: from the Mrima coast (op-
posite Zanzibar), Bagamoyo and Sadani, inland to the
Nyamwezi country and the Arab settlement at Tabora,
then: northwest, round the western shore of Lake Victoria to Uganda; west to Ujiji and across Lake Tanganyika to the Congo, or southwest, round the southern end of
Lake Tanganyika to Congo.
        c) The Northern route: from ports such as Pan-
gani and Tanga to Kilimanjaro region, then: west to
eastern shores of Lake Victoria or north into Kenya.

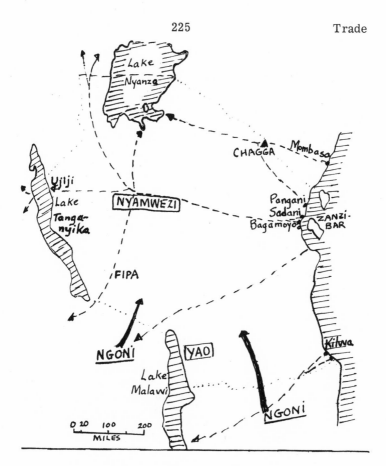

Trade Routes of the Early 19th Century

        Africans had started to build up long distance
trade before the Arabs, based on the three routes mentioned.   The Yao were the first to develop such trade.
Chiefs had sent caravans to the coast.   The southern
route became the major source of slaves in East Africa.
The Nyamwezi were the main supply of caravan porters
and organizers in the 19th century.   They had their own
caravans travelling to the coast in early 1800's.   The
chief item of trade in the central route was (and remained) ivory.   Slave trade increased so that 40,000 to
50,000 were sold annually in Zanzibar by 1840 and
70,000 in the 1860's.
        The East African Coast was used as a supply de-
pot by Americans for their whaling expeditions and later

as an outlet for Massachusetts white cotton cloth (meri-
kani) which became a currency along trade routes to the
interior.   A treaty of commerce was signed with the
Sultan in 1833 whereby American merchants could trade
freely.   In 1837 an American consulate was established
in Zanzibar.
　　　France signed treaties with the Sultan in 1844 and
the Hanseatic Republic did the same in 1859.   By 1859
Zanzibar's exports were valued at: Ivory, £146,666;
Cloves, £65,666; Cowries, £51,444; Sesamum, £20,800;
and Capital, £37,166.   By 1870 the German trade had
grown to approximately one-fifth of the total trade and
was larger than any other interest except British India.
Attempts were made to open up trade routes on the mainland by Sir William Mackinnon in 1876.   Negotiations
started with the Sultan for concession to trade and administer the interior.   These failed, due partly to the
British Government's reluctance to get further involved
in East African affairs at that time.   Commercial rivalry
between French, German and British Consuls in Zanzibar,
seeking concessions from the Sultan to develop trade and
communications on the mainland led to the Scramble in
East Africa and its partitioning.
　　　The building of railway lines in Tanganyika promoted the growth of towns as commercial, agricultural
and administrative centers.   The world slump in trade
from 1929-1930's affected the plantation owners also.
Asians played a dominant part in commerce and business.
　　　Domestic trade is carried on mainly through cooperatives and government-owned corporations.
　　　Sisal, coffee and cotton have formed over 50 percent of the export trade and all agricultural products
form 80 percent.   Sisal was leading until 1966 when cotton
took over.   By 1959 UK and India took the largest amount
of Tanganyika's cotton; the U. S. A. took the largest quantities of sisal, coffee, hides and skins and India most of
the cashewnuts and gum arabic.   Cotton piece goods were
imported from the U. K. , India, Japan and Hong Kong.
Machinery was mainly imported from the U. K. and Germany.   There was a favorable balance of trade with exports valued at £41.7 million and imports at £31.5 million.   Vehicles, petrol and oil accounted for about a
quarter of the imports reflecting the importance of motor
transport and of mechanization in agriculture.   Invisible
exports include money brought in through tourist trade
not usually shown on a pie chart.
　　　By 1974 there was a deficit in the balance of pay-

ments as exports valued Shs. 2, 074 million and imports Shs. 2, 540 million. Over a third of the imports were goods and spare parts.

TRADE SCHOOLS. In 1961 the two trade schools at Ifunda and Moshi had a total of 740 students. The subjects studied were: carpentry, 115; masonry, 93; painting, 70; plumbing, 72; electrical work, 76; and engine mechanics, 314. In January 1964 Ifunda led to become a full-fledged secondary school and Moshi followed two years later.

TRADE UNIONS. By 1947 there were five unions. The Stevedores and Dockers' Union had a membership of 1500. The TFL was formed in 1958 with 17 regional trade unions. That same year the Sisal Workers, 30, 000 strong, belonged to the National Plantation Workers Union. The Unions engineered strikes. From 1955-60 a total of 771 stopages were reported involving 298, 161 workers with 2. 4 million man-days lost. One and a half million accounted for 1960. From 1961-64 there were 862 strikes and 99, 382 workers and 613, 778 man-days were lost. From 1965-70 there were 74 strikes involving 9308 workers with 26, 518 man-days lost. From 1971 to September 1973, 31 strikes were reported involving 22, 708 workers and 63, 646 man-days lost. The right to strike was restricted by the Trade Disputes (Settlement) Act of 1962.

TRANSPORTATION. Two major transport complexes are available. One is centered in the northeast where road and rail systems lead from the port of Tanga through the Usambara Mts. to Moshi and Arusha. A second complex cuts through the center from Dar es Salaam on the coast to the Lakes on the west. An all weather highway and the Great Uhuru Railway are opening a third complex. The move of the capital to Dodoma is aimed at increasing the transport facilities in Central Tanzania. See also AVIATION; RAILWAYS; ROADS; and SHIPPING.

TREATIES. 1) 1886, 1890--Anglo-German agreements on the boundary lines of their possessions; 2) Trade treaties with the Sultan: 1837--American; 1844--French; 1859-- Hanseatic Republics; 3) Anti-Slavery treaties: 1822-- Moresby Treaty and 1873--British-Sultan; 4) To establish German protectorate: 1884, 85 Karl Peters with native chiefs; 5) 1 August, 1890: Treaty at Tabora between Emin Pasha and Arabs; abolition of slave trade but not

end of commerce; Arabs accepted German suzerainty;
6) 1967--Treaty for East African Cooperation set up East
African Community.

TRIBES.   See individual tribes under their names.   Tanzania
has more than 120 tribes and none in majority.   The largest in number is only about one-tenth of the total population.   See map of selected tribal areas below for names
and locations of important tribes.

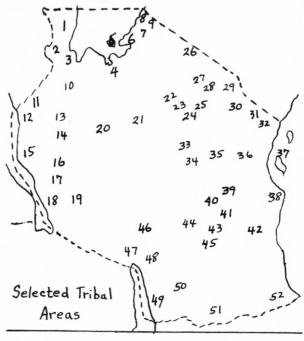

Selected Tribal
Areas

1. Haya	14. Tongwe	27. Meru	40. Sagara
2. Subi	15. Holoholo	28. Arusha	41. Vidunda
3. Zinza	16. Konongo	29. Chagga	42. Rufiji
4. Sukuma	17. Bende	30. Pare	43. Mbunga
5. Kerewe	18. Fipa	31. Shambaa	44. Hehe
6. Jita	19. Rungwa	32. Bondei	45. Pogoro
7. Zanaki	20. Nyamwezi	33. Sandawe	46. Sangu
8. Luo	21. Iramba	34. Gogo	47. Nyakyusa
9. Kuria	22. Kindiga	35. Kaguru	48. Bena
10. Sumbwa	23. Iraqw	36. Zigua	49. Nyasa
11. Ha	24. Dorobo	37. Shirazi	50. Ngoni
12. Jiji	25. Masai	38. Zaramo	51. Yao
13. Vinza	26. Sonjo	39. Luguru	52. Makonde

TSERE, LUCIANO (1916-). An Iraqw who was born in 1916
at Mbulu and was educated in local Catholic mission
schools.   He attended Makerere from 1942-48 and studied
medicine.   He was a member of the Action Group and a
master mind of TAA elections in 1950.   In 1944 he was
the house physician at Sewa Haji Hospital in Dar es Salaam. He was transferred to Tanga in 1950.   He studied
in the Liverpool School of Tropical Medicine in 1959 and
spent most of his years as a medical practitioner in
Tanzania.

TSETSE FLY.   Infects large areas of the Eastern Plateau
and more than two-thirds of the Central Plateau as they
live on the miombo trees and breed.   The species is a
variety.   The tsetse fly infects man and beast with
Trypanosomiasis (sleeping sickness).   It afflicts cattle
with nagana and human beings with a form of sleeping
sickness.   Losses due to nagana are estimated at 40
million to 50 million yearly.   Charles Swynnerton wrote
a standard book on Tsetse Flies of East Africa.   In an
effort to eradicate the tsetse fly, Land Clearance is being
carried out.

TUBERCULOSIS.   The Tanganyika Association Against Tuberculosis (TAAT) was established in 1962 to fight the common infection.   TB is a more serious problem in high
population densities, both rural and urban.   The main
method of control is through drug treatment of active
cases and vaccination.   It is estimated that more than 1
out of 100 suffers from TB at any given time or 140,000
in total.   Every 1 out of 10 dies who is affected and not
treated properly.   About 30,000 contract TB yearly.
Mobile X-ray units and vaccination with BCG vaccine
reach only a segment of the population.

TUMBATU (tribe).   A mixed race of African and Asiatic immigrants who arrived on the island northwest of Zanzibar
about the end of the 12th century.   After a gap of more
than five centuries, the first recorded sheha ruling the
island was a woman named Mwana wa Mwana who is believed to have married Hassan, the Mwenyi Mkuu of the
Hadimu, who died in 1845.   Either the Tumbatu were
exempt from the payment of all taxes due to his wife, or
they declined to pay any impositions, for they displayed
their traditional spirit of independence.   The Tumbatu occupied the area north of the 6th parallel of latitude in a
general rule.   Mwana wa Mwana's son Ali did not succeed

his father, the Mwenyi Mkuu and the sheha of Tumbatu
was filled by many prodigy until Sultan Majid, in the
early 1860's appointed Msellem as sheha.   Msellem was
not a hereditary successor and was not accepted very
well by the Tumbatu as sheha or as Mwenyi Mkuu as
Sultan Majid decreed.   The Tumbatu use Koranic charms
to a very large extent and make greater use of the numbers 3 and 4 and their total.

TUMBO, CHRISTOPHER KASSANGA (1934-   ).   Born in
    Sikonge, Tabora Region and educated at Tabora Govern-
    ment Secondary School to 1957.   The following year he
    attended the Apprentices' Course of the Railway School
    at Tabora and joined the East African Railways and Har-
    bours as a Station Clerk at Mwanza in 1959.   He re-
    signed from the job after 3 months in order to join Tan-
    ganyika Railway African Union as its Secretary General
    and served until 1962.   He was also a member of the
    National Assembly.   In 1962 he was appointed High Com-
    missioner in London.   That same year he formed the
    People's Democratic Party and became its president.   He
    was regarded as a "black chauvinist" and he fled to Kenya
    in 1963 to escape preventive detention when Tanganyika
    had become a one-party state.   In the aftermath of the
    1964 mutinees, Kenya expelled him as an undesirable im-
    migrant, extraditing him to Tanganyika where he was put
    in preventive detention.   He was freed in July 1966.   He
    returned to Sikonge and became a prosperous farmer and
    joined up with a Ujamaa village.

TUNGSTEN.   Tanzania has relatively small deposits usually
    in reef or alluvial form.   Tungsten is found in Bukoba
    District and has a declining output in the small-scale
    mining.

TURNBULL, SIR RICHARD.   Governor of Tanganyika as of
    July 1958 and Governor General in the Responsible Gov-
    ernment era; he left Tanganyika on 9 December, 1961.
    Turnbull was educated at University College School and
    then University College, London, as a physical chemist
    and received his degree in 1929.   He spent one year in
    a colonial course at Cambridge.   His first appointment
    as a cadet was to Tanganyika.   By the time he arrived
    in Africa, he was transferred to fill the vacancy of a
    District Officer in Kenya.   He completed nearly 27 years
    in Kenya from August 1931 to April 1958.   Having served
    in Kenya during unrest, he desired to move ahead well

when he became Governor of Tanganyika.   He worked well
with Nyerere and introduced elements of a nonracial policy for representation.   The Executive Council was replaced by a Council of Ministers of whom five were
elected TANU members.   He eased the tensions more
than once when conflicts between the nationalists and
British officials seemed to reach a breaking point.   His
diplomacy with both sides aided a smooth handover of
power to independence.

TWALIPO, COL. ABDALLAH.   Regional Commissioner of
West Lake in 1974 when he was promoted to Major General and appointed TPDF Commander.

TWINING, SIR EDWARD (1899-1967).   Born on 29 June, 1899,
the son of the Vicar of St. Stephen's, Rochester Row.
After attending preparatory school and Lancing College,
he entered Royal Military College at Sandhurst.   He
served with the KAR in Uganda from 1923-28 and then
ten more years in routine work in Uganda until he transferred to Mauritius in 1939 as Deputy Director of Labour.
In 1943 he was made a C. M. G. and appointed Governor
of St. Lucia in the Windward Islands.   From 1946-49 he
served as Governor and Commander-in-Chief in North
Borneo.   Lady Twining was a first class doctor.   Governor Twining arrived in Tanganyika in 1949 and opened
up its economic resources.   Export taxes on sisal paid
for a 59-mile Tanga-Korogwe Road and for Colito Bar-
racks outside Dar es Salaam.   He opposed TANU enough
to provide a good foil, yet only barred Nyerere for three
months from speaking all over the country.   After the
Meru Case he ordered tightening of regulations that civil
servants were barred from political organization membership.   This affected TAA.   On 14 April, 1954, a Societies Bill made it compulsory for all organizations to be
registered with the name of officers, its rules and regulations included.   He left Tanganyika in mid-1958.

- U -

UGWENO.   This kingdom in North Pare had a loose political
system before the end of the 15th century which was established and controlled by the blacksmiths.   The blacksmiths traded iron for cattle with the Chagga at Mamba.
As the communities became more complex, the blacksmiths could no longer satisfy their needs.   So a reform

was initiated from within about the beginning of the 16th century.   One Msuya was a member in charge of affairs at the court.   This commoner clan, Wasuya, engineered the reform.   Many Washana blacksmiths were eliminated during the Civil War.   Mranga was a foremost reformer of this period and centralized power through the initiation schools and created a large bureaucracy and a hierarchy of councils.   The Ugweno Kingdom was stable and carried into the 19th century.

UHURU.   The Swahili word for Freedom.   Uhuru na Kazi (Freedom and Work) was a popular slogan at independence.

UHURU RAILWAY   see   GREAT UHURU RAILWAY

UJAMAA.   The Swahili word for the concept of family or brotherhood.   It includes many things, but refers in particular to the mutual cooperation and egalitarianism characteristic of traditional African society.   It describes the sense of obligation that men have for the welfare of their fellowmen.

UJAMAA VILLAGES.   Set up as a way of life in place of the settlement transformation schemes.   The development of villages is shown as:

YEAR	VILLAGES	PEOPLE
1968	180	58, 500
1971	4, 500	1. 5 m.
1974	5, 500	3. 5 m.
1976	6, 000	10. 2 m.
1977	7, 000	12. 5 m.

UJIJI.   An Arab trading post for the caravans, it had a military station established at its location in 1896.   By 1905 there were 14, 000 people.   Census figures often combine Ujiji and Kigoma populations and call them "twin cities" or towns as both are located on Lake Tanganyika adjacent to each other.

ULUGURU MOUNTAINS.   Located between the east central region to Lake Nyasa.   The climate is cool and moist and rainfall is moderate.   There are tropical rain forests on the lower slopes.   Sheet mica is obtained here.   The Luguru tribe lives in the mountains and has a dense population.

UMATI see FAMILY PLANNING ASSOCIATION OF TANZA-
NIA.

UMMA PARTY. Formed just before the July 1963 elections
in Zanzibar due to a long-standing ideological conflict
within ZNP. Umma's leader, Babu, had a Marxist orien-
tation towards Cuban and Chinese revolutionary ideologies.
Umma stressed the goals of multiracial political representation with a strong African peasant base. Umma was
effectively organized and attracted many by its ability to
unite antigovernment groups. It did not contest the 1963
elections due to a lack of adequate preparation and candidates. Immediately after the revolution in January 1964,
Umma merged with the ASP.

UMOJA WA WANAWAKE WA TANZANIA (UWT) see UNITED
WOMEN OF TANGANYIKA

UNIFIED TEACHING SERVICE (UTS). Effective 1 January,
1963, for all government or non-government teachers to
enjoy: same terms of service; same privileges and benefits; and a contributory pension scheme. Before UTS,
there was a difference in privileges and fringe benefits
between government teachers and voluntary agency teachers. Most teachers, including expatriates, join UTS and
no promotions are granted or pensions without membership in UTS. UTS is the teachers' organization affiliated
with NUTA and has its own machinery for dealing with
disciplinary matters, grievances, appeals and promotions
at Central or local levels.

UNITED NATIONS VISITING MISSIONS. 1st--1948: The
Visiting Mission and the colonial administration advocated
the establishment of multiracial provincial, county and
local councils and the inclusion of non-Africans in district
councils. Some of the comments in its report raised a
storm of protest in England.
        2nd--1951: The Mission and report was more op-
timistic, the Meru Case being the only "fly in the oint-
ment, " so it caused very little reaction.
        3rd--1954: The members of the Mission held
strong political views and hotly disagreed with each other:
Mason Sears, the American member, was sympathetic to
Africans and desired earliest independence; Rikhi Jaipal,
the Indian member, agreed and cooperated with Sears;
Chairman John S. Reid from New Zealand sympathized
with the British administration and clashed with Sears so

much that eventually he refused to sign the report; and
the El Salvador representative tried to remain neutral
but, by inclination, sided with Reid. They recommended
that a date be set for granting independence or at least
a "time table" of the steps to be taken, in consultation
with the people towards self-government. It backed
TANU's demand that independence be granted in 25 years.
    4th--1957: The Mission reported considerable
dissatisfaction with the emphasis on agricultural and
practical training and advocated acceleration of the integration policy.
    5th--1960: The most impressive was the peace-
ful and harmonious atmosphere of goodwill.

UNITED REPUBLIC OF TANGANYIKA AND ZANZIBAR. The
    name given to the Union of the two countries on 26 April,
    1964, until the United Republic of Tanzania was selected
    as its new name later that year (October 1964).

UNITED TANGANYIKA PARTY (UTP). Wanted a multi-racial
    government and was founded in 1956 by advice of Governor
    Twining. UTP included many members of the Legislative
    Council and influential people. Articles 2, 4, and 10 of
    the UTP Manifesto declared belief in equality. Its aims
    were to respect the established government, to expose all
    attempts at unconstitutional or seditious changes in the
    constitution, to raise the standard of living and of educa-
    tion, and to promote the utilization of natural resources,
    free enterprise and cooperative effort. On 17 February,
    1956, the UTP Manifesto was printed and signed by 12
    Europeans, 12 Asians, 8 Africans and 1 descendant of
    the Sultan of Zanzibar. David Makwaia and Chief Harun
    M. Lugasha signed it and lost influence among the young
    Africans. The Europeans and Asians aimed at reaching
    agreement with TANU leaders. They supported a lim-
    ited, qualified franchise and modified their stand later.
        Ivor Bayldon was the UTP Chairman and Brian
    Willis the General Director. He was succeeded by Hus-
    sein Juma. By July 1957 the UTP had 7,127 members
    in 19 branches. The average monthly enrollment was
    650. The membership was 9.5 percent European, 24.9
    percent Asian and 65.6 percent African. The party was
    disbanded after the 1958 elections.

UNION OF WOMEN OF TANZANIA (Swahili: UMOJA WA
    WANAWAKE WA TANZANIA). Mainly concerned with
    social development through the mobilization of the ener-

gies of women citizens. The UWT was a creation of the
post-Independence era. It was set up on a voluntary basis with government and TANU support for the development of women in the domestic sphere. Bibi Titi Mohammed, a former junior minister of the Ministry of
Community Development and National Culture, was its
first President. The UWT was parastatal in nature and
was one of the departments of TANU. It provided an appointed member to the National Assembly. The 7th Bi-
annual Meeting in December 1976 was a time of self-
evaluation before the UWT would abdicate for a more
revolutionary women's organization in the new political
party CCM to be formed in early 1977.

UNIVERSAL PRIMARY EDUCATION. First set for 1989, then
    1980, and speeded up to 1977 when the majority of Tan-
    zanians had moved to Ujamaa villages.

UNIVERSITIES MISSION TO CENTRAL AFRICA (UMCA).
    After David Livingstone gave his report in England in
    1857 of his journey to Africa, the UMCA was formed for
    the main purpose of preaching the Gospel to tribes along
    Lake Nyasa. So Charles MacKenzie was consecrated
    bishop and he left with a number of missionaries for Lake
    Nyasa. On the way the Bishop and a number of them
    died from fever in 1862 and others returned to the coast.
        Upon Bishop Tozer's arrival in 1863, he decided
    to make the UMCA headquarters in Zanzibar. They were
    allowed to look after ex-slaves. Bishop Tozer resigned
    in 1873 and Bishop Steere became his successor. The
    cornerstone for the Cathedral in Zanzibar was laid in
    1873 on the grounds of the famous Slave Market. In
    1875 John Swedi became the first African deacon. Bishop
    Steere's Handbook of the Swahili Language was published
    in 1865.
        The period from 1875 to 1880 was one of great
    expansion especially among the Yao. The first mission
    station on the mainland had been opened at Muheza in
    1869 and closed later; but reopened in 1875. In 1876
    Bishop Steere took a number of ex-slaves and started off
    on a journey back to their home along Lake Nyasa. How-
    ever, the journey seemed long, and when they got to Ma-
    sasi, they asked to settle there.
        William P. Johnson and Charles Jensen led another
    group to Lake Nyasa in 1882. They built a station on the
    island called Likoma in 1885. The missionaries joined
    the pieces of the ship they had carried overland with them

and could reach many places around the Lake with it.
The Diocese of Nyasaland was formed in 1892.

In 1926 the Diocese of Masasi was cut out of the
Diocese of Zanzibar and in 1952 the Diocese of Southwest
Tanganyika was formed out of the Nyasaland Diocese.   In
1965 the UMCA merged with the SPG and took the name
of USPG (United Society for Propagation of the Gospel).
Two more dioceses were formed: Tanga and Ruvuma.
See ANGLICAN CHURCH for the explanation of the merger
of UMCA and CMS.

UNIVERSITY COLLEGE OF DAR ES SALAAM.   Established
by a Provisional Council Ordinance passed by the National
Assembly in February 1961.   It opened in October 1961
with a Faculty of Law and 14 students in a building leased
by TANU on Lumumba St.   The first degrees were awarded through a special relationship with the University of
London.   After the University of East Africa was formed
in 1963, it granted its own degrees.   In 1964 University
College moved to Observation Hill eight miles west of
town on a 1625 acre campus.   The Faculty of Arts and
Social Sciences was opened in 1964, the Faculty of Science
in 1965, the Faculty of Medicine in 1968, Faculty of Agriculture in 1969 and was then nationalized on 1 July,
1970.   University College also included the Institute of
Public Administration, Institute of Fisheries, Institute of
Swahili Research, Economic Research Bureau, Bureau of
Resource Assessment and Land Use Planning, Institute of
Education and Institute of Adult Education.

The University College's enrollment rose from 14
in 1961 to 873 in 1966/67, and to 1400 in 1969/70.   Students entry was direct from post-Form VI studies or
through mature application and acceptance.

The administration of the institution and power was
vested in the College itself, but it was responsible to the
needs of the country and tailored its offerings to the manpower targets of the government.   It has adhered to government emphasis on practical studies and training for
community service.   Government bursaries largely determine the composition of the student body.   Priorities were
placed on scientific and technical fields and on education.

In October 1966, when the students demonstrated
against the National Service Act, 393 students were expelled, about half of the undergraduate student body.
Many were accepted after a year on their apologies.   The
University College, Dar es Salaam, was renamed University of Dar es Salaam after its nationalization on 1 July,
1970.

UNIVERSITY OF DAR ES SALAAM. Preceded by the University College, Dar es Salaam, which was a part of the University of East Africa. When the Tanzanian-based institution was nationalized on 1 July, 1970, the East African union began its disintegration process. A Faculty of Swahili was established, the Faculty of Engineering was opened on 10 December, 1974, and Forestry and Applied Hydrology had its first graduates in 1975. Under a directive from the National Executive Committee of TANU, mature entry places were expanded and direct entry limited in 1975. There were 708 mature entries who were considered to be on "leave without pay" and receiving the direct entry Shs. 400 allowance fee then.

UNIVERSITY OF EAST AFRICA. Decided upon in 1960 to combine the University College of Makerere in Uganda, the Royal College of Nairobi and the University College at Dar es Salaam then in formation. An act of the East Africa Common Services Organization linked them in 1962 and on 29 June, 1963, the University of East Africa came into being with President Julius Nyerere as its first Chancellor. The University of East Africa granted its own degrees. Each college had its own faculties which were meant to complement its sister institution. The University College of Dar es Salaam was nationalized on 1 July, 1970, and the University of East Africa began a disintegration process.

URBAN AREAS. By 1948 there were four large towns: Dar es Salaam with 69, 227 residents; Tanga with 20, 619; Tabora with 12, 768; and Mwanza with 11, 296. There were four towns with populations between 8000 to 10, 000: Dodoma, Lindi, Morogoro and Moshi. Iringa and Arusha had over 5000; Bagamoyo had more than 4000 and Bukoba, Mbeya and Musoma had around 3000. Other centers with township status were Kilwa Kivinje and Pangani with over 2000; Kilosa, Korogwe, Kimamba and Chunya with over 1000; Lushoto and Songea with over 600 each.
    By the 1957 census Tanganyika had 33 gazetted towns and was 4. 1 percent urban although other figures put 3. 3 percent town dwellers in the late 1950's. Zanzibar was 26. 5 percent urban and 73. 5 percent rural in 1958.
    Only 32 out of the 50 towns proclaimed in the British era were considered urban in the 1967 census. Five percent of the population then lived in urban areas. The list is shown below along with the 1975 population

and 1977 estimations (given in thousands):

	1967	1975	1977
Dar es Salaam	272,820	517	609
Tanga	61,658	89	98
Mwanza	34,861	57	63
Arusha	32,482	82.3	104
Moshi	26,864	46	53
Morogoro	25,262	39	44
Dodoma	23,559	37	41
Iringa	21,746	43	51
Tabora	20,994	27	29
Musoma	15,412	28	33
Mtwara	13,369	26	27
Lindi	13,351	16	17
Ujiji	12,950	27	28
Kigoma	8,419		
Mbeya	12,479	20	22
Bukoba	8,186	12	13

- V -

VASCO DA GAMA (c. 1469-1524).   A Portuguese who made a
    trading voyage from 1497-99 to India at the command of
    King Manuel of Portugal.   He visited Mozambique, Mom-
    basa and Malindi on the way.   In 1502 he returned with
    15 ships for conquest as well as trade.   He forced Kilwa
    to pay tribute to Portugal.   He retired after that voyage,
    but during the next 20 years he acted as adviser to King
    Manuel and his successor, King John III.

VASEY, SIR ERNEST.   Twice Mayor of Nairobi and Minister
    of Finance in the Kenya Government, became Head of the
    Treasury in Tanganyika in February 1960.   In September
    1960 he was appointed Minister for Finance in the inde-
    pendent government.   He resigned from the post in Janu-
    ary 1962 since he was not eligible for citizenship and was
    Adviser to Finance.   He left Tanzania in November 1962.

VICTORIA FEDERATION OF COOPERATIVE UNION, LTD.
    The cooperative movement began in 1951 as Lake Pro-
    vince Growers Association.   By 1953 the cooperative had
    captured 13 percent of the total cotton crop.   In that year
    38 cooperative societies joined to form the Victoria Fede-
    ration of Cooperative Unions, VFCU.   By 1956 they were
    marketing 60 percent of the crop and in 1959 all 100 per-

cent of it. The VFCU owned their first ginnery in 1956
and completed their second one in 1958. By 1960 there
were 360 primary societies in 19 unions and a membership of 140,000. They marketed 170,000 bales of cotton,
operated 6 ginneries, a hostel and a headquarters building. In 1965 there were 450 member societies with a
membership of 200,000 cotton farmers. They operated
11 ginneries which processed 65 percent of the total crop,
3 cottonseed oil mills, 2 rice mills and 2 sisal factories
and rented out 158 tractors. In 1967 the Union was dissolved by government and reconstructed as the Victoria
Union of Cooperative Societies.

VICTORIA UNION OF COOPERATIVE SOCIETIES. The new
name for Victoria Federation of Cooperative Unions, Ltd.
which was dissolved in late 1967. The new institution is
a reconstruction with new by-laws and whose management
has been appointed by government.

VIDUNDA (tribe). In the southern part of Kilosa, they are a
matrilineal people who are changing in many ways. They
claim to originate from the Hehe and consider themselves
closely related to the Hehe and Sagara. They had a kind
of paramount chief in the pre-colonial times. He organized warriors against raiders and received annual tribute
in foodstuffs, free labor in cultivation and housebuilding
and the ivory of all elephants slain in his chiefdom. He
was also in charge of rites to ensure fertility, purifica-
tion and rainmaking in the area. The Vidunda were deeply involved in the 1905 Maji-Maji Rebellion and suffered
bitter reprisals from the Germans. The Kilombero Sugar
Estate, established in the south of Vidunda in the early
1960's, has had an enormous economic and social impact
on the tribe. The staple crop in the flood plains is rice
and on the hills is maize. They are energetic cultivators
in rice and tobacco, are growing rapidly and pushing up
to Sagara.

VILLAGE DEVELOPMENT COMMITTEE (VDC). The local
political organization involving directly or indirectly the
largest number of people and was responsible for community self-help projects such as the building of schools,
dispensaries, roads and laying of water pipelines. The
Committees were 7000 in number and were largely composed of local TANU leaders with the TANU Chairman
generally its head. Other members were teachers, cooperative society officials and local government officers.

Its efficiency varied as it depended on the local people's
concept of its function and the agreement between development officers and local politicians.

VILLAGE SETTLEMENT SCHEME. Designed to enable the
African peasant cultivators to become self-reliant, parti-
cipating in the economic development of his native land.
Tanganyika Agricultural Corporation (TAC) inherited three
undertakings from the ill-fated Groundnut Scheme: Nachingwea, Mtwara Region--cooperative farms and a farming
settlement; Urambo, Tabora Region--tobacco growing and
farm settlement; and Kongwa, Dodoma Region--a breeding
ranch and farming settlement scheme. It was an ambitious program embarked upon by the government in 1962.
Some other pilot village projects were also begun in
regions where development of economic resources seemed
feasible. Land surveys were carried out, formerly un-
cultivated land was prepared for use and the first groups
of families moved onto the land. The schemes required
great sums of capital investment. It was intended that up
to 250 families would live on one project, either brought
in or relocated or grouped within an area. The scheme
involved a tenancy grant of ten to fifty acres to selected
peasant farmers. Agricultural instruction, marketing
facilities, farm machine operations and other technical
aspects of the venture were provided by the TAC. The
scheme was very costly. Again, it was not popular with
African peasants. The results of the first few years were
varied; some were abandoned and others flourished. On
the whole, the Scheme was not considered successful.
This triggered the idea of Umamaa villages beginning from
small, indigenous, self-help schemes.
    By 1967 the Government was still upholding a poli-
cy of villagization but the stress was on small numbers of
villagers in one Ujamaa village. And, instead of large
capital expenditures, self-help was the watchword. This
new type of villagization continued to mushroom.

VINZA. Town near Lake Tanganyika, produced salt from brine
springs as early as the 19th century. Salt and iron hoes
were used as currency.

VISRAM, ALLIDINA (1863-1916). The largest early trader
in East Africa was born in Kera in the province of Kutch
and arrived in Zanzibar in 1877 as a young apprentice to
an old-established firm. He moved on soon afterward to
Bagamoyo as an assistant of Sewa Haji. The caravans

penetrated beyond the borders of German East Africa in
a fashion typical of Kutch merchants of that time. By
the 1890's he had extended his operations all along the
old caravan routes and opened branches of his firm in
Dar es Salaam, near Bagamoyo, Tabora, Ujiji and Kili-
ma in the Congo. In 1896 he opened an agency in Zanzibar. His caravans reached Mwanza that year and, two
years later, reached Kampala. In 1899 he opened a
store in Mombasa. After his death, his estate was
valued at well over three million rupees.

VOLUNTARY AGENCIES. Played a significant role in providing education in Tanganyika. Missions and TAPA
operated and managed about two-thirds of the schools in
the country until independence. The agency received
capital grants-in-aid, salaries for teachers and an equipment grant. Any other expenses were met by the agency. It was also necessary that, in return, the agency
provide an education in accordance with government
standards. Schools were nationalized in 1970. At that
time the Education Secretary of the agency lacked a job.
Voluntary Agencies also provided much informal education
for adults.

VON PRINCE, LT. TOM (nicknamed BWANA SAKKARANI).
Sent by the German government to bring the Africans
under German control. He met no resistance in 1893
from Kiumbu chiefs, but fought fiercely with Isike of the
Wanyamwezi and Mkwawa of the Hehe. He left in 1900.

- W -

WAGES. Between a top manager and a worker, the ratio of
minimum wages at 1961 was 80:1. By 1974 the top in-
comes fell 25 percent and the bottom had risen 250 percent so that the ratio was then 15:1. The minimum agricultural wage then was 240 shillings per month while the
non-agricultural minimum wage was Shs. 340.

WAKIL, IDRIS ABDUL (1926-). Born in Zanzibar and
finished secondary education in 1948, went on to Makerere
College (1949-51) where he received a Diploma in Education. He taught in Zanzibar schools for ten years, including teacher training. He then resigned from the head
teachership in the primary schools to run in the 1963
elections which he won, becoming a member of the Zanzi-

bar National Assembly.   After the revolution, he was a member of the Revolutionary Council and Minister of Education and National Culture in the People's Republic. He joined the Union Cabinet in April 1964 as Minister of Information and Tourism.   Since then he has held ambassadorial posts in the Federal Republic of Germany and Guinea.   He was recalled in December 1976.

De la WARR COMMISSION.   Formed in 1938, it was the first commission to advocate education for social change rather than for the status quo.   It supported an interaction between African theory of tradition and European theory of progress.   They considered poverty, superstitious prejudice, malnutrition and unhygienic conditions to be hindrances to advancement.   They felt that the apathy of the older generation was the greatest obstacle to combating illiteracy.   The Commission recommended a rapid expansion of higher education facilities, including the development of Makerere to the full status of a university college as soon as possible.

WATTLE BARK.   Extraction of tannic acid from the wattle bark in Lushoto District began in 1965 by two expatriates, W. L. Richards and R. Idsinger from England and Netherlands respectively.   They established the Giraffe Extract Co., Ltd.   An African General Manager was appointed in 1968.   By 1972/73 more than 2000 tons of wattle extract was produced.   Production is steadily rising making an annual profit of more than Shs. 1.1 million before taxation.

WELFARE.   In the traditional society, welfare assistance was a function of the extended family or lineage.   Mutual assistance operates within kinship units.   The first African welfare centers were organized in 1945.   The National Provident Fund, to which both employers and employees contribute, provides benefits which include retirement, illness and survivors' pension.   A College of Social Welfare trains recruits for the governmental department workers.   In addition, voluntary agencies such as the Community Development Trust Fund, Salvation Army, the Red Cross and churches are active in social welfare programs.

WESTERN RIFT.   Of the Rift Valley, it is often referred to as the Central African Rift.   It consists of a series of faults and contains Lakes Tanganyika, Rukwa and Nyasa

which are on the border of Tanzania with Burundi, Rwanda and Malawi. The rough terrain east of Lake Tanganyika rises to form the western edge of the Central Plateau. Lake Rukwa is a shallow depression varying in
size in accordance with the seasonal precipitation. There
is 30 to 40 inches of annual rainfall. Soils are moderately fertile, ranging from very sandy to very clayey
soils.

WHEAT. Recorded as being cultivated by Arabs in Tabora
    and Karagwe in 1852. It was grown in the Northern
    Province from 1942-45 and reduced the import require-
    ments during World War II. The 11,660 tons of 1960
    rose to 45,022 tons in 1970, an increase of 286 percent.
    Forty percent of Tanzania's wheat is grown on the slopes
    of Mt. Kilimanjaro. The National Milling Corporation
    purchased 25,802 metric tons from the farmers in
    1975/76. There was a significant increase in the 1976
    crop. Most of the crop is used locally.

WHITE FATHERS. The Society of the Missionaries of Af-
    rica (Société de Notre Dame d'Afrique) are more com-
    monly known as White Fathers because of their white
    clothes, not because they were Caucasian. They were
    given responsibility for Western Tanganyika. They ar-
    rived at Bagamoyo in 1878 and were ready to move in-
    land at the same time the Holy Ghost Fathers wanted to
    do so. They set off for Tabora where they divided into
    two groups, one going on to Bukumbi near Mwanza and
    on to Uganda and the other going to Karema on Lake
    Tanganyika. A few remained at Tabora where their re-
    lations with freed slaves were excellent.
        In 1879 they settled at Kibanga, the peninsula op-
    posite Ujiji. Their plantations produced a variety of
    crops and attracted voluntary settlers. The White
    Fathers suffered at Tabora and around Lake Tanganyika
    at the hands of the Arabs, Tippu Tip and Rumaliza, but
    in 1889 Emin Pasha's expedition with the German troops
    suppressed them. Settlements built up again at Unyany-
    embe, Tabora, Sukumaland and around Lake Tanganyika
    and lastly in Bukoba District. In 1905 Unyanyembe had
    61 African catechists against 43 European missionaries,
    there were more than 10,000 catechumens and 2500
    neophytes.
        Tukuyu divided into three sections during 1932--
    Mbeya, Karema and Kigoma. They were all given the
    status of a diocese in 1953. When Bishop Holmes-Seedle

was transferred in 1958 from Karema to Kigoma, a local, Charles Msakila was consecrated Bishop in his place on 27 December, 1958.

The Unyanyembe territory became a Vicariate Apostolic in 1897. In 1925 its name was changed from Unyanyembe to Tabora. Tabora became an Arch-Diocese in 1953 with Archbishop Cornelius Bronsveld in charge. He resigned in 1960 and Archbishop Mark Mihayo was installed in his place.

On the establishment of the Uganda Protectorate in 1894, Bishop Huth confined his pastorate to the German shore of Lake Victoria. Mwanza was included in this Vicariate of Nyanza. In 1946 three districts--Musoma, North Mara and Maswa--were separated from Mwanza and Shinyanga District was taken from Tabora to be joined to Mwanza. Shinyanga and Maswa were later handed over to the Maryknolls in 1956. A Social Training Centre, Nyegezi, near Mwanza, opened in 1960. They offered social training, but in 1963 journalism was added.

The Vicariate of Bukoba was erected in 1929 and from thence a number of dioceses were formed. The first four priests to be ordained in Tanganyika were ordained in Bukoba in 1917. His Eminence, Laurian Cardinal Rugambwa held jurisdiction over the Diocese of Bukoba. He was first elected a Bishop in 1951 and in 1960 made a Cardinal. The "Lourdes of Africa" is in this diocese at Nyakijoga.

There were five Africans already made Bishops by 1961--Cardinal Rugambwa, Archbishop Mihayo, Bishop Msakila of Karema, Auxiliary Bishop Butibubage of Mwanza and Auxiliary Bishop Nkalanga of Bukoba. Of the 303 African priests in the Catholic Church by 1962, the White Fathers had trained 58 percent of them.

In 1903 Rubya Seminary was opened near Bukoba and in 1909 a major seminary was added. In 1917 the first two priests of Tanganyika were ordained. A minor seminary was built near Tabora in 1908. In 1909 another was opened in Southwestern Tanzania. In 1921 a major seminary was erected at Utinta to serve all the regions. Two priests were ordained here in 1923. It transferred to Kipalapala in 1925.

The White Fathers amalgamated with other orders to form the present Tanzania Episcopal Conference (TEC).

WILDLIFE. Included are mammals, reptiles, amphibians and birds of several types or habitats. These are protected

in government reserves, game parks and conservation
areas.   Wildlife is a significant economic asset since it
attracts tourists and provides for foreign exchange.
Some of the most common animals are antelope, elephants, giraffes, hippos, lions, rhinos, wildebeest and
zebra.   The peak season was in 1973 when 84 thousand
kilograms of trophies were sold at a cost of Shs. 23 million in foreign currency.   Smuggling is a problem and it
is estimated that Tanzania loses Shs. 2 million annually
to "hide" smugglers.   However, the shooting of a limited
number of animals for sport is the most economical form
of game cropping.   The sale of game licenses in Tanganyika for the years 1955 to 1959 brought an average annual
revenue of £57,000.

WILLIAMSON, JOHN THORBURN (1907-1958).   Born in Que-
    bec, Canada in 1907 and studied law and later, mining.
    After graduating from McGill University, he took up a
    post with the Quebec Geological Survey and at twenty-one
    accompanied a professor to the Rand in South Africa and
    became interested in diamonds.   He found his first dia-
    mond near Shinyanga in March 1940.   The Tanganyika
    Government and DeBeers Diamond Corporation operated
    the mine jointly.

WINE.   Two Roman Catholic priests began cultivating vine-
    yards at Bihawana near Dodoma and were successful.
    This led to the Dodoma wine industry which has mush-
    roomed through Ujamaa villagization.   In 1975 the Nat-
    ional Milling Corporation produced around 150,000 bottles
    of Rose and Sweet Wines worth Sh. 2.5 million.   In April
    1976 they were getting around 10,000 litres of wines
    from Bihawana.

WISSMAN, GOV. HERMANN.   Travelled in East Africa as
    an Imperial Commissioner and in 1888 was sent to quell
    the rebellion under Abushiri.   He gained control of Baga-
    moyo in May 1889 and in the next few months gained
    control over the coast.   He sent troops to Kilwa Kivinje
    and Lindi in May 1890 and conquered there by 1891.
    Then he led an expedition to Kilimanjaro to subdue Sina.
    He was appointed Governor of German East Africa in
    1895 and continued to suppress tribes which resisted Ger-
    man rule.   He returned to Germany in mid-1896.

WITCHCRAFT.   A common belief of all tribes.   It is as-
    sumed that some persons are capable of inflicting harm

on others by their control of supernatural power.   A
"witch" is believed to be innately wicked and seeks to
hurt people for reasons of envy, jealousy or greed.
Sickness and death are commonly attributed to the action
of witches and sorcerers, often thought to be close rela-
tives of the person afflicted.

WOMEN'S POLICE DIVISION   see   POLICE

WORLD WAR I.   An attempted invasion of German East Africa by British and Indian troops in 1914 was repulsed by
the German forces.   In July 1915 the German battleship,
Konigsberg, was destroyed by the British ships and planes
on the Rufiji delta.   In early February 1916, General
J. C. Smuts, a Boer soldier, arrived from South Africa
to take command of the British forces.   No large-scale
attack had been made until February 1916 when a large
body of British, South African, Rhodesian and Indian
troops defeated the Germans near Kilimanjaro and occupied the town of Moshi in March 1916.   In April the
Belgians attacked and occupied Rwanda.   The British
continued southwards and Dar es Salaam was captured on
4 September, 1916.   By the end of 1916 all German East
Africa north of the Central Line was occupied by the
British and Belgian forces (from Belgian Congo).   On 1
January, 1917, a provincial civil administration was set
up with Horace Byatt as Head.   Smuts resigned his post
in January 1917.   The allied advance resumed mid-1917.
The Germans under General von Lettow-Verbeck were
finally driven across the Ruvuma River into Portuguese
territory in November 1917.   He returned in September
1918 but the next month he was forced to retreat into
Northern Rhodesia and remained there until the Armistice
was signed.
          Zanzibar had declared war against Germany on 5
August, 1914.   Many natives served as carriers for the
KAR.

WORLD WAR II.   Not fought in Tanganyika but its soldiers
went abroad and participated bravely in Somaliland and
Ethiopia against the Italians, in Madagascar and in Burma.   About 92,000 Tanzanians joined the KAR, the highest ratio of volunteers in British territories.   They
served under General Wavell in Somaliland and Abyssinia
and took part in the victorious entry into Addis Ababa on
6 April, 1941.   The KAR had a share in garrisoning
Diego Suarez in Madagascar and later in occupying the

rest of the island. When the war was extended to South
East Asia, the KAR fought in the Burma campaign. They
were in the vanguard of the advance down the Kabaw Valley, the famous Valley of Death. It was a test of endur-
ance and the casualties were high. They fought bravely
and well and returned to Tanganyika in 1946.

- Y -

YAO (tribe). Of southeastern Tanzania, they were very busy
    by the 17th century selling ivory at Kilwa in exchange for
    beads and cloth with which to buy iron hoes in their
    homeland for the smiths. They were also involved in the
    slave trade.

YOUNG AFRICAN SPORTS CLUB (YANGA). First known by
    other names, Jangwani, Navigation, Taliana, and New
    Youngs. When they formed the Navigation in 1926 many
    of the members were workers of the East Africa Cargo
    Handling Services. The New Youngs won the Kassum
    Cup. In 1937 there was a split in the New Youngs and
    a group of Sunderland Sports Club withdrew. In 1940 the
    Higginson Cup was taken. Yanga has gained in skill
    since independence and has attained the following record:
    1963, won Healtho Cup and Afro-Shirazi Party Cup; 1964,
    the Revolution Cup; 1965, the TAAA Cup; 1966, the Star
    Cup; 1967, the Shield of FAT, Taxi Drivers' Cup and
    Workers May Day Cup; 1971, the National, Kamanda Kon-
    do, Marini Cup and 10th Anniversary, Dodoma; 1968-72,
    the Taifa (National) Cup; 1974, the Taifa Cup; and 1975
    the East and Central Africa Cup.

YOUNG MEN'S CHRISTIAN ASSOCIATION (TANZANIA). Began
    in Moshi on a temporary basis in 1959, but in 1961 YMCA
    Sweden sent a Fraternal Secretary and YMCA in Tanzania
    was organized and registered nationally. The Moshi
    branch was officially opened and one year later a branch
    was registered in Arusha. More branches were opened
    until they totalled eleven by 1977. YMCA serves the
    refugees at Muyenzi, operates an agricultural school at
    Marangu and a secondary school at Masama, Moshi, and
    is concerned with poultry raising. In September 1976 it
    opened a vocational Training Centre for the training of
    instrument mechanics, refrigeration and air-conditioning.
    The school enrolls Std. VII leavers for a two-year course.
    It is associated with the Christian Council of Tanzania
    (CCT).

YOUNG WOMEN'S CHRISTIAN ASSOCIATION (TANZANIA).
YWCA was introduced at Marangu, Moshi in 1959 by E.
Mswia and C. Elfving. Later, in November 1964, it
was officially registered in government and its head of-
fice moved to Dar es Salaam. There are branches in
Dar es Salaam, Arusha, Moshi, Morogoro, Mwanza and
Tanga. YWCA had 765 members in mid-1970's and their
activities included needlework, cooking, arts and crafts,
language, general education, child care, debates and
speeches. They run pre-school classes at Dar es Salaam,
Moshi and Arusha. There is a hostel at Dar es Salaam.
With the self-reliance activities, each girl can produce
Shs. 250 a month which covers her living expenses.
YWCA became a member of CCT in 1963.

- Z -

ZANAKI (tribe). A small tribe of about 50,000 who are a
    mixture of several tribes whose members fled east of
    Lake Victoria because of famine or for personal reasons.
    Zanaki were divided into two nations, Biru and Baturi.
    President Nyerere comes from Biru. Brideprice was
    paid by cattle. A man could divorce his wife if barren,
    ugly, or unfit (for field work) or adulterous or guilty of
    murder or theft. She could not divorce him for murder,
    theft or arson but could divorce him if he bodily harmed
    her or disgraced her by stealing or setting on fire her
    fellow-tribesman's property. The Germans broke the
    tribe into 12 tiny chiefdoms and appointed its Mwami,
    Buhoro, as chief. His cousin Nyerere succeeded him in
    1912 and remained chief until 1942. When the British
    took over, the Zanaki were united into a tribe, but under
    Governor Cameron, they broke into seven chiefdoms
    which formed a federation in 1932 under Chief Ihunyo of
    Busegwe.

ZANZIBAR (history). It is generally accepted that the name
    "Zanzibar" is derived from the Persian word Zangh,
    meaning a negro, and bar a coast. The Arabic form and
    meaning of the name are similar, making the name Zinj-
    bar. It seemed to apply, according to Arab geographers,
    to the greater region of East Africa, and, in the course
    of centuries, came to indicate a small island (the rever-
    sal of many applications).
        The original population was composed of the Hadi-
    mu and Tumbatu. They claim Shirazi origin--maybe were

slaves of the Omanis.   Little is known of what happened
inside the island before the coming of the Portuguese to
East Africa.   Immigrations of Africans from the mainland
and various peoples from Arabia, Persia and India took
place.   The entire East African coast was subject for
centuries to trading ventures with some colonization from
Persia, Arabia, India and Somaliland and indirectly from
China and the Mediterranean Sea.   By the 10th century
A. D. the many city-states along the East African coast
of predominantly Muslim ruling groups were of Persian
and Arabian origin mixed with locals.   Two important
rulers in the 15th century were Husain bin Ahmed and
Ishaq bin Hasan.

The Portuguese first called at Zanzibar in early
1499 under Vasco da Gama, then attacked Zanzibar in
1503 and 1509 and destroyed the principal town.   The local ruler accepted his submission as vassal of the King
of Portugal.   Zanzibaris took part in the destruction of
Mombasa in 1528.   In 1654 Cabreira was forced during
his second term of office to carry out a punitive expedition, in the course of which the town was destroyed and
the Queen expelled.   Queen Fatima of Zanzibar had been
a friend of the besieged at Fort Jesus, so she sent supplies and harbored relief ships.   She was eventually allowed
to return home and her son was given the title of ruler.
During the 18th century Zanzibar remained loyal to the
Omani government.   When the ruling family of Oman
changed from the Yaarubi to the Albusaid, only Zanzibar
among the East African dependencies remained faithful
to the new Sultan.

Sultan Said of Muscat ushered in a Golden Age in
the 19th century.   The whole commerce of slaves, ivory,
cloves, etc. passed through Zanzibar.   Trade treaties
were signed with foreign countries.   A British Agency
was established in 1841 under the direction of the Bombay
Government and continued to 1873 when the Government of
India continued until 1883.   Then the Imperial Government
took over.   The Agency was headed by a Consul General
and later by a Resident in 1913.   In November 1890
Britain assumed her protectorate over the Sultan of Zanzibar's dominion.

Sultan Said was succeeded by his four sons and a
few more Sultans.   The Tumbatu and Hadimu were not
under the Sultan's power until 1890.   Seyyid Khalifa bin
Harub who ruled from 1911-60 developed Zanzibar into a
modern state.   The responsibility for Zanzibar passed
from the British Foreign Office to the Colonial Office in
1913.

When the Resident assumed control of the government, he appointed British officials in place of the Arabs and presided over the Executive and Legislative Councils. The Sultan was reduced to no more than a figurehead. The first elections were held in 1957. The development of nationalism and the growth of racialism began in the 1950's, so the situation changed rapidly after Sultan Khalifa's death in 1960.

Independence was granted on 10 December, 1963, two days before Kenya. On 12 January, 1964, the Government was overthrown, the new government was led by an alliance of ASP and UMMA parties. The President was Abeid Karume, Vice President Hanga, Foreign Minister Babu and Minister of Education was Othman Shariff. The Sultan fled to Tanganyika and on to Britain. On January 19 more than 100 Tanganyika police were sent to maintain law and order. On 26 April, 1964, Zanzibar and Tanganyika joined to form the United Republic of Tanzania. Zanzibar continued to manage its affairs locally except in certain areas where they were considered to be on the Union level.

On 7 April, 1972, President of Zanzibar, A. Karume and Vice President of the Republic, was assassinated. He was succeeded in office by A. Jumbe.

ZANZIBAR (island). A coral island, the highest point less than 400 feet above sea level. It is only 22½ miles from the mainland at the narrowest point. It is located 5° to 7°S latitude and has an area of 640 square miles. Its maximum mean temperature is 85.7°F. and its minimum temperature is 77.1°F. The island has an average rainfall of 60 inches. The west coast enjoys rainfall and an abundance of water that is the envy of the opposite mainland. Portuguese General Francisco de Barreto described Zanzibar in 1571 as the finest part of Africa. It had a population of about 170,000 in 1905, 197,199 in 1914, and 235,000 in 1921. The inhabitants are 80 percent Moslem and there are a few Christian churches: UMCA, Roman Catholic, Lutheran and Friends Industrial Mission. After the Revolution of 1964, it was estimated that only one-tenth of the 70,000 Arabs had remained and about one-third of the 16,000 Asians of Indian and Pakistani origin had remained.

ZANZIBAR (town). Founded in 1824 by Sultan Said. It has a well-protected, natural deepwater harbor and was the center of slave trade and all trade in the East African

Coast. The Beit al Ajaib (The Palace of Wonders) was
built by Sultan Barghash in 1883 as a ceremonial palace
and is a tourist attraction as well as the old slave market. Zanzibar town is a typical Arab town with tall,
stone houses, Arab-style embossed doors and narrow,
winding streets. It is the only town of importance in
Zanzibar and contains one-third of the island's population.
It is the center of the government, trade and commerce.
Steamers call regularly at its port. It had 35,000 inhabitants in 1910 and 58,000 in 1958. After the 1964
Revolution the number did decrease since only one-tenth
of the Arabs and one-third of the Asians on the island
had remained by 1967. The town now has some modern
apartment blocks.

ZANZIBAR AND PEMBA PEOPLE'S PARTY (ZPPP). The
     People's Party had been organized in 1956 to avoid domi-
     nation of either the Arab-led ZNP or the African Asso-
     ciation. In 1959 Shirazi Association of Pemba merged
     with this party. The ZPPP broke away from ASP in
     1959 and was led by Sheikh Mohammed Shamte. The
     ZNP and ZPPP formed a coalition government in 1961
     with Shamte as Chief Minister. Shamte became Prime
     Minister in 1963 with the ZNP in power. The Revolution
     of 12 January, 1964 toppled the government and ushered
     in the ASP.

ZANZIBAR NATIONAL UNION (ZNU). Formed in the early
     1950's by the Arabs in hopes of gaining the cooperation
     of the Africans, thus leading to a multi-racial community.
     The early attempt at unity failed largely because civil
     servants were prohibited to participate in politics and be-
     cause other African support was not attracted.

ZANZIBAR NATIONALIST PARTY (ZNP). Founded in 1955
     as an outgrowth of the National Party of the Subjects of
     the Sultan of Zanzibar (NPSS). It grew from a rural
     African peasant league into an Arab-dominated urban
     nationalist movement; it preached multi-racialism but
     practiced racialism. The President, Sheikh Ali Muhsin
     Barwani, was the most powerful leader and an Arab.
     ZNP was predominantly Arab and radical. In 1957 it
     failed to obtain much African support and polled a small
     percentage of the total vote but paid off in 1961. The
     ZNP and ZPPP formed a coalition government in 1961
     with Shamte as Chief Minister. The ZNP was in power
     1963 when Shamte became Prime Minister at independence.

The ZNP Government was overthrown on 12 January, 1964.

ZANZIBAR POLICE FORCE. Organizationally, they are integrated with the police on the mainland, but remain separate in some respects. The force was begun in 1908 to replace a military force of 500 men who served the Sultan. At independence many of the force were African mainlanders. They were instrumental in executing the revolutionary coup of January 1964. Miscellaneous duties of the force are: destruction of crows and stray dogs and cats; Fire Brigade duties.

ZANZIBAR PROTECTORATE. Included the islands of Zanzibar and Pemba and was announced in the Anglo-German agreement on East Africa of 1890. The Protectorate occurred as a result of the British pressures to end the slave trade and as a move to prevent a German takeover. The Consul General was the chief British representative. The coastal strip of 10 miles wide which belonged to the Sultan, from the Ruvuma River to the Tanganyika-Kenya border, became a part of German East Africa and north of the border to Tana River was rented by the British Government and administered by Kenya. Control of internal affairs and determination of successors to the Sultanate were left in the hands of the traditional rulers and Britain took over foreign affairs. The Foreign Office handed over the responsibility for the Protectorate to the Colonial Office in 1913 and a Resident replaced the Consul General. He replaced most Arab rulers with British officers and the Sultan became a figurehead. In 1926 the Executive Council and Legislative Council were introduced. The Legislative Council had some limited lawmaking responsibilities and, as such, began the gradual constitutional change that led to independence. In 1955 a Privy Council was formed to advise the Sultan. Political activities began in the 1950's and there were a number of political parties formed. The ZNP and ASP took part in the 1957 elections. After the granting of self-government in June 1963, the ZNP/ZPPP and ASP contested seats. Zanzibar received its independence from Great Britain on 19 December, 1963, and the Sultan became a constitutional monarch.

ZARAMO (tribe). The largest African ethnic group in Dar es Salaam, they are mainly urban dwellers. They had the tradition of two leading clans, the Shomvi at the coast

and the Pazi in the hills. They do much wood-carving
and produce the more classical figures, do some Makonde carvings and make drums. The tribe is characterized
by considerable family and marital instability. Their
traditional culture is intertwined with Islamic religion and
Islamic law.

ZELEWSKI, EMIL von. The commander of the German for-
    ces in 1891 who undertook a punitive expedition against
    the Hehe tribe. The Germans were ambushed at Lulu-
    Rugaro and nearly all were killed, including von Zelewski.

ZIGUA (tribe). They reside in western Tanga and northern
    Coast Region. They were considered by the Germans to
    be more warlike than their neighboring tribes and showed
    a great character. As a whole they have been conserva-
    tive and, in the past, showed a marked reluctance to
    connect themselves with modern enterprise. Cotton is
    the main crop. In 1957 they numbered 134, 000, and
    many Zigua reside outside their area as wage laborers
    and traders. Even in the 1890's there was a great quan-
    tity of coastal trade goods among the Zigua. Others
    made trading trips far inland. The early accounts of the
    area indicate that there was heavy raiding in the middle
    and end of the 19th century. Masai and Baraguyu raided
    the Zigua for livestock and Zigua raided their neighbors
    for slaves. Bwana Heri held power over large areas,
    though the matrilineal tribe never had paramount chiefs.
    Zigua raiding, slaving and trading often with Arab sup-
    port, placed them in strong opposition to the Germans
    and accounts for their fighting in the 1880's. Zigua be-
    lieve in witchcraft and divination. They are related to
    the Ngulu, Shambala and Bondei by their traditions.

ZIMBA. Not a tribe but a way of life, the Zimbas were eaters
    of human flesh. They are thought to have come from the
    Congo and were Bantu speaking. They were first mentioned
    in the middle of the 16th century on the north bank of the
    Zambezi River. There were approximately 5000 warriors
    in a band when they entered Kilwa in 1587; they slaughter-
    ed and ate some 3000 inhabitants and left the town vir-
    tually deserted and moved northwards in the same manner.
    They encountered the Segeju near Mombasa, Kenya and
    were annihilated almost to a man.

ZINJANTHROPUS. Discovered by Dr. and Mrs. Leakey in
    July 1959 in the lowest bed of Olduvai Gorge, Bed I.

The skull had enormous molars, thus earning the nickname "Nutcracker Man. " Zinj is an old East Africa
name. The skull was associated with a living floor which
contained fragments of small animals and birds believed
to have formed part of Zinjanthropus's diet. Scientists
have set the Bed level to be 1, 750, 000 years.

ZINZA (tribe). Of Northwestern Tanzania, they were famous
in the 19th century for their iron hoes, tools and weapons. They live along the Southwestern shore of Lake
Victoria.

ZIOTA II, CHIEF HUMBI (1922-). Of Nzega, he was educated at Tabora Secondary School, then was a clerk for
the railways and for the government before becoming a
chief of Usango in Nzega District in 1943. He studied
agriculture at Cambridge University and in Cyprus. In
1954 he was elected Chairman of the Unyamwezi Federal
Council and appointed a director of the Tanganyika Agricultural Corporation. He was nominated an unofficial
member of Legislative Council in 1957 and became an
Assistant Minister for Agricultural production the same
year. He was awarded the M. B. E. for exemplary service during the colonial regime. Towards the end of the
1950's he aligned himself with TANU and was elected a
member of Parliament in 1958. Chief Humbi served as
a Regional Commissioner in Morogoro and Shinyanga in
the mid-1960's. He was one of the few important traditional chiefs in Tanganyika to make a thoroughly successful entrance into the post-independence political arena,
serving the government in an administrative position with
the Ministry of Agriculture even to the mid-1970's.

BIBLIOGRAPHY

BIBLIOGRAPHY: TABLE OF CONTENTS

INTRODUCTION

INTRODUCTION

In addition to the government's official publications
during the German and British eras, of Tanganyika and Zanzibar as separate entities and of the union of the two, there
has been an appreciable amount of literature coupling Tan-
ganyika/Tanzania with the other East African countries, Kenya and Uganda, as well as official publications of the various
institutions within the East African federation.

In the latter half of the 1960's several books were published which gave very good general information about many
aspects of the mainland: MacDonald's Tanzania: Young Nation in a Hurry gave a journalist's point of view; The Area
Handbook for Tanzania--1968, edited by Herrick and Tanzania
Today published by the University Press of Africa in Nairobi
in 1968 were both good treatments. Another book of such
calibre is needed to be up-to-date in the last half of the
1970's. Zanzibar is best covered by Coupland, Gray and
Pearce.

The best authorities on archaeological materials are
L. S. B. Leakey and J. E. G. Sutton, Leakey specializing in
the excavational findings in his three volumes on Olduvai
Gorge and Sutton's greater interest on the East Africa Coast.
The most popular of the Swahili writers was Shaaban Robert.
I have not included his writings in the bibliography but listed
some of them in the entry under his name. The anthropological and scientific literature is scattered in many journals,
master's and doctoral dissertations and within books. Some
of the most prolific writers in the anthropological and sociological branches of the colonial government were Hans Cory,
A. H. J. Prins, T. O. Beidelman and G. W. B. Huntingford, each in his own general section of the country. Murdock has classified the tribes and given their characteristics
in Africa: Its Peoples and Their Cultural History. For a
survey of education from the past to the 1970's, I suggest
Cameron and Dodd's, Society, Schools, and Progress, Kurtz's
An African Education: The Social Revolution in Tanzania and
Resnick's Tanzania: Revolution by Education.

One of the best sources in the area of economics is the series of Weltforum Verlag Publications from Munich, Germany, which covers development from a geographical, economic and scientific point of view. Hans Ruthenberg gives the most thorough treatment on agriculture with an extensive bibliography. For a history of labor and unions, William Friedland seems to be well-versed. His latest book is Vuta Kamba: The Development of Unions in Tanganyika. The Economy of Tanzania, edited by K. E. Svensen, is one of the most recent books on this topic.

Some of the early explorers' writings have been included if the reader wishes to get a glimpse of Tanganyika and the East Coast before contact with the Western world had made its impact. Zamani, published regularly by the History Department of the University of Dar es Salaam, reports on pre-colonial historical research. Clarke's A Short History of Tanganyika is very readable for the student in secondary education. The three volumes of The History of East Africa, edited by Oliver and Gervase (vol. 1), Harlow et al. (vol. 2), and Low and Smith (vol. 3), as well as Kimambo and Temu's A History of Tanzania, Were and Wilson's East Africa through a Thousand Years, Robert's Tanzania Before 1900 and Ward and White's East Africa: A Century of Change, 1870-1970 can supply the reader with a good overall view of the history of Tanzania. A good Swahili source is Nsekela's Minara ya Tanganyika: Tanganyika hadi Tanzania. The best single coverage of the German period is Meyer's Das Deutsche Kolonialreich, I and of the British period is Moffatt's Tanganyika: A Review of Its Resources and Development or his revised Handbook of Tanganyika.

In the political science area, I would recommend the writings of Lionell Cliffe, John Iliffe, K. E. Svensen and J. F. Rweyemamu. Rural Cooperation in Tanzania, edited by Cliffe, Socialism in Tanzania: Vol. I, Politics; Vol. II, Policies, edited by Cliffe and Saul, and Towards Socialist Planning, edited by Rweyemamu, are the most recent and comprehensive treatment on the political thought and implementation in Tanzania. R. W. James is the best authority on Law in his Land Tenure and Policy in Tanzania, Customary Law of Tanganyika, and Law and Its Administration in a One-Party State. In A History of Zanzibar, Ayanyi gives a good coverage of its constitutional development.

Tanganyika/Tanzania Notes and Records is one of the best journals for a variety of historical, social and cultural topics. For convenience, I have used TNR in my references to it. I have also included only the German and Swahili publications which I felt were most relevant and important.

1. GENERAL

Travel and Description: Early Times

Burton, Sir Richard. The Lake Regions of Central Africa:
     a picture of exploration. London: Tinsley Bros.,
     1860. New York: Horizon Press, 1961.

_____. The Nile Basin, Parts I and II. London: Tinsley
     Bros., 1864.

Craster, J. E. E. Pemba, the Spice Island of Zanzibar.
     London: T. Fisher Unwin, 1913.

Fitzgerald, W. W. A. Travels in the Coastland of British
     East Africa and the Islands of Zanzibar and Pemba.
     London, 1898.

Johnston, H. H. The Kilima-Njaro Expedition. London:
     Kegan Paul, Trench and Co., 1886.

Krapf, L. Travels, Researches and Missionary Labours
     during an Eighteen years' residence in East Africa,
     together with journeys to Jagga, Usambara, Ukambani,
     Shoa, Abessinia and Khartum and a coasting voyage
     from Mombaz to Cape Delgado. London: Trubner and
     Co., 1860.

Richards, C. G. (ed.) Burton and Lake Tanganyika. Nairo-
     bi: East African Literature Bureau, 1965.

_____. (ed.) Some Historic Journeys in East Africa.
     Nairobi: OUP, 1967.

Stanley, Henry M. How I Found Livingstone. London: 1872.

_____. Through the Dark Continent. Vol. I, II. New
     York: 1878.

Waller, Horace. (ed.) Last Journals of David Livingstone in
     Central Africa, 1865 to His Death. Newark: F. C.
     Bliss, 1875.

Travel and Description: Current

Fosbrooke, Henry. Ngorongoro: The Eighth Wonder. London:
     Andre Deutsch Ltd., 1972.

_____. Ngorongoro's First Visitor. Nairobi: EALB, 1966.

Goldthorpe, J. E. and F. B. Wilson. Tribal Maps of East Africa and Zanzibar. (East African Studies, No. 13) Kampala: East African Institute of Social Research, 1960.

Grzimek, B. and M. Grzimek. Serengeti Shall Not Die. London: Hamish Hamilton, 1960.

Jensen, S. Regional Economic Atlas: Mainland Tanzania. Dar es Salaam: BRALUP, 1968.

Reuben, Joel and Howard Carstens. Tanzania in Pictures. New York: Sterling Publishing Co., 1972.

General Information

Bomani, Paul. Forward Tanzania. Nairobi: Patwa News Agency, Ltd., 1964.

Hatch, John. Tanzania: A Profile. London: Pall Mall, 1972.

Kaula, Edna Mason. The Land and People of Tanganyika. Philadelphia: Lippincott, 1963. (for children)

MacDonald, Alexander. Tanzania: Young Nation in a Hurry. New York: Hawthorn Books, 1966.

Meienberg, Hildebrand. Tanzanian Citizen. Nairobi: OUP, 1966.

Tanzania Society. A Decade of Progress: 1961-1971. TNR: No. 76, 1975.

Wilson, E. G. (ed.) Who's Who in East Africa, 1965-66. Nairobi: Marco Publishers, 1966.

Handbooks and Yearbooks

Admiralty War Staff, Intelligence Div. A Handbook of German East Africa. London: Her Majesty's Stationery Office, 1916, 1921.

Gordon-Brown, A. (ed.) The Year Book and Guide to East Africa. London: Robert Hale, 1965.

Herrick, Allen Butler, et al. Area Handbook for Tanzania-- 1968. DA Pam. No. 550-62 Washington: Gt. Printing Office, 1968.

Legum, Colin. (ed.) Africa Contemporary Record: Annual Survey and Documents, VOL. VII. 1974-75. New York: Africana Publishing Co., 1975.

Meyer, H. Das Deutsche Kolonialreich, 1. Leipzig and Wien: Bibliographisches Institut, 1909.

Moffett, J. P. (ed.) Tanganyika: a review of its resources and their development. Dar es Salaam: Gt. Printers, 1955.

_____. (ed.) Handbook of Tanganyika, 2nd edition. Dar es Salaam: Gt. Printers, 1958.

Sayers, Gerald F. (ed.) The Handbook of Tanganyika. London: Macmillan, 1930.

Steinberg, S. H. (ed.) Statesman's Yearbook. New York: St. Martin's Press, 1967-68.

Tanzania Today: a portrait of the United Republic. Nairobi: University Press of Africa, 1968.

Statistics

East Africa High Commission. East African Statistical Department. Economic and Statistical Review issues.

Tanzania Government. Central Statistical Bureau. Ministry of Economic Affairs and Development Planning. Statistical Abstract annual. Dar es Salaam: Gt. Printers.

Bibliographies

African Bibliography Series. East Africa. London: International African Institute, 1960.

Bates, M. L. A Study Guide for Tanzania. Boston: Boston University, 1969.

Decalo, Samuel. An Introductory Bibliography. Kingston, R. I.: University of Rhode Island, 1968.

East African Medical Research Council. A Bibliography of Health and Disease in East Africa. Nairobi: East African Literature Bureau, 1974.

Hall, R. deZ. "A Bibliography of Ethnological Literature for Tanganyika Territory." TNR, No. 7, 1939, 75-83.

Hanson, John W. and Geoffrey W. Gibson. African Education and Development Since 1960: A Select and Annotated Bibliography. East Lansing, Mich.: Michigan State University, 1966.

Jumba-Masagazi, Abdul R. K., compiler. Science and Technology in East Africa: A Bibliography and Short Commentaries. Nairobi: East African Academy, 1973.

Mutibwa, O. M. N., compiler. Education in East Africa; 1971: a selected bibliography. Kampala: Makerere University Library, 1972.

Rweyemamu, A. H. Government and Politics in Tanzania: A Bibliography. Nairobi: East African Academy, 1972.

Tanzania Library Services. Tanzania National Bibliography, # 1:1969. # 2:1970. Dar es Salaam: Tanzania Library Services.

Taylor, Barbara. Catalogue of Early German Material Relating to Tanzania in the Library of the Mineral Resources Division, Dodoma. Dodoma: Mineral Resources Division, 1968.

U.S. Library of Congress. General Reference and Bibliography Division. Official Publications of British East Africa. Part 2, Tanganyika. (compiled by Audrey A. Walker), Washington: 1962. Part 3, Kenya and Zanzibar. Washington: 1963.

2. CULTURAL

Archaeology

Fosbrooke, H. A. "Early Iron Age Sites in Tanganyika Relative to Traditional History. " Third Pan-African Congress on Pre-History, edited by J. Desmond Clark,
London, 1957.

Fosbrooke, et al. "Tanganyika Rock Paintings" TNR, 29,
1950, 1-61.

Freeman-Grenville, S. P. The Medieval History of the
Coast of Tanganyika: with special reference to recent
archeological discoveries. London: OUP, 1962.

_____. The French at Kilwa Island. Oxford: Clarendon
Press, 1965.

Kirkman, James S. Men and Monuments of the East African
Coast. London: Lutterworth Press, 1964.

Leakey, L. S. B. Olduvai Gorge. Vol. I, II, III. London:
Cambridge University Press, 1951.

_____. The Progress and Evolution of Man in Africa.
Nairobi: OUP, 1961.

Mathew, A. G. "The Culture of the East African Coast in
the 17th and 18th Centuries in the Light of Recent
Archaeological Discoveries. " Man, 56, 1956, 61.

Sutton, J. E. G. The East African Coast: an historical
and archaeological review. Nairobi: EALB, 1966.

Architecture

Flury, S. "The Kufic Inscriptions of the Kizimkazi Mosque,
Zanzibar. " Journal of the Royal Asiatic Society,
1922, 257-64.

Garlake, P. S. The Early Islamic Architecture of the East
African Coast. Oxford, 1966.

Art

Cory, Hans. Wall-Paintings by Snake Charmers in Tanganyika. London: Faber, 1953.

Stout, J. Anthony. Modern Makonde Sculpture. Dar
es Salaam: Kibo Art Gallery, 1966.

von D. Miller, Judith. Art in East Africa. London: Frederick Muller Ltd., 1975.

Communications

Giltrow, David R. "Young Tanzanians and the cinema: a
study of the effects of selected basic motion picture
elements and population characteristics on filmic com-
prehension of Tanzanian adolescent primary school
children." Doctoral dissertation, Syracuse University,
1973.

Language and Linguistics: Swahili Policy

Bryan, M. A. The Bantu Languages of Africa: Handbook of
African Languages. London: Oxford University Press,
1959.

Hollis, A. C. The Masai, Their Language and Folklore.
Oxford: Clarendon Press, 1905.

Whiteley, W. M. Swahili: The Rise of a National Language.
London: Methuen, 1968.

Wright, Marcia. "Swahili Language Policy, 1890-1940" Swahili, XXXV, no. 1, 1965, 40-48.

Language and Linguistics: Swahili Grammar

Guthrie, M. The Classification of the Bantu Languages.
London, 1948.

_____. "Some Developments in the Pre-history of Bantu
Languages" Journal of African History, III, 1962,
273-82.

Krumm, B. Words of Oriental Origin in Swahili. London, 1940.

Moore, Rae Arlene C. "The verbal derivations in Swahili." Doctoral dissertation, University of Texas, 1966.

Olinick, Judith O. "A transformation generative grammar of certain noun phrases in Swahili." Doctoral dissertation, University of Wisconsin, 1967.

Scotton, Carol. "Aspects of the Swahili extended verb system with special reference to some deep structure, syntactic and semantic restrictions." Doctoral dissertation, University of Wisconsin, 1965.

Literature: General

Buttner, C. G. Anthologie aus der Suaheli-Literatur. 2 vol. Berlin, 1894.

Curr, A. and A. Calder. (eds.) Writers in East Africa. Nairobi: EALB, 1974.

Hinnebusch, Thomas J. "An Introductory Study of Shaaban Robert and his contribution to Swahili literature." Master's thesis, Duquesne University, 1964.

Solenberger, Robert R. "An interpretation of material on the anthropology of East Africa based upon mediaeval Arabic writers." Master's thesis, University of Pennsylvania, 1940.

Literature: Poetry and Prose

Beidelman, T. O. "Eleven Kaguru Texts." African Studies (Johannesburg), XXVI, no. 1, 1967, 3-36.

_____. "Five Kaguru Texts." Anthropos, 58, nos. 5-6, 1963, 737-72.

_____. "Four Kaguru Tales." TNR, no. 61, Sept. 1963, 135-46.

_____. Further Adventures of Hyena and Rabbit: The Folktale as a Sociological Model." Africa, Jan. 1963, 54-69.

_____. "Further Kaguru Texts." Journal of African Languages, V, no. 2, 1966, 74-101.

_____. "Hyena and Rabbit: A Kaguru Representation of Matrilineal Relations." Africa, Jan. 1961, 61-74.

_____. "Some Kaguru Riddles." Man, LXIII, no. 195, Oct. 1963, 195-96.

_____. "Ten Kaguru Texts: Tales of an East African Bantu People." Journal of African Languages, III, no. 1, 1964, 1-37.

_____. "Three Tales of the Living and the Dead: The Ideology of Kaguru Ancestral Propitiation." Journal of the Royal Anthropological Institute, LXLIV, July-Dec. 1964, 109-37.

Farsi, S. S. Swahili Sayings from Zanzibar. Book II: Riddles and Superstition. Nairobi: EALB, 1973.

Harries, Lyndon. "Makua Song-Riddles from the Initiation Rites." African Studies, I, no. 1, 1942, 27-46.

_____. "Popular Verse of the Swahili Tradition." Africa (London) XXII, no. 2, 1952, 158-64.

_____. "Some Riddles of the Makua People." African Studies, I, no. 4, 1942, 275-91.

_____. Swahili Poetry. London: OUP, 1962.

_____. "Tales from Tanga: A Literary Beginning." East Africa Journal, III, no. 2, May 1966, 4-6.

Knappert, Jan. "Some Aspects of Swahili Poetry." TNR, no. 66, Dec. 1966, 163-70.

Sample, Ward A. "The Development of Style in Swahili Poetry." Master's thesis, Duquesne University, 1967.

Literature: Proverbs

Bull, A. F. "Asu (Pare) Proverbs and Songs." African, no. 6, 1933, 323-28.

Danielson, E. R.   "Proberbs of the Waniramba People of
     East Africa. "   TNR, nos. 47 and 48, June-Sept. 1957,
     187-97.

Duck, Carolyn A. P.   "Iwapo nia kuna njia: a study of the
     content and context of proverbs in Swahili. "   Master's
     thesis, University of Washington, 1970.

Farsi, S. S.   Swahili Sayings from Zanzibar, Book I: Pro-
     verbs.   Nairobi: EALB, 1973.

Olsen, H.   "Rimi Proverbs. "   TNR, no. 62, Mar. 1964, 73-
     82.

Seitel, Peter I.   "Proverbs and the structure of metaphor
     among the Haya of Tanzania. "   Doctoral dissertation,
     University of Pennsylvania, 1972.

Literature: Tales

Carnell, W. J.   "Four Gogo Folk Tales. "   TNR, no. 40,
     Sept. 1955, 30-42.

Institute of Adult Education.   Hadithi za Kinyamwezi.   Dar
     es Salaam: EALB, 1975.

_____. Hadithi za Kisukuma.   Dar es Salaam: EALB,
     1975.

_____. Hadithi za Kizanaki.   Dar es Salaam: EALB,
     1975.

Macdonald, Duff.   "Yao and Nyanja Tales. "   Bantu Studies,
     XII, no. 4, 1938, 251-85.

Woodward, H. W.   "Makua Tales. "   Bantu Studies, VI, no. 1,
     1932, 71-89.

Music

Beidelman, T. O.   "Some Baraguyu Cattle Songs. "   Journal
     of African Languages, IV, 1965, 1-18.

Tenraa, E. F.   "Sandawe Musical and Other Sound-Producing
     Instruments. "   TNR, no. 60, Mar. 1963, 23-48.

Tracy, Hugh. "The Development of Music in East Africa."
    TNR, no. 63, Sept. 1964.

van Thiel, Paul. "African Singing and Dancing in Divine
    Worship." African Ecclesiastical Review, Oct. 1967,
    341-48.

_____. "Text Tone and Tune in African Sacred Music."
    African Ecclesiastical Review, Jan. 1966, 53-62.

3.   ECONOMIC

Agriculture: General

Attems, Manfred. Smallholders in the Tropical Highlands of
    East Africa: The Usambara Mountains in the Transi-
    tion Period from Subsistence to Market Production.
    No. 25 (in German) Munchen: Weltforum Verlag, 1968.

Berry, L. et al. Human Adjustment to Agricultural Drought
    in Tanzania: Pilot Investigations. Dar es Salaam:
    Bureau of Research Assessment and Land Use Planning,
    1972.

Collinson, M. P. The Economic Characteristics of the Suku-
    ma Farming System. Dar es Salaam: Economic Re-
    search Bureau, 1972.

Colonial Reports. Annual Reports on Tanganyika Territory to
    the League of Nations, 1924-39. These are numbered
    in the Colonial Series.

_____. Annual Reports of the East African Agricultural
    Research Station, Amani, 1930-46. These are num-
    bered in the Colonial series.

de Wilde, John C. Experiences with Agricultural Development
    in Tropical Africa, 2 vols. Baltimore: John Hopkins
    Press for IBRD, 1967.

Donya, J. K. M. "The effects of the Plantation Economy on
    indigenous agriculture in the Northern Province, Tan-
    ganyika, 1950-1960." 3rd year dissertation, Universi-
    ty of Dar es Salaam, 1974.

Dumont, Rene. Tanzanian Agriculture after the Arusha Declaration. Dar es Salaam: Ministry of Economic Affairs and Development Planning, 1969.

Fuggles-Couchman, N. Agricultural Change in Tanganyika, 1945-1960. Stanford: Stanford University Press, 1964.

Iliffe, John. Agricultural Change in Modern Tanzania. Nairobi: East African Publishing House, 1971.

Lind, E. M. and M. S. Morrison. East African Vegetation. New York: Longmans, 1974.

Mhina, A. K. "Agricultural Change in Korogwe District, Bungu Division; a case study from pre-colonial period to 1974." 3rd year dissertation, University of Dar es Salaam, 1975.

Mothobi, Buzwani D. "A comparative analysis of agricultural development policy in Tanzania (mainland) and Kenya." Master's thesis, University of Toronto, 1970.

Reining, Priscilla C. "The Haya: the agrarian system of sedentary people." Doctoral dissertation, University of Chicago, 1966.

Ruthenberg, Hans. Agricultural Development in Tanganyika. Berlin: Springer-Verlag, 1964.

_____. Smallholder Farming and Smallholder Development in Tanzania; 10 case studies. Berlin: Springer-Verlag, 1968.

Schultz, J. Development Possibilities of Agriculture in Tanzania: The Agricultural Development on the Iraqw Highlands and its Margins. (in German with English summary) Munchen: Weltforum-Verlag, 1971.

Shapiro, Kenneth H. "Efficiency and modernization in African agriculture; a case study in Geita District, Tanzania." Stanford University doctoral dissertation, 1974.

Silberfein, Marilyn. "Constraints on the expansion of commercial agriculture in Iringa District, Tanzania." Doctoral dissertation, Ohio University, 1973.

Singleton, Carey B. Jr.   The Agricultural Economy of Tan-
    ganyika (U.S. Dept. of Agricultural Foreign Regional
    Analysis Division) Washington: Govt. Printing Office,
    1964.

Smith, Hadley E. (ed.)   Agricultural Development in Tanza-
    nia.   Nairobi: OUP, 1965.

Stanford Research Institute, Management and Social Systems
    Area.   An Economic Engineering Analysis of Alterna-
    tive Routes for Zambia/Tanzania Highway Link.   II:
    Agriculture Development Potential Crop Models.   and
    IV: Agricultural Development Potential Along the Al-
    ternative Routes for the TANZAM Highway.   Menlo
    Park: Stanford Research Institute, 1966.

Uchendu, V. E. and K. J. Anthony.   Agricultural Change in
    Geita District, Tanzania.   Dar es Salaam: EALB,
    1974.

Vesey-Fitzgerald, D.   East African Grasslands.   Nairobi:
    East African Publishing House, 1973.

Agriculture: Land Use

Tenure and Use

Bailey, A. P.   "Land Tenure: its sociological implications,
    with specific reference to the Swahili-speaking peoples
    of the East African coast."   Master's thesis, Univer-
    sity of London, 1965.

Gulliver, P. H.   Land Tenure and Social Change among the
    Nyakyusa.   East African Studies No. 11.   Kampala:
    East African Institute of Social Research, 1958.

Hekken, R. M. and H. U. G. Thoden von Velzen.   Land
    Scarcity and Rural Inequality in Tanzania: Some Case
    Studies in Mbungwe District.   The Hague: Mouton and
    Co., 1972.

James, R. W.   Land Tenure and Policy in Tanzania.   Dar
    es Salaam: EALB, 1973.

_____ and G. M. Fimbo.   Customary Land Law of Tan-
    zania (A Source Book).   Dar es Salaam: EALB, 1973.

Johnston, P. H. "Some notes on land tenure on Kilimanjaro and the vihamba of the Wachagga." TNR, XXI, June 1946, 1-20.

Lyall, A. B. "Land Law and Policy in Tanganyika, 1919-1932." Master's thesis, University of Dar es Salaam, 1973.

Maini, Krishan M. Land Law in East Africa. Nairobi: OUP, 1967.

Malcolm, D. W. Sukumaland: An African People and Their Country. London: OUP, 1953.

Middleton, John. Land Tenure in Zanzibar. London: HMSO, 1961.

Oldaker, A. A. "Tribal Customary Land Tenure in Tanganyika." TNR, no. 47 and 48, June-Sept. 1957, 117-44.

Pakenham, R. H. W. Land Tenure Among the Wahadimu at Chwaka, Zanzibar Island. Zanzibar: Gt. Press, 1947.

Rapp, Anders. (ed.) Studies of Soil Erosion and Sedimentation in Tanzania. Dar es Salaam: University of Dar es Salaam, Bureau of Resources Assessment and Land Use Planning, 1973.

Rotenham, Dietrich von. Land Use and Animal Husbandry in Sukumaland/Tanzania. (in German) Munchen: Weltforum Verlag, 1966.

Young, Roland A. and Henry A. Land and Politics Among the Luguru of Tanganyika. London: Routledge and Kegan Paul, 1960.

Meru Land Case

Japhet, Kirilo and Earle Seaton. The Meru Lands Case. Nairobi: East African Publishing House, 1967.

Mbise, Ismael R. Blood on Our Land. Dar es Salaam: Tanzania Publishing House, 1974.

Nelson, Anton. The Freemen of Meru. London: OUP, 1967.

Agriculture: Crops

Cloves

Zanzibar Government. Memorandum on Certain Aspects of the Zanzibar Clove Industry (G. D. Kirsopp) London: HMSO, 1926.

_____. Report on Clove Cultivation in the Zanzibar Protectorate (R. S. Troup) Zanzibar: Gt. Printers, 1932.

_____. Report of the Committee appointed to Discuss the Rationalization of the Clove Industry. Zanzibar: Gt. Printers, 1929.

_____. Report of a Mission appointed to Investigate the Clove Trade (of Zanzibar) (C. A. Bartlett and G. D. Kirsopp). London: HMSO, 1933.

_____. Report on the Zanzibar Clove Industry (B. H. Binder). Zanzibar: Gt. Printers, 1936.

Coffee

Mtei, B. F. "The fallacies of coffee cultivation in Kilimanjaro." 3rd year dissertation, University of Dar es Salaam, 1974.

Musikira, Mufungo A. D. "Tanzania's coffee: with special reference to diversification schemes." Master's thesis, Vanderbilt University, 1971.

Swynnerton, R. J. M. All About 'KNCU' Coffee. Moshi: The Moshi Native Coffee Board, 1948. (Also in Swahili).

Cotton

Hankins, Thomas D. "So you get out early to plant, who are you ahead of? The role of cotton planting time in Sukuma agriculture." Doctoral dissertation, Clark University, 1974.

Malima, Kighoma A. "The economics of cotton production in Tanzania: an examination of some of the factors that influence agricultural development." Doctoral dissertation, Princeton University, 1970.

Groundnuts

Anyonge, Nathan Jumba. "British groundnut scheme in East Africa: labour government's dilemma." Master's thesis, Kansas State University, 1966.

Wood, Alan. The Groundnut Affair. London: The Bradley House, 1976.

Maize

Miracle, Marvin P. Maize in Tropical Africa. Madison: University of Wisconsin Press, 1966.

Sisal

Ballali, Daudi T. "The sisal industry in Tanzania." Master's thesis, Catholic University of America, 1967.

Bruck, W. F. Die Sisalkultur in Deutsch-Ostafrika. Berlin, 1913.

Guillebaud, C. W. An Economic Survey of the Sisal Industry of Tanganyika. (3rd edition) Welwyn: James Nisbet, 1966.

Hindorf, Richard. Der Sisalbau in Deutsch-Ostafrika. Berlin, 1925.

Mascarenhas, Adolfo C. "Resistance and change in the sisal plantation system of Tanzania." Doctoral dissertation, Los Angeles, University of California, 1970.

Possinger, Hermann. Investigations into Productivity and Profitability of Smallholder Sisal in East Africa. (in German) Munich: Weltforum Verlag, 1967.

Tobacco

Kasaka, N. M. "Flue-Cured Tobacco Project in Chunya District, 1953-1974." 3rd year dissertation, University of Dar es Salaam, 1974.

Scheffler, Walter. Smallholder Production under Close Supervision: Tobacco Growing in Tanzania. A Socio-Economic Study. (in German) Munich: Weltforum Verlag, 1968.

Commerce: Trade

Anteneh, Addis. "Agricultural exports and economic development in Ethiopia and Tanganyika." Master's thesis, University of Illinois, 1961.

Bennett, A. L. B. "Short Account of the Work of the KNCU Ltd." East Africa Journal, Sept. 1935.

Gray, R. and D. Birmingham. (eds.) Pre-Colonial African Trade: Essays on Trade in Central and Eastern Africa before 1900. New York: OUP, 1970.

Hawkins, H. C. G. Wholesale and Retail Trade in Tanganyika. New York: Praeger, 1965.

Kainzbauer, Werner. Trade in Tanzania. Munchen: Weltforum Verlag, 1968 (in German).

Livingstone, Ian. "The Marketing of Crops in Uganda and Tanganyika." in I. G. Stewart and H. W. Ord (eds.) African Primary Products and International Trade. Edinburgh: Edinburgh University Press, 1965.

Mtinga, A. O. S. "The State Trading Corporation: Its role, organization and operation as an instrument of social development strategy." 3rd year dissertation, University of Dar es Salaam, 1972.

Mutaha, et al. Cooperatives in Tanzania. Dar es Salaam: Tanzania Publishing House, 1976.

Ngeze, Pius B. Ushirika Tanzania (Cooperatives in Tanzania). Dar es Salaam: Tanzania Publishing House, 1975.

Paulus, Margarete. The Role of Co-operatives in the Economic Development of East Africa, and Especially of Tanganyika and Uganda. (in German) Munchen: Weltforum Verlag, 1967.

Saul, J. "Marketing Co-operatives in a Developing Country: the Tanzania Case." in P. Worsley (ed.) Two Blades of Grass. London: Manchester University Press, 1970.

Sutton, J. Early Trade in East Africa. Nairobi: East Africa Publishing House.

Tanganyika Government. Report on the Kilimanjaro Native
    Co-operation Union. (Sessional Paper No. 4) 1937
    Dar es Salaam: Gt. Printers, 1937.

Widstrand, Carl G. (ed.) Cooperatives and Rural Development
    in East Africa. New York: Africana Publishing
    Corp., 1971.

Commerce: East African Federation

di Delupis, Ingrid D. The East African Community and Com-
    mon Market. London: Longmans, 1970.

Dunne, James R. "East African Federation: background and
    economic-political events of 1946-1964." Doctoral dis-
    sertation, Albany State University of New York, 1964.

Ford, V. C. R. The Trade of Lake Victoria. East African
    Studies, no. 3. Kampala: East African Institute of
    Social Research, 1955.

Franck, Thomas M. East African Unity through Law. New
    Haven, Conn.: Yale University Press, 1964.

The Governments of the United Republic of Tanzania, the
    Sovereign State of Uganda, and the Republic of Kenya.
    Treaty for East African Co-operation. Nairobi: Gov-
    ernment Press, 1967.

Hazlewood, A. D. Economic Integration: The East African
    Experience. London: Heinemann, 1975.

Hokororo, Anthony M. "An East African federation: Kenya,
    Uganda, and Tanzania." Master's thesis, Carleton
    College, 1964.

Hughes, A. J. East Africa: The Search for Unity, Kenya,
    Tanganyika, Uganda and Zanzibar. Baltimore: Pen-
    guin, 1963.

Jumba-Masagazi, Abdul-Hamid. "The political aspects of an
    East African federation, 1920-1966." Master's thesis,
    American University, 1966.

Leys, Colin and Peter Robson. Federation in East Africa:
    Opportunities and Problems. Nairobi: OUP, 1965.

Ndegwa, Philip. The Common Market and Development in
    East Africa: Nairobi: East African Publishing House,
    1965.

Segal, Aaron L. "Political independence and economic inter-
    dependence in East Africa." Doctoral dissertation,
    University of California (Berkeley), 1964.

Segal, David. "East African Common Market inequities of
    the 1960's: an arbitration scheme." Doctoral dis-
    sertation, Yale University, 1968.

Thomas, P. A. (ed.) Private Enterprise and East Africa
    Company. Dar es Salaam: Tanzania Publishing House,
    1969.

Development: Economic Change

Brett, E. A. Colonialism and Underdevelopment in East Af-
    rica: The Politics of Economic Change. Nairobi:
    Heinemann, 1973.

Hermats, Robert D. "Peasants and pressure: peasants as
    an active force in the process of change and develop-
    ment in rural Tanzania." Doctoral dissertation,
    Fletcher, Tufts University, 1970.

Kiyenze, B. K. S. "Economic change and underdevelopment
    in Shinyanga since pre-colonial times." 3rd year dis-
    sertation, University of Dar es Salaam, 1975.

McCarthy, Dennis M. P. "The politics of economic change
    in Tanganyika, 1919-1939." Doctoral dissertation,
    Yale University, 1972.

Winans, Edgar V. "The Political Context of Economic Adap-
    tation in the Southern Highlands of Tanganyika."
    American Anthropologist, LXVII, no. 2, Apr. 1965,
    435-551.

Development: Policy

Anderson, Lascelles F. "High level manpower and develop-
    ment alternatives for the Tanzanian economy." Doc-
    toral dissertation, New School for Social Research,
    1971.

Edogun, Clifford. "The politics of African economic develop-
    ment; two studies in African socialism: a comparison
    of aspects of the development strategies of Kenya and
    Tanzania." Master's thesis, Drew University, 1974.

Hunter, Guy. Manpower, Employment and Education in the
    Rural Economy of Tanzania. (Afr. Res. Mono. no. 9)
    Paris: UNESCO, International Institute for Educational
    Planning, 1966.

Khakee, Abdul. Development and Planning in Tanzania.
    Lund (Sweden): Studentlitteratur, 1971.

Leubuscher, C. Tanganyika Territory: a study of economic
    policy under mandate. London: OUP, 1944.

Seidman, Ann. Comparative Development Strategies in East
    Africa. Nairobi: East African Publishing House.

Skorov, George. Integration of Education and Economic Plan-
    ning in Tanzania. (Afr. Res. Mono. no. 6) Paris:
    UNESCO, International Institute for Educational Plan-
    ning, 1966.

Smith, Hadley E. (ed.) Readings on Economic Development
    and Administration in Tanzania. Dar es Salaam: OUP,
    1967.

Tanganyika. Development Plan for Tanganyika 1961/62-
    1963/64. Dar es Salaam: Government Printers, 1962.

Tobias, George. High-Level Manpower Requirements and Re-
    sources in Tanganyika, 1962-67. (Gt. Paper no. 2 of
    1963) Dar es Salaam: Gt. Printers, 1963.

United Republic of Tanganyika and Zanzibar. Tanganyika
    Five-Year Plan for Economic and Social Development,
    1st July, 1964-30th June, 1969. Dar es Salaam: Gt.
    Printers, 1964.

United Republic of Tanzania. Tanzania's Second Five-Year
    Plan for Economic and Social Development 1 July,
    1969 to 30 June 1974. Dar es Salaam: Gt. Printers,
    1969.

Ward, R. J. The Challenge of Development, Theory and
    Practice. Chicago: Aldine, 1967.

Development: General

Coulson, A.   A Simplified Political Economy of Tanzania.
     Dar es Salaam: Economic Research Bureau, 1974.

Gitelson, Susan A.   Multilateral Aid for National Development
     and Self-Reliance: A Case Study of the UNDP in Ugan-
     da and Tanzania.   Nairobi: EALB, 1975.

International Bank for Reconstruction and Development.   The
     Economic Development of Tanganyika.   Baltimore:
     Johns Hopkins Press, 1961.

Jensen, S.   Regional Economic Atlas: Mainland Tanzania.
     Dar es Salaam: BRALUP, 1968.

Konter, J. H.   Facts and Factors in the Rural Economy of
     the Nyakyusa.   Leiden: Afrika Studiecentrum, 1974.

Myers, Robert B.   "The structure and performance of a com-
     mercial farm settlement: an economic analysis of one
     of Tanzania's village schemes."   Doctoral dissertation,
     Syracuse University, 1973.

Pratt, R. C.   "The Administration of Economic Planning in
     a Newly Independent State: The Tanzanian Experience
     1963-1966."   Journal of Commonwealth Political Stu-
     dies, V, March 1967, 38-59.

Rutman, Gilbert L.   "An analysis of the economy of Tangan-
     yika with special reference to the role of government."
     Doctoral dissertation, Duke University, 1964.

Shelby, Martha J.   "Influence of tribalism, lingua franca, and
     mass communication on national development in East
     African states of Kenya, Uganda and Tanzania."   Doc-
     toral dissertation, University of Texas, 1970.

Svendsen, K. E. (ed.)   The Economy of Tanzania.   Dar es
     Salaam: Tanzania Publishing House, 1974.

_____   and Marete Teisen. (eds.)   Self-reliant Tanzania.
     Dar es Salaam: Tanzania Publishing House, 1969.

Finance

Armstrong, Audrey B. "Toward a systems approach to
foreign wealth deprivation in less developed countries:
the Tanzania case." Doctoral dissertation, University
of Washington, 1972.

Binhammer, H. H. The Development of a Financial Infra-
structure in Tanzania. Nairobi: EALB, 1975.

Blumenthal, Edwin. The Present Monetary System and Its
Future: Report to the Government of Tanganyika.
Dar es Salaam: Gt. Printers, 1963.

Freeman-Grenville, G. S. P. "A New Hoard and Some Un-
published Variants of the Coinage of the Sultans of
Kilwa." Numismatic Chronicle, N. S. 14, 1954, 220-
24.

_____. "Coinage in East Africa before Portuguese Times."
Numismatic Chronicle, N. S. 17, 1957, 151-75.

_____. "East African Coin Finds and Their Historical
Significance." Journal of African History, I, 1960,
31-43.

Gitelson, Susan A. Multilateral Aid for National Development
and Self-Reliance: A Case Study of the UNDP in Uganda and Tanzania. Nairobi: EALB, 1975.

Hicks, Ursula. "The Revenue Implications of the Uganda and
Tanzania Plans." Journal of Development Studies, II,
no. 3, Apr. 1966, 234-53.

Kimble, Helen. Price Control in Tanzania. Nairobi: East
African Publishing House.

Knight, J. B. The Costing and Financing of Educational Development in Tanzania (Afr. Res. Mono. no. 4) Paris:
UNESCO, International Institute for Educational Planning, 1966.

Kregan, Warren. "Tanganyika's Five-Year (1964-1969) Development Plan." in Tom J. Farer (ed.), Financing
African Development. Cambridge: MIT Press, 1965,
pp. 11-40.

Lee, Eugene. Local Taxation in Tanganyika. Berkeley:
    University of Cal. Press, 1965.

Msuya, J. R. "Money Supply and the East Africa Currency
    Board." 3rd year dissertation, University of Dar es
    Salaam, 1974.

Myers, Robert. "An Accounting Model Useful for Rural
    Transformation." Occasional Paper No. 26. Syra-
    cuse: Syracuse University, 1967. (mimeo)

Newlyn, Walter and D. C. Rowan. Money and Banking in
    British Colonial Africa. Oxford: Clarendon Press,
    1954.

Peacock, A. T. and D. G. M. Dosser. The National Income
    of Tanganyika, 1952-54. Colonial Research Publica-
    tion No. 26. London: HMSO, 1958.

Penner, R. G. Financing Local Government in Tanzania.
    Nairobi: East African Publishing House, 1970.

Tanzania Government. Background to the Budget. Annual.
    Dar es Salaam: Govt. Printers.

Yaffey, M. J. H. Balance of Payments Problems of a De-
    veloping Country: Tanzania: Munchen: Weltforum
    Verlag; New York: Humanities, 1970.

Housing

Bienefeld, M. A. A Long-Term Housing Policy for Tanza-
    nia. Economic Research Bureau Paper no. 70.9
    Dar es Salaam: University College, 1970.

Hutton, John. (ed.) Urban Challenge in East Africa. Nai-
    robi: East African Publishing House.

Stern, Richard E. Urban Inequality and Housing Policy in
    Tanzania: The Problem of Squatting. Berkeley, Cal.:
    Institute of International Studies, 1975.

Industries

Bituro, B. T. "The structure and growth of the Fishing in-

dustry in Mwanza Region, 1945-1973. " 3rd year dissertation, University of Dar es Salaam, 1974.

Coles, Diana M. The Vegetable Oil Crushing Industry in
      East Africa. Nairobi: OUP, 1968.

Kessel, Dudley M. "Effective protection rates and industrial-
      ization strategies in Tanzania. " Doctoral dissertation,
      Cornell University, 1969.

Little, Arthur D. , Inc. Tanganyika Industrial Development.
      Dar es Salaam: Gt. Printers, 1961.

Mbwilo, M. S. "Pottery Industry in Ukinga. " 3rd year dis-
      sertation, University of Dar es Salaam, 1974.

Mtango, G. "The impact of the sisal industry in the develop-
      ment of Tanzanian society (Pare). " 3rd year disserta-
      tion, University of Dar es Salaam, 1974.

Nimtz, Maxine L. "Decision-making in the fishing industry
      in Bagamoyo, Tanzania. " Doctoral dissertation, Uni-
      versity of Indiana, 1974.

Rweyemamu, Justinian. Underdevelopment and Industrializa-
      tion in Tanzania: A Study of Perverse Capitalist In-
      dustrial Development. Nairobi: OUP, 1973.

Schadler, Karl. Crafts, Small-Scale Industries and Indus-
      trial Education in Tanzania. New York: Humanities
      Press, 1968.

Stuhlmann, F. Handwerk und Industrie in Ostafrika. Ham-
      burg, 1910.

Tanzania Government. Tanzania: The Economic Survey,
      1971-72. Dar es Salaam: Gt. Printers, 1972.

Westergaatd, Paul W. and H. Y. Kayumbo. The Cashewnut
      Industry in Tanzania. Dar es Salaam: Economic Re-
      search Bureau, 1970.

Zajadacz, Paul. (ed.) Studies in Production and Trade in
      East Africa. Munchen: Weltforum Verlag, 1971.

Labor

Driskeli, Stanley W. "Causes of African labor migration: an economic schema with quantitative verification." Doctoral dissertation, Berkeley, California University, 1969.

Federation of Tanganyika Employers. Constitution and Rules. Arusha: Tanganyika Litho, 1965.

Friedland, Wm. H. "Cooperation, Conflict and Enforced Conscription: TANU: TFL Relations, 1955-1964." in A. A. Castagno and Jeffrey Butler (eds.), Boston University Papers on Africa: Transition in African Politics. Boston: Boston University Press, 1964, 67-95.

_____. Unions and Industrial Relations in Underdeveloped Countries. Ithaca, N.Y.: Cornell University Press, 1963.

_____. Vuta Kamba: The Development of Unions in Tanganyika. Stanford, Cal.: Hoover Institute Press, 1969.

Gappert, Gary M. "The economics of labor migration in an African society: labor aspects of resettlement policy in southern Tanzania." Doctoral dissertation, Syracuse University, 1971.

Greham, James D. "Changing patterns of wage labor in Tanzania: a history of the relations between African labor and European capitalism in Njombe District, 1931-1961." Doctoral dissertation, Northwestern University, 1967.

International Labour Organisation. UNDP. Report to the Government of the United Republic of Tanzania on the Setting up of a National Provident Fund in Tanganyika. Geneva: ILO, 1966.

Mapolu, Henry. Workers and Management. Dar es Salaam: Tanzania Publishing House, 1976.

Mwanda, M. "Bureaucracy and political development. NUTA: its organisation, operation and role in post-Arusha era." 3rd year dissertation, University of Dar es Salaam, 1972.

285   Bibliography

Nyalabi, F. L. Aspects of Industrial Conflicts. Nairobi:
    EALB, 1975.

Orde-Browne, Granville St. John. Labour Conditions in
    East Africa. London: HMSO, 1946.

Roberts, B. C. and Greyfie de Bellecombe. Collective Bar-
    gaining in African Countries. New York: Macmillan,
    1967.

Tanganyika Government. Report of the Committee appointed
    to Consider and Advise on Questions relating to the
    Supply and Welfare of Native Labour in the Tanganyika
    Territory. Dar es Salaam; Gt. Printers, 1938.

_____. The Welfare of the African Labourer in Tangan-
    yika (K. T. Charton) An Outline of Post-war Develop-
    ment Proposals. Dar es Salaam: Gt. Printers, 1944.

Tordoff, William. "Trade Unionism in Tanzania" The Journal
    of Development Studies, II, no. 4, July 1966, 408-30.

Tumbo, N. S. K. "Towards NUTA: the search for perma-
    nent unity in Tanganyika's trade union movement."
    3rd year dissertation, University of Dar es Salaam,
    1969.

Vest, Benny D. "Labor migration and nationalism in Kenya
    and Tanzania." Master's thesis, University of West
    Virginia, 1969.

Transportation and Communication

Curran, James C. Communist China in Black Africa: The
    Tan-Zam Railway, 1965-1970. Carlisle Barracks,
    Pa.: U.S. Army War College, 1971.

Hafmeier, Rolf. Transport and Economic Development in
    Tanzania with special reference to roads and road
    transport. Munchen: Weltforum Verlag, 1973.

Hall, Richard and Hugh Peyman. The Great Uhuru Railway:
    China's Showpiece in Africa. London: Victor Gollanz
    Ltd., 1976.

Hazelwood, Arthur. Rail and Road in East Africa: Transport
    Coordination in Underdeveloped Countries. Oxford:
    Basil Blackwell, 1967.

Hill, M. F. Permanent Way. II: The Story of the Tangan-
    yika Railways. Nairobi: East African Railways and
    Harbours, 1957.

Mackay, James A. East Africa: The Story of East Africa
    and Its Stamps. London: Philatelic Publishers Ltd.,
    1970.

Obell, Onegi. "The East African Railways and Harbours Ad-
    ministration: its economic role." Master's thesis,
    University of Toronto, 1964.

Van Dongeu, Irene S. "The British East African Transport
    Complex (Kenya, Uganda, and Tanganyika)." Mas-
    ter's thesis, Columbia University, 1953.

4. HISTORIC

General

Austen, Ralph A. Northwest Tanzania under German and
    British rule: Colonial Policy and Tribal Politics,
    1889-1939. New Haven: Yale University Press,
    1968.

Clarke, P. H. C. A Short History of Tanganyika. Nairobi:
    Longmans, 1963.

Harlow, Vincent with E. M. Chilver and Alison Smith.
    (eds.) History of East Africa, II: 1890-1945. Lon-
    don: OUP, 1965.

Holmes, Charles F. "A History of the Kakwimba of Usuku-
    ma, Tanzania, from earliest times to 1945." Doc-
    toral dissertation, Boston University, 1968.

Kimambo, I. N. and A. Temu. (eds.) A History of Tanza-
    nia. Nairobi: East African Publishing House, 1969.

Low, D. A. and Alison Smith. (eds.) History of East Afri-
    ca, Vol. III: 1945-1963. London: OUP, 1976.

Mustafa, Sophia. The Tanganyika Way. London: OUP,
    1962.

Nsekela, Amon J. Minara ya Historia ya Tanganyika; Tanganyika hadi Tanzania. Dar es Salaam: Longmans, 1971 3rd edition.

Oliver, Roland and Gervase Mathew. History of East Africa. Vol. I. London: OUP, 1963.

Ward, W. F. and L. W. White. East Africa: A Century of Change, 1870-1970. London: George Allen and Unwin, 1971.

Were, Gideon S. and Derek A. Wilson. East Africa Through a Thousand Years. London: Evans Bros., 1970.

Pre-Colonial: General

Allen, J. W. T. "Rhapta." TNR, no. 27, 1949, 52-59.

Azelson, Eric V. South-East Africa, 1488-1530. London: Longmans, 1940.

———. The Portuguese in South-East Africa, 1600-1700. Johannesburg, 1960.

Baumann, Oscar. Usambara und seine Nachbargebiete. Berlin: Dietrich Reimer, 1891.

Bennett, Norman R. "The Arab power of Tanganyika in the nineteenth century" Doctoral dissertation, Boston University, 1960.

———. (ed.) Leadership in Eastern Africa: Six Political Biographies. Boston: Boston University Press, 1968.

———. Mirambo of Tanzania, c1840-1884. New York: OUP, 1971.

———. From Zanzibar to Ujiji. Boston: Boston University Press, 1969.

Brown, Beverly B. "Ujiji: the history of a lakeside town, c1800-1914." Doctoral dissertation, Boston University, 1973.

Brown, Walter Thaddeus. "A pre-colonial history of Bagamoyo: aspects of the growth of an East African coastal town." Doctoral dissertation, Boston University, 1970.

Cole, Sonia. The Prehistory of East Africa. New York: Macmillan, 1963.

De Kiewiet, M. J. "History of the Imperial East Africa Company, 1876-1895. " Doctoral dissertation, London University, 1955.

Duffy, James. Portuguese Africa. Cambridge, Mass.: Harvard University Press, 1959.

Feierman, Steven. The Shambaa Kingdom: a history. Madison: University of Wisconsin Press, 1974.

Ford, J. and R. de Z. Hall. "The History of Karagwe. " in TNR, XXIV, Dec. 1947, 3-27.

Fouquer, R. P. Mirambo. Paris, 1966.

Freeman-Grenville, G. S. P. The East African Coast: select documents. Oxford: Clarendon Press, 1962.

_____. The French at Kilwa Island. Oxford: Clarendon Press, 1965.

Gailey, Harry A., Jr. History of Africa from Earliest Times to 1800. New York: Holt, Rinehart and Winston, 1970.

Hallet, Robin. Africa to 1875: A modern history. Ann Arbor: The University of Michigan Press, 1970.

Hartwig, G. W. The Art of Survival in East Africa: The Kerebe and Long-distance Trade, 1800-1895. New York: Africana, 1975.

Jacobs, Alan H. "The traditional political organization of the pastoral Masai. " Doctoral dissertation, Oxford University, 1965.

July, Robert W. A History of the African People. New York: Charles Scribner's Sons, 1970.

Katoke, Israel K. The Making of the Karagwe Kingdom. Dar es Salaam: East African Publishing House, 1970.

Kimambo, Isaria N. A Political History of the Pare of Tanzania, c1500-1900. Nairobi: East African Publishing House, 1969.

Kunambi, Patrick. "An analytic study of the Bantu tribal political systems of Tanganyika and the impact upon them of European and Arabic colonization." Master's thesis, Duquesne University, 1964.

Lee, C. Elton in the Southern Highland of Tanganyika. Nairobi: EALB, 1968.

Loftus, E. A. Speke and the Nile Source. Nairobi: EALB, 1964.

Makundi, J. E. S. "Pre-colonial forces against the creation of one Chagga nation." 3rd year dissertation, University of Dar es Salaam, 1969.

Marsh, Zoe. East Africa through Contemporary Records. London: Cambridge University Press, 1961.

_____ and George Wm. Kingsnorth. An Introduction to the History of East Africa. 3rd edition. New York: Cambridge University Press, 1965.

Mulugula, Njelu E. and Aylward Shorter. Nyunga-ya-Mawe: Mtawala Shujaa wa Kinyamwezi. Nairobi: EALB, 1971.

Oliver, Roland. (ed.) The Dawn of African History. London: OUP, 1961.

Pouwels, Randall Lee. "Origins of the Arabic settlement of East Africa to the tenth century." Master's thesis, Duquesne University, 1971.

Poznansky, M. (ed.) Prelude to East African History. Oxford: OUP, 1966.

Roberts, Andrew. (ed.) Tanzania before 1900. Nairobi: East African Publishing House, 1968.

Robinson, A. E. "Shirazi Colonisations of East Africa." TNR, no. 7, 1939.

Rotberg, Robert I. and H. Neville Chittick. (eds.) East Africa and the Orient: Cultural Synthesis in Pre-colonial Times. New York: Africana, 1975.

Schweitzer, G. Emin Pasha, His Life and Work. 2 vols. London: 1898.

Simpson, Donald. Dark Companions: the African Contribu-
    tion to the Exploration of East Africa. London: Paul
    Elek, 1976.

Smith, I. R. The Emin Pasha Relief Expedition, 1886-1890.
    London, 1972.

Strandes, Justus. The Portuguese Period in East Africa.
    Dar es Salaam: EALB, 1971.

Stuart-Watt, E. Africa's Dome of Mystery ... History of
    the Wachagga People of Kilimanjaro. London:
    Mashall, Morgan & Scott, 1930.

Thomson, J. Through Masai Land. 2nd edition. London,
    1885.

Thurnwald, Richard C. Black and White in East Africa.
    London, 1935.

Pre-colonial: Slave trade

Alpers, Edward A. Changing Patterns of International Trade
    to the Later 19th Century. London: Heinemann, 1975.

_____. The East African Slave Trade. Nairobi: East
    African Publishing House, 1967.

_____. Ivory and Slaves in East Central Africa. Berke-
    ley: University of California Press, 1975.

Beachey, R. W. The Slave Trade in Eastern Africa. Lon-
    don: Rex Collings, 1976.

Cooper, Frederick. "Plantation slavery on the East Coast
    of Africa in the 19th century." Doctoral dissertation,
    Yale University, 1974.

Coupland, Reginald. East Africa and Its Invaders. New
    York: Russell and Russell, 1965.

_____. The Exploitation of East Africa, 1856-1890: The
    Slave Trade and the Scramble. Evanston: North-
    western University Press, 1967.

_____. From the Earliest Times to the Death of Seyyid
    Said in 1856. London: OUP, 1962.

Farrant, L. Tippu Tip and the East African Slave Trade.
    London: Hamish Hamilton, 1975.

Gray, Richard and David Birmingham. Pre-Colonial African
    Trade: Essays on Trade in Central and Eastern Afri-
    ca Before 1900. London: OUP, 1970.

Lodhi, Abdulaziz. The Institution of Slavery in Zanzibar and
    Pemba. Uppsala: Scandinavian Institute of African
    Studies, 1975.

Loftus, E. A. Elton and the East African Coast Slave-Trade.
    London: Macmillan, 1952.

Nicholls, C. S. The Swahili Coast: Politics, Diplomacy and
    Trade on the East African Littoral, 1795-1856. Lon-
    don: George, Allen and Unwin, 1971.

Sullivan, G. L. Dhow Chasing in Zanzibar Waters. London:
    Dawsons of Pall Mall, 1967; and London: Sampson
    Low and Co., 1873.

Waller, H. The Case of Our Zanzibar Slaves. Why not
    liberate them? London: Westminster, 1896.

Zanzibar Government Publications. The most relevant papers
    during the period are: 1895, C. 7707; 1896, C. 8275;
    1897, C. 8394; 1900, Cd. 96; 1901, Cd. 593; 1903, Cd. 1389;
    1905, Cd. 2330.
        On the Abolishing of Slave Trade are: 1897, C. 8394;
    C. 8433; 1898, C. 8858; 1899, C. 9502; 1909, Cd. 4732.

Pre-Colonial: Zanzibar

Burton, Sir Richard. Zanzibar: City, Island and Coast. 2
    vols. London: Tinsley Bros., 1872.

Gray, John. History of Zanzibar from the Middle Ages to
    1856. London: OUP, 1962.

Hamilton, Genesta. Princes of Zinj: The Rulers of Zanzi-
    bar. London: Hutchinson, 1957.

Hollingsworth, L. W. Zanzibar Under the Foreign Office,
    1890-1913. London: Macmillan, 1953.

Ingrams, W. H.   Chronology of Genealogies of Zanzibar
    Rulers. Zanzibar: Govt. Printers, 1926.

_____. Zanzibar, Its History and Its People.   London:
    H. F. and G. Witherby, 1931.

Lyne, R. N.   Zanzibar in Contemporary Times.   London:
    Hurst and Blackett, 1905.

Playne, Somerset and F. H. Gale. (eds.) East Africa (Brit-
    ish): Its History, People, Commerce, Industries and
    Resources.   London: The British, Foreign and Colo-
    nial Compiling and Publishing Co. , 1908.

Said-Ruete, Rudolph.   Said bin Sultan (1791-1856).   London:
    Alexander-Ouseley Ltd. , 1927.

Versteijnen, Frits.   Zanzibar Through Contemporary Records.
    Bagamoyo: RC Mission, 1968.

Zanzibar Papers, 1841-1898.   Shannon: Irish University
    Press, 1971.

German Period: General

Brode, Heinrich.   British and German East Africa.   Eng.
    trans. London: Arnold, 1911.

Brown, Beverly B.   "Ujiji: the history of a lakeside town,
    c. 1800-1914. " Doctoral dissertation, Boston Univer-
    sity, 1973.

Calvert, A. F.   German East Africa.   London: T. Werner
    Laurie, 1917 and New York: Negro University Press,
    1970.

Dukes, Jack R.   "Heligoland, Zanzibar, East Africa: colo-
    nialism in German politics, 1884-1890. " Doctoral
    dissertation, University of Illinois, 1969.

Dundas, Hon. C. C. F.   A History of German East Africa.
    Dar es Salaam: 1923.

Eberlie, R. F.   "The German achievement in East Africa. "
    TNR, LV, Sept. 1960, 181-214.

Gardner, Brian. German East. London: Cassell and Co.,
    Ltd., 1963.

Holmes, Charles F. "A History of the Kakwimba of Usuku-
    ma, Tanzania from earliest times to 1945." Doctoral
    dissertation, Boston University, 1968.

Hubbell, Paul E. "The Heligoland-Zanzibar Treaty of 1890."
    Doctoral dissertation, University of Michigan, 1938.

Iliffe, John. Tanganyika Under German Rule, 1905-1911.
    London: East African Publishing House, 1969.

Meyer, H. Das Deutsche Kolonialreich, I. Leipzig and
    Wien: Bibliographisches Institut, 1909.

Muller, Fritz F. Deutschland-Zanzibar-Ostafrika: Geschich-
    te einer Deutschen Kolonialeroberung 1884-1890. Ber-
    lin, 1959.

Peters, Carl. New Light on Dark Africa. London: Ward,
    Lock and Co., 1891.

Pierard, Richard V. "The German Colonial Society, 1882-
    1914." Doctoral dissertation, University of Iowa,
    1964.

Rodemann, H. William. "Tanganyika; 1890-1914: selected
    aspects of German administration." Doctoral disserta-
    tion, University of Chicago, 1961.

Schnee, Heinrich. German Colonization, Past and Future.
    Eng. trans. London, 1926.

Tetzlaff, Rainer. Koloniale Entwicklung und Ausbeutung:
    Wirtschafts-und Sozialgeschichte Deutsch-Ostafrikas,
    1885-1914. Duncker und Humblot, 1970.

German period: Maji-Maji Uprising

Bell, R. M. "The MajiMaji Rebellion in the Liwale District."
    TNR, no. 28, Jan. 1950, 38-57.

Gwassa, G. C. K. and John Iliffe. (ed.) Records of the
    Maji-Maji Rising. Nairobi: East African Publishing
    House, 1967.

Mapunda, O. B. and G. B. Mpangara. The MajiMaji War
    in Ungoni. Dar es Salaam: East African Publishing
    House, 1968.

World War I:

Dane, E. British Campaigns in Africa and in the Pacific,
    1914-1918. London: Hodder and Stoughton, 1919.

Dolbey, R. V. Sketches of the East Africa Campaign. Lon-
    don: John Murray, 1918.

Fendall, C. P. The East African Force, 1915-1919. Lon-
    don: Witherby, 1921.

Great Britain. Official History of the Great War. Vol. I-IV.
    HMSO: 1920-1924.

Sibley, Major J. R. Tanganyikan Guerrilla: East African
    Campaign, 1914-18. Pan Books Ltd., 1973.

von Lettow-Vorbeck, General P. My Reminiscences of East
    Africa. London: Hurst and Blackett, 1920.

_____. East African Campaigns. New York: Speller,
    1957.

British period: Zanzibar

Crofton, R. H. The Old Consulate at Zanzibar. London:
    1935.

_____. Zanzibar Affairs, 1914-1953. London: Francis
    Edwards, 1953.

Lofchie, Michael F. Zanzibar: Background to Revolution.
    Princeton: Princeton University Press, 1965.

Lyne, R. N. An Apostle of Empire, being the Life of Sir
    Lloyd William Mathews, K. C. M. G. London: Allen
    and Unwin, 1936.

Middleton, John and Jane Campbell. Zanzibar: Its Society
    and Its Politics. London: OUP, 1965.

Moutafakis, George J. "Desturi and Heshima--Aspects of
    the Evolution of the Arab Community in the Zanzibar
    Sultanate 1890-1950. " Paper delivered at the African
    Studies Association Meeting, Chicago, 1964.

British Period: Mainland

Bates, M. L. "Tanganyika under British Administration,
    1920-1955. " Doctoral dissertation, Oxford University,
    1956.

Cameron, D. My Tanganyika Service and Some Nigeria.
    London: Allen and Unwin, 1939.

Chidzero, B. T. G. Tanganyika and International Trustee-
    ship. London: OUP, 1961.

Cohen, Sir A. B. British Policy in Changing Africa. Lon-
    don: Routledge and Kegan Paul, 1959.

Morris-Hale, Walter. British Administration in Tanganyika
    from 1920-1945: with special references to the prepa-
    ration of Africans for Administrative Positions. Gene-
    va: Imprime, 1969.

Low, D. A. and Alison Smith. (eds.) History of East Afri-
    ca, Vol. III. (1945-1963) London: OUP, 1976.

Symes, Stewart. Tour of Duty. London: Collins, 1946.

Independence: Zanzibar

Kharusi, Ahmed Seif. The Agony of Zanzibar: a victim of
    the new colonialism. Richmond: Foreign Affairs
    Publishing Co., 1969.

_____ . Zanzibar, Africa's first Cuba: a case study of
    the new colonialism. 68 Hudson Road, Southsea,
    Hants., 1966.

_____ . Zanzibar Cries for Help. Southsea, Hants., 1975.

5. POLITICAL

Colonial Rule and Political Development

Austen, Ralph Albert. Northwest Tanzania under German and British Rule: Colonial Policy and Tribal Politics, 1889-1939. New Haven: Yale University Press, 1968.

Barongo, E. B. M. Mkiki Mkiki wa Siasa Tanganyika (The Political Struggle in Tanganyika towards Independence). Nairobi: EALB, 1966.

Datta, Ansu Kumar. Tanganyika: A Government in a Plural Society. The Hague: Nijhoff, 1955.

Diamond, Stanley and Fred G. Burke. (eds.) The Transformation of East Africa. New York: Basic Books, 1966.

Friedland, William H. "The Evolution of Tanganyika's Political System." Occasional Paper no. 10. Syracuse: Syracuse University, 1964.

Hyden, Goran. Political Development in Rural Tanzania. Nairobi: East African Publishing House, 1969.

Kimambo, Isariah N. Popular Protest in Colonial Tanzania. Nairobi: East African Publishing House, 1971.

Lema, Alea O. "The role of Machame Chiefdom in the politics of the Wachagga since 1930's." 3rd year dissertation, University of Dar es Salaam, 1969.

Liebenow, J. Gus. Colonial Rule and Political Development in Tanzania: The Case of the Makonde. Nairobi: East African Publishing House, 1971.

_____. "A Tanganyika Federation: the Sukuma." in East African Chiefs, edited by Audrey Richards. London: Faber and Faber, 1960, 229-59.

Listowel, Judith. The Making of Tanganyika. London: Chatto and Windus, 1965.

Maruma, Oliver J. "Chagga Politics: 1930-1952." 3rd year dissertation, University of Dar es Salaam, 1969.

Morrison, David R. Education and Politics in Africa: The
    Tanzanian Case. London: C. Hurst, 1976.

Mutahaba, G. R. Portrait of a Nationalist--The Life of Ali
    Migeyo. Nairobi: East African Publishing House,
    1969.

Mwanjisi, R. K. Sheikh Abeid Amani Karumi. Nairobi:
    East African Publishing House, 1967.

Ranger, Terence O. "Connections between 'primary resist-
    ance' movements and modern mass nationalism in
    East and Central Africa." Nairobi: University of
    East Africa Social Science Conference, 1966.

Richards, Audrey I. (ed.) East African Chiefs: a study of
    political development in some Uganda and Tanganyika
    tribes. New York: Praeger, 1960; London: Faber
    and Faber, 1960.

Schmidt, Rochus. Geschichte des Araberaufstandes in Ost-
    Afrika. Frankfurt, a.O., 1892.

Skeffington, A. Tanganyika in Transition. London: Fabian
    Commonwealth Bureau, 1960.

Stephens, Hugh W. The Political Transformation of Tanganyi-
    ka, 1920-1967. New York: Praeger, 1968.

Strayer, Robert, Edward I. Steinhart and Robert Mason.
    Protest Movements in Colonial East Africa: Aspects
    of Early African Response to European Rule. Syra-
    cuse, N.Y.: Syracuse University Press, 1973.

Taylor, J. Clagett. The Political Development of Tanganyika.
    Stanford, Calif.: Stanford University Press, 1963.

Von Clemm, M. F. M. "People of the White Mountain: the
    interdependence of political and economic activity
    amongst the Chagga in Tanganyika." Doctoral disser-
    tation, Oxford University, 1962.

Constitution

Ayany, Samuel G. A History of Zanzibar: a study in con-
    stitutional development, 1934-1964. Nairobi: EALB,
    1970.

Cole, J. S. R. and W. N. Denison. The British Commonwealth: The Development of Its Laws and Constitution
XII: Tanganyika. London: Steven, 1964.

McAuslan, J. P. "The Republic Constitution of Tanganyika."
International Comparative Law Quarterly, 4th series,
XIII, no. 2, Apr. 1964, 502-73.

Tanzania. Laws, Statutes, etc. The Interim Constitution of
Tanzania, 1965. Dar es Salaam: Gt. Printers, 1965.

Winans, Edgar V. Shambala: the constitution of a traditional
state. London: Routledge and Kegan Paul, 1962.

Elections

Cliffe, Lionel. (ed.) One Party Democracy: the 1965 Tanzania General Elections. Dar es Salaam: East African Publishing House, 1973, 2nd edition.

Election Study Committee. Socialism and Participation:
Tanzania's 1970 National Elections. Dar es Salaam:
Tanzania Publishing House, 1974.

Kjekshus, Helge. The Elected Elite: A Socio-Economic Profile of Candidates in Tanzania's Parliamentary Election
1970. Uppsala: The Scandinavian Institute of African
Studies, 1975.

Foreign Relations

Cooley, John K. East Wind Over Africa: Red China's African Offensive. New York: Walker, 1965.

Fournier, Gordon, W. F. "Tanzania--Neither East nor
West. " World Mission, Summer, 1966, 73-84.

Legum, Colin. Pan-Africanism: A Short Political Guide.
New York: Praeger, 1965.

Mwamba, Zuberi Uddi. "The foreign policy of the United Republic of Tanzania from 1964 to 1969. " Doctoral dissertation, Howard University, 1972.

Nye, Joseph S. , Jr. Pan-Africanism and East African Integration. Cambridge: Harvard University Press, 1965.

Shaw, T. M. The Foreign Policy of Tanzania, 1961-1964. Nairobi: East African Publishing House.

Stephens, Robert F. "An analysis of the foreign relations of Tanzania and Kenya: a comparative study." Doctoral dissertation, University of Michigan, 1973.

Stoltzfus, Miriam. "Refugees in Tanzania: a reflection of Tanzania's commitment to African unity." Master's thesis, Duquesne University, 1971.

Yu, George. China's African Policy: A Study of Tanzania. New York: Praeger, 1975.

Government: General

Adedeji, A. The Tanzanian Civil Service a Decade after Independence. Ile-Ife: Ife University Press, 1974.

Bailey, Martin. The Union of Tanganyika and Zanzibar: A Study in Political Integration. Syracuse: Syracuse University Press, 1973.

Halimoja, Y. L. Bunge la Tanzania. Nairobi: EALB, 1973.

Martin, Robert. Personal Freedom and the Law in Tanzania: A Study of Socialist State Administration. Nairobi: OUP, 1974.

von Sperber, K. W. Public Administration in Tanzania. Munchen: Weltforum Verlag, 1970.

Government: Local Administration

Dryden, Stanley. Local Administration in Tanzania. Nairobi: East African Publishing House, 1968.

Hailey, Lord. Native Administration in the British Africa Territories, Vol. I. London: HMSO, 1950.

Heussler, Robert. British Tanganyika: An Essay and Documentation of a District Administrator. Durham: Duke University Press, 1971.

Liebenow, J. G. "Chieftainship and Local Government in

Tanganyika: a study in institutional adaptation. " Doctoral dissertation, Northwestern University, 1955.

Lumely, E. K. Forgotten Mandate: A British District Officer in Tanganyika. London: C. Hurst, 1976.

Maguire, G. Andrew. Towards 'Uhuru' in Tanzania: The Politics of Participation. Cambridge: Cambridge University Press, 1969.

Mutahaba, Gelase R. "Decentralized administration in Tanzania: Bukoba and Ngara District Councils, 1962-1969. " Doctoral dissertation, University of California (Berkeley), 1973.

Rea, Sam. "Local education authorities in Tanzania, 1926-1969: a study in local government. " Doctoral dissertation, Columbia University, 1970.

Samoff, Joel. Tanzania: Local Politics and the Structure of Power. Madison: The University of Wisconsin Press, 1974.

Shellabarger, Samuel. "The politics of institutional transfer; local authorities in Tanzania, 1962-1969. " Doctoral dissertation, Columbia University, 1971.

Yeager, Rodger D. "Micro-politics and transformation: a Tanzania study of political interaction and institutionalization. " Doctoral dissertation, Syracuse University, 1968.

Law

Castelnuovo, Shirley. "Legal and Judicial Integration in Tanzania: A study of law and politics and social change. " Doctoral dissertation, University of California (Los Angeles), 1969.

Clark, Cedric. "Dispute settlement in Tanzania: a model of system support through the communication of legitimacy. " Doctoral dissertation, Michigan State University, 1968.

Cory, Hans. Sukuma Law and Custom. London: HMSO, 1953.

_____ and M. M. Hartnoll. Customary Law of the Haya
    Tribe. London, 1945.

DuBow, Fredric. "Justice for people: law and politics in
    the lower courts of Tanzania." Doctoral dissertation,
    University of California (Berkeley), 1973.

Dundas, Hon. C. D. "Native Law of Some Bantu Tribes."
    Journal of Royal Anthropological Institute, LI, 1921,
    217-78.

Jackson, Tudor. Guide to the Legal Profession in East Afri-
    ca. London: Sweet and Maxwell, 1970.

James, R. W. and F. M. Kassim. Law and Its Administra-
    tion in a One-Party State. Nairobi: EALB, 1973.

Kingdon, H. E. The Conflict of Laws in Zanzibar. Zanzi-
    bar: Gt. Printers, 1940.

Neville, Richard R. "Institutional transfer and change in Af-
    rica: the introduction of British court structure in
    Tanganyika Territory, 1920-1946." Doctoral disserta-
    tion, Syracuse University, 1971.

Nicholson, Mary R. "Legal change in Tanzania as seen
    among the Sukuma." Doctoral dissertation, University
    of Minnesota, 1968.

Sawyerr, G. F. A. East African Law and Social Change.
    Nairobi: East African Publishing House, 1967.

Seaton, Earle and Sostenes T. Maliti. Tanzania Treaty Prac-
    tice. New York: OUP, 1973.

Zanzibar Government. Sultan's Decrees, 1908-21. Zanzibar:
    Gt. Printers.

Party: TANU

Barnekov, Timothy K. Demand-Stress Regulations: The
    Merger of Party and State in Tanzania. Occasional
    Paper no. 35. Syracuse: Syracuse University, 1967.
    (mimeo)

Bienen, Henry. Tanzania: Party Transformation and Economic Development.   Princeton, N.J.:   Princeton University Press, 1967.

Chilivimbo, Alifeyo B.   "Tanganyika Mono-Party Regime: A Study in the problems, conditions, and processes of the emergence and development of the One-Party State on the mainland of Tanzania." Doctoral dissertation, University of California (Los Angeles), 1968.

Glickman, Harvey.   "One Party System in Tanganyika." Annals of the American Academy of Political and Social Science, CLVIII, Mar. 1965, 136-49.

Hopkins, R.   Political Roles in a New State: Tanzania's First Decade.   New Haven: Yale University Press, 1971.

Klerruu, Wilbert.   One-Party System of Government.   Dar es Salaam: Mwananchi Publishing Co., 1964.

Lowenkopf, Martin.   "Political Parties in Uganda and Tanganyika." Master's thesis, London School of Economics, 1961.

Mabadiba, R. R.   "UWT: Its role in Tanzania." 3rd year dissertation, Dar es Salaam University, 1974.

Muzo, et al.   The Party: Essays on TANU.   Dar es Salaam: Tanzania Publishing House, 1976.

Neal, Robert S.   "Political Parties as agents of modernization: a comparison of the party systems of Tanzania and Uganda." Master's thesis.   Kansas City (Missouri) University, 1970.

O'Barr, Jean and Joel Samoff. (eds.) Tanu Cell Leaders in Tanzania.   Nairobi: East African Publishing House, 1974.

Proctor, J. H.   The Cell System of the Tanganyika African National Union.   Dar es Salaam: Tanzania Publishing House, 1970.

Smith, Daniel R.   "Independence for Tanganyika: an analysis of the political developments which led to the emancipation of the trust territory, 1946-1961." Doctoral dissertation, St. John's University, 1974.

Party: Zanzibar

Lofchie, Michael F. "Party Conflict in Zanzibar" Journal of
    Modern African Studies, I, no. 2, June 1973, 185-208.

_____. "Zanzibar" in Political Parties and National Inte-
    gration in Tropical Africa, edited by James S. Cole-
    man and Carl Rosberg, Jr. Berkeley: University of
    California Press, 1964, 482-511.

Vincent, Jean E. "The social bases of party conflict in Zan-
    zibar, 1956-1963." Master's thesis, University of
    Chicago, 1965.

Rural Development and Nation Building

Cliffe, Lionel, et al. (eds.) Rural Cooperation in Tanzania.
    Dar es Salaam: Tanzania Publishing House, 1975.

Finucane, James R. Rural Development and Bureaucracy in
    Tanzania: The case of Mwanza Region. Uppsala:
    Bohnslaningelors AB, 1974.

Hyden, Goran. Political Development in Rural Tanzania.
    Nairobi: East African Publishing House, 1969.

Ingle, Clyde R. From Village to State in Tanzania: The
    Politics of Rural Development. Ithaca and London:
    Cornell University Press, 1972.

Institute for Development Research. Dualism and Rural De-
    velopment in East Africa. Copenhagen: Institute for
    Development Res., 1973.

McHenry, D. E. "Tanzania: The Struggle for Development."
    Doctoral dissertation, University of Dar es Salaam,
    1971.

Macpherson, George. First Steps in Village Mechanisation.
    Dar es Salaam: Tanzania Publishing House, 1974.

Mfoulou, Jean. "Ideology and nation building: the Tanzania
    case." Doctoral dissertation, Boston University,
    1974.

Miller, Norman N. "Village leadership and modernization in

Tanzania: rural politics among the Nyamwezi people of Tabora Region. " Doctoral dissertation, University of Indiana, 1966.

Rald, Jorgen and Karen. Rural Organisation in Bukoba District, Tanzania. Uppsala: Scandinavian Institute of African Studies, 1975.

Rural Development Research Committee. Rural Cooperation in Tanzania. Dar es Salaam: Tanzania Publishing House, 1974.

Rweyemamu, A. H. Nation-Building in Tanzania. Nairobi: East African Publishing House, 1970.

_____ and B. U. Mwansasu. (eds.) Planning in Tanzania: Background to Decentralisation. Nairobi: EALB, 1974.

Rweyemamu, J. F. , et al. Towards Socialist Planning. Dar es Salaam: Tanzania Publishing House, 1974.

Shivji, Issa G. Class Struggles in Tanzania. Dar es Salaam: Tanzania Publishing House, 1975.

_____. The Silent Class Struggle. Dar es Salaam: Tanzania Publishing House, 1973.

_____. (ed.) Tourism and Socialist Development. Dar es Salaam: Tanzania Publishing House, 1973.

Shoka, John L. "Ideology and nation-building in Tanzania: a microstudy of Shinyanga District, 1961-1970. " Doctoral dissertation, University of Washington, 1972.

Spence, William R. "Design and implementation of a development project system in Tanzania. " Doctoral dissertation, University of Toronto, 1972.

Thomas, Gary. Community Development and Nation Building in Transitional Tanganyika. Occasional Paper no. 11. Syracuse, N.Y.: Syracuse University, 1964. (mimeo)

Ujamaa and Socialism

Burke, Fred G. "Tanganyika: The Search for Ujamaa. " in

African Socialism, edited by Wm. H. Friedland and
Carl Rosberg, Jr. Stanford, Calif.: Stanford University Press, 1964, 194-219.

Cliffe, Lionel and John S. Saul. Socialism in Tanzania.
Vol. I: Politics. Nairobi, East African Publishing
House, 1972.

_____. Socialism in Tanzania. Vol. II: Policies. Nai-
robi: East African Publishing House, 1973.

Duggan, William and John Civille. Tanzania and Nyerere:
A Study of Ujamaa and Nationhood. Maryknoll, N.Y.:
Orbis Books, 1976.

Kahama, Kabakama. "Rural development as a stragety of
modernization: a case study of Ujamaa villages in
Tanzania." Doctoral dissertation, Claremont University, 1973.

Karioki, James N. "The philosophy and politics of Julius K.
Nyerere: an analysis of African statesmanship."
Doctoral dissertation, American University, 1969.

Karume, Abeid Amani. Karume na Siasa ya Mapinduzi. (Ka-
rume and Political Revolution in Vol. I: Karume and
Political and Revolutionary Development in Vol. II)
Zanzibar: Gt. Printers, 1973.

Maluki, Eliud I. "The Influence of Traditionalism upon Nyerere's 'Ujamaa-ism'." Doctoral dissertation, University of Denver, 1965.

Mapolu, H. "The Social and Economic Organisation of Ujamaa Villages." Master's thesis, University of Dar es
Salaam, 1973.

Mohiddin, Ahmed. "The formulation and manifestations of
two socialist ideologies: democratic African socialism
of Kenya and the Arusha Declaration of Tanzania."
Doctoral dissertation, McGill University, 1973.

Musoke, I. K., et al. Building Ujamaa Villages in Tanzania.
Dar es Salaam: Tanzania Publishing House, 1975.

Nellis, John R. A Theory of Ideology: The Tanzanian Example. New York: OUP, 1972.

Nyerere, Julius K. The Courage of Reconciliation. Dar es
        Salaam: Gt. Printers, 1964.

_____ . Democracy and the Party System. Dar es Salaam:
        Tanganyika Standard Ltd. , 1963.

_____ . Education for Self-Reliance. Dar es Salaam: Gt.
        Printers, 1967.

_____ . Freedom and Development (Uhuru na Maendeleo):
        A Selection from Writings and Speeches, 1968-1973.
        London: OUP, 1973.

_____ . Freedom and Socialism (Uhuru na Ujamaa): A
        Selection from Writings and Speeches, 1965-1967.
        London: OUP, 1968.

_____ . Freedom and Unity: A Selection from Writings
        and Speeches, 1952-1965. (Uhuru na Umoja) London:
        OUP, 1966.

_____ . Man and Development. (Binadamu na Maendeleo)
        London: OUP, 1974.

_____ . Nyerere on Socialism. London: OUP, 1969.

_____ . To Plan Is to Choose. Dar es Salaam: Gt.
        Printers, 1969.

_____ . Principles and Development. Dar es Salaam: Gt.
        Printers, 1967.

_____ . The Second Scramble. Dar es Salaam: Tanganyi-
        ka Standard Ltd. , 1962.

_____ . Socialism and Rural Development. Dar es Salaam:
        Gt. Printers, 1967.

_____ . TANU na Raia. Dar es Salaam: TANU Press,
        1962.

_____ . Ujamaa-Essays on Socialism. London: Oxford,
        1968.

Proctor, J. H. (ed.) Building Ujamaa Villages in Tanzania.
        Dar es Salaam: Tanzania Publishing House, 1971.

Ruhimbika, G. (ed.) Towards Ujamaa. Nairobi: EALB, 1974.

Smith, Wm. Edgett. Nyerere of Tanzania. Nairobi: Transafrica Publishers, 1974.

_____. We Must Run While They Walk: A Portrait of Africa's Julius Nyerere. New York: Random House, 1971.

Svendsen, K. E. and Marete Teisen. Self-Reliant Tanzania: A Series of Articles. Dar es Salaam: Tanzania Publishing House, 1969.

Tanganyika African National Union. The Arusha Declaration and TANU's Policy on Socialism and Self-Reliance. Dar es Salaam: Gt. Printers, 1967.

6. SCIENTIFIC

Geography

Altschul, Dieter R. "The arrangement and dimensions of rural settlements of the northeast coastal zone of Tanganyika, Pangani District." Doctoral dissertation, University of Illinois, 1966.

Berry, L. Tanzania in Maps. London: University of London Press, 1971.

Davis, Raymond L. "A brief ecological survey of a portion of the Mwanza District. Tanganyika Territory." Master's thesis, University of Pennsylvania, 1927.

Gageru, Axel von. The African Settlers and How They Organise Their Life in the Urambo Scheme (Tanzania). No. 38 (in German). Munchen: Weltforum Verlag, 1969.

Geilinger, W. Der Kilimanjaro, sein Land und seine Menschen. Bern-Berlin: Verlag Hans Haber, 1938.

Georgulas, Nikon. "Structure and communication: a study of the Tanganyika Settlement Agency." Doctoral dissertation, Syracuse University, 1967.

Gillman, Clement. "A Vegetation-Type Map of Tanganyika
    Territory." Geographical Review, XXXIX, 1949, 7-37.

Harris, Lawrence D. "Some structural and functional attri-
    butes of a semi-arid East African ecosystem." Doc-
    toral dissertation, Michigan State University, 1971.

Jatzold, Ralph and E. Baum. The Kilombero Valley (Tan-
    zania): Characteristic Features of the Economic Geo-
    graphy of a Semi-humid East African Flood Plain and
    Its Margins. No. 28. Munchen: Weltforum Verlag,
    1968.

Kendall, Robert L. "An ecological history of the Lake Vic-
    toria basin." Doctoral dissertation, Duke University,
    1968.

Mihalyi, Louis J. "The Usambara Highlands: a geographical
    study of the changes during the German Period, 1885-
    1914." Doctoral dissertation, University of California
    (Los Angeles), 1968.

Morgan, W. T. W. Geography of East Africa. London:
    Longmans, 1973.

O'Connor, A. M. An Economic Geography of East Africa.
    New York: Praeger, 1966.

Rapp, Anders. (ed.) Studies of Soil Erosion and Sedimenta-
    tion in Tanzania. Dar es Salaam: University of Dar
    es Salaam, Bureau of Resource Assessment and Land
    Use Planning, 1973.

Russel, E. W. (ed.) The Natural Resources of East Africa.
    Nairobi: Hawkins Press, 1962.

Silberfein, Marilyn. "The regional impact of Tanzanian
    settlement schemes." Doctoral dissertation, Syracuse
    University, 1972.

Vesey-Fitzgerald, D. East African Grasslands. Nairobi:
    East African Publishing House, 1973.

Geology

Coetzee, Gerrard L. "The origin of the Sangu carbonate

complex and associated rocks, Karema Depression,
Tanganyika Territory, East Africa. " Doctoral dissertation, University of Wisconsin, 1962.

Dixey, F.   The East African Rift System (Colonial Geology
and Mineral Resources Supplement Series), London:
HMSO, 1956.

Hay, Richard L.   Geology of the Olduvai Gorge: A Study of
Sedimentation in a Semi-arid Basin. Berkeley: University of California Press, 1976.

Mannard, George W.   "The Geology of the Singida kimberlite
pipes, Tanganyika. " Doctoral dissertation, McGill
University, 1963.

Quennel, A. M. , et al.   Summary of the Geology of Tanganyika. Dar es Salaam: Gt. Printers.

Tremblay, M.   "The geology of the Williamson Diamond Mine,
Mwadui, Tanganyika. " Doctoral dissertation, McGill
University, 1956.

Hydrology

Coster, F. M.   Underground Water in Tanganyika. Dar es
Salaam: Gt. Printers, 1960.

Gillman, Clement.   A Reconnaissance Survey of the Hydrology
of Tanganyika Territory in Its Geographical Setting.
Dar es Salaam: Gt. Printers, 1940.

_____ . The Geography and Hydrography of the Tanganyika
Part of the Ruvuma Basin. Dar es Salaam: Gt.
Printers, 1943.

Kuepper, William G.   "Rainfall deficiencies on the plateau of
Tanzania. " Doctoral dissertation, University of Wisconsin, 1968.

White, G. F.   Drawers of Water: Domestic Water Use in
East Africa. Chicago: University of Chicago Press,
1972.

Woodhead, T.   Studies of Potential Evaporation in Tanzania.
Nairobi: East African Agricultural For. Research
Organization, 1968.

Medicine

African Medical and Research Foundation. The Health Ser-
    vices of Tanganyika: A Report to the Government.
    London: Pitman Medical Publishing Co., 1964.

Brock, J. I. and M. Antret. Kwashiorkor in Africa (FAO
    Nutritional Studies, no. 8) Rome: FAO, 1952.

Christie, J. Cholera Epidemics in East Africa. London:
    Macmillan, 1876.

Clyde, D. F. History of the Medical Services of Tanganyika.
    Dar es Salaam: Gt. Printers, 1962.

_____. Malaria in Tanzania. London: OUP, 1967.

East African Trypanosomiasis Research Organization Report--
    1965. Entebbe: EASCO, 1966.

Ford, J. "Distributions of Glossina and Epidermiological
    Patterns in African Trypanosomiases." Journal of
    Tropical Medicine and Hygiene, LXVIII, no. 9, Sept.
    1965, 211-25.

Goatly, K. D. and P. Jordon. "Schistosomiasis in Zanzibar
    and Pemba." East African Medical Journal, XLII,
    no. 1, Jan. 1965, 1-9.

Latham, Michael. Human Nutrition in Tropical Africa: A
    Textbook for Health Workers with Specific Reference
    to Community Health Problems in East Africa. Rome:
    FAO, 1965.

Marealle, A. L. D. Tanzania Food Tables. Nairobi: EALB,
    1975.

Nhonoli, A. M. "An Enquiry into the Infant Mortality Rate
    in Rural Areas of Unyamwezi." East African Medical
    Journal, XXXI, no. 1, Jan. 1954, 1-12.

Reid, Marlene B. "Persistence and change in the health con-
    cepts and practices of the Sukuma of Tanzania, East
    Africa." Doctoral dissertation, Catholic University of
    America, 1968.

Richards, Audrey I. and Priscilla Reining. "Report of Fer-

tility Surveys in Buganda and Buhaya, 1952. " in Culture
and Human Fertility, edited by Frank Lorimer. Paris:
UNESCO, 1954, 351-403.

Robson, J. R. K.   "Malnutrition in Tanganyika. " TNR, Nos.
58 and 59, Mar. and Sept. 1962, 258-67.

Stirling, L. Bush Doctor. London: Westminster, 1947.

Sturrock, R. F. "Hookworm Studies in Tanganyika. " East
African Medical Journal, XLI, no. 11, Nov. 1964,
520-29.

Tanner, R. E. S. "Sukuma Fertility: An Analysis of 148
Marriages in Mwanza District, Tanganyika. " East
African Medical Journal, III, no. 3, Mar. 1956, 96-99.

Walter Reed Army Institute of Research. Tanganyika (Health
Data Publication No. 17). Washington: Walter Reed
Army Medical Center, 1962.

Natural Sciences and Zoology

Buxton, Patrick A. The Natural History of Tsetse Flies.
London: Lewis, 1955.

Kruuk, Hans. Hyena: The Life of Hyenas and Other Animals
in the Serengeti. London: OUP, 1975.

Lind, E. M. and M. S. Morrison. East African Vegetation.
New York: Longmans, 1974.

Nash, Leanne T. "Social behavior and social development in
baboons (Papio Anumis) at the Gembe Stream National
Park, Tanzania. " Doctoral dissertation, University
of California (Berkeley), 1973.

Ransom, Timothy W. Ecology and social behavior of baboons
(Papio anubia) in the Gombe National Park. " Doctoral
dissertation, University of California (Berkeley), 1971.

Spry, J. F. "The Sea Shells of Dar es Salaam. " Part I
and II, TNR, No. 56, Mar. 1961 and TNR, No. 63,
Dec. 1967, 20-47.

7. SOCIAL

Anthropology: General

Brown, G. G. and A. Hutt. Anthropology in Action; an experiment in the Iringa Province of Tanganyika Territory. London: OUP, 1935.

Castle, E. B. Growing Up in East Africa. London: OUP, 1966.

Gulliver, Philip H. Alien Africans in Tanga Region. Dar es Salaam: Govt. Printers, 1956.

Jerrard, R. C. Tribes of Tanganyika: Their Districts, Usual Dietary, and Pursuits. Dar es Salaam: Gt. Printers, 1936.

Oliver, Roland. "The problem of Bantu expansion." Journal of African History, VII, no. 3, 1966, 361-76.

Anthropology: Marriage and the Family

Beidelman, T. O. "Kaguru Omens, an East African People's Concepts of the Unusual, Unnatural and Supernormal." Anthropological Quarterly, XXXVI, no. 2, Apr. 1963, 43-59.

_____. The Matrilineal Peoples of Eastern Tanzania. London: International African Institute, 1967.

_____. "A Note on Luguru Descent Groups." Anthropos, LV, 1960, 882-85.

_____. "Pig ('guluwe'): An Essay on Ngulu Sexual Symbolism and Ceremony." Southwestern Journal of Anthropology, XX, no. 4, Winter 1964, 359-405.

_____. "Utani: Some Kaguru Notions of Death, Sexuality, and Affinity." Southwestern Journal of Anthropology, XXII, no. 4, Winter 1966, 354-80.

Cory, Hans. African Figurines: Their Ceremonial Use in Puberty Rites in Tanganyika. London: Faber, 1956.

_____. "The Sambwa Initiation Rites for Boys." TNR, Nos. 58, 59, Mar., Sept. 1962, 274-82.

Gray, Robert F.   "Sonjo Brideprice and the Question of Afri-
    can 'Wife Purchase'. " American Anthropologist, LXII,
    no. 1, Feb. 1960, 34-57.

Huber, H.   Marriage and the Family in Rural Bukwaya.
    Fribourg, Switz.: University Press, 1973.

Moller, M. S. G.   "Bahaya Customs and Beliefs in Connection
    with Pregnancy and Childbirth. " TNR, no. 50, June
    1968, 112-17.

Pfister, George F.   "Marriage Among the Central Basukuma. "
    Anthropological Quarterly, XXXV, no. 2, Apr. 1962,
    134-42.

Swantz, Marja-Liisa.   Ritual and Symbol in Transitional Za-
    ramo Society. Uppsala: Scandinavian Institute of Af-
    rican Studies, 1970.

Wilson, M.   "Nyakyusa Ritual and Symbolism. " American
    Anthropologist, LVI, no. 2, 1954, 228-41.

Wise, R.   "Some Rituals of Iron-making in Ufipa. " TNR,
    no. 51, Dec. 1958, 232-37.

Anthropology: Witchcraft and Sorcery

Abrahams, R. G.   "Aspects of Nyamwezi Witch Belief. "
    East African Institute of Social Research Conference
    Paper, No. 97, 1958. (mimeo)

Beidelman, T. O.   "Three Tales of the Living and the Dead:
    The Ideology of Kaguru Ancestral Propitiation. " Jour-
    nal of the Royal Anthropological Institute, LXLIV,
    July-Dec. 1964, 109-37.

Brain, J. L.   "More Modern Witchfinding. " TNR, no. 62,
    Mar. 1964, 44-48.

Carnell, W. J.   "Sympathetic Magic Among the Gogo of
    Mpwapwa District. " TNR, No. 54, Mar. 1960, 14-26.

Gray, Robert F.   "The Shetani Cult Among the Segeju of Tan-
    ganyika. " in Spirit Mediumship and Society in Africa,
    edited by J. Beattie and J. Middleton. London: Rout-
    ledge and Kegan Paul, 1969.

Harwood, Alan. Witchcraft, Sorcery and Social Categories Among the Safwa. London: OUP, 1970.

Hatfield, Colby R., Jr. "The Nfumu in tradition and change: a study of the position of religious practitioners among the Sukuma of Tanzania, East Africa." Doctoral dissertation, Catholic University of America, 1968.

Imperato, P. J. "Witchcraft and Traditional Medicine Among the Luo of Tanzania." TNR, no. 66, Dec. 1966, 193-201.

Middleton, John and E. H. Winter. Witchcraft and Sorcery in East Africa. New York: Praeger, 1963.

Ndee, Abdullah M. "Some Experiences of Witchcraft." TNR, Sept. 1961, 149-51.

Tanner, R. E. S. Witch Murders in Sukumaland. New York: Africana, 1970.

Winans, Edgar V. "Variation in the Incidence of Magic and Witchcraft in Uhehe, Tanganyika." American Anthropological Association Annual Meeting Paper, Washington D. C., 1967.

Winans and Edgerton, R. B. "Hehe Magical Justice." American Anthropological, LXVI, Aug. 1964, 745-64.

Demography and Population

Blacker, J. G. D. Population in East Africa. Nairobi: OUP.

East African High Commission. East African Statistical Dept. African Population of Tanganyika Territory, (Geographical and Tribal Studies). Nairobi: EHC, 1950.

_____. Tanganyika Population Census 1957: Analysis of total population; Certain analyses by Race and Sex, Geographical Area, Age, Religion and Nationality. Dar es Salaam: Gt. Printers, 1958.

Fosbrooke, H. A. "Tanganyika's Population Problem: an historical explanation." Human Problems of British Central Africa, No. 23, 1958, 54-58.

Gillman, Clement. "Dar es Salaam, 1860-1940: a story of growth and change." TNR, XX, 1945, 1-23.

Hirst, M. S., B. W. Langlands and G. Jamal. Studies in the Population Geography of Uganda and Tanzania. Makerere: Geography Occasional Paper no. 14, 1970.

Jurgens, Hans W. Investigations into Internal Migration in Tanzania. No. 29. (in German) Munchen: Weltforum Verlag, 1968.

Kucyski, R. R. Demographic Survey of the British Colonial Empire, II: East Africa. London: OUP, 1949.

Maro, Paul S. "Population and land resources in northern Tanzania: the dynamics change, 1920-1970." Doctoral dissertation, University of Minnesota, 1974.

Martin, C. J. "A Demographic Study of an Immigrant Community: the Indian Population of East Africa." Population Studies, VI, no. 3, Mar. 1953.

_____. "Estimates of Population Growth in East Africa, with special reference to Tanganyika and Zanzibar." in Essays on African Population, edited by Kenneth Michael Barbour and R. M. Prothero. New York: Praeger, 1961, 49-61.

Roberts, D. F. and R. E. S. Tanner. "A Demographic Study of an Area of Low Fertility in North-East Tanganyika." Population Studies, XIII, no. 1, July 1959, 61-80.

Southall, Aiden W. "Population Movements in East Africa." in Essays on African Population, edited by Barbour and Prothero. New York: Praeger, 1961, 157-192.

Tanganyika Government. African Census Report 1957. Dar es Salaam: Gt. Printers, 1963.

_____. Report on the Census of the Non-African Population Taken on the Night of the 13th Feb. 1952. Dar es Salaam: Gt. Printers, 1954.

Education: Adult Education

Hall, B. L. Adult Education and the Development of Social-

<u>ism in Tanzania.</u> Nairobi: EALB, 1976.

_____ and K. Remtulla. <u>Adult Education and the National</u>
<u>Development in Tanzania.</u> Nairobi: EALB, 1973.

Institute of Adult Education. <u>Adult Education Handbook.</u> Dar
es Salaam: Tanzania Publishing House, 1973.

King, Jane. <u>Planning Non-Formal Education in Tanzania.</u>
Afr. Res. Mono. no. 16. Paris: UNESCO, IIEP,
1967.

Millonzi, Joel C. "Citizenship in Africa: the role of adult
education in the political socialization of Tanganyikans,
1891-1961." Doctoral dissertation, Columbia University, 1972.

National Adult Education Association of Tanzania. <u>Adult Edu-</u>
<u>cation and Development in Tanzania.</u> Vol. 1. Dar es
Salaam: Executive Committee, NAEA, 1975.

Ryan, John. <u>Adult Education: the Tanzanian Experience.</u>
Teheran: International Institute for Adult Education,
1975.

Education: General

Cameron, John and W. A. Dodd. <u>Society, Schools, and Pro-</u>
<u>gress.</u> London: Pergamon Press, 1970.

Carter, J. Roger. <u>The Legal Framework of Educational</u>
<u>Planning and Administration in East Africa.</u> Afr. Res.
Mono. no. 7. Paris: UNESCO, IIEP, 1966.

Courtney, Dorothy. "Certification--a Trojan horse in Africa:
a perspective on educational and social change in
mainland Tanzania." Doctoral dissertation, Syracuse
University, 1973.

Hector, Henry J. "African post-primary education in Tanganyika, 1919-1939." Master's thesis, Columbia University, 1966.

Heijnen, J. D. <u>Development and Education in the Mwanza</u>
<u>District: a case study of migration and peasant</u>
<u>farming.</u> Groningen: Bronder-Offset, 1968.
A C.E.S.O. publication.

317   Bibliography

Hornsby, George. "A Brief History of Tanga School up to
1914." TNR, LVIII-LIX, March/Sept. 1962, 148-50.

_____. "German Educational Achievement in East Africa."
TNR, LXII, Mar. 1964, 83-90.

Jones, Thomas Jesse. Education in East Africa. East Africa Commission for the Phelps-Stokes Fund. London:
Edinburgh House Press, 1925.

Lema, Anza Amen. Partners in Education in Mainland Tanzania. Arusha: Evangelical Lutheran Church of Tanzania, 1972.

Mwingira, A. C. and Simon Pratt. The Process of Educational Planning in Tanzania. Afr. Res. Mono. no. 10.
Paris: UNESCO, IIEP, 1967.

Nyiti, Raphael M. "Intellectual development in the Meru
children of Tanzania." Doctoral dissertation, University of Illinois, 1973.

Ostheimer, John Maurice. "The achievement motive among
the Chagga of Tanzania." Doctoral dissertation, Yale
University, 1967.

Shann, Nevil. "The educational development of the Chagga
tribe." Overseas Education, XXVI, 1954, 47-65.

Skorov, George. Integration of Education and Economic
Planning in Tanzania. Afr. Res. Mono. no. 6. Paris: UNESCO, IIEP, 1966.

Smith, Anthony. "The Contribution of Missions to the Educational Development and Administrative Policy in Tanganyika from 1918 to 1961." Master's thesis, Shef-
field University, 1963.

Education: Higher

Ashby, Eric. Universities--British, Indian, African: A
Study in the Ecology of Higher Education. Cambridge:
Harvard University Press, 1966.

Barkan, Joel D. An African Dilemma: University Students
Development and Politics in Ghana, Tanzania and Uganda. Dar es Salaam: OUP, 1975.

Goldthorpe, J. E. An African Elite: Makerere College
    Students, 1922-1960. London, OUP, 1966.

Harbison, Frederick. "The African University and Human
    Resources Development. " Journal of Modern African
    Studies, III, no. 1, May 1965, 53-62.

Kelly, Chester S. "The role of an African university as an
    institution for national development. " Doctoral disser-
    tation, Columbia University, 1970.

Mbirika, Abukese V. E. P. "An examination of the functions
    of the University of East Africa in relation to the
    needs of the people. " Doctoral dissertation, New York
    University, 1969.

Southall, Roger. Federalism and Higher Education in East
    Africa. Nairobi: East African Publishing House,
    1974.

Van Onselen, Jurgens J. "The social, economic and political
    influences on higher education in Tanganyika since in-
    dependence (1961-1970). " Doctoral dissertation, Uni-
    versity of Houston, 1970.

Education: Policies

Colonial Government. Education Policy in British Tropical
    Africa. Cmd. 2374. London: HMSO, 1925.

Dodd, William A. Education for Self-Reliance in Tanzania:
    A Study of Its Vocational Aspect. New York: Colum-
    bia University Press, 1969.

Dolan, Louis F. "Transition from colonialism to self-re-
    liance in Tanzanian education. " Doctoral dissertation,
    University of Michigan, 1969.

Hinkle, Rodney J. "Educational Problems and Policies in
    Post-Independent Tanzania. " Doctoral dissertation,
    Teachers College, Columbia University, 1969.

Ishumi, Abel G. M. Education: A review of concepts, ideas
    and practices. Dar es Salaam: Institute of Education,
    University of Dar es Salaam, 1974.

Kurtz, Laura S. An African Education: The Social Revolu-
     tion in Tanzania. New York: Pageant-Poseidon Press,
     1972.

Resnick, Idrian N. (ed.) Tanzania: Revolution by Education.
     Arusha: Longmans of Tanzania, 1968.

Zanolli, N. V. Education Toward Development in Tanzania.
     Basel, Switz.: Pharos-Verlag, 1971.

Education: Primary

C. E. S. O. Primary Education in Sukumaland. Groningen,
     Neth.: Wotters-Noordhoff, 1969.

Dubbeldam, L. F. B. The Primary School and the Communi-
     ty in Mwanza District. Groningen, Neth.: Wotters-
     Noordhoff, 1970.

Education: Secondary

Anderson, Eugene L. "An experimental evaluation of pro-
     grammed agricultural instruction in a private Tanza-
     nian secondary school." Doctoral dissertation, Uni-
     versity of Wisconsin, 1973.

Court, David. "Schooling experience and the making of citi-
     zens: a study of Tanzanian secondary students."
     Doctoral dissertation, Stanford University, 1970.

Education: Teacher Training

Corbin, Hugh I. "A study of the contribution of TEEA tutors
     in teacher training colleges in East Africa." Doctoral
     dissertation, Columbia University, 1972.

Holland, Arden W. "The transformation of the African teach-
     ing profession in Tanzania." Doctoral dissertation,
     Columbia University, 1971.

Renes, P. B. Teacher Training at Butimba: a case study
     in Tanzania. Groningen, Neth.: Wotters-Noordhoff,
     1970.

Ethnology: Asians

Bhavra, G. E. "The Sikhs in East Africa: a political, social and economic analysis of a community. " 3rd year dissertation, University of Dar es Salaam, 1968.

Delf, George. Asians in East Africa. London: OUP, 1963.

Ghai, Dharam P. (ed.) Portrait of a Minority: Asians in East Africa. Nairobi: OUP, 1965.

Hollingsworth, L. W. Asians of East Africa. London: Macmillan, 1960.

Mangat, J. S. A History of the Asians in East Africa c1886 to 1945. Oxford: Clarendon Press, 1969.

Nanjira, Daniel. The Status of Aliens in East Africa: Asians and Europeans in Tanzania, Uganda and Kenya. New York: Praeger, 1976.

Rotberg, Robert I. and H. Neville Chittick. East Africa and the Orient: Cultural Synthesis in Pre-Colonial Times. New York: Africana, 1975.

Schneider, Karl-Ginther. Dar es Salaam, Stadtentwicklung unter dem Einfluss der Araber und Inder. Wiesbaden; Franz Steiner Verlag GmbH, 1965.

Smith, Daniel R. "The problems and possibilities of survival facing the Asian population of post-uhuru Tanzania. " Master's thesis, St. John's University, 1971.

Ethnology: Ethnographic Survey

Beidelman, T. O. The Matrilineal Peoples of Eastern Tanzania. "East Central Africa, " Part XVI. London: International African Institute, 1967.

Huntingford, G. W. B. The Southern Nilo-Hamites. East Central Africa, Pt. VIII, 1953.

Prins, A. H. J. The Swahili-speaking peoples of Zanzibar and the East African Coast. East Central Africa, Pt. XII, 1961.

Taylor, Brian. The Western Lacustrine Bantu. East Central
     Africa, Pt. XIII, 1962.

Tews, Mary. People of the Lake Nyasa Region. East Cen-
     tral Africa, Pt. I, 1950.

Willis, Roy G. The Fipa and Related Peoples of South-West
     Tanzania and North-East Zambia. East Central Afri-
     ca, Pt. XV, 1966.

Ethnology: Europeans

Georgulas, Nikos. Minority Assimilation in Africa: The
     Greeks in Moshi--an Example. Occasional Paper no. 22,
     Syracuse University, 1967. (mimeo)

Ethnology: Tribes

Arens, William E. "Mto wa Mbu: a study of a multi-tribal
     community in rural Tanzania." Doctoral dissertation,
     University of Virginia, 1970.

Dibble, Jarnes B. The Plains Brood Alone: Tribesmen of
     the Serengeti. Grand Rapids, Mich.: Zondervan,
     1973.

Guillotte, Joseph V., III. "Becoming one people: social and
     cultural integration in a multi-ethnic community in
     rural Tanzania." Doctoral dissertation, Tulane Uni-
     versity of Louisiana, 1973.

Kollmann, Paul. The Victoria Nyanza: The Land, the Races
     and Their Customs with Specimens of Some of the Dia-
     lects. Trans. by H. A. Nesbitt. London: Swan Son-
     nenschein Co., Ltd., 1899.

Murdock, G. P. Africa: Its Peoples and Their Culture His-
     tory. New York: McGraw-Hill, 1959.

Oliver, Roland. "The problem of Bantu expansion." Journal
     of African History, VII, no. 3, 1966, 361-76.

van Pelt, P. Bantu Customs in Mainland Tanzania. Tabora:
     TMP Book Dept., 1971.

Bibliography 322

Arusha

Gulliver, Philip H. Social Control in an African Society: A Study of the Arusha. Boston: Boston University Press, 1963.

Steinhauser. "Waarushcha." in Beantwortung des Fragebogens uber die Rechte der eingeborenen in den deutschen Kolonien c. 1914, copies in the National Museum.

Thomas, Anthony. "Notes on the Formal Education of the Arusha 'Muran' at Circumcision." TNR, no. 65, Mar. 1966.

Barabaig

Klima, George J. The Barabaig: East African Cattle Herders. New York: Holt, Rinehart and Winston, 1970.

Baraguyu

Beidelman, T. O. "The Baraguyu." TNR, no. 55, Sept. 1960, 245-78.

Bena

Culwick, A. T. and G. M. Ubena of the Rivers. London: Allen & Unwin, 1935.

Langness, Lewis L. "Bena Bena social structure." Doctoral dissertation, Washington State University, 1963.

Mwenda, E. A. "Historia na Maendeleo ya Ubena." Swahili, XXXIII, no. 2, 1963, 99-123.

Chagga

"The Tanzania Notes and Records," TNR, No. 64 of March 1965 concentrated on this tribe and the surroundings.

Dundas, Hon. C. C. F. Kilimanjaro and Its People. London: Witherby, 1924.

_____. Asili na Habari za Wachaga. London, 1932.

Geilinger, W. Der Kilimanjaro, sein Land und seine Menschen. Bern-Berlin: Verlag Hans Haber, 1938.

323   Bibliography

Gutman, B. Des Recht der Dschagga. Munich; Beck, 1926.

Marealle, Chief P. I. "Notes on Chagga Customs. " (Trans.
    by R. D. Swai) TNR, no. 60, Mar. 1963, 69-90.

Ntiro, S. J. Desturi za Wachagga. Nairobi: EALB, 1953.

Raum, O. F. Chaga Childhood. Oxford, 1940.

Stahl, Kathleen M. History of the Chagga People of Kiliman-
    jaro. London: Mouton, 1964.

Gogo

Claus, H. Die Gogo. Berlin: Baessler Archives, 1911.

Mnyampala, M. E. Historia Mila na Desturi za Wagogo wa
    Tanganyika. Nairobi: EALB, 1971.

Rigby, Peter. Cattle and Kinship among the Gogo: A Semi-
    Pastoral Society of Central Tanzania. London: Cor-
    nell University Press, 1969.

Schaegelen, T. "La Tribu des Wagogo. " Anthropos, 33,
    1938, i/ii, 195-217; iii/iv, 515-67.

Ha

Scherer, J. H. "The Ha of Tanganyika. " Anthropos, LIV,
    nos. 5 and 6, 1959, 841-903.

Hadzapi, Kindiga, Tindiga

Bleek, D. F. "The Hadzapi or Watindiga of Tanganyika Ter-
    ritory. " Africa, IV, 1931, 273-86.

Cooper, B. "The Kindiga. " TNR, no. 27, June 1949, 8-15.

Woodburn, J. C. "The Future of the Tindiga, a Hunting
    Tribe in Tanganyika. " TNR, nos. 58, 59, Mar./Sept.,
    269-73.

Hehe

Nigman, Ernst. Die Wahehe. Berlin, 1908.

Kilindi

'lAjjemy, Abdullah Hemedi. Habari za Wakilindi. Nairobi:
    EALB, 1962.

Luguru

Hadumbarhinu, R. L. Waluguru na Desturi Zao. Nairobi:
    EALB, 1968.

Mzuando, C. Historia ya Uluguru. Dar es Salaam: Pri-
    vately published for the Luguru Native Authority, 1958.

Luo

Crazzolara, J. P. The Lwoo. 3 vols. Verona: Missioni
    Africane, 1950-54.

Ominde, S. H. The Luo Girls: From Infancy to Marriage.
    Nairobi: EALB, 1952.

Masai

Tanganyika Notes and Records. December 1948. (Dedicated
    to the Masai.)

Bleeker, Sonia. The Masai. New York: Morrow, 1963.

Sankan, S. S. The Maasai. Nairobi: EALB, 1971.

Mbugu

Green, E. C. "The Wambugu of Usambara." TNR, no. 61,
    Sept. 1963, 175-89.

Mbugwe

Gray, Robert F. "The Mbugwe Tribe: Origin and Develop-
    ment." TNR, no. 38, Mar. 1955, 39-50.

Meru

Puritt, Paul. "The Meru of Tanzania: a study of their so-
    cial and political organization." Doctoral dissertation,
    University of Illinois, 1970.

Ndendeuli

Gulliver, Philip H. Labour Migration in a Rural Economy: a study of the Ngoni and Ndendeuli of Southern Tanganyika. Kampala: East African Institute of Social Research, 1955.

Ngoni

Ebner, Elzear. History of the Wangoni. Peramiho, 1959.

Haplinger, J. Land und Leute von Ungoni. 1901.

Nyakyusa

Charsley, Simon. The Princes of Nyakyusa. Nairobi: EALB, 1969.

Konter, J. H. Facts and Factors in the Rural Economy of the Nyakyusa. Leiden: Afrika Studiecentrum, 1974.

Wilson, Marcia. Good Company: a study of Nyakyusa age-villages. London: OUP, 1951.

_____. Communal Rituals of the Nyakyusa. London: OUP, 1959.

_____. Rituals of Kinship among the Nyakyusa. London: OUP, 1957.

Nyamwezi

Abrahams, R. G. The People of Greater Unyamwezi, Tanzania. East Central Africa, Pt. XVII, ed. Daryll Forde. London: International African Institute, 1967.

African Bibliography Series. East African volume. International African Institute, 1960.

Yongolo, W. D. Maisha na Desturi ya Wanyamwezi. London: 1956.

Sonjo

Gray, Robert F. The Sonjo of Tanganyika: An Anthropological Study of an Irrigation-based Society. London: OUP, 1963.

Sukuma

Malcolm, D. W. Sukumaland: an African people and their
      country. London: OUP, 1953.

Swahili

Brock, Clara. 'Kazi za Waswahili (Work of the Swahili). "
      Master's thesis, Duquesne University, 1964.

Caplain, Ann Patricia. Choice and Constraint in a Swahili
      Community: Property, Hierarchy and Cognatic Descent
      on the East African Coast. Nairobi: OUP, 1975.

Kline, William E. "An inquiry into the birth and burial cus-
      toms of the Waswahili. " Master's thesis, Duquesne
      University, 1962.

Petrock, Kenneth M. "Marriage and Divorce among the
      Waswahili. " Master's thesis, Duquesne University,
      1964.

Zaramo

Mwaruka, R. Masimulizi juu ya Zaramo. London: Mac-
      millan, 1965.

Swantz, Lloyd W. The Zaramo of Tanzania. Dar es Salaam:
      Nordic Tanganyika Project, 1965.

Religion: General

Mamuya, Matthew S. "Religion and Society in Tanganyika:
      an encounter of Western civilization with traditional
      culture. " Master's thesis, University of Pennsylvania,
      1965.

Muga, Erasto. "The impact of western Christian religion on
      the development of leadership groups in East Africa
      (Kenya, Uganda and Tanzania). " Doctoral dissertation,
      New School for Social Research, 1967.

Oliver, Roland. The Missionary Factor in East Africa. Lon-
      don: Longmans, 1952.

Religion: Islam

Gallagher, Joseph T. "Islam and the emergence of the Nden-
    deuli." Doctoral dissertation, Boston University, 1970.

Klamroth, M. Der Islam in Deutsch-Ostafrika. Berlin,
    1912.

Martin, Earl R. "The Ahmadiyya Movement in Tanzania."
    Master's thesis, Southern Baptist Theological Semina-
    ry, 1966.

Nimitz, August H. "The role of the Muslim Sufi order in
    political change; an overview and micro-analysis from
    Tanzania." Doctoral dissertation, University of In-
    diana, 1973.

Trimingham, J. Spencer. Islam in East Africa. London:
    OUP, 1964.

Walji, Shirin R. "Ismailis on Mainland Tanzania, 1850-
    1948." Master's thesis, University of Wisconsin,
    1969.

Religion: Native

Balina, Aloys, et al. Sukuma Expression of Traditional Re-
    ligion in Life. Kipalapala, Tanz.: Kipalapala Semi-
    nary.

Beattie, J. and J. Middleton. (eds.) Spirit Mediumship and
    Society in Africa. London: Routledge and Kegan
    Paul, 1968.

Cory, Hans. "Religious Beliefs and Practices of the Sukuma/
    Nyamwezi Tribal Group." TNR, no. 54, Mar. 1960,
    14-26.

Finch, F. G. "Hambageu, Some Additional Notes on the God
    of the Wasonjo." TNR, nos. 47 and 48, June and
    Sept. 1957, 203-08.

Fosbrooke, H. A. "Hambageu, the God of the Wasonjo."
    TNR, no. 35, July 1953, 38-42.

Harjula, Raimo. God and the Sun in Meru Thought. Helsin-
    ki: Forssan Kirjapaino Oy, 1969.

Hatfield, Colby R., Jr. "The Nfumu in tradition and change: a study of the position of religious practitioners among the Sukuma of Tanzania, East Africa." Doctoral dissertation, Catholic University of America, 1968.

Johnson, C. B. "Some Aspects of Iraqw Religion." TNR, no. 65, Mar. 1966, 53-56.

Komba, James J. God and Man: Religious Elements of the Ngoni of Southwestern Tanganyika Viewed in the Light of Christian Faith. Rome: Pontifica Universitas Uribanina de Propoganda Fide, 1961.

Mbiti, John S. African Religions and Philosophy. London: Heinemann, 1969.

Ruel, M. J. "Religion and Society Among the Kuria of East Africa." Africa, XXXX, no. 3, July 1965, 295-306.

Simenauer, E. "The Miraculous Birth of Hambague, Hero-God of the Sonjo: A Tanganyika Theogony." TNR, no. 38, Mar. 1955, 23-30.

Tanner, R. E. S. Transition in African Beliefs. Maryknoll, N.Y.: Maryknoll Publications, 1967.

Religion: Protestants

Anchak, G. Ronald. "An experience in the paradox of indigenous church building: a history of the Eastern Mennonite Mission in Tanganyika, 1934-1961." Doctoral dissertation, Michigan State University, 1975.

Anderson-Mershead, A. E. M. The History of the Universities Mission to Central Africa. I: 1859-1909. 6th edition. London, 1955.

Bennett, Norman R. (ed.) From Zanzibar to Ujiji: The Journal of Arthur W. Dodgshun, 1877-1879. Boston: Boston University Press, 1969.

Blood, A. G. The History of the Universities' Mission to Central Africa. Vol. II 1907-1932. London: UMCA, 1957.

Bloom, A. G. The History of the Universities Mission to

Central Africa. Vol. III: 1933-1957. London: UMCA, 1962.

Broomsfield, G. W. Towards Freedom: History of the UMCA. London, 1957.

Frank, C. N. The Life of Bishop Steere. Nairobi: EALB, 1953.

Johnson, V. E. The Augustana Lutheran Mission of Tanganyika Territory, East Africa. Rock Island, Illinois, 1939.

Lovett, Richard. The History of the London Missionary Society. 2 vol. London, 1899.

Mshana, E. E. "Religion and Revelation in Christ with special reference to the Wapare tribe." M.S.T. thesis, Union Theological Seminary, New York, 1966.

Shenk, David. Mennonite Safari. Scottdale, Pa.: Herald Press, 1971.

Smith, Maynard. Frank, Bishop of Zanzibar. London: 1926.

Stock, Eugene. History of the Church Missionary Society. 3 vol. London: 1899.

Wilson, C. H. History of the Universities Mission to Central Africa. London: 1935.

Wolf, James B. Missionary to Tanganyika, 1877-1888: The Writings of Edward Corde Hore, Master Mariner. London: Frank Cass, 1971.

Wright, Marcia. German Missions in Tanganyika 1891-1941: Lutherans and Moravians in the Southern Highlands. New York: OUP, 1971.

Religion: Roman Catholics

Attwater, D. The White Fathers in Africa. London, 1937.

Bouniel, J. The White Fathers and Their Missions. London, 1929.

Carney, Joseph P. "The history of the functional structure
of the Maryknoll Mission in Musoma and Shinyanga,
Tanzania." Doctoral dissertation, St. John's University, 1973.

Kittler, Glenn D. The White Fathers. New York: Harper,
1957.

Matheson, E. An Enterprise So Perilous. Nairobi: EALB,
n. d.

Sociology: Sociological Change

Brain, James L. "Patterns of continuity and change in the
context of planned settlement in Tanzania." Doctoral
dissertation, Syracuse University, 1968.

Noble, Charles. "Voluntary associations of the Basukuma of
northern mainland Tanzania." Doctoral dissertation,
Catholic University of America, 1969.

O'Barr, William. "An ethnography of modernization: Pare
traditionality and the impact of recent change." Doctoral dissertation, Northwestern University, 1970.

Roth, Warren J. "Three cooperatives and a credit union as
examples of culture change among the Sukuma of Tanzania." Doctoral dissertation, Catholic University of
America, 1965.

Varkevisser, C. M. Socialization in a changing society:
Sukuma childhood in rural and urban Mwanza, Tanzania. Den Haag: Cent. Stud. Educ. Changing Societies, 1973.

Sociology: Urbanization

De Blij, H. J. Dar es Salaam: A Study in Urban Geography.
Evanston: Northwestern University Press, 1963.

Gillman, Clement. "Dar es Salaam: 1860-1940: a story of
growth and change." TNR, XX, 1945, 1-23.

Kalugendo, P. F. "The Development of Bukoba town up to
the end of German rule." 3rd year dissertation, University of Dar es Salaam, 1975.

Leslie, J. A. K.   A Survey of Dar es Salaam.   London:
     OUP, 1963.

Mascarenhas, Adolfo.   "Urban Development in Dar es
     Salaam. "   Master's thesis, University of California
     (Los Angeles), 1966.

Sutton, J. E. G. (ed.)   Dar es Salaam: City, Port and
     Region.   TNR, no. 71, 1971, for the Tanzania So-
     ciety, Dar es Salaam.